OXFORD TEXTUAL PERSPECTIVES

*Reimagining the Past in the
Borderlands of Medieval England
and Wales*

GENERAL EDITORS

Elaine Treharne   Greg Walker

Reimagining the Past in the Borderlands of Medieval England and Wales

GEORGIA HENLEY

OXFORD
UNIVERSITY PRESS

Great Clarendon Street, Oxford, OX2 6DP,
United Kingdom

Oxford University Press is a department of the University of Oxford.
It furthers the University's objective of excellence in research, scholarship,
and education by publishing worldwide. Oxford is a registered trade mark of
Oxford University Press in the UK and in certain other countries

© Georgia Henley 2024

The moral rights of the author have been asserted

All rights reserved. No part of this publication may be reproduced, stored in
a retrieval system, or transmitted, in any form or by any means, without the
prior permission in writing of Oxford University Press, or as expressly permitted
by law, by licence or under terms agreed with the appropriate reprographics
rights organization. Enquiries concerning reproduction outside the scope of the
above should be sent to the Rights Department, Oxford University Press, at the
address above

You must not circulate this work in any other form
and you must impose this same condition on any acquirer

Published in the United States of America by Oxford University Press
198 Madison Avenue, New York, NY 10016, United States of America

British Library Cataloguing in Publication Data
Data available

Library of Congress Control Number: 2023951782

ISBN 9780192856463
ISBN 9780192856470 (pbk.)

DOI: 10.1093/oso/9780192856463.001.0001

Printed and bound by
CPI Group (UK) Ltd, Croydon, CR0 4YY

Links to third party websites are provided by Oxford in good faith and
for information only. Oxford disclaims any responsibility for the materials
contained in any third party website referenced in this work.

To Lyle, Elliott, and Jack

SERIES EDITOR'S PREFACE

Oxford Textual Perspectives is a series of informative and provocative studies focused upon texts (conceived of in the broadest sense of that term) and the technologies, cultures, and communities that produce, inform, and receive them. It provides fresh interpretations of fundamental works, images, and artefacts, and of the vital and challenging issues emerging in English literary studies. By engaging with the contexts and materiality of the text, its production, transmission, and reception history, and by frequently testing and exploring the boundaries of the notions of text and meaning themselves, the volumes in the series question conventional frameworks and provide innovative interpretations of both canonical and less well-known works. These books will offer new perspectives, and challenge familiar ones, both on and through texts and textual communities. While they focus on specific authors, periods, and issues, they nonetheless scan wider horizons, addressing themes and provoking questions that have a more general application to literary studies and cultural history as a whole. Each is designed to be as accessible to the non-specialist reader as it is fresh and rewarding for the specialist, combining an informative orientation in a landscape with detailed analysis of the territory and suggestions for further travel.

Elaine Treharne and Greg Walker

ACKNOWLEDGEMENTS

I am grateful to the editors of this series, Elaine Treharne and Greg Walker, for believing in this book project and seeing it to fruition. It began as the nucleus of an idea during my Ph.D. programme, and I owe a great debt to Catherine McKenna, Nicholas Watson, Elaine Treharne, Paul Russell, and Daniel Donoghue for their support during that time. I am grateful to the American Council of Learned Societies for the generous funding that enabled me to write this book while a Fellow in 2021–2, and to Saint Anselm College's Faculty Summer Research Grant initiative for funding travels to archives in 2019. I thank the librarians and staff at the British Library, the Bodleian Libraries, the National Library of Wales, the Pierpont Morgan Library, and the Hanna Holborn Gray Special Collections Research Center at the University of Chicago Library for their assistance with accessing manuscripts and digital images. I am also indebted to Mary Violette for facilitating my Associateship with the Department of Celtic Languages and Literatures at Harvard University and access to Harvard Libraries. I am grateful to a number of readers for their helpful comments on drafts of various chapters: the anonymous reader at Oxford University Press for comments on the manuscript; Megan Cook, Elizaveta Strakhov, Damian Fleming, Joshua Byron Smith, and Zachary Hines for comments on drafts of Chapters 1 and 2; Joey McMullen for feedback on the Introduction and Conclusion, Paul Russell for reading an early draft of Chapter 5 and segments of the Introduction; and Ben Guy, Joshua Byron Smith, and Lindy Brady for generously taking the time to read and workshop the entire book. I also thank David Parsons, Robert Bartlett, Daniel Huws, Manon Bonner Jenkins, and Philip Hume for sharing unpublished material with me, and Chris Given-Wilson for answering queries. I am grateful to audiences of various conferences over the years (the Oxford Celtic Seminar, the Medieval History Workshop at Harvard University, the Mortimer History Society's Online Seminar Group on Medieval Wales and the Marches, the Celtic Studies Association of North America Annual Meetings, the

International Congress of Celtic Studies at Bangor University, the Center for Medieval and Renaissance Studies' lecture series at Stanford University, and the international medieval conferences at Leeds and Kalamazoo) for insightful comments on various iterations of this work, and to Ben Guy, Nia Wyn Jones, Joshua Byron Smith, Lindy Brady, Patrick Wadden, Rebecca Thomas, Barry Lewis, Myriah Williams, and Sarah Zeiser for enlivening conversations about Welsh history and literature over the years. I also thank my colleagues at Saint Anselm College, particularly Bindu Malieckal, for their support. And finally, to Lyle, Elliott, Jack, and my mother, who have witnessed the piles of books grow taller at home—thank you for your encouragement and love.

CONTENTS

List of Illustrations	*x*
Abbreviations	*xi*
Introduction	1
1 Rewriting Geoffrey of Monmouth	33
2 Royal Aspirations	75
3 Ancestral Memory	116
4 Romance and Identity	153
5 Elegies for Welsh Princes	195
Conclusion: *Literary Borderlands*	228
Appendix A	242
Appendix B	250
Bibliography	252
General Index	274
Index of Manuscripts	297

LIST OF ILLUSTRATIONS

Front Matter: The March of Wales in the Fourteenth Century		xiii
1.1.	London, British Library, Cotton Titus D. xxii, fols. 21^v–22^r	38
1.2.	The Lordship of Glamorgan	47
1.3.	London, British Library, Cotton Nero A. iv, fols. 2^v–3^r	65
1.4.	London, British Library, Harley 3725, fols. 40^v–41^r	71
2.1.	Gwladys pedigree, Chicago, University Library, 224, fols. 51^v–52^r	89
2.2.	Mortimers and the House of York	100
3.1.	London, British Library, Cotton Julius D. x, fols. 29^v–30^r	123
3.2.	The lords of Brecon according to the *Genealogy of the Lords of Brecknock*	128
3.3.	The ancestry of John II Hastings according to Dugdale 18, items 2a and 2b	138
3.4.	The ancestry of Ada of Huntingdon according to Dugdale 18, item 3	145
3.5.	Descendants of William Brewer according to Dugdale 18, item 4	146
3.6.	Descendants of William Marshal according to Dugdale 18, item 5	147
4.1.	The Fitz Warin family	158

ABBREVIATIONS

Annales Cambriae B text	Henry W. Gough-Cooper, 'Annales Cambriae: The B Text, from London, B-text National Archives, MS E164/1, pp. 2–26', *Welsh Chronicles Research Group*, http://croniclau.bangor.ac.uk/editions.php.en
Annales Cambriae C text	Henry W. Gough-Cooper, 'Annales Cambriae: The C Text, from London, C-text British Library, Cotton MS Domitian A. i, ff. 138^r–155^r, with an appended concordance of intercalated notices', *Welsh Chronicles Research Group*, Bangor University, http://croniclau.bangor.ac.uk/editions.php.en
Armitage	*Sir Gawain and the Green Knight*, trans. Simon Armitage (New York, 2007)
Burgess	*Two Medieval Outlaws: Eustace the Monk and Fouke Fitz Waryn*, trans. Glyn S. Burgess (Cambridge, 1997)
CCCC	Cambridge, Corpus Christ College
CMCS	*Cambridge Medieval Celtic Studies/Cambrian Medieval Celtic Studies*
DGB	Geoffrey of Monmouth, *De gestis Britonum*, ed. Michael Reeve, trans. Neil Wright, *Geoffrey of Monmouth:The History of the Kings of Britain: An Edition and Translation of De Gestis Britonum (Historia regum Britanniae)* (Woodbridge, 2007)
EHR	*English Historical Review*
FFW	*Fouke Le Fitz Waryn*, ed. E. J. Hathaway, P. T. Ricketts, C. A. Robson, and A. D. Wilshere, Anglo-Norman Texts Society, 26–8 (Oxford, 1975)

GCH	T. B. Pugh (ed.), *Glamorgan County History*, vol. iii. *The Middle Ages* (Cardiff, 1971)
HGK	*Historia Gruffud vab Kenan*, in *A Mediaeval Prince:The Life of Gruffudd ap Cynan*, ed. and trans. D. Simon Evans (Lampeter, 1990)
HWM	*The History of William Marshal*, ed. A. J. Holden, trans. S. Gregory, with notes by David Crouch, Anglo-Norman Text Society, Occasional Publications Series, 4, 3 vols (London, 2002–6)
JMH	*Journal of Medieval History*
MWG	*Medieval Welsh Genealogy: An Introduction and Textual Study*, Studies in Celtic History, 42 (Woodbridge, 2020)
NLW	National Library of Wales
NLWJ	*National Library of Wales Journal*
ODNB	*Oxford Dictionary of National Biography Online* (Oxford, 2004)
SC	*Studia Celtica*
TRHS	Transactions of the Royal Historical Society
VGC	*Vita Griffini Filii Conani: The Medieval Latin Life of Gruffudd ap Cynan*, ed. and trans. Paul Russell (Cardiff, 2005)
WGP	*The Works of the Gawain Poet: Sir Gawain and the Green Knight, Pearl, Cleanness, Patience*, ed. Ad Putter and Myra Stokes (London, 2014)
WHR	*Welsh History Review*

The March of Wales in the Fourteenth Century.
Note: Maelor Saesneg and Hopedale were at this time part of Flintshire.

Introduction

Late in 1282, Llywelyn ap Gruffudd, the last prince of independent Wales, penned a letter to John Peckham, Archbishop of Canterbury, rejecting King Edward I's demand that he surrender and forfeit the principality of Wales.[1] The archbishop's efforts at diplomacy between the two men had broken down, and Edward's army was assembled at Rhuddlan in north-east Wales for a final assault. Llywelyn explained his rejection of Edward's terms, which had included an offer of clemency and an earldom in England in exchange for the territory of Snowdonia, by invoking ancient British history.

Referencing the relevant passages in Geoffrey of Monmouth's *De gestis Britonum* (*Historia regum Britanniae*), Llywelyn explained that he could not forfeit those lands that he held by right of ancient inheritance, passed down to him through his descent from Camber, son of Brutus, eponymous founder of Britain.[2] He referenced the legendary British past described in *De gestis Britonum* (hereafter *DGB*), in which the kingdom of Britain was divided upon Brutus' death between his three sons, Locrinus, Camber, and Albanactus.[3] These three territories became present-day England, Wales, and Scotland. Llywelyn

---

[1] *Registrum Epistolarum Fratris Johannis Peckham, Archiepiscopi Cantuariensis*, ed. Charles Trice Martin, 3 vols (London, 1882–5; repr. 1965), ii.468–71; J. Beverley Smith, *Llywelyn ap Gruffudd: Prince of Wales* (Oxford, 1998), 335; *The Acts of the Welsh Rulers, 1120–1283*, ed. Huw Pryce (Cardiff, 2005), 626. Unless otherwise noted, translations are my own.

[2] *Registrum*, ed. Martin, ii.468, 470; *Acts*, ed. Pryce, 626. I use the title *De gestis Britonum* instead of the more commonly known *Historia Regum Britanniae* because this is the title used by Geoffrey and in the earliest manuscripts of the text; for discussion, see *DGB*, p. lix.

[3] *DGB* ii.23.5–11, pp. 30–1. See Matthew Fisher, 'Genealogy Rewritten: Inheriting the Legendary in Insular Historiography', in Raluca L. Radulescu and Edward Donald Kennedy (eds), *Broken Lines: Genealogical Literature in Medieval Britain and France*, Medieval Texts and Cultures of Northern Europe, 16 (Turnhout, 2008), 123–42, at 125–8, for discussion of Edward I's use of *DGB* as the basis for his right to rule Scotland.

was invoking what he considered his inviolable, hereditary right to Cambria. And yet his articulation of the supremacy of Locrinus, heir to England, over Camber, heir to Wales, carefully placed Edward above himself in a royal hierarchy.[4] Here, legendary history and contemporary politics merged: Llywelyn was prepared to admit that he held Cambria by permission of the English Crown, but he would not forfeit his lands, which he held by right of ancient inheritance, nor abandon his people.

Peckham, agreeing to engage in this discursive mode, fired back with a different invocation of the legendary past: while he understood Llywelyn's position, he wrote, he did not understand the prince's desire to trace his roots back to a rebellious people who chose exile after defending the adultery of Paris.[5] The Trojans and their descendants, Peckham noted, were known for their disorganization, rebelliousness, idol-worship, and adulterous nature, which generations of legitimate marriages were unable to repair: *Non oportet autem, simplice, in radice adulterina, processu idololatriae, et usurpationis spoliis gloriari* 'It is not necessary, frankly, to boast of adulterous origins, the advancement of idolatry, and the possession of spoils'.[6] Negotiations between Llywelyn and the archbishop failed, and Llywelyn died one month after the letter was written. With his death, independent Wales became the stuff of historiography and prophecy.

This episode illustrates the seriousness with which the legendary history of Britain and Wales was taken in the political arenas of conquest and statecraft in this period. Perhaps these appeals to the past were opportunistic; perhaps they were made in earnest. At the very least, it is clear that legendary history was well suited to high-stakes political argument.[7] And yet, the standard narrative of English and Welsh interactions in the Middle Ages is that, after Edward I's conquest of Wales in 1282–4, England grew progressively more powerful while Wales lapsed into

---

[4] J. Beverley Smith, *Llywelyn ap Gruffudd*, 278, 335; J. Beverley Smith, *Yr Ymwybod â Hanes yng Nghymru yn yr Oesoedd Canol: Darlith Agoriadol/The Sense of History in Medieval Wales: An Inaugural Lecture* (Aberystwyth, 1991).

[5] *Registrum*, ed. Martin, ii.473–4.

[6] Ibid.

[7] For further discussion, see Georgia Henley, 'The Reception of Geoffrey of Monmouth as Political Influence', in Ben Guy and Patrick Wadden (eds), *Propaganda and Pseudo-history in the Medieval Celtic World: Interrogating a Paradigm* (forthcoming).

obscurity, with the exception of a handful of rebellions. I show instead that Welsh and British historical memory and historiography were in fact enduringly potent political instruments in the centuries following the conquest, as Wales was further incorporated under English and marcher governance, and that the narrative of British–Welsh history, as told by Geoffrey of Monmouth, had an outsized influence on the political landscape of late medieval Britain.[8] Geoffrey's narrative, and its accompanying ideologies of conquest, settlement, and unification, was a flexible and productive medium of political influence in the medieval period. It is no surprise, therefore, that *DGB* succeeded as the primary historical framework for British history until the sixteenth century. Its broad utility as a tool for negotiating and defining identity through historical memory also contributed to its success as popular secular literature: throughout the Middle Ages, interpretations of Geoffrey's historical scheme took the form of vernacular translations, prophetic poetry, commentaries, and romances that permeated the literatures of Europe.

The potency of *DGB* as a political instrument is best understood through the medium of literary production in the March of Wales, a contested, militarized borderland between England and Wales ruled by a colonial aristocracy of distinctive identity, social circumstances, and concerted ambition that ruled former Welsh territories and profited vastly from them in wealth and political power.[9] As a meeting

---

[8] It is necessary to speak of British and Welsh history together, as the two are inextricably intertwined in Geoffrey, and medieval readers would have viewed British history as the immediate predecessor of Welsh history in this context.

[9] The March of Wales encompassed the conquest lordships of southern and eastern Wales as well as the western fringes of the counties of Cheshire, Shropshire, and Herefordshire. The lordships that constituted the March of Wales by the fourteenth century (the date of much of the literature discussed in this book) were: Denbigh, Dyffryn Clwyd, Flint, Bromfield and Yale, Mold, Hawarden, Hopedale, Maelor Saesneg, Chirk, Oswestry, Caus, Montgomery, Cedewain, Ceri, Clun, Bishop's Castle, Maelienydd, Wigmore, Cwmwd Deuddwr, Gwerthrynion, Radnor, Huntington, Elfael, Glasbury, Builth, Clifford, Hay, Ewyas Lacy, Archenfield, Monmouth, Usk, Chepstow, Abergavenny, Caerleon, Gwynllŵg, Glamorgan, Blaenllyfni, Brecon, Cantref Bychan, Gower, Kidwelly, Iscennen, Ystlwyf, Llanstephan, Emlyn, Cilgerran, St Clears, Narberth, Laugharne, Pembroke, Haverford, Pebidiog, Cemais, and Llawhaden. The boundaries of the March of Wales, and the boundary between Wales and England, were not well defined (see discussion in R. R. Davies, *Lordship and Society in the March of Wales, 1282–1400* (Oxford, 1978), 16), so it is appropriate to use the term 'borderlands' to describe the figurative border zone overlaid on the marcher lordships. The term 'borderlands' constitutes any site

point of Welsh, Anglo-Norman, Breton, Flemish, and Irish peoples, the region was a particularly rich site of cross-cultural contact. Despite its geographically peripheral position in relation to England's centres of power, it came to have a considerable influence on medieval Britain's political landscape, which was to some degree shaped by the historical narratives and views of the past that interested marcher families. The present study examines a range of texts produced for or adjacent to the barons of marcher lordships between the mid-twelfth century and the late fifteenth century, an era that fundamentally redefined the relationship between England and Wales. During this time, baronial families in the March of Wales, who conquered and governed former Welsh kingdoms and intermarried with Welsh nobility throughout generations, became particularly attuned to and interested in British and Welsh history. They leveraged their ancestral and political ties to Wales in order to strengthen their political power, both regionally and on a national scale, through the patronage of historical and genealogical texts that reimagined the Welsh historical past on their terms. These literary activities advanced their political power and increased the symbolic value of Welshness, to the extent that Edward IV emphasized his Welsh ancestry in genealogies around the year 1470, and Henry Tudor evoked his Welsh background during his accession to the English throne in 1485. This use of Welshness runs counter to contemporary assumptions of the marginality of Wales and the Welsh to English culture.

In addition, the texts examined in this book reveal a body of 'marcher literature', a baronial literature produced by and for marcher lords, their families, and descendants. This marcher literature, located in a region whose borders frequently shifted with the winds of political fortune and whose territories were a mosaic of individual lordships and counties, was characteristically variable, distinctive by region and time period, and fundamentally multilingual in character. Nevertheless, common threads run through it, including interest in Geoffrey's *DGB*, fiercely defending rights to land, and a considerable degree of access to and familiarity with Welsh culture, customs, and laws, in part due to marcher families' frequent intermarriage with Welsh noble families.

of encounter between Welsh and English in this general geographical area, regardless of whether the lords of a given area claimed marcher legal status.

By examining how marcher families explored and exploited their Welsh heritage and political ties, I trace the development of one of the most politically potent historical myths of the period: the idea that English and Welsh nobility shared a common ancestry, since both claimed descent from the kings of Britain, who were themselves descended from Trojan refugees. By implication, both English and Welsh royal lines inherited a legacy of flight, resettlement, and divine claim to rule over the island of Britain. These two lines were brought together by marcher families, who vocally claimed both Welsh and English noble ancestry and, in some cases, used this dual ancestry to their advantage.

The activities of marcher barons as patrons of literature had important consequences for literary transmission. The process of textual transmission and literary contact between Wales and England took place not across a border line between two countries, as one might expect, but rather through a porous border zone with its own interests, needs, and circumstances particular to a border culture. As marcher lords reimagined, reinterpreted, and rewrote narratives of British–Welsh history, they played a vital role in exporting, transmitting, and popularizing that history to a broader audience outside Wales, where ideas of British–Welsh history had far-reaching impact. These literary activities shaped the lines of transmission that drew Welsh texts out of Wales and into England, and amplified Welsh influence on English understandings of the past. This study therefore shows that Wales did not fade into obscurity after the conquest of 1282, but rather exerted a continuous pull on the English historical imagination.

Further, this book reveals the importance of historical literature, including chronicles, genealogy, and prophecy. These genres have been overlooked in literary studies and are only recently being recognized as delivering coherent rhetorical arguments. I also show that conditions of warfare and conquest such as that experienced by the border culture on the March do not act as barriers to cultural exchange; rather, the literature that develops in troubled border zones is shaped by conflict, and, in turn, shapes the forces of conquest, particularly when literary production is used as a tool by conquerors and their descendants.

The formation of the March of Wales as a political and cultural borderland has been well-discussed by historians, who have focused on its development as a borderland shaped by a unique political position and hybrid identity.[10] Marcher literature, on the other hand, is an understudied field. There is broad recognition of the March as a zone of cultural contact, and several recent studies attend to individual texts or themes, but there are no synthetic surveys.[11] Historically, studies of literary contact between Wales and England tend to trace links between the two countries directly, without attending to the multilingual border region through which much textual transmission occurred (with a few important exceptions).[12] For example, scholars have long noticed common literary motifs in Welsh and English Arthurian romances,[13]

---

[10] Max Lieberman, *The Medieval March of Wales: The Creation and Perception of a Frontier, 1066–1283*, Cambridge Studies in Medieval Life and Thought, 78 (Cambridge, 2010); Max Lieberman, *The March of Wales, 1067–1300: A Borderland of Medieval Britain* (Cardiff, 2008); Brock W. Holden, *Lords of the Central Marches: English Aristocracy and Frontier Society, 1087–1265* (Oxford, 2008); R. R. Davies, *Lordship and Society in the March of Wales, 1282–1400* (Oxford, 1978); see, more recently, Ben Guy, Howard Williams, and Liam Delaney (eds), 'Borders in Early Medieval Britain', *Offa's Dyke Journal*, 4 (2022); Philip Hume (ed.), *The Welsh Marcher Lordships*, i. *Central & North* (Eardisley, 2021); David Stephenson, *Patronage and Power in the Medieval Welsh March: One Family's Story* (Cardiff, 2021); David Stephenson, *Medieval Wales, c.1050–1332: Centuries of Ambiguity* (Cardiff, 2019), 63–83; Matthew Siôn Lampitt, 'Networking the March: A History of Hereford and its Region from the Eleventh through Thirteenth Centuries', *Journal of the Mortimer History Society*, 1 (2017), 55–72; see also a new project by Helen Fulton, 'Mapping the March: Medieval Wales and England, c.1282-1550: Mapping Literary Geography in a British Border Region', https://blog.mowlit.ac.uk/, accessed 29 December 2023.

[11] Daniel Helbert, *Arthur between England and Wales: Arthurian Literature in the Anglo-Welsh Borderlands* (Liverpool, forthcoming); Emily Dolmans, *Writing Regional Identities in Medieval England: From the Gesta Herwardi to Richard Coer de Lyon* (Cambridge, 2020), 97–132; Matthew Siôn Lampitt, 'Networking the March: The Literature of the Welsh Marches, c.1180–c.1410' (unpublished Ph.D. dissertation, King's College London, 2019); Helen Fulton, 'The Red Book and the White: Gentry Libraries in Medieval Wales', in Aisling Byrne and Victoria Flood (eds), *Crossing Borders in the Insular Middle Ages*, Texts and Cultures of Northern Europe, 30 (Turnhout, 2019), 23–46; Joshua Byron Smith, *Walter Map and the Matter of Britain* (Philadelphia, 2017); Emily Dolmans, 'Locating the Border: Britain and the Welsh Marches in Fouke le Fitz Waryn', *New Medieval Literatures*, 16 (2016), 109–34; Ralph Hanna, 'The Matter of Fulk: Romance and History in the Marches', *Journal of English and Germanic Philology*, 110/3 (2011), 337–58; Simon Meecham-Jones, 'Where Was Wales? The Erasure of Wales in Medieval English Culture', in Ruth Kennedy and Simon Meecham-Jones (eds), *Authority and Subjugation in Writing of Medieval Wales* (New York, 2008), 27–56.

[12] For recent work on multilingual contact zones, see Thomas O'Donnell, Jane Gilbert, and Brian Reilly, 'Introduction', in Thomas O'Donnell, Jane Gilbert, and Brian Reilly (eds), *Medieval French Interlocutions: Shifting Perspectives on a Language in Contact* (York, forthcoming).

[13] See discussion in Ceridwen Lloyd-Morgan and Erich Poppe, 'The First Adaptations from French: History and Context of a Debate', in Ceridwen Lloyd-Morgan and Erich

La3amon's relationship to Wales,[14] Welsh subtexts and Celtic sources in *Sir Gawain and the Green Knight*,[15] and echoes of Welsh metrics in the Harley lyrics.[16] These studies have tended to take a comparative approach, evaluating observable parallels in Welsh and English literature, but less often discussing how the sources for such texts may have been transmitted. In a significant study, Simon Meecham-Jones argues that the silence about Wales and the Welsh in much of Middle English literature represents a purposeful erasure of Wales by English writers and their critics, a deliberate forgetting in service to colonization.[17] Similarly, Michael Faletra asserts that several works of insular historiography erase Wales and the Welsh from the historical record in service to a colonial project.[18] These works are more interested in the direct relationship between Wales and England than in the role of the borderlands. Study of the literatures of Wales and England remains almost entirely separate, with the divide between disciplines maintained by an entrenched belief in medieval studies that each literary tradition is defined by a single vernacular language.

That said, a few recent works have contributed to our understanding of cross-cultural contact and textual transmission in the insular world. An important, recent model for the present work is the volume *Crossing Borders in the Insular Middle Ages* (Turnhout, 2019), edited by Aisling Byrne and Victoria Flood, which takes a broadly insular view of transmission and contact that breaches the traditional divides between disciplines and languages. The volume frames interactions between

Poppe (eds), *Arthur in the Celtic Languages: The Arthurian Legend in Celtic Literatures and Languages*, Arthurian Literature in the Middle Ages, 9 (Cardiff, 2019), 110–16.

[14] Jennifer Miller, 'La3amon's Welsh', in Rosamund Allen, Jane Roberts, and Carole Weinberg (eds), *Reading La3amon's Brut: Approaches and Explorations* (Amsterdam, 2013), 589–622; Michael A. Faletra, 'Once and Future Britons: The Welsh in Lawman's *Brut*', *Medievalia et Humanistica*, 28 (2002), 1–23; Françoise Le Saux, 'La3amon's Welsh Sources', *English Studies*, 67/5 (1986), 385–93.

[15] Ordelle G. Hill, *Looking Westward: Poetry, Landscape, and Politics in Sir Gawain and the Green Knight* (Newark, 2009); Lynn Arner, 'The Ends of Enchantment: Colonialism and Sir Gawain and the Green Knight', *Texas Studies in Literature and Language*, 48/2 (2006), 79–101; Nicolas Jacobs, 'The Green Knight: An Unexplored Irish Parallel', *CMCS* 4 (1982), 1–4.

[16] A. T. E. Matonis, 'An Investigation of Celtic Influences on MS Harley 2253', *Modern Philology*, 70/2 (1972), 91–108.

[17] Meecham-Jones, 'Where Was Wales?', 35.

[18] Michael A. Faletra, *Wales and the Medieval Colonial Imagination: The Matters of Britain in the Twelfth Century* (New York, 2014), 3.

Wales and its neighbours as evidence for a broader pattern of insular connections and characterizes the island region of north-west Europe as a zone of contact.[19]

Another major lens through which relations between medieval England and Wales has been considered is that of postcolonial theory.[20] Owing to the theoretical framework adopted from Homi Bhabha, Gayatri Spivak, Edward Said, and others, and the need to disrupt a general indifference in literary studies towards the colonial relationship between Wales and England, these studies are chiefly interested in the relationship between colonizer (English/Anglo-Norman) and colonized (Welsh). The March plays an oblique role in this discourse, with the border zone giving rise to the hybridity of the colonial subject, as in Jeffrey Jerome Cohen's and Faletra's studies of Gerald of Wales.[21] Unlike this book, however, these studies do not focus on the complex role that the borderlands played in the colonial relationship.[22] Moreover, in explaining how the Welsh were the colonial 'other' or subaltern, at times postcolonial studies risk a replication of colonial norms, further 'othering' the Welsh by conducting a discourse that too often operates outside Welsh-language scholarship or editions of texts.

The present book departs from previous studies of relations between Wales and England in several crucial respects. First, it brings together an understudied group of texts, mainly chronicles and genealogies, associated with baronial families in the March of Wales whose literary activities reimagined British and Welsh history. Out of ten Latin and Anglo-Norman French texts under discussion, only half are available in modern print editions and translations. The rest are unedited, and they have never been brought together for consideration in a scholarly study before.

---

[19] See also Joshua Byron Smith, *Walter Map*; Lindy Brady, *Writing the Welsh Borderlands in Anglo-Saxon England* (Manchester, 2017).

[20] See, e.g., Faletra, *Wales*; Patricia Clare Ingham, *Sovereign Fantasies: Arthurian Romance and the Making of Britain* (Philadelphia, 2001); Jeffrey Jerome Cohen, 'Hybrids, Monsters, Borderlands: The Bodies of Gerald of Wales', in Jeffrey Jerome Cohen (ed.), *The Postcolonial Middle Ages* (New York, 2000), 85–104; Michelle R. Warren, *History on the Edge: Excalibur and the Borders of Britain, 1100–1300* (Minneapolis, 2000); Michelle R. Warren, 'Making Contact: Postcolonial Perspectives through Geoffrey of Monmouth's "Historia regum Britannie"', *Arthuriana*, 8/4 (1998), 115–34.

[21] Cohen, 'Hybrids'; Faletra, *Wales*, 135–72.

[22] I do take it as given that Welsh conquest and colonization (and, later, defence of those actions) was a major goal for marcher lords and that marcher baronial literature not only reflects that goal but was used in service to it.

Second, this book is unusually interdisciplinary, bringing together Latin, a range of vernaculars, and multiple genres under a regional focus, rather than pursuing a single language or literary form. It views the genres of history and genealogy, not as passive vehicles of information, but as deliberate creations shaped by authors' rhetorical strategies. It demonstrates that literary influence is not a passive undercurrent in the background of the production of literature, but a phenomenon generated by the purposeful behaviours of specific actors who choose to bring texts across political, linguistic, and cultural boundaries.

Third, the book's multilingual focus also has broad implications for the way languages are positioned in the subfields of medieval studies. The literature of a particular people or nation is not limited to works in the vernacular; rather, Latin belongs as much to regional and national literatures as vernaculars do, redefining what should be accepted as worthy of literary study. This book also has consequences for historians, demonstrating the outsized influence that conceptions of the British past had on the political landscape. It rehabilitates Geoffrey of Monmouth, who is often dismissed as a fanciful writer of pseudohistory, as a crucial force of influence on how the peoples of medieval Britain viewed themselves and their positions in the wider world. It demonstrates the importance of medieval historical narrative, continuously renegotiated and reimagined to fit new circumstances, as a source for understanding the attitudes and mindsets of the marcher nobility whose world view it animated.

Fourth, this book redraws the disciplinary boundaries of Welsh and English literary history. Marcher writers had unprecedented access to both Welsh and English monastic libraries and textual sources and, using that access for its own gain, became a major conduit through which literary contact between Wales and England took place. This conduit was fundamentally shaped by the interests of marcher families, as they found their places in the shifting political and ecclesiastical hierarchies of the March. The book urges the disciplines of Welsh and Celtic Studies to consider marcher literature as an important, influential category of literature that shaped Welsh literary tradition. Welsh literary studies would benefit from continued incorporation of French, Latin, and Middle English texts into its purview, even if only better to understand the rich set of influences at work in medieval Welsh literature. Similarly, English literary studies would be greatly enriched by increased attention to the influence of marcher and Welsh literature and politics, especially at the present moment, when there is a great deal of scholarly interest in borderlands, borders, and cultural exchange. In particular, literature produced in the West Midlands, which forms a significant proportion of extant literature in Middle English, was subject to the influence of marcher culture and ought to be studied in this light, as I discuss further in the Conclusion. With increased attention given by both disciplines to marcher literature and to the 'foreign' literature on the other side of the borderlands, a more comprehensive, diverse, multilingual picture of the literary history of medieval Britain can emerge. This study therefore knits together a lacuna that has persisted between subfields for many decades, but that is not reflected in medieval sources; rather, these sources display active transmission in the borderlands throughout the Middle Ages.

In addition to highlighting the important role that the reimagined Welsh and British past played in the English political arena, this study highlights the importance of the baronial families of the March of Wales in facilitating interaction between English and Welsh literatures, demonstrating the effect of marcher networks on the circulation and availability of texts, but also discussing the different ways that England and Wales felt ownership over the March—both politically, through disputed conquest territory, and ideologically, through an understanding of common descent from the kings of Britain. This sense of common inheritance contributed to the cultural hybridity of marcher society. This study's transnational and multilingual approach to literary contact in western Britain helps account for the ambivalent treatment of the Welsh in English literary works of this period, the presence of literary analogues in the vernacular literatures of England and Wales, and the indelible presence of these two countries in their overlapping historical narratives, as medieval writers negotiated both foreignness and proximity.

The history and character of the March of Wales

While the scholarly language used to describe the medieval English–Welsh borderlands very often relies on the image of a line or a boundary that must be traversed between two distinct countries—Wales and England, separated by an ambiguous border that was both cultural and geographical—the area across which contact between medieval Wales and England occurred was in fact a distinct zone.[23] It was known as the March of Wales, a contested borderland ruled in part by a semi-independent aristocratic society of mixed Norman, Welsh, English, and Breton descent.[24] The term for this zone is the 'March', from Old French *marche* 'border, border territory' and Latin *marcha, marchia* (ultimately from Old English *mearc* 'boundary, borderland', from which the name of the early English kingdom of Mercia also derives).[25] The term 'March' refers to a geographical area, defined by R. R. Davies as 'a broad zone on or beyond the frontiers of a country or an ill defined and contested district between two countries'.[26] As I discuss in further detail below, its medieval usage seems to have evolved over time, beginning life as a geographical term, and becoming in the thirteenth century a specific legal designation, referring specifically to borderlands that were under marcher law (*lex Marchiae*).

Beyond this legal definition, the term is also useful in a literary sense, referring to a broad contact zone between Welsh, English, and other cultures in the borderlands, which were sites of encounter between different peoples, languages, and texts. A range of scholars have described the Welsh border and/or borderlands as a fluid, ambiguous zone of contact.[27] Faletra characterizes the Welsh border as 'a persistently and perhaps troublingly fluid one'.[28] Michelle Warren, writing specifically of Monmouthshire, describes a colonial culture, a contact zone 'where people lived interactive, improvised border lives of transient identities'.[29] For Cohen, colonial subjects inhabit an 'interstice' between Wales and England, 'a place of overlap where "cultural

---

[23] Conceiving of a border as a zone rather than a line to be crossed is an idea that emerged from Fredrik Barth (ed.), *Ethnic Groups and Boundaries: The Social Organization of Culture Difference* (Boston, 1969).

[24] Some areas of the March, depending on location and time period, were ruled by Welsh princes and/or by the English Crown.

[25] *OED: Oxford English Dictionary Online*, s.v. 'march, n. 3', 'mark, n. 1' (Oxford, 2016), www.oed.com, accessed 14 March 2022.

[26] R. R. Davies, *Lordship and Society*, 15. For the contested nature of the region, which frequently saw battles and raids, see Stephenson, *Medieval Wales*, 66–74.

[27] See, most recently, Lindy Brady, 'The Fluidity of Borderlands', *Offa's Dyke Journal*, 4 (2022), 3–15.

[28] Faletra, *Wales*, 5.

[29] Warren, 'Making Contact', 117.

differences 'contingently' and conflictually touch".[30] Cohen's Welsh–English borderland is a frontier between a so-called advanced culture and a primitive culture, 'an ambiguous middle location caught between a distant, dominant, domestic center and a proximate, absolute, alien outland'.[31] His March is 'an uneasy composite' of Welsh and Anglo-Norman, 'linguistically, architecturally, and culturally ... a mixed form ... *biformis* like a centaur, a minotaur'.[32] But the materials discussed in this book do not reveal the March as a binary hybrid of two conjoined cultures—instead, more than two cultures and languages were at play, and marchers at times saw themselves as constituting a separate, third category, in terms of both identity and law.

Meecham-Jones writes instead of a substrate–superstrate relationship between Wales and England, with marcher society characterized by an 'unresolvable contention between promoted and suppressed cultures'.[33] It is a 'penumbra', in other words, a series of frontiers, both psychological and geographic, marked by garrisoned settlements of English people.[34] The suppressed, substrate Welsh culture lurks behind English texts, emerging in passing in the form of Welsh place names or other lexical items, but its appearance is vanishingly brief owing to suppression by the superstrate. Others have theorized the March in terms of a centre–periphery model that considers the position of the March in relation to other major loci of Middle English literature. As discussed in more detail in Chapter 4, Ralph Hanna characterizes the county of Shropshire as particularly conscious of its position on a periphery, 'looking back into England from the edge', similar to Meecham-Jones's theory of frontiers.[35] In contrast, Matthew Siôn Lampitt sees marcher culture as self-consciously global and internationally connected, 'present[ing] itself not as the western periphery of an English power to which it is assimilable', but as situated in a 'global geography'.[36] The difficulty in defining the position of centre

---

[30] Cohen, 'Hybrids', 88.
[31] Ibid., 95.
[32] Ibid., 97.
[33] Meecham-Jones, 'Where Was Wales?', 32.
[34] Ibid., 34.
[35] Hanna, 'Matter of Fulk', 355.
[36] Lampitt, 'Networking the March: Literature', 104; see also Dolmans, 'Locating the Border'.

versus periphery in this context may be due to the overlay of contemporary scholarly attitudes towards medieval perceptions of geography and identity: modern scholars see Wales and the Welsh borderlands as peripheral, and, even as canonical English literature emerges from the West Midlands, West Midlands Middle English is considered primarily in the orbit of English literature's other geographical areas, such as London, and the literature of Wales is (as Meecham-Jones points out) too often suppressed and ignored. In contrast, medieval marcher lords, to the extent that they considered the civility of Wales and the Welsh from their position on a militarized frontier, were deeply engaged in relations with Wales and the Welsh, while also often heavily involved in the politics of the English 'centre'—that is, the royal court. As a result, they do not seem to have been overly concerned with perceptions of their peripherality: even Gerald of Wales, uncomfortably aware of his dual Welsh and Norman descent and its effect on his career, readily celebrated the accomplishments of the marchers (*marchiones*). In order to cleave as closely as possible to contemporary usage, I use the narrow legal definition of the term 'March of Wales' as it was used during the medieval period to refer to the baronial marcher lordships, which in fact covered a very extensive area encompassing not only the north–south borderlands between Wales and England, but much of South Wales itself (see frontispiece for map).

The boundaries of the March of Wales fluctuated along with the political fortunes of its inhabitants and rulers. The baronial society of the marcher lords was a product of a unique set of circumstances, influences, and military needs.[37] It was defined by its own identity, separate from English or Welsh; its own loose set of laws; a strongly militarized structure; and an interdependent set of relationships both internally and with the families of native Wales. It was also characterized by a considerable degree of access to, and familiarity with, Welsh culture, customs, and laws, in part owing to a frequent practice of intermarriage with Welsh noble families, to the extent that the anachronistic identity term 'Cambro-Norman' is sometimes used. Nevertheless, marcher society was not quite Welsh, nor English, legally or culturally. Instead, as I discuss further below, it was a 'third category', a border culture that encompassed multiple identities, languages, and states of being.

[37] See Lieberman, *Medieval March*, 173–88.

The March of Wales in the period covered by this book existed as an outcome of the Norman conquest of 1066, and I will briefly describe here the history of the March insofar as it is useful for understanding the region's position in relation to Wales, England, and the conquest and colonization of Wales.[38] Following the Norman conquest of 1066, Normans spread into South Wales initially in the 1070s, establishing a set of castles along the southern border of former Mercia that were used to launch campaigns into Wales.[39] Normans did not make significant gains in the area until after the Welsh king of Deheubarth, Rhys ap Tewdwr, was killed in 1093 by the army of Bernard de Neufmarché, a Norman aristocrat who had served William I.[40] With Rhys fell the Welsh kingdoms of Brycheiniog, Dyfed, Ceredigion, and Ystrad Tywi, resulting in what has been called a 'wholesale land grab' in South Wales.[41] At this point, several important and long-standing Norman lordships—what we would now call marcher lordships—were established, including the lordship of Brecon and the earldoms of Shrewsbury, Hereford, and Chester. Over the next two centuries, much of Wales was conquered in piecemeal fashion, with the exception of the northern kingdom of

---

[38] Though I focus on the post-Norman-conquest period, it must be noted that the marcher zone took shape much earlier. It was a disputed border region prior to the Norman conquest, when Offa's Dyke was constructed and the Welsh kingdom of Ergyng was brought under Mercian control, and took shape as early as the first and second centuries AD, as it was the borderland between Roman Britain and Celtic-speaking Britain; see Keith Ray, 'The Organisation of the Mid–Late Anglo-Saxon Borderland with Wales', *Offa's Dyke Journal*, 4 (2022), 132–53; Ben Guy, 'The Changing Approaches of English Kings to Wales in the Tenth and Eleventh Centuries', *Offa's Dyke Journal*, 4 (2022), 86–106; Brady, *Writing the Welsh Borderlands*; Wendy Davies, *Wales in the Early Middle Ages* (Leicester, 1982), 195; Wendy Davies, 'Land and Power in Early Medieval Wales', *Past and Present*, 81 (1978), 3–23, at 5–6.

[39] Stephenson, *Medieval Wales*, 9–10; Philip Hume, 'The Marcher Lordships and their Distinctive Features', in Hume (ed.), *Welsh Marcher Lordships*, 1–9, 13–17, at 3–5; Philip Hume, 'The Arrival of the Normans 1066–1100 and Establishment of Early Marcher Lordships', in Hume (ed.), *Welsh Marcher Lordships*, 41–56; David Crouch, 'The Transformation of Medieval Gwent', in Ralph A. Griffiths, Tony Hopkins, and Ray Howell (eds), *The Gwent County History*, volume 2. *The Age of the Marcher Lords, c.1070–1536* (Cardiff, 2008), 1–45; R. R. Davies, *The Age of Conquest: Wales, 1063–1415* (Oxford, 2000), 27–9.

[40] See J. E. Lloyd, 'Rhys ap Tewdwr (d. 1093)', rev. David E. Thornton, *ODNB*, accessed 14 March 2022; Robert S. Babcock, 'Rhys ap Tewdwr, King of Deheubarth', *Anglo-Norman Studies*, 14 (1994), 21–36; Paul Courtney, 'The Norman Invasion of Gwent: A Reassessment', *JMH* 12/4 (1986), 297–313.

[41] Courtney, 'Norman Invasion', 309; J. E. Lloyd, *A History of Wales from the Earliest Times to the Edwardian Conquest*, 2 vols, 2nd edn (London, 1912), ii.400–22.

Gwynedd, which, after a brief takeover in the 1080s following the battle of Mynydd Carn, was independent until Edward I conquered it in 1282, a date that conventionally marks the end of independent Welsh rule in Wales.[42]

The activities of Norman barons such as Robert fitz Hamon in Glamorgan and Bernard de Neufmarché in Brecon in the years following these initial acquisitions of Welsh territory in the eleventh century illustrate the interdependent relationship between secular and ecclesiastical structures of power, important for present purposes, because the relationships between marcher lords and ecclesiastical institutions influenced opportunities for and patterns of textual production later on. These lords granted Welsh churches, located in newly acquired swathes of territory, to monasteries in the March under their patronage, thus strengthening their hold on Welsh territory and forging new points of contact between native Welsh and Anglo-Norman monasteries.[43] New Benedictine foundations in Wales and the March, which number at least nineteen, demonstrate an important relationship between military conquest and ecclesiastical foundation, with the initial Norman conquest of Wales achieved and stabilized with the help of ecclesiastical authority. This process, in turn, had a considerable effect on the transmission of texts between various locations in the borderlands, and a corresponding increase in interest in the Welsh historical past on the part of new marcher arrivals, because ecclesiastical institutions were often also sites of textual production, particularly histories and genealogies.

The twelfth and thirteenth centuries saw the development of what Max Lieberman calls a 'border aristocracy', formed by families such as the Mortimers, Fitz Alans, Corbets, Lacys, and Braoses, as well as

---

[42] These events are, of course, more nuanced than what is offered in this brief narrative. See Stephenson, *Medieval Wales*, 7–27; Lieberman, *Medieval March*, 1–5; C. P. Lewis, 'The Shape of the Norman Principality of Gwynedd', in K. J. Stringer and A. Jotischky (eds), *The Normans and the 'Norman Edge': Peoples, Polities and Identities on the Frontiers of Medieval Europe* (London, 2019), 100–28; J. Beverley Smith, *Llywelyn ap Gruffudd*.

[43] As is well known, the identity term 'Anglo-Norman' is fraught and anachronistic, but is retained here for ease of use. It remains useful for present purposes even after the traditional cut-off of 1204, when some would argue that the identity term 'English' becomes more appropriate, because the baronial families of Norman heritage in the March of Wales continued to use French in communication and literature. See R. R. Davies, *Domination and Conquest: The Experience of Ireland, Scotland, and Wales, 1100–1300* (Cambridge, 1990), 112–17.

families like the Clares and Marshals, whose interests exceeded the March even as their power bases were located there.[44] These families ruled over territories conquered from the Welsh as well as portions of English counties, and they formed a recognizable set: Lieberman writes, 'the March may have been perceived as a discrete territory because it was seen to coincide with the lands of a certain group of lords', who came to be called the *barones Marchie*.[45] They may not have operated politically as a unified entity at all times, but they were recognized as a distinct, powerful group.

With the Edwardian conquest of Wales in 1282–4, the principality of Gwynedd came under royal control, and the geography of the March expanded.[46] Stephenson observes that, in the post-conquest era, the term 'March' denoted any land that was not in the principality of Wales.[47] At this time, Edward I created new marcher lordships in the north-east from lands forfeited by Llywelyn ap Gruffudd and Gruffudd Fychan (specifically Ceri, Cedewain, Denbigh, Bromfield and Yale, Chirk, and Dyffryn Clwyd), as well as in the south (Iscennen and Cantref Bychan) and gave them to his barons.[48] Hopedale, Teigengl, and Maelor Saesneg became part of the county of Flintshire, and the counties of Anglesey, Merionethshire, and Caernarfonshire were created.[49] R. R. Davies notes that the conquest created a 'new Marcher aristocracy' in North Wales that held land by permission of the king and acted out his pacification of Wales.[50] Following the conquest, Wales was overall divided between the marcher lordships in the south, east, and north-east, and the principality, consisting of Anglesey, Caernarfon, Meirionnydd, Ceredigion, and Carmarthen in the west and north. With the collapse of the military border that had separated the Welsh kingdom(s) of Powys from the English county of Shropshire, the lordships

---

[44] Lieberman, *Medieval March*, 56–101; Stephenson, *Medieval Wales*, 11.
[45] Lieberman, *Medieval March*, 56.
[46] Edward I's conquest of 1282–4 is conventionally thought of as the singular event of Welsh loss of independence. For a recent, more nuanced view, see Stephenson, *Medieval Wales*, 5, 155–6, who argues that Edward I continued a process that was already well underway, and the landscape of ministerial governance of royal and marcher lands continued as it had done in the thirteenth century. There is perhaps more continuity in governance and society before and after 1282 than is sometimes acknowledged.
[47] Stephenson, *Medieval Wales*, 12, 122–3.
[48] R. R. Davies, *Lordship and Society*, 26–9; Stephenson, *Medieval Wales*, 12; Hume, 'Marcher Lordships', 6.
[49] R. R. Davies, *Age of Conquest*, 364.
[50] Ibid., 363.

of Cedewain, Ceri, and Chirk were given to the Mortimers, who introduced English governance systems to those areas (see frontispiece for map).[51] In the counties, offices of justiciar and sheriff were implemented, and people from England migrated to the new lordships in the north-east and to towns on a large scale, displacing Welsh people to poorer farmland.[52]

Owing to advantageous marriages, the deaths of some prominent marcher lords, a general lack of male heirs, and other political factors, the early fourteenth century saw the emergence of new families, including the Bohuns and Despensers, as significant players in the March; additional families like the Mortimers were able to gain a stronger foothold following the collapse of independent Gwynedd. Power shifted to these new families, and even more lands shifted to the Crown, such as the 1322 forfeiture to Edward II of Brecon, Bromfield and Yale, Chirk, Wigmore, and Iscennen. Generally speaking, such shifts in power relations reflect the characteristic fluidity of marcher political geography, which was dependent on individual fortune: 'the extent of the March was determined not by legal or constitutional criteria but by the flow of historical events ... [and] by the forcefulness and ability of the Marcher lords themselves.'[53] Though further political changes occurred in the later fourteenth century following the population decline and economic difficulties of the plague, the geography of the region was relatively stable (though its rulers were not) from c.1300 until the Acts of Union of 1536 and 1542 fully incorporated the marcher lordships into English government.[54] During the fifteenth century, many marcher lordships (as well as marcher genealogies, as discussed in Chapter 3) were sites of conflict and negotiation in the Wars of the Roses.

The nature of marcher culture and identity

The terms of identity used in this book, which relate to geography, polity, and language, have nuances that are difficult to capture. I use the terms 'Welsh', 'English', and 'marcher' as labels to describe different

---

[51] Lieberman, *Medieval March*, 257–8.
[52] Stephenson, *Medieval Wales*, 28–9, 125–6; R. R. Davies, *Age of Conquest*, 365, 370–3.
[53] R. R. Davies, *Lordship and Society*, 32, 278–83.
[54] Ibid., 425–43, 19.

groups of people in medieval Britain. That 'Welsh' and 'English' were (and are) distinct ethnic identity terms is rightly taken a given in medieval studies. 'Welsh' typically describes people of Wales (living in *pura Wallia*, to use a medieval term, but also living in marcher lordships), who generally spoke Welsh, practised Welsh cultural customs, and lived under Welsh law, while English describes people of England, who generally spoke English, practised English cultural customs, and lived under English law. However, even the most superficial examination of the literature and history of these two countries reveals the problems inherent in defining identity terms according to language, law, and custom, as these were, in reality, multilingual societies that intermingled with one another in many ways. These distinctions become even more difficult after 1282, when, for example, English law and rulers pertained in a colonized Wales. Nevertheless, it would be reductive and incorrect to abandon these terms and to say that there are no cultural distinctions between 'Welsh' and 'English' in the medieval period, or that these identity markers have no meaning, because they did (and do) have meaning. The distinction between 'English' and 'Welsh' in the post-conquest period was in fact institutionalized and loomed large in contemporary documentation.[55] Therefore, I use the adjective 'Welsh' to describe people, objects, or customs generally emerging from Wales (*pura Wallia*), but not necessarily resident there, and the adjective 'English' to describe people, objects, or customs generally emerging from England, though not necessarily resident there either.[56] Both of these groups could (and did) live in the March of Wales as well as elsewhere. I use these identity terms to describe people from the twelfth to the fifteenth centuries, while acknowledging that their meanings evolved over time and reveal considerable nuances as soon as one takes a closer look. The terms 'Norman' and 'Anglo-Norman' are also necessarily used. Though the term 'Anglo-Norman' is widely acknowledged to be anachronistic, as mentioned previously, it is difficult to find a substitute term that describes the francophone culture that emerged in Britain following the Norman conquest. This term will be used as shorthand, however imperfect, from time to time.

---

[55] For discussion, see R. R. Davies, *Age of Conquest*, 419–21.
[56] For discussion of what 'Wales' meant in the medieval period, see Stephenson, *Medieval Wales*, 4–5.

Deliberately muddying the waters of the above ethnic identity terms is the word 'marcher', which I use to refer to a third category of people that emerged in the March of Wales in the medieval period. In scholarship to date, 'marcher' is most often used to describe the baronial class of hybrid Norman–Welsh-English descent that ruled the marcher lordships. This is the narrowest definition of the term. I use it to describe the customs, culture, and character of *any* people residing in the borderlands, or March of Wales, where a distinct 'border culture' emerged. 'Border culture' is a term I borrow from border studies and border theory, referring to culture that arises at or alongside political borders.[57] The people of the March of Wales were neither wholly English, Norman, nor Welsh, but an emergent third category. The term 'third category' comes from Gloria Anzaldúa's work on borderlands and borderland consciousness, and echoes Bhabha's concept of the 'third space'.[58] For the purposes of this book, the term 'marcher' most often refers to the ethnically hybrid baronial class that arose in the March of Wales in the medieval period and sought to make sense of its position in society, geography, and politics, and drew upon the different ethnic identity markers at its disposal depending on the context. However, one must keep in mind that other groups were 'marcher' as well, by nature of residing in the borderland. For example, people whom scholars typically think of as Welsh (Welsh-speaking, with Welsh names, with ancestors who had lived in independent Wales), and who would have identified themselves as Welsh, also lived in the March of Wales. The same goes for people who were ethnically English, Norman, Flemish, or Irish. By my definition, these people were 'marcher' as well, because they resided in the March of Wales and to some degree had a particular awareness of inhabiting a borderland.

---

[57] Victor A. Konrad and Anne-Laure Amilhat Szary, *Border Culture: Theory, Imagination, Geopolitics* (Abingdon and New York, 2023), 6.

[58] Gloria Anzaldúa, *Borderlands/La Frontera: The New Mestiza* (San Francisco, 1987); Homi Bhabha, *The Location of Culture* (London and New York, 1994); later, Alicia Español, Giuseppina Marsico, and Luca Tateo, 'Maintaining Borders: From Border Guards to Diplomats', *Human Affairs*, 28/4 (2018) 443–60, at 457–8, posit a 'triadic system' of inside, border, and outside. Emily Dolmans has independently suggested that the March of Wales is a 'third space'; see Dolmans, *Writing Regional Identities*, 105, citing Jonathan Rutherford, 'The Third Space: Interview with Homi Bhabha', in Rutherford, *Identity: Community, Culture, Difference* (London, 1990), 207–21.

Borderlands, according to border theorists, are 'sites that can enable those dwelling there to negotiate the contradictions and tensions found in diverse cultural, class, and other forms of difference'.[59] Because borders are socially constructed, they have a psychological dimension, existing in the minds of the people who dwell there. Border theorists posit that border-dwellers are aware of the 'in-between space' they inhabit; they are able to negotiate living in 'multiple worlds' and have a different perspective on 'systems of difference' than people who do not live in a borderland.[60] They learn to 'navigate different social worlds'.[61] This state of mind is described by Anzaldúa as a 'mestiza consciousness'.[62] Similarly, Konrad and Amilhat Szary argue that 'political borders, at all scales, constitute a kind of space that allows very well for grasping tensions and links through both their symbolic and material existence'.[63] This is the border culture represented by the term 'marcher'.[64]

This third category, 'marcher', is difficult to define (in any way other than geographically) because of the legacy of the academic disciplines in which we operate, which categorize national literatures according to language. How can one talk about cultural identity when it is not anchored to a particular language, a currently existing country, or an academic discipline? Marcher identity encompasses many identities, languages, perspectives, and experiences. It is uncoupled from language and nation. It must be evaluated and defined carefully, and on a case-by-case basis, with practitioners always acknowledging that it is changeable and fluid, the product of people residing in a borderland. The medieval

---

[59] Nancy A. Naples, 'Borderland Studies and Border Theory: Linking Activism and Scholarship for Social Justice', *Sociology Compass*, 4/7 (2010), 505–18, at 507, citing Pablo Vila, 'The Limits of American Border Theory', in Pablo Vila (ed.), *Ethnography at the Border* (Minneapolis, 2003), 306–41.

[60] Naples, 'Borderland Studies', 507, citing AnaLouise Keating (ed.), *Entre Mundos/Among Worlds: New Perspectives on Gloria E. Anzaldúa* (New York, 2005), 1.

[61] Naples, 'Borderland Studies', 508.

[62] Anzaldúa, *Borderlands*, 77. This is a culturally specific term that would be inappropriate to adopt here, but it must be acknowledged.

[63] Konrad and Amilhat Szary, *Border Culture*, 6.

[64] The distinction between border-dwellers and non-border-dwellers risks essentializing and homogenizing the cultures that were being crossed by border-dwellers. One must be careful, in emphasizing the nature of border culture, not to create a monolith of the cultures that surround the borderland, as human experience there was varied and multiple as well. One must also allow for the possibility that some border-dwellers reinforced borders rather than crossed them. For discussion, see Naples, 'Borderland Studies', 507, citing Vila, 'Limits', 307; Konrad and Amilhat Szary, *Border Culture*, 7–8.

March of Wales, as a border culture, was a hybrid mix of many cultures; it was multilingual, and its inhabitants were self-aware of their position in a borderland and of their cultural and ethnic difference.[65] Therefore, when I make a distinction between 'Welsh' and 'marcher' literary culture, for example, what I mean by 'Welsh' is 'non-borderland, within Wales', while what I mean by 'marcher' is 'borderland, within the March of Wales'—while also acknowledging that the 'marcher' person could still be Welsh or English (or Norman, or French, or Flemish, or Irish) in some way. This third category emerges because of the mixing of and encounters between multiple cultures and languages and the lived experiences of people dwelling in a borderland.

One must also acknowledge the binary inherent in border studies. The March of Wales is, by definition, a border region that arose between England and Wales because of conquest and colonization. In a recent study of border culture, Konrad and Amilhat Szary argue: 'If we consider that borders are the limits of national containers, then they ostensibly form a space of confrontation between two cultural entities.'[66] Though Wales and England are not monoliths, they are different countries that claim different identities and national origins, and, by necessity, the March is defined against the countries on either side of the borderland. For this reason, it is difficult to escape the binary of 'Welsh' versus 'English' in discussions of the March.[67] The borderland is defined against and according to its existence on a boundary between two comparatively well-defined countries. However, the term 'marcher' in fact troubles the binary between 'English' and 'Welsh', because the people inhabiting the March of Wales could be both and neither of these ethnic identities.[68] They could be ethnically or linguistically English or Welsh, and identify as such, but, because they inhabited a borderland,

---

[65] For hybridity, see Bhabha, *Location of Culture*. This is not to say that people in other regions of medieval Britain were not multilingual or hybrid, but that the inhabitants of the March of Wales (in a centre–periphery model) had a different experience and perspective than they would have had if they lived in a non-borderland.

[66] Konrad and Amilhat Szary, *Border Culture*, 8.

[67] For challenges to the binaries inherent in discussions of borderlands, see Josiah McC. Heyman, 'Culture Theory and the US–Mexico Border', in Thomas M. Wilson and Hastings Donnan (eds), *A Companion to Border Studies* (Chichester, 2012), 48–65; Español et al., 'Maintaining Borders'.

[68] I do not think that the March renders the identity terms 'Welsh' and 'English' meaningless, as I do not think marcher inhabitants were ever unaware of or unresponsive to those identities; cf. Dolmans, *Writing Regional Identities*, 105.

they had a different experience from that of an English or Welsh person residing in England or Wales.[69] In other words, the Welsh–English binary loses its purchase in this region. What, for example, do we make of Welsh officials who worked for marcher lords, or the Herberts of Rhaglan, marcher lords who are widely viewed as being Welsh? What do we make of the poems written in Welsh to the Mortimer family, a family of marcher lords who are typically thought of as being English and/or Anglo-Norman in their ethnic orientation?[70] What did it mean to be 'Welsh' on the March (such as a member of the Welsh population of Oswestry), or 'Norman' or 'English' on the March? Such examples suggest that ethnic identities could be performed in different ways, both within and outside Wales and the March. The presence of Welsh or English people on the March does not refute the idea of marcher identity as a real entity but complicates it.

Konrad and Amilhat Szary describe the difficulty of defining the culture of border-dwellers, particularly when border-dwellers are self-aware of having come from somewhere else: 'Is [border culture] their former national culture? Is it the culture that they have negotiated throughout their journey? Is it the new hybridized culture that they attain? Or, is it a diasporic culture that spans all of these possibilities and draws from them differentially?'[71] Border-dwellers have a different experience of their ethnic identity, influenced by their position in a borderland, and perform this identity differently from non-border dwellers. Perhaps this constituted an increased awareness of cultural differences, as suggested by border theorists, or an ability to navigate other worlds using techniques such as code-switching. The term 'marcher', therefore, encompasses a wide range of possibilities for identity, which is variable according to situation and circumstance.

The degree to which marcher culture and identity shifted after the conquest of 1282–4 is an open question. Traditionally, historians have demarcated a sharp line between life in Wales before and after the

---

[69] I take it as given that there is a difference in experience of a Welsh, English, or Norman person living in the border culture of the March from that of a person living in a non-borderland area of Wales or England.

[70] See Chapter 2 of this book, which discusses the Mortimer family's identity further.

[71] Konrad and Amilhat Szary, *Border Culture*, 13.

conquest. However, more recent work has tempered this approach, suggesting that the conquest was a continuation of many earlier efforts already well established by the late thirteenth century.[72] Because of this new thinking, I hesitate to draw too sharp a line between marcher identity before and after 1282. While R. R. Davies charts a rise in new absentee landlords in the March of Wales after the conquest, whose estates in the March 'were only a means for them to pursue their ambitions elsewhere', and who lacked a marcher identity, I show that some fourteenth-century families self-consciously participated in the building of a marcher identity, to their advantage.[73] Perhaps there is less of a division between life before and after the conquest than between individual families, whose reasons for adopting and expressing marcher identities varied widely.

In the end, it is important not to homogenize any of the regions or identity terms discussed in this book, as all perspectives are the result of distinct, individual experiences. Because the March of Wales was a border culture, a space of 'struggle, contest, and negotiation where socio-spatial identities emerge to question or re-frame territorial accounts of political belonging/exclusion', the writing that emerged from this region was 'border writing'—preoccupied by a position within a borderland, navigating ethnic difference, articulating awareness of exclusion and belonging, and inhabiting multiple spheres of identity.[74] This book is interested in how these issues played out in border writing about the historical past, and constitutes a step forward in defining marcher identity, its culture, and interests.

It is most important to examine how the people of the March of Wales themselves conceived of the territory in which they lived, its borders, and their own identities within that context. In this next section, I address how the March of Wales as a geographical region has been defined at different points in the Middle Ages, using extant legal, literary, and historical sources.

---

[72] R. R. Davies, *Age of Conquest*, 376–8, suggests that Edward's conquest of 1282 'palpably diminished' the claim that marcher lords had as 'conquerors and defenders of Wales', because the conquest effort was largely royal and followed by direct challenges to marcher liberties; see also discussion in Stephenson, *Medieval Wales*, 123–5.
[73] R. R. Davies, *Age of Conquest*, 395.
[74] Konrad and Amilhat Szary, *Border Culture*, 37.

Defining the March of Wales

The term 'March' is contemporary, and it evolved as a legal and spatial signification, and as a term of identity, throughout the centuries.[75] The region is referred to varyingly in sources as *marcha, marchia, Marchia Walliae* (Latin), *y Mars* (Welsh), *marche* (Old French), and the *Marche of Walis* (Middle English). The earliest attested use of the term is in Domesday Book (1086), referring to manors in western Herefordshire.[76] The word *Marcha* first appears in the Pipe Rolls in 1165–6 in the entry for Shropshire.[77] In the Welsh vernacular chronicle *Brut y Tywysogion* ('History of the Princes'), the term seems to have been a geographic designation as well: in the entry for the year 1022, the chronicler describes an army being driven *hyt y Mars* 'as far as the March'.[78] To the thirteenth-century Welsh translators of this chronicle, the March is a distinct border region controlled by foreign noblemen.

By contrast, the thirteenth-century author of the *History of William Marshal*, a text discussed in Chapter 4, refers to William Marshal's supporters as *les marchis / De Wales* 'the marcher lords from Wales' (ll. 9902–3), suggesting that, to one author at least, the word had morphed into a term of identity decoupled from geographic origin.[79] Further evidence for the use of the word as an identity label is found in the writings of Gerald of Wales, the twelfth-century clergyman of Norman and Welsh descent from Pembrokeshire, who refers to his people as

---

[75] The following overview of the term relies on Max Lieberman, 'The Medieval "Marches" of Normandy and Wales', *EHR* 115/517 (2010), 1357–81; Kevin Mann, 'The March of Wales: A Question of Terminology', *WHR* 18 (1996), 1–13; R. R. Davies, 'Law of the March'.

[76] Critics hesitate to apply the term in this period to the broad region of the March that would later become widely known: for example, Lieberman takes *marcha* in Domesday Book as evidence of anomalous, local usage, while Mann suggests the word in this period should be translated simply as 'borderlands'; see Lieberman, 'Medieval "Marches"', 1358; Lieberman, *March of Wales*, 5–8; Mann, 'March of Wales', 4–5.

[77] R. R. Davies, *Conquest, Coexistence and Change: Wales, 1063–1415* (Oxford, 2000), 272; Lieberman, 'Medieval "Marches"', 1358; Mann, 'March of Wales', 1.

[78] Mann, 'March of Wales', 10; *Brut y Tywysogyon, or The Chronicle of the Princes, Red Book of Hergest Version*, ed. and trans. Thomas Jones (Cardiff, 1955), 22–3, 176–7, 222–3; some of these instances are also noted by Mann, 'March of Wales', 10. Importantly, this entry is probably not from 1022: this chronicle is a late-thirteenth-century translation into Welsh of a no-longer-extant Latin chronicle, and the terminology used by the original Latin chronicle is unknown.

[79] *HWM* i.502–3; Mann, 'March of Wales', 9.

marchiones, people who have grown up in the March of Wales (*gens in Kambrie marchia nutrita*).[80]

In Latin documentary sources, *marchia* also seems to have been an improper noun referring to 'borderlands, boundary, border', or 'frontier line', interchangeable with *fines*, and used broadly to refer to border regions not just in Wales but also in Normandy, Scotland, and Ireland.[81] In Middle English, too, the word was used as a more general term for borderlands. The difficulty of defining the geographic bounds of the March of Wales during a period of struggle for control of various lordships by non-Welsh barons, Welsh princes, and English kings probably contributed to this continued ambiguity. Given these nuances, it is perhaps more appropriate to follow R. R. Davies's broad definition and take the 'march', in those documentary and literary sources that are not referring specifically to a region governed by *lex Marchiae*, as referring to a borderland with poorly defined, contested boundaries that resided between two distinct countries with different customs, cultures, and languages.[82]

In sum, the term seems to have been used at first as a geographical designation, referring generally to 'borderlands', and was not used in any systematic way in legal documentation, or by the royal exchequer or chancery, until the thirteenth and fourteenth centuries. Then, it came to refer to an area governed by specific marcher liberties, laws that were separate from the legal systems of Wales and England.[83] Lieberman defines marcher liberties as 'the quasi-regal privileges claimed

---

[80] Gerald of Wales, *Descriptio Kambriae*, ii.8, ed. J. F. Dimock, *Giraldi Cambrensis Opera*, 6 (London, 1868), 220; Gerald of Wales, *Expugnatio Hibernica*, ii.38, ed. and trans. A. B. Scott and F. X. Martin, *Expugnatio Hibernica: The Conquest of Ireland by Giraldus Cambrensis*, A New History of Ireland, Ancillary Publications, 3 (Dublin, 1978), 246.

[81] Mann, 'March of Wales', 4, 12. The use of the Latin term *marchia* to refer to Scottish and Irish borderlands suggests that it may have referred to a militarized border specifically. For Ireland and Normandy, see Lieberman, 'Medieval "Marches"', 1360–9; for Scottish Marches, see Andy King, 'Best of Enemies: Were the Fourteenth-Century Anglo-Scottish Marches a "Frontier Society"?', in Andy King and Michel Penman (ed.), *England and Scotland in the Fourteenth Century: New Perspectives* (Woodbridge, 2007), 116–35; Anthony Goodman, 'The Anglo-Scottish Marches in the Fifteenth-Century: A Frontier Society?' in Roger A. Mason (ed.), *Scotland and England: 1286–1815* (Edinburgh, 1987), 18–33.

[82] R. R. Davies, *Lordship and Society*, 15; see also Lieberman, *Medieval March*, 10–11.

[83] It was used as a legal designation in Magna Carta, referring to land governed by *lex Marchiae*; R. R. Davies, 'Law of the March', 6–7, 16–19.

by the Marchers within their lordships ... which included the right to wage war, broker truces and adjudicate on arson and murder', all necessary elements of leadership in a militarized border zone.[84] Similarly, R. R. Davies describes the remarkable degree of independence that resulted from the circumstances of the March: while marcher families were subject to the king of England, and held their lands with his permission, 'within their Marcher lordships they claimed and exercised a measure of authority unsurpassed elsewhere within the king's dominions'; the most unusual of these rights was the right to wage war without royal permission.[85] Historians attribute the development of these liberties to the unique conditions of a militarized society that, by necessity, operated semi-independently of English administrative and legal authority. Such liberties were the result of necessity and survival, rather than a granted constitutional privilege.[86] Evidence for this legal designation and semi-independent status emerge in the thirteenth century, as marcher liberties were being contested by English kings and increasingly defended by marcher lords. *Marchia Walliae* in this period was quickly becoming 'a highly valuable territorial distinction' enabling landowners to exercise constitutional liberties under *lex Marchiae* that would otherwise be unavailable to them.[87] These struggles seem to have precipitated the solidification, to some extent, of the definition of the term.[88]

Given the liberties that were at stake, families controlling conquest territories had a vested interest in proving that their lands were part of *Marchia Walliae* and that they could rule with *lex Marchiae*.[89] An incident that perhaps represents the pinnacle of marcher liberties occurred in 1250, when a messenger bearing a letter from King Henry III was sent to Walter III de Clifford, lord of Clifford, Glasbury, and Cantref Selyf. In a rage, Walter demonstrated that the king had no authority in

---

[84] Lieberman, 'Medieval "Marches"', 1359; see also Hume, 'Marcher Lordships', 8–9.
[85] R. R. Davies, 'Kings, Lords and Liberties in the March of Wales, 1066–1272', *TRHS* (Fifth Series), 29 (1979), 41–61, at 41; R. R. Davies, 'Law of the March', 13.
[86] Holden, *Lords*, 7–8; R. R. Davies, 'Kings', 44.
[87] Lieberman, 'Medieval "Marches"', 1380; R. R. Davies, 'Kings'; Sara Elin Roberts, 'The Law of the March', in Hume (ed.), *The Welsh Marcher Lordships*, 9–13.
[88] Mann, 'March of Wales', 2–3. For the difficulties surrounding the definition of the March, particularly as it pertains to Herefordshire, see further discussion in Mann, 'March of Wales'; Lieberman, 'Medieval "Marches"'.
[89] Ibid., 1358–9.

the March by forcing the royal messenger to eat the letter and its seal.[90] Proving marcher status would have been increasingly important after 1282, when Edward I took over vast areas of land in the March and in Wales and acted aggressively to curtail marcher power.

A representative, much-discussed example of the deployment of marcher liberties is William VI de Braose's protracted legal battle with the county administration of Carmarthen and the royal courts between 1302 and 1312, during which time he sought to prove that his lordship, Gower, was independent of English control because it was part of the March.[91] William seems to have capitalized on Gower's legally vague status, defending a previous failure to appear in court by invoking marcher liberties: *il tyent e doyt tenir, e ses aunscestres devaunt ly unt tenu, tote la terre de Gowere entierement of totes les fraunchises, fraunches custumes, e fraunches usages a la dite terre aportenauntz* 'he holds, and ought to hold, and his ancestors before him held, all the land of Gower in its entirety, with all the franchises, free customs, and free usages pertaining to the said land'.[92] In response, the constable of Carmarthen, Walter of Pederton, argued that Gower was under royal administrative control as part of the county of Carmarthen, and William's summons to court therefore compulsory.[93] Countering Walter, William asked for justice for the wrongs committed against the liberties his family had enjoyed since the time of King John, when his charter was made (a vague definition that reflects the fact that marcher liberties were customary laws). His liberties include:

---

[90] Brock Holden, 'The Making of the Middle March of Wales, 1066–1250', *WHR* 20/2 (2000), 207–26, at 207; Emma Cavell, 'Aristocratic Widows and the Medieval Welsh Frontier: The Shropshire Evidence', *TRHS* 17 (2007), 57–82, at 59 n.4.

[91] Michael Richter, 'William ap Rhys, William de Braose and the Lordship of Gower, 1289 and 1307', *SC* 32 (1998), 189–209; J. Beverley Smith and T. B. Pugh, 'The Lordship of Gower and Kilvey', in *GCH* 205–84, at 231–47. The Parliamentary Rolls of 1292 make a distinction between *comitatus* 'county', referring to Hereford, Carmarthen, and Cardigan, and *pars* 'region', referring to Gower, Kidwelly, Ewyas, and Grosmont; see Edward I, Roll 5, in 'Original Documents: Edward I Parliaments, Roll 5', in *Parliament Rolls of Medieval England*, ed. and trans. Chris Given-Wilson et al. (Woodbridge, 2005), *British History Online*, http://www.british-history.ac.uk/no-series/parliament-rolls-medieval/roll-5, accessed 27 October 2022.

[92] Edward I, Roll 11, in 'Original Documents: Edward I Parliaments, Roll 11', in *Parliament Rolls of Medieval England*, ed. and trans. Given-Wilson et al. (Woodbridge, 2005), *British History Online*, http://www.british-history.ac.uk/no-series/parliament-rolls-medieval/roll-11, accessed 27 October 2022.

[93] Ibid.

quod ipse habere debet cancellariam suam et [cancellarium] suum, et sigillum suum in eadem cancellaria, hominibus et tenentibus suis terre predicte de Gowere deserviencia cum neccesse fuerit, judicium vite et membrorum, et eciam cognicionem omnium placitorum tam corone quam aliorum quorumcumque infra dictam terram inter quascumque personas emergencium, **ut de terra in marchia** et extra comitatum predictum de Kermyrdyn, et extra potestatem vicecomitis ejusdem comitatus existente.

that he is entitled to have his own chancery and his own chancellor, and his seal in the same chancery, to serve the men and tenants of the aforesaid land of Gower whenever necessary, judgment of life and limb, and also cognisance of all pleas both of the crown and all others originating within the said land between any persons, **as in marcher land** and outwith the aforesaid county of Carmarthen, and outwith the authority of the sheriff of the same county.[94]

William claims that Gower enjoys the same rights as *terra in marchia* 'marcher land' and should continue to do so. This case suggests that Gower was not considered part of the March per se (perhaps, as in the Pipe Rolls, it is a *pars* 'region'), but that William was trying to define it as such to remain independent of the Crown.

Marcher liberties were in this sense extremely valuable, ensuring independence from English administrative control. These parliamentary proceedings indicate that the border between the March and England was one of administrative control and legal status, and marcher lords who wished to enjoy marcher liberties would have interest in defining their lands as *in Marchia*, rather than *in Anglia*, where stricter English laws pertained. It would follow that *Wallia* would refer to places operating under Welsh law.[95] The Braose case further suggests that a lordship enjoying marcher liberties and jurisdiction by definition had its own seal and chancery—in other words, the material, symbolic, and economic abilities to exercise governance.

In the Gower court documents, it is difficult to discern exactly which liberties were being claimed. They are described vaguely as 'liberties enjoyed by the ancestors of the men of Gower', and therefore seem to

---

[94] Edward I, Roll 11, in 'Original Documents', ed. and trans. Given-Wilson.
[95] The Treaty of Aberconwy of 1277 corroborates this suggestion, at least until 1284, when the Statute of Rhuddlan placed Wales under English law. For discussion, see R. R. Davies, 'Law of the March', 1.

reside in popular memory, referenced wholesale and tacitly understood, rather than delineated in written law. This vague definition is probably a symptom of the organic creation of marcher liberties over time as customary law, never granted by royal decree. What the conquest lordships and the border counties had in common were culture, languages, legal independence from England, proximity to both Welsh and English cultures, intermarriage with both Welsh and English nobility, and—most importantly to the present study—an interest in Welsh historical narrative and ideologies regardless of political boundaries. This distinct society played an integral role in the transmission of ideas of history from medieval Wales to England.

Reimagining the past in marcher literature

In this book, I argue that the baronial families of the March used their ancestral ties to Wales to strengthen their political positions, both regionally and nationally, and, in doing so, conducted investigations into and written displays of their family history set in the broader legendary context of British–Welsh history derived from Geoffrey of Monmouth. A consequence of this reimagining of the Welsh past, as mentioned above, was the drawing of Welsh texts out of Wales and into the March and England, amplifying the influence of Welsh historical narrative on late medieval Britain's political landscape. This conduit was fundamentally shaped by the interests of marcher gentry patrons in the history of Wales and Britain, which they reimagined for their own purposes.

My definition of marcher literature is regional: literature produced in the region of the March of Wales, in any language, in the medieval period. In examining this body of 'marcher literature', written for and by marcher baronial families, several interlinked themes, interests, and concerns have emerged. These are: an interest in the British–Welsh past based in the narrative of Geoffrey's *DGB* (with its attendant focus on political prophecy, the unification of the kingdoms of Britain, and justification of conquest); fierce defence of marcher families' rights to land, particularly conquest territories of Wales and areas under threat of royal ownership, with an accompanying preoccupation with recording the succession of lordships within a particular baronial family, often through a female line; and, lastly, the incorporation of a range of perspectives on Welsh people, culture, and history, sometimes manifested as an affinity for or interest in Welsh princes. These emergent themes in marcher literature are a consequence of dwelling in a borderland, where elite readers and writers of texts were situated in a multilingual, militarized society undergoing frequent political upheavals, battles, and changes in leadership. Their location in this society was the result of incremental conquest, at times precarious and threatened, in need of defending, and characterized by a heightened awareness of ethnic difference. At times, self-conscious expressions of that particular position emerge from contemporary writings, and a coherent marcher identity is realized.[96]

The themes of marcher literature centre around issues of succession, historical narrative, and relationships with the Welsh, because this is what interested baronial families. Any one of these items could be of interest to a baronial family in a different region. Interest in Geoffrey of Monmouth, or in issues of inheritance and succession, are by no means unique to the baronial families of the March. However, what sets this body of literature apart from general baronial interests is the way in which Geoffrey's narrative is interpreted and used. *DGB* is the key text that allows for a confluence of different cultures, kingdoms, and influences to be imagined in the March of Wales, a border culture that (as will be seen in this book) is characteristically preoccupied with borderland issues of identity, place, and belonging, and the consolidation of power and influence in that context. These issues manifest as defensive ownership of territory, rewriting historical narrative so that residence in the March is justified, and an interest in the precedent Geoffrey set for the different kingdoms of Britain to be united, here in the form of marcher leadership.[97]

---

[96] Gerald of Wales, for example, makes marcher identity visible in *Expugnatio Hibernica*; he writes: *Gens in Kambrie marchia nutrita, gens hostilibus parcium illarum conflictibus exercitata, compententissima; puta formatis a convictu moribus, audax et expedita* 'That breed of men which has been brought up in the March and trained in the warfare that goes on in those parts, is the most capable, being resolute and quick to act because they have been refined by habits shaped by their environment' (Gerald of Wales, *Expugnatio Hibernica*, ii.38, ed. and trans. Scott and Martin, *Expugnatio Hibernica*, 246–7.

[97] These interests are not necessarily distinct from the interests of Welsh gentry (the *uchelwyr* who succeeded the native princes of Wales following the conquest of Wales in 1282), but, as discussed further in Chapter 1, the perspective of the colonizer is distinct from the perspective of the colonized with respect to reading and interpreting narratives of British–Welsh history. Marcher barons may have readily taken on aspects of Welsh identity and capitalized on Welsh ancestry to increase their political power, as I show in this book, but these behaviours did not preclude their point of origin in the March of

The second key dynamic that distinguishes literature of the March of Wales from other literatures written for medieval barons is a particular relationship to Wales, Welsh princes and gentry, and the British–Welsh past. This book is, therefore, not about the influence of Geoffrey on marcher literature, but about the nature of marcher literary culture as it emerged from a multilingual border zone, with a focus on articulations of marcher identity, the positionality of marcher readers towards the Welsh past and their reinterpretation of that past, and the role that marcher literary activities played in the exportation of ideas of the British–Welsh past to audiences beyond Wales.

In Chapter 1, I examine an adaptation of Geoffrey's *DGB* called the *Epitome historiae Britanniae*, whose transmission from the marcher lordship of Glamorgan in South Wales to the marcher town of Ludlow in Shropshire demonstrates the mobility of narratives of Welsh history in the medieval English–Welsh borderlands. For the first time, I place this text in its literary, political, and historical contexts, and demonstrate how marcher interest in the Welsh past drew Welsh historical texts out of Wales and refashioned them for new audiences. The stakes of this process of transmission are set out further in Chapter 2, in which I discuss the most remarkable and high-profile instance of marcher use of the British–Welsh past: the Mortimer family's interest in its Welsh ancestry in a flurry of textual production that argued in favour of Roger Mortimer's claim to the throne of England. Chapter 2 demonstrates the value of narratives of British–Welsh history and assertions of Welsh identity and heritage to the arenas of English statecraft and politics at the highest level. It shows that marcher families and their historians worked together to generate new narratives of the historical past for the benefit of a family that laid claim to a marcher identity. Chapter 3 therefore takes a closer look at the relationship between several of these families and the monasteries they patronized, which, in these specific cases, were sites of textual production. Several key genealogical and historical texts produced at Llanthony Priory for the lords of Brecon, as well as short histories of the earldoms of Gloucester and Hereford, some of which I have edited for the first time, demonstrate the importance of the relationship between monastery and patron for the writing of family histories, a relationship that was foundational to the preservation of family memory and therefore status. Chapter 3

Wales, which was a result of colonization and conquest of Welsh kingdoms. Their position towards Wales and Welsh culture is distinct from that of the *uchelwyr*.

lays out the mechanisms of literary production that animated marcher reshaping of British–Welsh history.

The final two chapters of the book focus on literature and identity, examining the depiction of marcher and Welsh figures and their identities in marcher literature.[98] Chapter 4 examines two francophone marcher texts, the romance of *Fouke le Fitz Waryn* and the biography of William Marshal, set against the Middle English *Awntyrs off Arthure at the Terne Wathelyn* as a point of comparison from the Anglo-Scottish Marches. These literary texts bring a marcher point of view into focus: defensive claims to land, difficulties of inheritance, succession, and English royal overreach, an interest in Welsh princes, and an adoption of Geoffrey of Monmouth as the major narrative framework for understanding their place in the contemporary political landscape. Finally, Chapter 5 takes a broader view of perceptions of the British–Welsh past outside Wales, examining reverberations of that past in English chronicles. Elegies to Welsh princes in English chronicles demonstrate how the formerly threatening power of Welsh princes was deliberately diminished in post-conquest chronicle narratives, even as marcher families elsewhere grew powerful by association with Wales.

In sum, the reimagining of British–Welsh historical narratives played a key role in the development of marcher identity and political strategy in the medieval period. The expansion of marcher power and the distinctiveness of the March as a borderland society was in part due to the ability of individual families to shape their narratives of origin. They did this by drawing upon familial connections to Welsh nobility and access to Welsh texts, and, in doing so, solidified their placement in the shifting landscape of political relations between England and Wales. Their efforts had profound implications for English and Welsh literary history and gave Wales a place in the historical imagination and political landscape of medieval Britain that is more significant than previously imagined.

---

[98] This book does not focus primarily on literature written in Welsh, nor on literature in any one language, because its focus is regional rather than language based. This region happened to use several languages to write literature and history, and resists categorization under any one national literature.

1

Rewriting Geoffrey of Monmouth

In the fraught English–Welsh borderlands of the late fourteenth and early fifteenth centuries, during the decades spanning Owain Glyndŵr's rebellion and the beginning of the Wars of the Roses, when ideas about Welsh history and prophecy were particularly potent, a short chronicle abbreviating Geoffrey of Monmouth's *De gestis Britonum* (*Historia regum Britanniae*) made its way from South Wales to Shropshire. It crossed boundaries of language and country, transcended local reading communities, and articulated new ways of relating to the past in the light of the colonization and conquest that dominated medieval Wales and the March of Wales. This chronicle is known as *Epitome historiae Britanniae*.

Geoffrey's *De gestis Britonum* (hereafter *DGB*), a malleable work that was frequently adapted to fit different societies and languages throughout medieval Europe, was in this context fashioned to suit two different reading communities with divergent interests. Though these audiences shared a common interest in the British–Welsh past, that interest was rooted in rather different motivations. First was the religious institution of Llandaf in the late fourteenth century, diocesan seat of the multilingual, colonized lordship of Glamorgan, a former Welsh kingdom conquered by Robert fitz Hamon in the late eleventh century and governed at this time by the powerful Despenser family. This marcher lordship was populated by Welsh speakers, including gentry patrons who read Welsh literature, history, and law, and whose interest in the

Galfridian past was that of a colonized people coping with their loss of independence. Second was an audience in Ludlow, a town in the borderlands in the county of Shropshire, a multilingual patchwork of marcher lordships and English hundreds. Ludlow, which also had a substantial Welsh population, was controlled by the powerful Mortimer earls of March. Their interest in the Galfridian past was from the position of the colonizing outsider, and their adaptation of Welsh texts to suit their own uses drew those texts out of Wales to reach wider audiences.[1] This chapter shows how the thread of interest in Geoffrey of Monmouth that runs through the marcher literature discussed in this book was bolstered by transmission of materials out of Wales and into new marcher contexts. The adaptation of a Galfridian chronicle to fit a marcher readership represents a key aspect of marcher identity: the use of the British–Welsh past to understand (and sometimes, to shape) contemporary circumstances.

The distinction I am making here between the identities of people in Glamorgan and people in Shropshire is complicated. I view the initial audience for the *Epitome historiae Britanniae* in the diocese of Llandaf as Welsh-identifying, Welsh-speaking, and with a perspective on Welsh history that is sympathetic to Welsh people, and the later audience in Ludlow as 'marcher'—a third category of identity that was influenced by Welsh, English, and other cultures, and adopted different aspects of those identities to suit different contexts (such as the Galfridian past), as befits a border culture.[2] We do not know how readers of the *Epitome* in Ludlow would have labelled themselves, or to what extent their identities mapped onto language choices. The Mortimer lords in Shropshire, while they were not native Welsh gentry, adopted and were aligned with various aspects of Welsh culture—see, for example, the praise poem written for Roger Mortimer in Welsh, 'Moliant Syr Rosier Mortimer', composed by Iolo Goch in the 1390s and discussed in Chapter 2.[3] However, while the Mortimers did adopt aspects of Welsh culture in this manner, I still see them and their milieu as 'colonizing outsiders', because the family's dominance in the region was the result of conquest and colonization, even as they did assimilate to some degree. I call them

---

[1] This is discussed further in Ch. 2, pp. 105–14. Unless otherwise noted, translations are my own.

[2] For further discussion of these identity terms, see the Introduction.

[3] See pp. 95–7.

'marcher' as a way of addressing the complexity of this identity issue. The residents of Ludlow similarly would have had multiple identities and ways of expressing them.[4]

In any case, in this chapter, I trace the evolving contexts of the *Epitome historiae Britanniae* in the March of Wales. I frame the text as an important instance, not only of the transmission of narratives of the British–Welsh past beyond Wales, but also of the ways in which such narratives were transformed by writers outside Wales who were interested in adapting a conquered country's history for their own purposes. The medieval copies of this text demonstrate an active network of Welsh and marcher scribes whose interest in the ancient history of Britain superseded the boundaries (linguistic, political, and cultural) that are often wrongly assumed to restrict the transmission of ideas.

Below, I contrast the way the *Epitome* was read in Wales and/or by readers whose identities were Welsh (as an explanation for Welsh loss with a promise of future regeneration in the era of rapid political change leading up to the rebellion of Owain Glyndŵr) with how it was read in the March and/or by marcher people (as a summary of the historical past and royal lineage that marcher lords had now inherited). This contrast shows how the literary activities of adaptation, textual transmission, and reinterpretation of the past were central to articulations of medieval marcher identity.

In the first section of the chapter, I place the chronicle for the first time in the context of late-fourteenth-century Glamorgan's literary activities and climate of colonization and rebellion. I read its trajectory of British–Welsh kingship in this light, reflecting a time when Welsh rebellions against English and marcher rule were informed by Welsh history, genealogy, and prophecy. I then discuss the chronicle's transmission to Ludlow in Shropshire and Hailes Abbey in Gloucestershire (in a full version at Ludlow in the context of a Ludlow-area chronicle, and in an excerpted form as part of the *Register and Chronicle of the Abbey of Aberconwy* at Hailes). Owing to its transmission to Ludlow, Hailes,

---

[4] Additionally, some notable members of the Welsh gentry moved comfortably in marcher society as officials in the late thirteenth and early fourteenth centuries, as David Stephenson has recently discussed, showing that the rift between the two worlds of Welsh and English, as it is often described, does not capture the full picture of post-conquest Welsh life; see David Stephenson, *Medieval Wales, c.1050–1332: Centuries of Ambiguity* (Cardiff, 2019), 137–52; David Stephenson, *Patronage and Power in the Medieval Welsh March: One Family's Story* (Cardiff, 2021), 110.

and perhaps Aberconwy Abbey, this chronicle constitutes an important example of marcher interest in Welsh history, and in Welsh historical texts finding a readership outside Wales.[5] In this, the text seems to have bridged what R. R. Davies calls 'the greatest chasm between the worlds of the Welsh *uchelwyr* and the English gentry ... their interpretations of the past and the future', a move that was made possible by the border culture of the March of Wales and the interests of marcher readers.[6] The chronicle's explanations of the classical origins of the Britons, the loss of Welsh independence, and the foundation of the church in Glamorgan were adapted to fit the political geography of the March of Wales in the early fifteenth century, when control over South Wales was being reasserted after the failure of Owain Glyndŵr's rebellion.

The *Epitome historiae Britanniae*'s narrative scope

The *Epitome historiae Britanniae* offers a condensed version of British history based on Geoffrey's *DGB*, with details added from the life of a local Welsh saint, the first *Life of St Dyfrig*.[7] It covers the origin myth of Brutus' arrival in Britain; the legendary foundation of the church of Llandaf in Glamorgan; a sketch of Welsh history from the ninth-century Welsh king Rhodri Mawr (Rhodri 'the Great') to the death of Llywelyn ap Gruffudd, last prince of independent Wales (*c*.1233–82); a precis of fourteenth-century Glamorgan history to 1375 (a *terminus ante quem*

---

[5] It was read, for example, by David Winchcombe, monk of Hailes and later abbot of Aberconwy.
[6] R. R. Davies, *The Revolt of Owain Glyn Dŵr* (Oxford, 1995), 55.
[7] St Dyfrig was an important fifth- or sixth-century Welsh saint in Glamorgan and Gwent (both kingdoms in South Wales), and bishop of Ergyng (Archenfield in English) in what became Herefordshire. For the first *Life of St Dyfrig*, see Ben Guy, 'The Life of St Dyfrig and the Lost Charters of Moccas (Mochros), Herefordshire', *CMCS* 75 (2018), 1–37.

for the composition of the chronicle); and an eschatological timeline.[8] I discuss its narrative in more detail below.

The chronicle is accompanied in its earliest extant manuscript (London, British Library, Cotton Titus D. xxii, AD 1429) by a range of religious texts in Latin and Welsh (see Table 1.1 for contents; see Figure 1.1. for manuscript images).[9] Daniel Huws suggests that this bilingual

TABLE 1.1   Contents of London, British Library, Cotton Titus D. xxii

Text	Language	Foliation
Description of Judgement Day (*Yr Anghrist a Dydd y Farn*)	Welsh	4^r–22^r
Epitome historiae Britanniae	Latin	22^r–37^r
Latin Life of the Welsh saint Gwynllyw	Latin	37^v–52^v
Latin Life of the Welsh saint Cadog (the *Vita Prima* by Lifris of Llancarfan)	Latin	54^r–137^r
Welsh Life of St David, patron saint of Wales (*Buchedd Dewi*)	Welsh	138^r–155^v
Welsh translation of the *Sunday Letter* (*Ebostol y Sul*)	Welsh	155^v–159^r
Welsh Life of St Margaret of Antioch (*Buchedd Fargred*)	Welsh	159^r–175^r
Welsh Life of St Katherine of Alexandria (*Buchedd Catrin*)	Welsh	175^r–185^r

---

[8] The title *Epitome historiae Britanniae* is not contemporary; it was given this title by its first editor; see *Lives of the Cambro-British Saints*, ed. and trans. W. J. Rees (London, 1853), 278–86, 612–22. I am retaining this title because it has been used in what little scholarship has been published on the text. Selections are edited in *Cartae et Alia Munimenta quae ad Dominium de Glamorgan Pertinent*, vol. iv. *1215–1689*, ed. G. T. Clark (Cardiff, 1893), 90–3; an abbreviated version in Peniarth 32 is edited by Diana Luft, 'The NLW Peniarth 32 Latin Chronicle', *SC* 44 (2010), 47–70, at 65–70. I discuss the *Epitome* further in 'The Reception of Gerald of Wales in Welsh Historical Texts', in Sadie Jarrett, Katharine Olson, and Rebecca Thomas (eds), *Memory and Nation: Writing the History of Wales* (Cardiff, forthcoming).

[9] An early modern transcription of this witness, probably in the antiquary Robert Vaughan's hand, is in Aberystwyth, NLW, Peniarth 383 (pp. 276a–h).

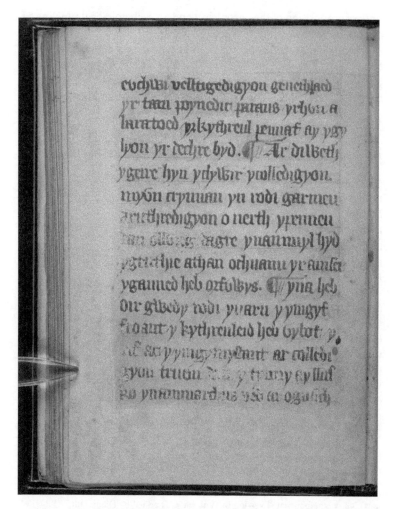

FIGURE 1.1 London, British Library, Cotton Titus D. xxii, fols. 21ᵛ–22ʳ. *Epitome historiae Britanniae* begins on fol. 22ʳ, l. 8, with the scribe code-switching from Welsh to Latin.

© The British Library Board

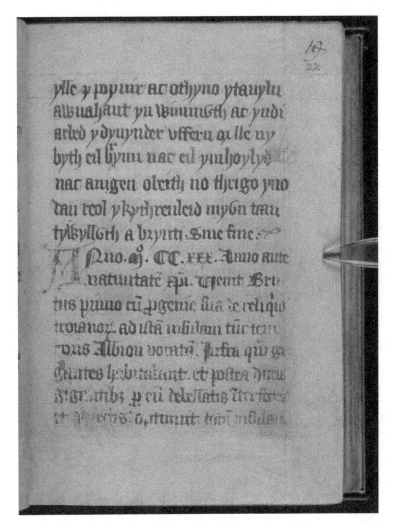

FIGURE 1.1   (*Continued*)

manuscript may have been written in the diocese of Llandaf, and Chris Given-Wilson argues that the chronicle itself was probably composed at or for the Llandaf community.[10] Cotton Titus D. xxii's contents and use of Latin corroborate origin in a religious institution, and Llandaf itself has a precedent for being interested in the history of the diocese in the twelfth-century codex known as the Book of Llandaf (Aberystwyth, NLW, 17110E, s. xii) and in the genealogical text *Gwehelyth Morgannwg*.[11] By combining the first *Life of St Dyfrig* with Geoffrey's *DGB* and other historical sources, the *Epitome* offers a sophisticated rendering of the diocese's history in its broader historical and biblical context.

An additional, abbreviated copy was created in or near Llantarnam Abbey in Monmouthshire, AD 1404 (*Y Llyfr Teg* 'The Fair Book', Aberystwyth, NLW, Peniarth 32, fols. 112ᵛ–114ᵛ), indicating that it was of sufficient interest to have circulated in a limited fashion in late-fourteenth- and early fifteenth-century Glamorgan and Monmouthshire in the years immediately preceding and during the rebellion of Owain Glyndŵr.[12] The compilation of the chronicle seems to have occurred between 1375 and 1399 (see Table 1.2).[13]

The *Epitome historiae Britanniae*, though it has not been the focus of sustained contextual study, has been discussed by Diana Luft and Chris

[10] Daniel Huws, *A Repertory of Welsh Manuscripts and Scribes, c.800–c.1800*, 3 vols (Aberystwyth, 2022), i.666; Chris Given-Wilson, 'Chronicles of the Mortimer Family, c.1250–1450', in Richard Eales and Shaun Tyas (eds), *Family and Dynasty in Late Medieval England: Proceedings of the 1997 Harlaxton Symposium* (Donington, 2003), 67–86, at 79 n. 34; Luft, 'NLW Peniarth 32', 50–1. Another possible point of origin is Cardiff Priory, because the chronicle mentions the building of the town of Cardiff in 1081 (perhaps more likely the Dominican or Franciscan priory than the Benedictine priory, owing to their focus on Welsh parishioners and sympathy for Owain Glyndŵr's rebellion).

[11] For the Book of Llandaf, see Patrick Sims-Williams, *The Book of Llandaf as a Historical Source*, Studies in Celtic History, 38 (Woodbridge, 2019); John Reuben Davies, *The Book of Llandaf and the Norman Church in Wales*, Studies in Celtic History, 21 (Woodbridge, 2003). For *Gwehelyth Morgannwg*, which was revised at Llandaf in the twelfth century and c.1500, and also incorporates information about St Dyfrig, see *MWG* 147–50, 345–8. I am grateful to Ben Guy for bringing this item to my attention.

[12] Luft, 'NLW Peniarth 32'; Huws, *Repertory*, i.349.

[13] The chronicle's last dated annalistic entry, in all copies of the text, is 1375. Handily, near the end of the chronicle is a statement about how many years have elapsed between the birth of Christ and now. A copy of the chronicle in London, British Library, Cotton Nero A. iv, discussed further below, gives this date as 1399. Peniarth 32 gives a date of 1404, and Cotton Titus D. xxii gives a date of 1429. The *terminus ante quem* for compilation is therefore 1399. Moreover, the appearance of this date in the Cotton Nero A. iv witness, which must have been copied from an exemplar, given that the manuscript is paleographically late fifteenth century, gives us proof that yet another copy of the text existed.

TABLE 1.2   Dating the *Epitome historiae Britanniae*

1375	The chronicle's last dated entry, in all copies
1399	The witness in Cotton Nero A. iv states that 1399 years have passed since the birth of Christ, a date carried over from Cotton Nero A. iv's exemplar
1404	The witness in Peniarth 32 states that 1404 years have passed since the birth of Christ
1429	The witness in Cotton Titus D. xxii states that 1429 years have passed since the birth of Christ
Late fifteenth century	Date of Cotton Nero A. iv based on palaeography

TABLE 1.3   Structure of *Epitome historiae Britanniae*

Part 1	Galfridian history from the arrival of Brutus to the departure of Kadwaladrus, 1230 BC–AD 689
Part 2	A sketch of Welsh history, with a Glamorgan emphasis, 689–1375
Part 3	Miscellaneous notes interested in world geography and reckoning of time

Given-Wilson.[14] Luft focuses on the manner in which it abbreviates Geoffrey and its possible place of origin. She takes primary interest in the abbreviated copy from Llantarnam, which she edits. Given-Wilson discusses the chronicle in the context of a range of other materials relating to the Mortimer family.

The chronicle can be divided into three major parts (see Table 1.3). First, it sketches the broad outlines of Galfridian history from the arrival of Brutus to Britain (which it dates to the year 1230 BC) to Kadwaladrus,

---

[14] Luft, 'NLW Peniarth 32'; Given-Wilson, 'Chronicles of the Mortimer Family'. It is briefly summarized by Ben Guy, 'Historical Scholars and Dishonest Charlatans: Studying the Chronicles of Medieval Wales', in Ben Guy, Georgia Henley, Nia Wyn Jones (published under Owain Wyn Jones), and Rebecca Thomas (eds), *The Chronicles of Medieval Wales and the March: New Contexts, Studies and Texts*, Medieval Texts and Cultures of Northern Europe, 31 (Turnhout, 2020), 69–106, at 105; Ben Guy, '*Epitome Historiae Britanniae*', Welsh Chronicles Research Group, Bangor University, http://croniclau.bangor.ac.uk/hist-britanniae.php.en, accessed 3 February 2022.

the last British king (689 AD).[15] In this section it is tightly focused on three episodes: the coming of Brutus, the coming of Christianity, and the coming of the Saxons. In a very abbreviated paraphrase of *DGB* I.20–2, Brutus vanquishes the giants inhabiting the island and founds New Troy (London) on the bank of the Thames. Next is a conversion legend: Lucius, king of the Britons, writes to Pope Eleutherius and sends for the missionaries Faganus and Diwanus, who convert the Britons in AD 156.[16] Three hundred years later, Germanus of Auxerre and Lupus of Troyes are sent to Britain to stamp out the Pelagian heresy.[17] Germanus and Lupus found the metropolitan church of Llandaf by permission of Meurig ap Tewdrig, king of Morgannwg, in AD 447.[18] This was, of course, important information for the probable Llandaf audience of the chronicle.

Paraphrasing *DGB*, the chronicle frames Vortigern's destructive decision to invite Hengist to Britain—which leads to the collapse of British independent rule—around the concept of Merlin's prophecies.[19] In this episode, Merlin prophesies that the kingdom of Britain will suffer many tribulations, with the Britons giving up their nobility to degenerate foreign nations (*per externas degeneres naciones*) until a later time when they will be freed from oppression. True to these words, Hengist arrives in 449 and unites with Vortigern against Uther Pendragon and Aurelius Ambrosius. Much of this section is abridged from Geoffrey, including

---

[15] This 1230 BC date is consistent with Geoffrey's own statement that Brutus settled New Troy when Eli was ruling in Judea, though Geoffrey does not give a specific date; see *DGB* i.22.506–9, pp. 30–1.

[16] This is called the 'Lucius legend' and is also found in Geoffrey, William of Malmesbury, and the Book of Llandaf.

[17] The chronicle repeats this story twice, in slightly different ways, suggesting an imperfect combining of textual sources.

[18] Meurig ap Tewdrig's role in Llandaf's foundation is also mentioned in *Gwehelyth Morgannwg*, §1; *MWG* 347.

[19] In this sense, it is distinct from Wace's *Brut*, which famously shies away from translating Geoffrey's *Prophetiae Merlini*. See Jean Blacker, 'Where Wace Feared to Tread: Latin Commentaries on Merlin's Prophecies in the Reign of Henry II', *Arthuriana*, 6/1 (1996), 36–52. The Anglo-Norman Prose *Brut* and the Middle English Prose *Brut* include Merlin's prophecy to Vortigern about the red and white dragon, but not Geoffrey's *Prophetiae Merlini*; see *The Oldest Anglo-Norman Prose Brut Chronicle*, ed. and trans. Julia Marvin, Medieval Chronicles, 4 (Woodbridge, 2006), 140–5; *The Brut: Or, The Chronicles of England*, ed. Friedrich W. D. Brie, 2 vols, Early English Text Society, OS 131, 136 (London, 1906–8, repr. 1960), i.59.

the bloody 'treachery of the long knives' episode, wherein the Saxons slaughter a large group of British nobles in the guise of brokering a peace treaty.[20]

The lives of King Arthur and St Dyfrig are woven together in the next section, drawing on material from DGB and the first *Life of St Dyfrig*.[21] St Dyfrig crowns Arthur at Cirencester in 506 before withdrawing to Ynys Enlli (Bardsey Island) to die.[22] St Teilo succeeds him in the archbishopric. Out of temporal sequence, but reflecting its probable place of origin and hagiographical source, the chronicle mentions that Dyfrig's relics are translated to Llandaf in the year 1120.[23] It then resumes the story of Arthur, who is fatally wounded by Mordred and passes to Avalon. It lists Arthur's successors before landing on Gormundus' battle with Kareticus and finally Kadwaladrus' withdrawal from Britain.[24] The chronicle turns to prophecy again, this time conveyed by an angel, who delivers God's message to Kadwaladrus, telling him that the Britons can no longer rule over Britain until the time comes that was prophesied by Merlin to Arthur. The chronicler states that contemporary belief in this prophecy is reflected in the authentic books of Welsh bards.

Thus concludes the first section of the chronicle, most of which is sourced from Geoffrey. Its second section begins with the Britons'

---

[20] Interestingly, the *Epitome* uses the wording *Draw ȝour sexis* rather than the standard reading from Geoffrey, *nimet oure saxas*, suggesting influence from a Middle English chronicle. The Middle English Prose *Brut*, as edited by Brie, uses the verb *draw*; see *Brut*, ed. Brie, i.54, while Laȝamon's *Brut* uses *nimeð*; see *Layamon: Brut: Edited from British Museum Ms Cotton Caligula A. IX and British Museum Ms Cotton Otho C. XIII*, ed. G. L. Brook and R. F. Leslie, 2 vols (London, 1963–78), i.394, l. 7610.

[21] As mentioned below, it is possible that this information is coming from the saint's life or from *De primo et statu Landauensis ęcclesię*, which begins with part of the saint's life. Both are in the Book of Llandaf.

[22] The crowning of Arthur by St Dyfrig is also mentioned in *Gwehelyth Morgannwg*, §4; *MWG* 348.

[23] For this episode in the first *Life of St Dyfrig*, which also discusses the 1120 translation, see §20 of 'Vita Sancti Dubricii (Liber Landavensis / Vespasian A. xiv)', ed. and trans. Ben Guy, *Seintiau: The Cult of Saints in Wales* (Aberystwyth, 2019), https://saint2.llgc.org.uk/texts/prose/VDub_LL-V/edited-text.eng.html, accessed 4 May 2022.

[24] This section of the *Epitome* includes a detailed description of Gormundus' wasting of Britain. It describes his siege of Cirencester, during which he burns the city by attaching fire to the tails of sparrows. This episode is not in Geoffrey or the Middle English Prose *Brut*, but it is in Laȝamon's *Brut*, potentially suggesting that Laȝamon was a source for the *Epitome* compiler, or that they were drawing on a common story. See *Layamon: Brut*, ed. Brook and Leslie, ii.766, ll. 14601–22.

loss of their name, their transformation into the Welsh people, and their flight to Cambria (Wales), where they reside today. The chronicle states that the last prince to rule over a unified Wales is Rhodri Mawr, whose sons divide Wales after his death into three principalities: Gwynedd, Deheubarth, and Powys.[25] The chronicle explains that Powys and Deheubarth both lost the status of principality, lists the rulers of Deheubarth up to Lord Rhys ap Gruffudd (d. 1197), and notes that North Wales retained its status of principality while the other two kingdoms diminished. It then jumps to the *magna discordia* 'great disagreement' between King Edward I of England and Llywelyn ap Gruffudd, the last prince of independent Wales. The killing of Llywelyn in 1282 by Edward's supporters marked the end of independent rule in Wales and the beginning of total control by the English Crown and marcher lords. Following Llywelyn's death, the chronicle describes the Welsh having to relinquish all the castles of North Wales; many relics, including a piece of the True Cross (called the *Croes Neide*); and the crown of Arthur in a symbolic transfer of power to the English.[26] The rest of this portion of the chronicle whips through a series of noteworthy wars and plagues, including the capture and death of Dafydd ap Gruffudd in 1283, the rebellions of Morgan ap Maredudd in 1296 and Llywelyn Bren in 1315, and the Black Death in 1348.[27] As previously mentioned, the last entry is for 1375, noting a fourth coming of the plague.

The third and final section of the chronicle turns to time and geography before ending in a jumble of miscellaneous items. It reckons time from Creation to the Flood (2,242 years), from the Flood to the Nativity (2,958 years), and from the Nativity to today (1,429 years in the Llandaf

---

[25] The earliest record of Rhodri's division of Wales among his three sons, the 'Rhodri Mawr origin story', is in Gerald of Wales, *Descriptio Kambriae*, i.2 (c.1194). Powys was not a major kingdom in Rhodri Mawr's time; it did not become prominent until the twelfth-century rule of Madog ap Maredudd. This statement is therefore anachronistic but reflects contemporary understanding of Welsh history. For discussion, see *MWG* 118–21.

[26] For the *Croes Neide*, a relic of the True Cross that had belonged to Llywelyn ap Gruffudd and was taken by Edward I to Westminster Abbey, see R. R. Davies, *The Age of Conquest: Wales, 1063–1415* (Oxford, 2000), 355–6.

[27] Dafydd ap Gruffudd (d. 1283) held out against Edward I for a few months after his brother Llywelyn ap Gruffudd's death. Morgan ap Maredudd (fl. 1270–1316) led a rebellion in Glamorgan against the Clare lords of Glamorgan after being dispossessed of his lands. Llywelyn Bren (d. 1318) led a rebellion in Glamorgan and Gwent against Edward II and several marcher lords.

manuscript, Cotton Titus D. xxii).[28] It discusses the division of the world into three parts by the sons of Noah and names each country in Asia, Africa, and Europe. It gives a rhyme about the nine worthies,[29] says that the Antichrist will rule in the future, and lastly notes the building of the town of Cardiff in the year 1081.

Cumulatively, *Epitome historiae Britanniae* abbreviates *DGB* in a manner that is tightly focused on major highlights, but with a particular emphasis on Llandaf. Like Geoffrey, the *Epitome* gives the Britons a Trojan origin, accounts for their loss of rule over the island of Britain, and contextualizes their deeds in salvation history. It also extends Geoffrey's narrative to the present day, with its final section reminding readers that the action is taking place within a much wider historical, geographical, and providential context. One of its most notable features is the emphasis on the history of Llandaf and St Dyfrig, more pronounced because the rest of the history is so abbreviated.

The general sense one gets from this chronicle is that it came to be through a process of accretion. The first section is tightly organized and thematically unified, as if it were the work of a single person who knew Geoffrey's work very well, while the second and third parts are less organized, as if added later, possibly by multiple people recording annalistic entries and notes at different times. Any such compilatory activity is buried below the surface of this clean copy, but one suspects its exemplar was a bit messier.

The *Epitome historiae Britanniae*'s geographical, political, and cultural context

Fourteenth-century Glamorgan's broader landscape of colonization, foreign governance, tension, and rebellion provides valuable evidence

---

[28] This date of 1429, if accurately reckoned, would indicate that this third section of the chronicle was written later than the second section, which ends at 1375, perhaps by a different author, or that the scribe of Cotton Titus D. xxii has updated the date to 1429.

[29] *Hector, Alex[ander], Iulius, | Iosue, Dauid, Machabe | Arthurus, Karolus, | et precellens Godofridus. | Isti sunt ter tres | trine secte meliores* 'Hector, Alexander, Julius, | Joshua, David, Maccabeus, | Arthur, Charles, | and distinguished Godfrey. | Those are three times three, | the best men of the triple division' [i.e. classical, biblical, and 'medieval']. I am grateful to Joshua Byron Smith for discussing these verses with me.

for how the *Epitome historiae Britanniae* would have been read by audiences in Wales and/or audiences who were Welsh in their identity.[30] It is necessary now to give some historical context in order to understand the chronicle's intentions, achievement, and early reception before moving on to how it was reframed by marcher chroniclers.

Glamorgan was one of the wealthiest and most influential of the marcher lordships, controlled by the powerful Clare family, then by the Despensers, and later by Richard Neville, earl of Warwick (1428–71), and Jasper Tudor, duke of Bedford (c.1431–95). As R. R. Davies and others have shown, one can imagine Glamorgan as divided into two worlds.[31] These two worlds were reflected in its administrative division between Bro Morgannwg, the lowlands along the coastline where the long-standing English settlements and the cathedral of Llandaf were located, and Blaenau Morgannwg, the highlands, composed of Welsh-governed lordships such as Afan and Senghenydd (see Figure 1.2).[32] In other words, Glamorgan was located on a borderland, but it also contained, within its bounds, an internal border zone of cultural contact and conflict.[33] This geopolitical reality attests to the shifting nuances of the March of Wales more broadly, with its multiple, overlapping, and shifting cultural–political boundaries and ethnic identities.

Like most ecclesiastical communities in the conquest territories of medieval Wales, Llandaf in the fourteenth century would have drawn from the local Welsh population for personnel, while higher offices were reserved exclusively for Englishmen.[34] Furthermore, during the time that the *Epitome* was compiled and Cotton Titus D. xxii was written, the see of Llandaf had no fewer than seven bishops from 1382 to 1407,

---

[30] I follow Huws's suggestion that Cotton Titus D. xxii may have been created in the diocese of Llandaf. There, it would plausibly have been available to a Welsh readership, given that the community at Llandaf drew from the local Welsh population for its members.

[31] R. R. Davies, *Revolt*, 58–9, though see recent nuance in Stephenson, *Medieval Wales*, 137–52.

[32] The Welsh lords of Morgannwg (specifically, Senghenydd, Ruthin, and Afan) owed allegiance to the lords of Glamorgan but governed otherwise independently under Welsh law. See J. Beverley Smith, 'The Kingdom of Morgannwg and the Norman Conquest of Glamorgan', in *GCH* 1–43, at 26–7.

[33] J. Beverley Smith, 'Kingdom of Morgannwg', 30–3, 38.

[34] Glanmor Williams, 'The Church in Glamorgan from the Fourteenth Century to the Reformation', in *GCH* 135–66, at 138. For nuanced discussion of relations between Welsh communities and marcher lords, see Stephenson, *Medieval Wales*, 130–6.

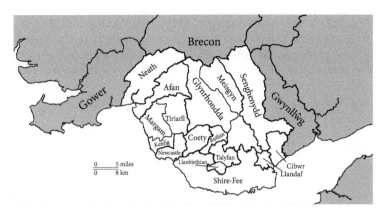

FIGURE 1.2   The Lordship of Glamorgan.

only one of whom was Welsh.[35] Precisely during the time of the chronicle's composition, the community at Llandaf suffered from considerable upheaval and the machinations of political games.

In the secular sphere, the ruling elite was rooted in a francophone, 'Anglo-Norman' culture, while the majority population of the lordship was Welsh-speaking, and included the Welsh gentry, known in the post-conquest period as *uchelwyr* ('nobility'), who were themselves also interested in francophone literature and trends.[36] The *uchelwyr* were responsible for a flourishing of literature in the Welsh vernacular.[37] Glamorgan had a long history of Norman, Anglo-Norman, and

---

[35] Glanmor Williams, 'Church in Glamorgan', 139; R. R. Davies, *Revolt*, 58.

[36] Patrons—most famously Hopcyn ap Tomas in Gower and Rhydderch ab Ieuan Llwyd in Ceredigion, but also lesser-known men such as Ifor Hael of Monmouth and Madog Fychan of Tiriarll—had a wide range of literary tastes, commissioning translations of contemporary French romances into Welsh and contemporary poems in Welsh, as well as ensuring the preservation of older vernacular literature. See discussion in Helen Fulton, 'Literary Networks and Patrons in Late Medieval Wales', in Helen Fulton and Geraint Evans (eds), *The Cambridge History of Welsh Literature* (Cambridge, 2019), 129–54; Catherine McKenna, 'Reading with Rhydderch: *Mabinogion* Texts in Manuscript Context', in Anders Ahlqvist and Pamela O'Neill (eds), *Language and Power in the Celtic World: Papers from the Seventh Australian Conference of Celtic Studies* (Sydney, 2011), 205–30.

[37] The careers of several of these men are described by Stephenson, *Medieval Wales*, 137–49. Conventionally included in Glamorgan's literary orbit are two major manuscript compilations of Middle Welsh literature: the White Book of Rhydderch (Aberystwyth,

English settlement and interaction between the Welsh population and foreigners from the eleventh century onwards, leading to a high degree of literary exchange between multiple languages and cultures and complex expressions of identity. It is this multilingual environment that produced the *Epitome*.

Politically, the era was characterized by intense social change and inequality, including the deaths of five important marcher lords between 1397 and 1399, which created a vacuum of leadership.[38] Tensions exploded in the revolt of Owain Glyndŵr (c.1359–c.1416) in 1400, which began in north-east Wales but quickly spread to national significance before dispersing by c.1412 (see Table 1.4). Importantly, the *Epitome* fits a readership that sympathized with the rebellion: Glanmor Williams argues that in the diocese of Llandaf, 'many of the lower clergy of Welsh descent may have viewed [Owain's] cause with sympathy as their fellows elsewhere in Wales did'.[39] These circumstances impact the interpretation of the history and the prophecy present in the text.

For readers who were Welsh, Geoffrey's history set a precedent for future Welsh independence and established an ancient noble lineage for native Welsh families, who in the present-day reality had very little say in governance or leadership (with some minor exceptions).[40]

NLW, Peniarth 4 and 5, c.1350), probably written in Ceredigion, and the Red Book of Hergest (Oxford, Jesus College, 111, AD 1382–1405), probably written at patron Hopcyn ap Tomas's residence in Ynysforgan, Gower, or (as is sometimes suggested) at Neath Abbey or Margam Abbey in Glamorgan. See discussion in Helen Fulton, 'The Geography of Welsh Literary Production in Late Medieval Glamorgan', *JMH* 41/3 (2015), 325–40, at 327; Ceri W. Lewis, 'The Literary Tradition of Morgannwg down to the Middle of the Sixteenth Century', in *GCH* 449–554. Gower became part of Glamorgan in 1535, and it is presumably for this reason that the Red Book of Hergest is typically included in surveys of Glamorgan literature despite its probable origin in Gower, a separate marcher lordship.

[38] R. R. Davies, *Age of Conquest*, 442.

[39] Glanmor Williams, 'Church in Glamorgan', 148. The most loyal to the rebellion in Glamorgan may have been the Franciscans in Cardiff, whose flock was Welsh. Owain Glyndŵr caused significant damage to Llandaf, Neath, Margam, Ewenny, and Tintern, and burned the whole town of Cardiff in 1404—to the extent that Cardiff's Benedictine priory was dissolved and/or reduced to a parish church—but he did not touch the Franciscan friary. This is a significant example of loyalty to Owain Glyndŵr very near Llandaf. For discussion, see Glanmor Williams, 'Church in Glamorgan', 148, 150; T. B. Pugh, 'The Marcher Lords of Glamorgan, 1317–1485', in *GCH* 167–204, at 184.

[40] For my definition of Welsh identity, see the Introduction.

TABLE 1.4   Timeline of Owain Glyndŵr's rebellion

1400	Owain Glyndŵr is declared Prince of Wales by an assembly of supporters; they burn various towns in north-east Wales. Henry IV travels to North Wales, offers pardons to rebels, and declares Owain's lands forfeit
1401	Owain's cousins capture Conwy Castle; Owain wins a battle in Ceredigion and attacks Welshpool and Caernarfon Castle
1402	Owain attacks Ruthin and Maelienydd, is joined by Edmund Mortimer, wins Battle of Bryn Glas. English parliament enacts restrictive statutes; Prince Henry burns Owain's properties
1403	Owain attacks castles and towns in South Wales; Henry Percy (Hotspur) joins him, loses a battle at Shrewsbury. Henry IV campaigns in South Wales
1404	Owain captures Aberystwyth, Harlech, and Cardiff castles, attacks Archenfield, enters into a formal treaty with Charles VI of France, and assembles a parliament at Machynlleth
1405	Owain assembles a parliament at Harlech, enters into Tripartite Indenture with Edmund Mortimer and Henry Percy agreeing to a tripartite rule of Wales and improvements to the status of the church in Wales, and attacks towns in South Wales
1406	Gower, Ystrad Tywi, Ceredigion, Anglesey formally submit to English Crown
1408	Aberystwyth Castle captured by Prince Henry; Henry Percy dies
1409	Owain raids Shropshire and one of his sons is killed; Harlech is captured by English; Owain's wife and two daughters are captured and taken to London
1415	Owain disappears or goes into hiding

Note: For discussion, see Michael Livingston, 'Owain Glyndŵr's Grand Design: "The Tripartite Indenture" and the Vision of a New Wales', *Proceedings of the Harvard Celtic Colloquium*, 33 (2013), 145–68; R. R. Davies, *Revolt*, 166–72. Dates are taken from Llinos Smith, 'Glyn Dŵr [Glyndŵr], Owain [Owain *ap* Gruffudd Fychan, Owain Glendower]', *ODNB*, accessed 4 May 2022.

In this sense, Geoffrey provided an expansive vision of a former era of independent rule and nobility and a model for good kingship through negative example.

Geoffrey's popularity in Wales is usually addressed through discussion of the multiple translations of his history into Middle Welsh, known as *Brut y Brenhinedd* ('History of the Kings').[41] But the *Epitome*, written in Latin, is also part of the Welsh reception of Geoffrey. Its compilers drew on the themes that pervaded Welsh historical consciousness at the time, not only because they were drawing directly from Geoffrey's Latin history, which was itself grounded in popular themes of Welsh history, but because they were making a deliberate appeal to Welsh readers. These themes include the idea of British history as a continuum from the ancient Mediterranean past to the present day, the long-standing nobility of Welsh people descended from Trojan refugees, a narrative arc of loss and decline, the unification of national identity beyond local identities, and the promise of future deliverance by a messianic leader. These themes would have appealed to a dispossessed, colonized audience suffering from social disruption, pessimism, and despair.[42] Though the *Epitome* was its own adaptation of Geoffrey that relied directly on the Latin text, it sketches out the narrative of British–Welsh history in response to the same political concerns and cultural needs.

First, it implicitly draws connections between present-day Wales and ancient Mediterranean history through references to biblical history, Troy, and Rome.[43] Second, its considerable time span highlights the long-standing nobility of the Welsh, descended from Trojans and converted to Christianity at an early time. Third, it follows the themes of loss and decline, which are pervasive in medieval Welsh historical writing and are widely viewed as reflecting a grievance about the present-day oppressed and colonized predicament of Welsh readers.[44] Its trajectory of British history begins at a high point, with a moment of

[41] Patrick Sims-Williams, 'The Welsh Versions of Geoffrey of Monmouth's "History of the Kings of Britain"', in Axel Harlos and Neele Harlos (eds), *Adapting Texts and Styles in a Celtic Context: Interdisciplinary Perspectives on Processes of Literary Transfer in the Middle Ages: Studies in Honour of Erich Poppe*, Studien und Texte zur Keltologie, 13 (Münster, 2016), 53–74.

[42] Glanmor Williams, 'Church in Glamorgan', 151.

[43] For the theme of Rome in Welsh historiography, see Brynley F. Roberts, 'Geoffrey of Monmouth and Welsh Historical Tradition', *Nottingham Medieval Studies*, 20 (1976), 29–40, at 33–4, 37.

[44] For the theme of loss in Welsh historiography, see Roberts, 'Geoffrey of Monmouth', 34–6.

triumph (the defeat of the giants of Albion) marking the Britons' transition from wandering exiles from Troy to righteous settlers of a land that rightfully belongs to them. This episode implicitly comments on the present-day injustices of dispossession and colonization at work in Wales, and makes an argument that the Britons, or Welsh, even today, have a divine right to rule over the island.

But the prophecy of deliverance by a messianic leader, known in Welsh as the *mab darogan* or 'son of prophecy', is the theme that most powerfully accords with the political circumstances just discussed. In the chronicle, the high point of their successes—the settlement of the island by Brutus, the foundation of New Troy, and the success of their peaceful conversion to Christianity—is interrupted in the text by Merlin's prophecy, which warns of devastations to come:

> [P]rophetauit Merlinus multas inauditas tribulaciones et futuras desolaciones regibus et regno Brittanie. Prophetauit enim dictum populum Britanicum per externas degeneres naciones a nobilitate sua pro tempore fore depositurum et iterum in fine temporum releuaturum.
>
> Merlin prophesied many novel tribulations and future devastations to the kings and to the kingdom of Britain. For he prophesied that the aforementioned British people would be forced away from their nobility by degenerate foreign nations for a time, and in the end of time they would be lifted up again.

This is a far more straightforward prophetic message than what is in the chronicle's source material, as if the compilers have simplified and distilled the prophecy of Merlin for their readership. Geoffrey's *Prophetiae Merlini* is famously difficult to interpret and does not transmit nearly as clear a message about the fortunes of the Welsh. By contrast, the *Epitome* gets straight to the point. The placement of the prophecies in this section of the *Epitome* is also significant. In *DGB*, the prophecies occur during the reign of King Vortigern. By moving Merlin's prophecies to this earlier point in the narrative, during the arrival of Brutus, the compilers write Merlin's prophecy into Brutus' settlement of Britain, anticipating Vortigern's later, destructive decision to invite the Saxons to the island. This has the effect of emphasizing the inevitability of the Britons' loss of independence. Thereafter, the Britons' trajectory is characterized by a consistent decline, compounded by successive deaths and failures of rulers. Each defeat further diminishes their status.

Hope is kept alive by the dynasty of Gwynedd, which retains its status as a principality into the late thirteenth century, but that too is extinguished upon Llywelyn ap Gruffudd's death, recounted in great detail. The emphasis on the emotional reaction of the Welsh people to the death of a leader is striking, and common in Welsh historical writing and poetry, as Chapter 5 discusses.[45] The episode describing Llywelyn's death is more vividly detailed than other sections of the chronicle. Edward I is described as hateful and cruel, the Welsh as brave, and Llywelyn as captured through *ymaginata fraude* 'contrived deceit'. The account is sympathetic to the Welsh side:

> Tempore uero istius Lewelini orta est magna discordia inter ipsum et Edwardum regem Anglie, dictum Longe Schankys, qui ei diu mortaliter inuidebat propter quod congregauit excercitum et ingressus est Walliam cum multitudine, graui gentem et patriam igne et gladio crudeliter deuastabat. Quod cum Wallenses tantam persecucionem senciebant, sumptis viribus viriliter congressi sunt cum eis. Et ex eis tam armatorum quam peditum per mors exterminauerunt. Sed nichil eis in fine profuit, nam denocte ymaginata fraude Lewelinus princeps suus captus fuit per Rogerum de Mortuomari affinem suum et per eum interfectus et decollatus. Post cuius mortem nullum hucusque habuerunt principem de genere suo. De cuius morte territi sunt Wallenses vltra modum.[46]

> In the time of that Llywelyn, a great disagreement arose between him and Edward, king of England, called Longshanks, who mortally hated him for a long time, for which reason he gathered an army and entered Wales with a great number, and cruelly devastated the people and the nation by dreadful fire and sword. When the Welsh felt such persecution, they took hold of their strength and met them manfully in battle. And they expelled by death from that great number as many armed men as foot soldiers. But in the end, none of it benefited them, for in the night Llywelyn their prince was captured through contrived deceit by Roger Mortimer, his relative, and he was killed and beheaded. After his death up to this time they have had no prince from his line. On account of his death, the Welsh were terrified beyond measure.

---

[45] See pp. 199–202, 206.
[46] External sources attribute his death, not to Roger Mortimer (1231–82), who predeceased Llywelyn, but to Roger's son Edmund Mortimer.

Displaying a structural unity of narrative, Llywelyn's death cements the loss set into motion by Vortigern centuries earlier.

With all of that said, the placement of Merlin's prophecy at the beginning of the text, while it emphasizes the inevitability of the Britons' fall, also predicts their future rise. The prophecy frames the Britons' loss of their kingdom as divinely engineered, following familiar themes of Christian theology. It frames the Welsh loss of sovereignty as engineered by God, who has temporarily taken away their right to rule over the island but will return it in the future.

An additional convention of Welsh history fulfilled by the *Epitome* is the unity of Britain and the unification of national Welsh identity beyond local identities.[47] The Britons, later the Welsh, are one people, and though they are divided into three regional kingdoms after the reign of Rhodri Mawr, they experience oppression and later renewal as one people. The concept of descent from the Britons, a single kingdom ruled by a single king, reinforces this sense of common identity. Such historical mythologizing had been a response to dispossession and loss in Wales since the ninth century, and would have been meaningful to Welsh gentry readers, who took consolation in poetry that described their noble descent and future deliverance.[48]

The *Epitome historiae Britanniae* and Welsh prophetic poetry

The prophecy in the *Epitome* reflects contemporary Welsh interest in prophecy, which is well documented by outsiders. For example, the archbishop of Canterbury wrote to the bishop of St Asaph in 1284 asking that the Welsh people abandon the dreams and visions that led them to believe they were descended from Trojans.[49] The author of the c.1325 *Vita Edwardi Secundi* scorned the prophetic beliefs of the Welsh, while a

---

[47] For the theme of unity in Welsh historiography, see Roberts, 'Geoffrey of Monmouth', 37–8.

[48] R. R. Davies, *Age of Conquest*, 56–81; Dafydd Johnston, 'The Aftermath of 1282: Dafydd ap Gwilym and his Contemporaries', in Fulton and Evans (eds), *Cambridge History of Welsh Literature*, 112–28, at 113.

[49] *Registrum Epistolarum Fratris Johannis Peckham, Archiepiscopi Cantuariensis*, ed. Charles Trice Martin, 3 vols (London, 1882–5, repr. 1965), ii.741–2.

1402 law forbade Welsh poets from fomenting rebellion with prophecies and lies.[50]

Welsh interest in prophecy is evident in collections of prophecy such as the Red Book of Hergest (Oxford, Jesus College, 111, AD 1382–1405) and *Y Cwta Cyfarwydd* ('The Short Guide', Aberystwyth, NLW, Peniarth 50, c.1445), which contains a collection of prophetic poetry in Latin, English, and Welsh.[51] The prophetic poems in these manuscripts give frequent reference to the English conquest of Wales and repeated attempts by the Welsh to resist it. Nearly every prophetic poem foretells the victory of the Welsh over the English. For example, the poems 'Cyfoesi Myrddin' and 'Moch Daw Byd' in the Red Book of Hergest prophesy the deliverance of the Welsh from the English by Cadwaladr and others. Numerous poems in *Y Cwta Cyfarwydd* reference Owain Glyndŵr specifically, positioning him as a messianic figure.[52] R. R. Davies writes that Welsh prophecy 'bound a mythical past, a despairing present, and the prospect of future deliverance into one. It was also a powerful instrument in forging a measure of unity in an otherwise politically fragmented and decentralised society, for it presented a vision which could be converted into a programme of action to which

---

[50] *Rotuli parliamentorum, ut et petitiones, et placita in parliament*, ed. J. Strachey, 6 vols (London, 1767–77), iii.508; discussed by Manon Bonner Jenkins, 'Aspects of the Welsh Prophetic Verse Tradition in the Middle Ages: Incorporating Textual Studies of Poetry from "Llyfr Coch Hergest" (Oxford, Jesus College, MS cxi) and "Y Cwta Cyfarwydd" (Aberystwyth, National Library of Wales, MS Peniarth 50)' (unpublished Ph.D. thesis, University of Cambridge, 1990), 12.

[51] Jenkins, 'Aspects', 187–94; Aled Llion Jones, *Mab Darogan: Prophecy, Lament, and Absent Heroes in Medieval Welsh Tradition* (Cardiff, 2013), 128–40; Ceridwen Lloyd-Morgan, 'Prophecy and Welsh Nationhood in the Fifteenth Century', *Transactions of the Honourable Society of Cymmrodorion* (1985), 9–26, at 18–20.

[52] Poems 18 (*baedd Glyn Dyfórdwy* 'boar of Glyn Dyfrdwy'), 228b (*gorvot, yn dyuot o [E]deyrnion* 'victory, coming from Edeirnion'), and 229c (*tref Rythyn* 'town of Ruthin'); discussed by Jenkins, 'Aspects', 214, 330–1, 337. Owain is a conventional name in Welsh prophetic poetry, referring also to Owain Gwynedd (d. 1170) and Owain Lawgoch (d. 1378), and the many mentions of Owain in this body of verse may have had multiple resonances for fifteenth-century readers. Furthermore, Owain Glyndŵr himself drew on Geoffrey's history in the Tripartite Indenture, consulting the patron of the Red Book of Hergest, Hopcyn ap Tomas, as a master of *brut* ('prophecy') in 1403; see *Original Letters Illustrative of English History*, ed. Henry Lewis, 4 vols (London, 1827), i.21–3; Helen Fulton, 'Owain Glyn Dŵr and the Uses of Prophecy', *SC* 39 (2005), 105–21.

all Welshmen might subscribe'.[53] *Epitome historiae Britanniae* fits this need precisely, weaving the past tribulations of the Welsh into a promise of future deliverance.

While this interest in prophecies is typically interpreted by outsiders at this time as fanciful, an antiquated and obscure practice, it in fact reflects a strong thread of independence that runs subtly through Middle Welsh literature. For example, the *cywyddwyr*, a class of poets active in post-conquest Wales who served Welsh gentry, probably had a more subtle, metaphorical understanding of political prophecies than they were often accorded, in that the prophecies were innately tied to ideas of loss of inheritance and loss of independence—present conditions that would someday be reversed, according to Merlin. These concerns are reflected in, for example, an elegiac poem by Iolo Goch (fl. 1345-97) for Tudur Fychan (d. 1367, an ancestor of the Tudor line), which states,

> Ni chollai wan, gwinllan gwŷr,
> Tref ei dad tra fu Dudur;
> Ni thitid câr amharawd,
> Odid od wtlëid tlawd.[54]

> No defenceless person would lose—vineyard of the people
> His father's land while Tudur was alive;
> No unprepared kinsman was indicted,
> Rarely was a poor man outlawed (ll. 79-82).

The importance of holding on to one's land and inheritance (*tref ei dad* 'land of his father, patrimony, inheritance') is clear here. This statement in praise of Tudur Fychan indicates that, in the eyes of his family and any other audiences for this poem, a leader's ability to protect his people against loss of patrimony was the strongest mark of leadership—even as the conquest was finished, and Welsh governance conditional and limited by marcher lords and the English Crown. Texts like the *Epitome* therefore were meant to offer solace, an imagined alternative in the face of difficult circumstances, and a promise of future deliverance.

---

[53] R. R. Davies, *Age of Conquest*, 80.
[54] *Gwaith Iolo Goch*, ed. D. R. Johnston (Cardiff, 1988), 16-21, at 18.

The *Epitome historiae Britanniae* and the Book of Llandaf

The *Epitome* does more than express the traditions of Welsh history and prophetic poetry. It also contains important moments of innovation, the most significant of which is its weaving of local religious history, focused on the activities of St Dyfrig at Llandaf, into the Galfridian narrative. As mentioned above, St Dyfrig was a fifth- or sixth-century Welsh saint and bishop based in southern Wales.[55] Though he does appear as a character in *DGB*, crowning Arthur at the age of 15 and urging his men to battle with an impassioned speech,[56] a number of details about him in the *Epitome* are instead more aligned with the first *Life of St Dyfrig* and the *Life of St Teilo* from the Book of Llandaf, a source that could have been accessed by chroniclers at Llandaf, than with *DGB*.[57] For example, in the *Epitome*, Dyfrig is the archbishop of Llandaf, not Caerleon, as he is in Geoffrey. In addition, the *Epitome* elaborates on *DGB* by including a segment on the foundation of Llandaf that places a strong emphasis on the saint as the first archbishop of southern Britain (*dextralis Britanie*), consecrated by Germanus of Auxerre and Lupus of Troyes, who were sent to Britain to eradicate the Pelagian heresy:

> Preceperunt assensu et consensu Ma[u]ricii filii Teudrici, tunc regis Morgannuc, edificare et de nouo [con]struere unam sedem metropolitanam super a[uam Taaf] 3 honore [sanctorum] apostolorum Petri et Pauli. Et post completum opus dictus rex eam diuersis territoriis, priuilegiis, redditibus honorifice dotauit sicut in graffo sancti Thelyai plenarie reperitur, et in eam dicti religiosi viri Dubricium virum sanctum et famosum doctorem eciam archiepiscopum et **dextralis Britanie** primatem consecrauerunt.[58]

---

[55] Joshua Byron Smith, 'Benedict of Gloucester's *Vita Sancti Dubricii*: An Edition and Translation', *Arthurian Literature*, 29 (2012), 53–100, at 54–5.

[56] *DGB* ix.143, ix.147, pp. 192–5, 196–201.

[57] Daniel Huws notes that knowledge of the Book of Llandaf is reflected in Cotton Titus D. xxii; see Huws, *Medieval Welsh Manuscripts* (Aberystwyth, 2000), 150, n. 42. Geoffrey in fact mentions Llandaf only briefly, in reference to St Teilo as a priest of Llandaf; see *DGB* ix.158.406–9, pp. 214–15.

[58] Text in brackets has been supplied from the Peniarth 32 abbreviation of the text edited by Luft, 'NLW Peniarth 32 Latin Chronicle', 65, or by me. The phrase *dextralis*

With the assent and consent of Meurig, son of Tewdrig, then king of Morgannwg, [Germanus and Lupus] directed the building and construction, for the first time, of a metropolitan seat by the river Taf in honour of the holy apostles Peter and Paul. And, after completing the work, the aforementioned king honourably endowed it with diverse territories, privileges, and rents, as can be learned fully in the book of St Teilo. And in it, the aforementioned religious men consecrated Dyfrig, holy man and famous doctor, and even now the archbishop and primate of **southern Britain**.

This passage is not in Geoffrey. The *Epitome* relies on the first *Life of St Dyfrig* as a source (or perhaps on the first few paragraphs of *De primo et statu Landauensis ęcclesię*, which begins with the first *Life of St Dyfrig*).[59] The *Epitome* also uses wording from the first *Life of St Dyfrig* and/or from the *Life of Elgar the Hermit* (the sources all seem to be related) when it discusses Dyfrig retiring to Ynys Enlli (Bardsey Island), where he lives out his life as a hermit and eventually dies, and the *Life of St Dyfrig* again when it describes the translation of Dyfrig's relics to Llandaf in 1120.[60]

These passages demonstrate the innovative incorporation of local sources into Geoffrey's history. Details from the lives of Dyfrig, Teilo, and Elgar, all in the Book of Llandaf, mark a significant departure from *DGB* in a reflection of local interest and provenance.[61] And yet, in this local context, the *Epitome* compilers appear to be following a trend.

Britanie refers to southern Wales and would only have been used by a Welsh author; J. Byron Smith, 'Benedict of Gloucester's *Vita Sancti Dubricii*', 63.

[59] The first *Life of St Dyfrig* has no Arthurian content and predates Geoffrey. It reads: *Postquam predicti seniores pelagianam heresim extirpauerant, episcopos in pluribus locis Britannię insulę consecrauerunt ... Hac dignitate ei a Germano et Lupo data, constituerunt ei episcopalem sedem, concessu Mourici regis, principum, cleri et populi, apud podum Lanntam, in honore sancti Petri apostoli fundatam* 'After the aforesaid elders had eradicated the Pelagian heresy, they consecrated bishops in many places in the island of Britain ... Once that status had been given to [Dyfrig] by Germanus and Lupus, they established an episcopal see for him, with the consent of King Meurig, the principal men, the clergy and the people, at the church of Llandaff, founded in honour of the apostle St Peter' ('Vita Sancti Dubricii', ed. and trans Guy).

[60] I discuss this in more detail in 'Scribal Authority and Hagiographical Adaptation in London, British Library, Cotton Titus D. xxii', in Myriah Williams, Silva Nurmio, and Sarah Waidler (eds), *Medieval Wales and the Medieval World: Context and Approaches, Knowledge and Exchange* (Turnhout, forthcoming).

[61] Unlike the other manuscripts discussed in this chapter, Cotton Titus D. xxii is decisively from an ecclesiastical context: the use of Latin, a regular scribal hand, religious

Back in the early twelfth century, the purpose of the Book of Llandaf, a collection of saints' lives, charters, and other materials, was to promote Llandaf's primacy in southern Wales against the dioceses of St Davids and Hereford.[62] At the centre of these efforts was St Dyfrig, promoted as the founder of the church in southern Wales and of Llandaf. The *Epitome* makes the same claim centuries later, reaffirming the same primacy during a very different time of political turmoil involving outsiders.[63] These moments in the text may have been read, given the political climate discussed above, as a subtle push against the control of the diocese by outside forces and the near constant upheaval of foreign bishops coming and going in the late fourteenth century.

Cumulatively, the *Epitome historiae Britanniae* would have been read by a South Wales audience between 1375 and 1399 as explanation for English conquest and Welsh loss with a promise of future regeneration. In the context of the copy of the text in Cotton Titus D. xxii, dated to c.1429, the rebellion of Owain Glyndŵr was quashed and the text offered reflection on the cyclical nature of Welsh history, characterized by frequent attempts to fulfil the prophecy of Merlin.

As a postscript to this discussion of the *Epitome* in Wales, it should be mentioned again that an abbreviation of the text was made at the Cistercian abbey of Llantarnam in the early fifteenth century, extant in *Y Llyfr Teg* 'The Fair Book' (Peniarth 32), a collection of historical, legal, and religious texts in Welsh written by a professional scribe.[64] Llantarnam, a daughter house of Strata Florida Abbey in Ceredigion, was located in Monmouthshire. It was probably the most Welsh-leaning of the southeast Welsh monasteries, and its abbot, John ap Hywel, supported the Glyndŵr rebellion.[65] The result of the abbreviation is a very brief survey of British–Welsh history from the arrival of Brutus to 1375, omitting

contents, and the divisions of the *passio* of St Cadog into lections for reading aloud indicate monastic production and use.

[62] Joshua Byron Smith, 'Benedict of Gloucester's *Vita Sancti Dubricii*', 57; John Reuben Davies, *Book of Llandaf*, 86.

[63] In combining the character of Dyfrig from the first *Life of St Dyfrig* with that in Geoffrey, the *Epitome* also follows the same impulse as a twelfth-century reworking of the *Life* by Benedict of Gloucester, who adapts it into a Galfridian narrative. The *Epitome* does not, however, use Benedict's Second *Life of St Dyfrig* as a source; it demonstrates no verbal parallels. The moments where the *Epitome* agrees textually with Benedict of Gloucester's Second *Life of St Dyfrig* are taken from their common source, *DGB*.

[64] Luft, 'NLW Peniarth 32'.

[65] David H. Williams, *The Welsh Cistercians* (Leominster, 2001), 53; Luft, 'NLW Peniarth 32', 60–1.

references to Llandaf. The existence of this abbreviated copy shows that the popularity of the text endured and that multiple versions were circulated in monastic contexts and resonated among those communities. As will be seen below, the same can be said of copies of the text outside Glamorgan and Monmouthshire in a marcher context.

The *Epitome historiae Britanniae* in Shropshire

Given how saturated the *Epitome* is in the themes of the Welsh historical imagination, it is striking that it was transmitted shortly after it was written to the town of Ludlow in Shropshire, where it appears as a prelude to a 'Ludlow Annal' (London, British Library, Cotton Nero A. iv, part i, fols. 2^r–62^v, s. xv/xvi).[66] This instance of transmission, and the incorporation of the *Epitome* into a larger regional chronicle of Ludlow, shows that readers in the Middle March took interest not only in the history of ancient Britain (corroborated by the circulation of the Prose *Brut* and other iterations of *DGB* in the region) but in the post-Galfridian history of Wales itself, despite the significant difference in marcher readers' positionality towards that history by comparison to Welsh readers.[67] Whereas the original Llandaf audience, as I argue above, would have read the text as supportive of the Glyndŵr rebellion and the hope for future Welsh independence, I see marcher readers such as the Mortimers, those who were sympathetic to the Mortimers, and those who wrote the Ludlow Annal, as having a different perspective. In the Ludlow manuscript, the standard narrative of British–Welsh

[66] This copy of the *Epitome* has been copied from an exemplar that dates to 1399, which predates the copy of the text from South Wales, in Cotton Titus D. xxii (AD 1429). However, given the Llandaf focus of much of the *Epitome*, the direction of transmission is most likely to be Llandaf to Ludlow, not the other way around. Furthermore, owing to the Ludlow focus of this annal, I am assuming that the *Epitome* was combined with the rest of the contents of the Ludlow Annal at a location in Shropshire or Ludlow itself, rather than an unknown, third location, because medieval chroniclers typically tend to include local information. For a brief description of the manuscript, see Huws, *Repertory*, i.662.
[67] I follow Given-Wilson in calling this chronicle the 'Ludlow Annal', though it is labelled *Chronicon Laudanenses* in the manuscript's early modern table of contents (fol. 1^r). Given its interest in Ludlow and Middle March events, I agree with Given-Wilson that it was compiled in Ludlow. He suggests origin in the Hospital of the Holy Trinity or the house of Augustinian friars; see Given-Wilson, 'Chronicles of the Mortimer Family', 79. The manuscript itself could be from Ludlow, though there is no evidence outside the chronicle to determine this for sure.

history as represented in the *Epitome* was an important contextual prelude to late-fourteenth-century, regional Ludlow history. In this section of the chapter, I consider the shift in interpretation of the *Epitome*, a powerfully evocative, politically current Glamorgan chronicle, when it reached a marcher audience whose ancestors and predecessors were caught up in the conquest of Wales and whose interests lay in maintaining power over their conquered territories. Their interest in Welsh history was political and bound up in their identities as marchers, as they sought to understand and solidify their place in the March of Wales and their relationship to Wales using history as a framework.

Medieval Ludlow was a market town some fifteen miles from the Welsh border, twenty-four miles from Hereford, and thirty miles from the larger market towns of Shrewsbury and Worcester. Its citizens were involved in the wool and cloth trades, making use of the trade route through Bristol up the Severn River and the cattle droving road from North Wales to London, which cut through Ludlow.[68] The town is not recorded in the Domesday Book survey, but is thought to have had around two thousand inhabitants *c*.1300.[69] Two per cent of its population had Welsh names.[70] It was home to three conventual houses (an Augustinian friary, a Carmelite priory, and the Hospital of John the Baptist), a parish church dedicated to St Laurence, and an active religious guild. Its lords were first the Lacys, then the Genevilles and the Verduns (families whose interests were chiefly in Ireland), and then the Mortimers for most of the fourteenth century. The Mortimers based themselves at Wigmore, seven miles to the west, though Joan de Geneville, wife of Roger Mortimer (1287–1330), lived in Ludlow itself.[71] Given that both Wigmore Abbey and Ludlow Priory were Augustinian, one can assume an ecclesiastical connection and communication between clerics in the two towns. Ludlow's connections with Wales were agricultural and economic: Ludlow farmers often grazed their cattle in central Wales, Ludlow merchants traded in Wales, and the town was home to Welsh immigrants.[72] The proximity to Wales and

---

[68] For discussion, see Michael Faraday, *Ludlow, 1085–1660: A Social, Economic, and Political History* (Chichester, 1991), 131–3.
[69] Faraday, *Ludlow*, 3, 157.
[70] Ibid., 137.
[71] Ibid., 7.
[72] Faraday notes names such as Dulcia la Walesche in 1266, 'le Galeys' before 1300, Iorvard le Mercer of la Pole in 1385, and David ap Rees before 1424; see ibid., 133, 137.

interactions between English and Welsh people in Ludlow reinforces the interest in Welsh history in the Ludlow Annal.

Moving from Ludlow to the county of Shropshire at large: the earldom was established after 1066 and given to Roger Montgomery (d. 1094); it was then governed by a succession of sheriffs and powerful baronial families in the centuries following, including the Fitz Alans, Corbets, and particularly the Mortimers, earls of March from 1328.[73] As in Glamorgan, this ruling elite was Anglo-Norman in origins (francophone or francophone-influenced), with baronial connections to England, Wales, and Ireland. Elites tended to marry locally, to other marcher or Welsh nobility.[74] Following the defeat of Edward II, the marcher lordships in western Shropshire (including Clun, Oswestry, and a number of others) effectively enjoyed legal jurisdiction independent of English royal authority, while the shires and hundreds of Shropshire were under English jurisdiction and common law.[75] The boroughs and lordships of western Shropshire on the border with Wales had substantial Welsh-speaking populations, particularly in Oswestry, Clun, and Caus.[76] These western border areas were populated by English and Welsh settlements that overlapped.[77]

The exceptionalism of Ludlow, an otherwise average market town in Shropshire, becomes apparent only when one considers its literary output, specifically that of the 'Harley scribe', a cleric and legal scribe

---

[73] *A History of Shropshire, Volume III*, ed. G. C. Baugh, The Victoria History of the Counties of England (London and Oxford, 1979), 1–53; Lieberman, *Medieval March*; Frederick C. Suppe, *Military Institutions on the Welsh Marches: Shropshire, AD 1066–1300*, Studies in Celtic History, 14 (Woodbridge, 1994).

[74] Lieberman, *Medieval March*, 84–99; Frederick Suppe, 'Interpreter Families and Anglo-Welsh Relations in the Shropshire–Powys Marches in the Twelfth Century', *Anglo-Norman Studies*, 30 (2008), 192–212; Emma Cavell, 'Aristocratic Widows and the Medieval Welsh Frontier: The Shropshire Evidence', *TRHS* 17 (2007), 57–82; David Stephenson, 'Welsh Lords in Shropshire: Gruffydd ap Iorwerth Goch and his Descendants in the Thirteenth Century', *Transactions of the Shropshire Archaeological Society*, 77 (2002), 32–7; Brock Holden, 'The Making of the Middle March of Wales, 1066–1250', *WHR* 20/2 (2000), 207–26, at 219–23.

[75] *History of Shropshire*, ed. Baugh, 39.

[76] David N. Parsons, *Welsh and English in Medieval Oswestry: The Evidence of Place-Names* (Nottingham, 2023), 9–18; David N. Parsons, 'Pre-English River Names and British Survival in Shropshire', *Nomina*, 36 (2013), 107–23; Lieberman, *Medieval March*, 42–51; Melville Richards, 'The Population of the Welsh Border', *Transactions of the Honourable Society of Cymmrodorion* (1970), 77–100; W. J. Slack, *The Lordship of Oswestry, 1393–1607* (Shrewsbury, 1951), 21–9.

[77] Lieberman, *Medieval March*, 42.

working in one or more wealthy households in the Ludlow area as a tutor or chaplain.[78] Between 1314 and 1349, during the time that Roger Mortimer and Joan de Geneville held Ludlow Castle and town, the Harley scribe wrote two important multilingual miscellanies and made additions to a third, amounting to over 120 texts in French, Latin, and Middle English. All three are in the British Library: Harley 2253, Royal 12 C. xii, and Harley 273.[79] Rather than producing these manuscripts for a single patron, the scribe seems to have collected these texts for himself over a long period of time.[80] Harley 2253 is the most thoroughly catalogued and best studied of the three, particularly by Middle English scholars, because it contains the Harley lyrics, a group of some thirty secular and religious lyrics in Middle English.[81] Some of the lyrics, as well as the romance *King Horn*, the *Harrowing of Hell*, and the *Short English Metrical Chronicle* in Royal 12 C. xii, represent major examples of the South West Midlands dialect of Middle English.[82] The Harley scribe also wrote French and Latin texts (in fact, almost all the texts in Harley 273, the earliest of the three manuscripts, are in French), including two French texts thought to be the scribe's own reworkings or translations of older texts: the romance of *Fouke le Fitz Waryn* in

---

[78] See Carter Revard, 'Scribe and Provenance', in Susanna Fein (ed.), *Studies in the Harley Manuscript: The Scribes, Contents, and Social Contexts of British Library MS Harley 2253* (Kalamazoo, 2000), 21–110, at 22–3. For a summary of scholarship to date, see Matthew Siôn Lampitt, 'Networking the March: The Literature of the Welsh Marches, c.1180–c.1410' (unpublished Ph.D. dissertation, King's College London, 2019), 57–64.

[79] Harley 2253 (fols. 49^r–140^v, 142r), Harley 273 (fols. 7^r, 85^v, 112^v, 181^v–197^v), and Royal 12 C. xii (fols. 1^r–16^v, 26^v–29^r, 30^v, 32^v–68^v, 76^v–107^r).

[80] Jason O'Rourke, 'Imagining Book Production in Fourteenth-Century Herefordshire: The Scribe of British Library, MS Harley 2253 and his "Organizing Principles"', in Stephen Kelly and John J. Thompson (eds), *Imagining the Book*, Medieval Texts and Cultures of Northern Europe, 7 (Turnhout, 2005), 45–69, at 55–9.

[81] It is in fact the earliest manuscript containing secular lyrics in Middle English. For discussion, see Susanna Fein, 'Compilation and Purpose in MS Harley 2253', in Wendy Scase (ed.), *Essays in Manuscript Geography: Vernacular Manuscripts of the English West Midlands from the Conquest to the Sixteenth Century*, Medieval Texts and Cultures of Northern Europe, 10 (Turnhout, 2007), 67–94; Fein (ed.), *Studies in the Harley Manuscript*.

[82] Frances McSparran, 'The Language of the English Poems', in Fein (ed.), *Studies in the Harley Manuscript*, 391–426; Language Profile (LP) 9260, in Michael Benskin, Margaret Laing, Vasilis Karaiskos, and Keith Williamson (eds), *An Electronic Version of a Linguistic Atlas of Late Mediaeval English* (Edinburgh, 2013), http://www.lel.ed.ac.uk/ihd/elalme/elalme.html, accessed 5 December 2021.

Royal 12 C. xii (the subject of Chapter 4 of this book), and *Old Testament Stories*, translated from the Vulgate Bible, in Harley 2253.[83] The English lyrics reveal a network of scribal copying that extended from Hereford to North Yorkshire.[84] Despite the appearance of such a literary achievement in the supposedly peripheral region of the West Midlands, readers and compilers of literature in Ludlow were well connected, francophone, and interested in a wide range of texts and genres of national and international interest.[85]

Nearly all the critical focus on medieval Shropshire's literary output has been devoted to the Harley scribe. Additionally, the editors of the *Linguistic Atlas of Late Mediaeval English* have identified a considerable number of surviving texts written in the Shropshire dialect of Middle English. Most of these are religious texts, but they also include romances, recipes, charters and other legal documents, a grammatical treatise, and a copy of Geoffrey Chaucer's *Canterbury Tales*.[86] The survival of popular, widely transmitted items in Shropshire manuscripts, though relatively low in number compared to some other counties, indicates a flourishing of Middle English literature on a par with other

---

[83] Susanna Fein, 'Literary Scribes: The Harley Scribe and Robert Thornton as Case Studies', in Margaret Connolly and Raluca Radulescu (eds), *Insular Books: Vernacular Manuscript Miscellanies in Late Medieval Britain*, Proceedings of the British Academy, 201 (Oxford, 2012), 61–79, at 67; Matthew Fisher, *Scribal Authorship and the Writing of History in Medieval England* (Columbus, 2012), 122–41; A. D. Wilshere, 'The Anglo-Norman Bible Stories in MS Harley 2253', *Forum for Modern Language Studies*, 24 (1988), 78–89; *King Horn: An Edition Based on Cambridge University Library MS Gg. 4.27*, ed. Rosamund Allen, Garland Medieval Texts, 7 (New York, 1984), 61–2; *FFW*, p. xxxvii.

[84] Lampitt, 'Networking the March: Literature', 64–8; Daniel Birkholz, 'Harley Lyrics and Hereford Clerics: The Implications of Mobility, c.1300–1351', *Studies in the Age of Chaucer*, 31 (2009), 175–230; Alison Wiggins, 'Middle English Romance and the West Midlands', in Scase (ed.), *Essays in Manuscript Geography*, 239–56.

[85] Keith Busby, 'Multilingualism, the Harley Scribe, and Johannes Jacobi', in Connolly and Radulescu (eds), *Insular Books*, 49–60, at 54; O'Rourke, 'Imagining Book Production', 49–50.

[86] The literary texts include Mirk's *Festial* (Southwell, Southwell Minster Library, VII (s. xv)), three copies of the *Prick of Conscience* (Oxford, Bodleian Library, Rawlinson Poet. 139 (s. xiv²), Oxford, Trinity College, 16A (s. xv¹), Manchester, John Rylands Library, 90 (s. xiv^ex–s. xv^in)), the *Stanzaic Life of Christ* (London, British Library, Add. 38666 (s. xv)), the *Canterbury Tales* (Oxford, Bodleian Library, Rawlinson Poet. 141 (s. xv)), the *Seege or Batayle of Troye*, *Kyng Alisaunder*, and *Of Arthour and of Merlin* (London, Lincoln's Inn, Hale 150 ((s. xiv²)), the C-version of *Piers Plowman* (London, British Library, Add. 34779 (s. xv^in)), and *The Seven Joys of Our Lady* (London, British Library, Harley 2010 (s. xv^{1/4})).

regions of England. One would expect to find Latin and French texts in Shropshire as well. One important French romance that was composed in Shropshire is the romance of *Fouke le Fitz Waryn*, written down with some degree of authorial adaptation by the Harley scribe.[87] One might also imagine Welsh literature being read and copied in Shropshire, given the substantial Welsh population of Oswestry, Clun, and Caus. A systematic study of Shropshire literature that accounts for multilingual contact, building upon David Parsons's work on place names, would be a worthy endeavour.[88]

The *Epitome historiae Britanniae* and Ludlow

If we consider the amount of scribal and authorial activity represented by just one documented individual working in fourteenth-century Ludlow, it is perhaps less surprising that a smallish market town like Ludlow had its own chronicle. The Ludlow Annal, which extends from the time of Brutus to 1338, is extant in Cotton Nero A. iv, part i (fols. 2^r–62^v), written in one gothic cursive hand (see Figure 1.3). The chronicle begins with the *Epitome historiae Britanniae* (fols. 2^r–7^v), which forms a sort of prelude to the Ludlow information that comes after.[89] Perhaps unusually for medieval chroniclers, the compilers of the Ludlow Annal did not adjust the Llandaf source to fit their perspective. The *Epitome* is slotted in without significant changes. Instead, their perspective must be inferred from what follows: essentially, a history of the nobility of the Middle March (the Genevilles, Verduns, and Mortimers) who succeeded the failed Welsh kings and princes of an earlier era. Interest in Welsh history, which spurred the transmission of historical texts across national boundaries in many cases, seems in this instance to have been motivated by an interest in the history of a neighbouring people that has already been conquered. The overall effect of the Ludlow Annal is a co-opting and subsuming of the British past—the story of the Britons and their eventual degeneration into the Welsh—into local Ludlow history. It is an example of a key theme of marcher literature, which explored

---

[87] See pp. 155, 157–9.
[88] Parsons, *Welsh and English*.
[89] The composite nature of this chronicle is discussed by Given-Wilson, 'Chronicles of the Mortimer Family', 69.

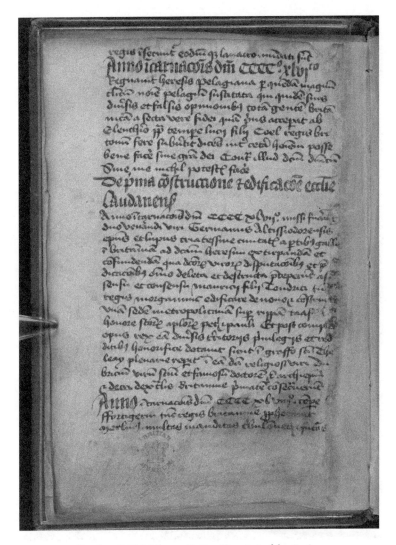

FIGURE 1.3   London, British Library, Cotton Nero A. iv, fols. 2ᵛ–3ʳ.
© The British Library Board

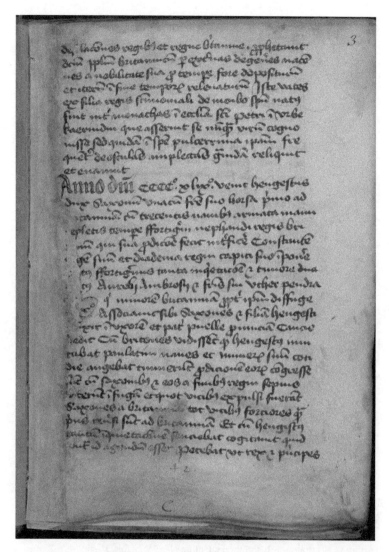

FIGURE 1.3 (Continued)

and solidified the place of marcher lords in the region: a realignment of British–Welsh historical narrative in a manner that promoted the families of the March.

I briefly recount the Ludlow Annal's contents here because there is no published edition. For the years immediately following the *Epitome*, the Ludlow Annal is fundamentally a chronicle of popes and emperors, beginning with Octavian. There is little attempt to unite the two sections: the final statement in the *Epitome*, stating that William Rufus built Cardiff in 1081, is followed by the beginning of the Ludlow Annal: a calculation of the time between the destruction of Troy, the foundation of Rome, and the birth of Christ according to Orosius. The annal briefly describes the reign of Octavian before turning to the Incarnation and early Christian history in the context of Roman emperors. It resumes information about Britain in the fifth century. Reflecting its composite nature, and a lack of reconciliation of different sources, the annal repeats information from the *Epitome*, describing Faganus' and Diwanus' conversion of the Britons (the 'Lucius legend') in AD 184 (fol. 13ᵛ), the arrival of Hengist and Horsa in 456 (fol. 22ᵛ), and Cadwaladr's withdrawal to Rome and the transfer of the Crown of the kingdom from the Britons to the Saxons (fol. 27ᵛ). It records St Patrick's mission to Ireland in 431 (fol. 22ʳ) and death in 495 (fol. 23ᵛ), the birth of St David in 457 (fol. 22ᵛ), a battle between Saracens and Arthur in 516 (fol. 24ʳ), Arthur's wounding by Mordred and retreat to Avalon in 543 (fol. 24ᵛ), St Augustine's mission to England in 594 (fol. 25ᵛ), followed by various activities of early English kings, plus the death of Bede in 740 (fol. 29ʳ).[90] The annal's mixture of English and Roman–Christian history emphasizes links between England and the church in Rome. It becomes a chronicle of English kings around fol. 29ᵛ, and then Anglo-Norman kings at fol. 36ʳ, and is thereafter similar to monastic chronicles such as the Annals of Waverley and the Annals of Worcester in its royal and ecclesiastical interests.

From about fol. 40 onward, the annal's focus in its twelfth- to fourteenth-century entries is primarily the Mortimer family's activities, mixed in with other marcher families (Braose, Clare, Lacy, Geneville, and Despenser). Given-Wilson argues persuasively that the annal was not written for one specific family, because it tends to report their deeds impassively or without support. In this sense, it is more of a regional chronicle than a family chronicle.[91] Its view is much wider than Ludlow:

---

[90] Bede is the likely source for early English history, with Arthurian items mixed in.
[91] Given-Wilson, 'Chronicles of the Mortimer Family', 80–1.

it is interested in events in Glamorgan, Hereford, and Gloucester, as well as Shropshire at large. This is not surprising, given how connected the aforementioned families were to those areas. In this sense, it is fundamentally a marcher chronicle, similar to the Cardiff and Margam chronicles in its regional interests.[92] It occasionally mentions locations in Wales (Neath, Strata Florida, Llandaf, and Gower), which attests to connections between religious houses in Glamorgan and those in other marcher lordships. Beyond this regional localization, it also takes interest in national events, particularly the activities of King Edward I in Wales and Scotland and the usurpation of the Crown by Roger Mortimer and Queen Isabella.

Following the Ludlow Annal is part ii of the manuscript (s. xiv$^{1/4}$), written in an earlier hand than part i.[93] It contains several popular prophetical texts of the era, including the *Prophecy of Merlin Silvester* and excerpts from *DGB*, including the *Prophetiae Merlini*.[94] However, it is unclear whether parts i and ii were brought together in the medieval period, or whether the composite nature of the manuscript is the result of Robert Cotton's compilatory activities, as is typical of many manuscripts from his library. Part ii lacks the Ludlow associations of part i. For these reasons, I am not including the prophetical texts of part ii in my discussion.

The readers of the Ludlow Annal would have been encouraged to interpret the prophetic messages in the *Epitome historiae Britanniae* rather differently from the Glamorgan audience, given that they are, in this chronicle, positioned as a preface to the marcher history to come. By mapping out the history of the Ludlow region in this way, the compilers offer a very different fulfilment of the Merlinic prophecies in the

---

[92] For the Cardiff chronicle, see Georgia Henley, 'The "Cardiff Chronicle" in London, British Library, Royal MS 6 B. xi', in Guy et al. (eds), *Chronicles of Medieval Wales*, 231–87; for the Margam chronicle, see Marvin L. Colker, 'The "Margam Chronicle" in a Dublin Manuscript', *Haskins Society Journal*, 4 (1992), 123–48; Robert B. Patterson, 'The Author of the "Margam Annals": Early Thirteenth-Century Margam Abbey's Compleat Scribe', *Anglo-Norman Studies*, 14 (1992), 197–210.

[93] The scribe of part ii also writes the prophetical texts in London, Lambeth Palace Library, 527; see Victoria Flood, 'Prophecy as History: A New Study of the Prophecies of Merlin Silvester', *Neophilologus*, 102/4 (2018), 543–59, at 547.

[94] These texts are the *Prophecy of Merlin Silvester* (fols. 63^r–65^r), a copy of Geoffrey's *Prophetiae Merlini* with marginal commentary and drawings identifying British and Angevin kings (fols. 65^r–76^r), a compilation of passages from *DGB* that refer to Merlin (fol. 76^v), and a chronicle of English history to 1274 (fols. 77^r–111^v).

Epitome than would have been considered by Llandaf supporters of the Glyndŵr rebellion: instead, the result is continued tribulations for the Welsh, transfer of the kingdom to the English, and rightful Mortimer, Braose, Lacy, and Clare control over formerly Welsh lands.

At the same time, the text's report on the activities of Llywelyn ap Gruffudd, Edward I's conquest of Wales, and the failed rebellions of later figures such as Rhys ap Maredudd and Llywelyn Bren would have appeared in a different light from most English monastic annals because of the use of the Galfridian material as the prelude to contemporary events, and the familiarity that marcher audiences would have felt with the Welsh by comparison to English readers, who were less familiar with Wales and the March of Wales. For example, the killing of Llywelyn ap Gruffudd by Edmund Mortimer (reported in the Ludlow Annal on fol. 47^v) and the aftermath of Llywelyn's death continues the downfall predicted by Merlin. The Ludlow manuscript in its entirety offers a very different context for this tale from the Llandaf manuscript, which was interested in Welsh saints' lives and eschatology, connecting the providential history and biblical timeline of the *Epitome* to the sanctity of early medieval South Wales. In the case of the Ludlow manuscript, the compilers instead use the *Epitome* as framing for the marcher history that follows. After the conquest of Wales, the Ludlow Annal moves forward briskly with the early fourteenth-century history of the marcher lords in which it is primarily interested: lengthy entries on the births, deaths, marriages, and national political significance of the Mortimers and their neighbours, complemented by battles fought by Edward I to gain control of Wales and Scotland. This regional and thematic focus, with the *Epitome* as a prelude, implicitly places the marcher lords (not the English or the Welsh) as the rightful successors of the kingdom of Britain. The stories of Brutus and Arthur detailed in the *Epitome* serve as a legendary prelude to the contemporary victories of the Mortimers and other marcher lords.

Thus far, I have postulated a readership for the Ludlow Annal in Cotton Nero A. iv that was 'marcher' in the sense that it was interested in a narrative that reinforced marcher baronial power. I must also acknowledge that the chronicle may have been of interest, for different reasons, to audiences in this region who identified as Welsh and spoke Welsh (for example, in the lordship of Oswestry, a heavily Welsh-speaking area of

Shropshire) and who were not in favour of marcher baronial power. They may have wanted to see a chronicle that folded the British history into local Ludlow history, because their ancestry was traced in that manner to the present day. However, I hesitate to go too far down this path of speculation, because language choice and identity do not always correlate with textual interpretation, nor political loyalties, particularly in a multilingual area like Ludlow. One can say instead that the flexibility of interpretation that this chronicle offered may have bolstered its popularity, as was the case with Geoffrey's *DGB* in many contexts.

The *Epitome historiae Britanniae* in Hailes and Aberconwy

The chronicle's popularity is suggested by another appearance of it in a marcher context, this time excerpted in a text compiled at Hailes Abbey, near Winchcombe in Gloucestershire. The short section of the *Epitome* concerning Welsh history from Rhodri Mawr to Llywelyn ap Gruffudd was excised from its larger context and placed in the *Register and Chronicle of the Abbey of Aberconwy* (London, British Library, Harley 3725, fols. 40^v–65^v, s. xv; see Figure 1.4).[95] Historically, the Cistercian abbey of Aberconwy in Gwynedd (founded as a daughter house of Strata Florida in Ceredigion) was patronized by the kings of Gwynedd (North Wales), whose histories are outlined in the *Epitome*. This text is preceded in Harley 3725 by a chronicle of Hailes Abbey (fols. 2^r–31^v), written by a different scribe. Though Rhŷs Hays argues that the *Register and Chronicle* was compiled at Aberconwy, David Stephenson argues for production at Hailes Abbey for one David Winchcombe, a monk of Hailes who became abbot of Aberconwy in 1482.[96] A range of Welsh Cistercian sources and English annalistic sources, Stephenson argues, were assembled at Hailes during the time that David Winchcombe became

---

[95] Huws, *Repertory*, i.684.
[96] Rhŷs W. Hays, *The History of the Abbey of Aberconway, 1186–1537* (Cardiff, 1963), 145; David Stephenson, *The Aberconwy Chronicle*, Kathleen Hughes Memorial Lectures on Mediaeval Welsh History, 2 (Cambridge, 2002), 7–17.

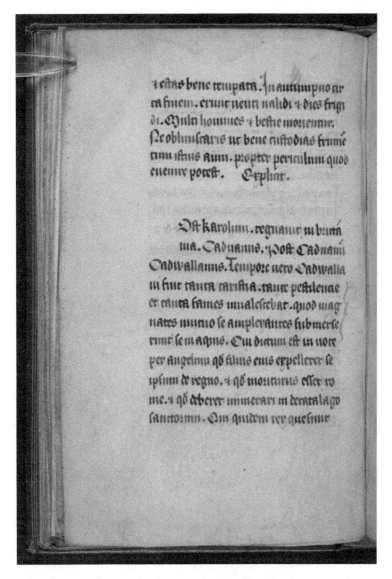

FIGURE 1.4 London, British Library, Harley 3725, fols. 40ᵛ–41ʳ.
© The British Library Board

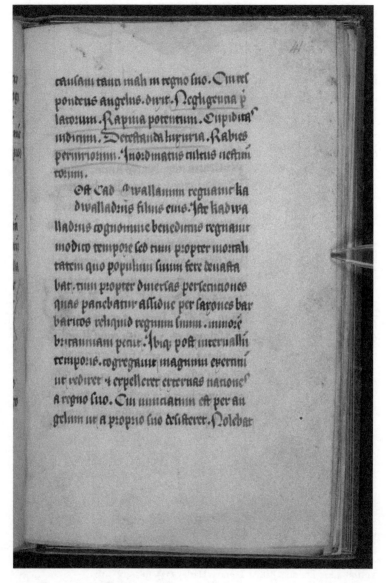

FIGURE 1.4 (*Continued*)

abbot of Aberconwy and monks were sent from Hailes to Aberconwy to institute reforms.[97]

Collectively, the appearance of the *Epitome* in two marcher contexts (Ludlow and Hailes) indicates that this short chronicle may have been quite popular in South Wales and the Middle March. It was popular enough to exit Wales (Glamorgan to Ludlow) and then return (Hailes to perhaps Aberconwy), an unexpected pathway of transmission that suggests several networks of copying. In fact, given the existence of multiple witnesses of the chronicle in extant manuscripts, we can postulate several more copies underlying this network of transmission.[98] This is an example of a Welsh text that achieved considerable popularity both within and outside Wales.

By placing contemporary marcher history in a Galfridian framework, the compilers of the Ludlow Annal make subtle ideological arguments for the primacy of marcher lords in the Middle March, including their right to occupy and govern the territory that their ancestors conquered from the Welsh, because Merlin predicted it and God allowed it. The Ludlow Annal is thus a new example of a broad co-opting of Galfridian history and Arthurian myth that was taking place in many arenas of textual production in medieval Britain. But in this case, unlike, for example, in the Middle English Prose *Brut*, Arthur is not presented as English. Rather, his successors are marcher. Marcher readers seem to have taken special inspiration from the themes of Geoffrey's *DGB*, particularly its argument that the throne of Britain would unite its three kingdoms, to the extent that interest in Geoffrey is a major presence in marcher literature. As descendants of Welsh, English, and Norman peoples, marchers were able to position themselves as uniquely qualified to rule in Britain. This argument reaches its fullest potential in a group of Mortimer genealogies discussed in the following chapter, which examines how Welsh genealogical sources were used by marcher compilers to construct an argument for the right of Roger Mortimer, 4th earl of March (1374–98), to the throne of England. The Ludlow Annal's presentation of marcher lords as successors to British–Welsh rulers, using

---

[97] Stephenson, *Aberconwy Chronicle*, 15–16.
[98] For a related study of textual transmission of chronicles between Wales and England, see Georgia Henley, 'Networks of Chronicle Writing in Western Britain: The Case of Worcester and Wales', in Francesca Tinti and David Woodman (eds), *Constructing History through the Conquest: Worcester c.1050–c.1150* (Woodbridge, 2022), 227–70, at 269.

Welsh historical sources to construct its argument, is paralleled in the Mortimer genealogies discussed presently. In both cases, Welsh sources were transmitted beyond Wales to be used in marcher texts for political and ideological effect, demonstrating that Welsh narratives of history and Welsh identities were not marginal to the articulation of British and English kingship in the medieval period, but fundamental.

2

Royal Aspirations

Geoffrey's *De gestis Britonum* (*Historia regum Britanniae*) was central to the interpretation of the historical past in medieval Britain. Throughout the medieval period, his history circulated widely in monastic institutions, households, and university libraries alike, and generated numerous commentaries, translations, and reinterpretations. It was read widely by laity and referenced by canonical English poets such as Chaucer and Lydgate as an authoritative source for the British past. It is very likely the flexibility—some might say the political ambivalence—of Geoffrey's narrative that permitted the emergence of so many interpretations. In England, this included, in addition to Arthurian romances and other generic offshoots, narrative adaptations such as Wace's *Roman de Brut*, Layamon's *Brut*, and the French Prose *Brut*, which was translated into Latin and Middle English. In Wales, this included a cluster of Welsh vernacular adaptations known collectively as *Brut y Brenhinedd* ('History of the Kings'), as well as other chronicles, genealogies, and Arthurian texts.

Geoffrey's history took on a particular kind of importance in the March of Wales, where baronial families worked on articulating their place in the borderlands, negotiating their position (both politically and in terms of identity) in relation to Wales and England, and defending their ownership of conquered land. These strategies are visible in historical writing associated with marcher lords. Geoffrey's history, of course, took on ideological importance in many contexts in medieval Britain, and Europe more broadly, but the ways in which it was interpreted in the March of Wales is the result of the specific circumstances of this border culture. Geoffrey provided a model for articulating the range of identities available to marcher people in a manner that promoted their dominance and control in the region (but also nationally, in the case of the Mortimer family). His vision of a multifarious kingdom able to be united under a single leader, guided by divine prophecies that predetermined and reinforced that leader's rule, were particularly appealing, and spurred new readings and new adaptations of his work in the marcher context. While many of these writings were highly localized and had a diffuse impact, the reimagining of Geoffrey's vision of the British–Welsh past by the Mortimers of Wigmore in the late fourteenth century reached national significance. In this chapter, I discuss histories and genealogies associated with this family, many of which are in an understudied fourteenth- and fifteenth-century manuscript, Chicago, University Library, 224, written in Latin and French by at least six scribes. The activities of this manuscript's compilers reveal the centrality of Geoffrey to the ideologies underlying the Mortimer family's politics as well as their distinct articulations of marcher identity.[1]

At the time of the manuscript's creation, Roger Mortimer, 4th earl of March (1374–98), was the presumptive heir to Richard II, king of England. These circumstances may have prompted chroniclers at Wigmore Abbey to draw together this compilation of historical and genealogical texts, several of which are edited by this author for the first time. As argued by Mary Giffin, the genealogies emphasize Roger's right to rule in an elaborate and striking presentation of hybrid English and Welsh ancestry: 'If scribes of the abbey, diligent in support of their patron, sought to advance the claim of the earl of March to the throne, they could not more effectively have shown him to be the descendant of all

---

[1] For general discussion, see Chris Given-Wilson, 'Chronicles of the Mortimer Family, c.1250–1450', in Richard Eales and Shaun Tyas (eds), *Family and Dynasty in Late Medieval England: Proceedings of the 1997 Harlaxton Symposium* (Donington, 2003), 67–86; Paul Dryburgh and Philip Hume (eds), *Mortimers of Wigmore 1066–1485: The Dynasty of Destiny* (Eardisley, 2023); J. J. Crump, 'The Mortimer Family and the Making of the March', in Michael Prestwich, R. H. Britnell, and Robin Frame (eds), *Thirteenth Century England VI: Proceedings of the Durham Conference 1995* (Woodbridge, 1997), 117–26. Unless otherwise noted, transcriptions and translations are my own.

the royal lines than in this genealogy.'[2] In this chapter, I demonstrate that these efforts to trace his Welsh and English ancestry back to the legendary founders of Britain, rhetorically doubling his claim to the throne, were the result of direct use of Welsh textual sources transmitted from Wales. The ideological argument in the genealogies is supported by other texts in the manuscript, including a version of the Latin Prose *Brut* and a Latin history of Wigmore Abbey. Mostly interested in continuing the scope of Geoffrey's history with king lists, one for each ethnic group of early medieval Britain, the version of the Latin Prose *Brut* is, like the genealogies, interested in demonstrating the Mortimers' Welsh lineage.

This creative refashioning of the past on the part of family chroniclers illustrates the leverage of Welsh connections by marcher families, which in turn stimulated textual transmission between Wales and the March. The compilers' efforts position Roger as uniquely qualified to unite the kingdoms of Britain and, furthermore, offered an important model for Edward IV and Henry Tudor's later use of Welsh ancestry to support their own royal claims.[3] Overall, the Mortimer interpretation of Geoffrey's history reveals the character of the March as discussed in the Introduction: it is a hybrid society, influenced by Welsh, English, and other literary cultures and political machinations, but its hybridity manifests not in a binary struggle between two worlds, but in a unique and cohesive entity, governed by its own internal interests, circumstances, and desires.

A brief history of the Mortimer family

The Mortimers started out as minor barons, with lands in the March of Wales granted to Ralph de Mortimer for service to William the Conqueror, and lands in Shropshire and Worcestershire granted to Roger

---

[2] Mary E. Giffin, 'The Wigmore Manuscript and the Mortimer Family' (unpublished Ph.D. dissertation, University of Chicago, 1939), 4; Mary E. Giffin, 'Cadwalader, Arthur, and Brutus in the Wigmore Manuscript', *Speculum*, 16 (1941), 109–20, at 110–11.

[3] Giffin, 'Cadwalader', 111; J. L. Laynesmith, 'Anne Mortimer's Legacy to the House of York', in Dryburgh and Hume (eds), *Mortimers of Wigmore*, 212–41, at 223–5.

Mortimer (d. 1214) for service to Henry II.[4] Roger and his sons, Hugh (d. 1227) and Ralph (d. 1246), conquered significant lands in the Welsh kingdoms of Maelienydd and Gwerthrynion, eventually extinguishing the Gwerthrynion dynasty in feuds with the descendants of Madog ab Idnerth (d. 1146).[5] Roger expanded into Wales, building a castle at Cymaron in 1195 and endowing the Cistercian monastery of Cwmhir in Maelienydd in 1200.[6] In a move that would become important to the future dynastic politics of the family, in 1229 his son Ralph married Gwladys Ddu (d. 1251), widow of Reginald de Braose (d. 1227/8) and the daughter of Llywelyn ab Iorwerth, prince of Wales (c.1173–1240) and Joan (d. 1237), natural daughter of King John. Through Gwladys, later generations of the family would claim descent from the great Welsh princes of Gwynedd, including Gruffudd ap Cynan (1054/5–1137), Rhodri Mawr (d. 878), Maelgwn Gwynedd (d. 547/9), and other figures typically found in Welsh genealogies. Mortimer interest in their Welsh descent appears to have been part of a broader engagement in Galfridian history for the purpose of justifying and solidifying the claim of Roger Mortimer, 4th earl of March, to the English throne at the end of the fourteenth century and resulted in the transmission of Welsh genealogical texts from Wales to the Augustinian abbey of Wigmore in Herefordshire (founded by Hugh de Mortimer in 1172).

In the second half of the twelfth century, heightened involvement in royal politics increased the Mortimers' status and wealth. They became a family 'whose ambition for power was a controlling factor in the history of England throughout three centuries'.[7] Eventually they held vast estates in England, Wales, and Ireland, with their family seat at Wigmore Castle.[8] The term 'March' reached new heights of political status

---

[4] For recent discussion, see Dryburgh and Hume (eds), *Mortimers of Wigmore*; Philip Hume, 'The Lordships of Radnorshire and North Herefordshire', in Hume (ed.), *The Welsh Marcher Lordships*, i. *Cedntral & North* (Eardisley, 2021), 129–88, at 133–44; Ian Mortimer, 'The Chronology of the de Mortemer Family of Wigmore, c.1075–1185, and the Consolidation of a Marcher Lordship', *Historical Research*, 89/246 (2016), 613–35.

[5] J. Beverley Smith, 'The Middle March in the Thirteenth Century', *Bulletin of the Board of Celtic Studies*, 24 (1970–2), 77–93; Crump, 'Mortimer Family', 117, n. 1.

[6] *Brut y Tywysogyon, or The Chronicle of the Princes, Red Book of Hergest Version*, ed. and trans. Thomas Jones (Cardiff, 1955), 174–5; B. G. Charles, 'An Early Charter of the Abbey of Cwmhir', *Transactions of the Radnorshire Society*, 40 (1970), 68–74.

[7] Giffin, 'The Wigmore Manuscript and the Mortimer Family', 3–4.

[8] Historians attribute their quick rise to Ralph's marriage to Gwladys Ddu and his son Roger's marriage to Maud de Braose, through which the Mortimer family gained the

when Roger Mortimer (1287–1330), who held vast lands in Herefordshire, Shropshire, Wales, and Ireland, was given the rank of earl in 1328, a result of his relationship with Queen Isabella and the displacement of King Edward II, and chose the title earl of March.[9] Roger forfeited this title just two years later, and in 1330 was executed for treason under the suspicion that he played a role in the king's death.[10] Despite this fall from grace, the family recovered. The marriage in 1369 of Roger's great-grandson Edmund Mortimer, 3rd earl of March (1352–81), to Philippa (daughter of Lionel, duke of Clarence, and granddaughter of Edward III) was particularly important to the family's success, as it united the earldom of Ulster with the Mortimer holdings in England and Wales and placed the couple's firstborn son, Roger, 4th earl of March and 6th earl of Ulster, directly in line to the English throne (see Table 2.1 for the family line).[11]

The creation of the earldom of March has been interpreted as a sign of a broad political transition in the region, from a period during which Norman and Anglo-Norman rule of the March was a piecemeal, individualized effort, focused on acquiring Welsh territories, to a new, post-conquest era, in which marcher families, including the Mortimers, consolidated their power and wealth through intermarriage.[12]

One of the ways in which the family supported its own ascent was by engaging with and utilizing the ideology of Geoffrey's *De gestis Britonum* (hereafter *DGB*) in a range of languages and contexts. By the fourteenth century, *DGB* was very well known. The Prose *Brut*, a

---

Braose and Marshal lands in Wales, Ireland, and the March; see J. J. Crump, 'Mortimer, Roger de, lord of Wigmore', *ODNB*, accessed 29 December 2021.

[9] See Given-Wilson, 'Chronicles of the Mortimer Family', 67; Hume, 'Lordships of Radnorshire', 139–41; Caroline Shenton, 'Edward III and the Coup of 1330', in J. S. Bothwell (ed.), *The Age of Edward III* (York, 2001), 13–34. Ludlow Castle had been granted to Roger Mortimer, 1st earl of March, and his wife Joan de Geneville by her grandfather in 1308. See discussion in John J. Thompson, 'Mapping Points of West of West Midlands Manuscripts', in Wendy Scase (ed.), *Vernacular Manuscripts of the English West Midlands from the Conquest to the Sixteenth Century* (Turnhout, 2007), 113–28, at 126–7; Michael Faraday, *Ludlow, 1085–1660: A Social, Economic, and Political History* (Chichester, 1991), 4–9.

[10] May McKisack, *The Fourteenth Century, 1307–1399* (Oxford, 1959), 58–88.

[11] Roger's younger brother Edmund (1376–1408/9) was allied with Owain Glyndŵr, and married Owain's daughter Catrin. Owain Glyndŵr is discussed in Ch. 1, pp. 48–9.

[12] For background, see Crump, 'Mortimer Family'; J. Beverley Smith, 'Middle March'.

TABLE 2.1 The Mortimer line

Roger de Mortimer (fl. 1054–c.1080)
Ralph de Mortimer (fl. c.1080–after 1115)
Hugh de Mortimer (d. 1185)
Roger de Mortimer, lord of Wigmore (d. 1214)
Ralph de Mortimer, lord of Wigmore (d. 1246), *marries Gwladys Ddu*
Roger Mortimer, lord of Wigmore (1231–82)
Edmund Mortimer, lord of Wigmore (d. 1304)
Roger Mortimer, 1st earl of March (1287–1330), *consort of Queen Isabella*
Edmund Mortimer (d. 1331)
Roger Mortimer, 2nd earl of March (1328–60)
Edmund Mortimer, 3rd earl of March (1352–81), *marries Philippa of Clarence*
Roger Mortimer, 4th earl of March (1374–98)
Edmund Mortimer, 5th earl of March (1391–1425)

narrative adaptation of the text that existed in French, Middle English, and Latin versions, was the primary vehicle through which laypeople knew Geoffrey.[13] The broad structure of the narrative is based on Geoffrey, with other sources incorporated into it, such as Wace's *Roman de Brut*, Geffrei Gaimar's *Estoire des Engleis*, and the Anglo-Norman poem *Des grantz geanz*.[14] The complex textual history of the Prose *Brut* in three of Britain's major literary languages attests to its widespread circulation across social classes, geographical regions, and several centuries of reinterpretation.

Dialect evidence shows that the earliest English translation of the Prose *Brut* is in a Herefordshire dialect, locating it in a marcher environment in the second half of the fourteenth century.[15] This was a border region home to Welsh, French, and English speakers and governed by

---

[13] See Lister M. Matheson, *The Prose Brut: The Development of a Middle English Chronicle* (Tempe, 1998), 4–8, 30–49.

[14] Ibid., 30–3.

[15] Ibid., 48. The earliest Middle English Prose *Brut* manuscripts with Herefordshire associations are Oxford, Bodleian Library, Rawlinson B. 171 (south-west Herefordshire, c.1400); Oxford, Bodleian Library, Rawlinson B. 173 (west Herefordshire, s. xv); Cambridge, University Library, Kk.1.12 (central Herefordshire, s. xv^{med}); and Oxford, Bodleian Library, Bodley 840 (Essex with Herefordshire remnants, c.1420–30).

the Mortimers. Despite this point of origin, few scholars have considered the Middle English Prose *Brut* as a product of the March or as marcher literature.[16] However, it may have been precisely the multicultural environment of the March, with Welsh, Latin, French, and English speakers and writers intermixing, in combination with the presence of Wales as a neighbour, that made English-speaking readers in this region so interested in defining English identity and nationhood.[17] The reception of *DGB* takes on special meaning in this context. Marcher baronial families, descended from both Anglo-Norman and Welsh nobility, seem to have been uniquely positioned to consider themselves as the true inheritors of British kingship because of their descent from both Welsh and English sides of Brutus' line.[18] The Mortimers in particular deliberately cultivated and emphasized these lines of descent during the time that the Prose *Brut* was widely disseminated. It is appropriate here to take a momentary detour into the Middle English Prose *Brut*'s Mortimer-focused passages to demonstrate popular views of the family in this period and the close relationship between vernacular and Latin narrative sources about them.

The family's popularity is evident in two Herefordshire-provenance manuscripts of the Middle English Prose *Brut*, which favour members

---

[16] Instead, interpretations have focused on the role it played in the formation of a specifically English identity. See, e.g., Thorlac Turville-Petre, *England the Nation: Language, Literature, and National Identity, 1290–1340* (Oxford, 1996), 81–2; Margaret Lamont, 'Becoming English: Ronwenne's Wassail, Language, and National Identity in the Middle English Prose *Brut*', *Studies in Philology*, 107 (2010), 283–309.

[17] Its marcher origins lend credence to John Gillingham's argument that English national identity was formed against neighbouring peoples' cultural difference; see Gillingham, *The English in the Twelfth Century: Imperialism, National Identity, and Political Values* (Woodbridge, 2000), 41–58. For multilingualism studies, see Lindy Brady, *Multilingualism in Early Medieval Britain*, Cambridge Elements: Elements in England in the Early Medieval World (Cambridge, 2023); Margaret Connolly and Raluca Radulescu (eds), *Insular Books: Vernacular Manuscript Miscellanies in Late Medieval Britain*, Proceedings of the British Academy, 201 (Oxford, 2012); Ad Putter and Judith Jefferson (eds), *Multilingualism in Medieval Britain (c.1066–1520): Sources and Analysis*, Medieval Texts and Cultures of Northern Europe, 15 (Turnhout, 2012); Elizabeth M. Tyler (ed.), *Conceptualizing Multilingualism in England, c.800–c.1250*, Studies in the Early Middle Ages, 27 (Turnhout, 2011); Jocelyn Wogan-Browne (ed.), *Language and Culture in Medieval Britain: The French of England c.1100–c.1500* (York, 2009).

[18] In other words, as people of both Welsh and English ancestry, they were symbolically uniting two of the kingdoms of Geoffrey's Britain: Cambria (understood to be Wales, the portion of Brutus' kingdom he gave to his son Camber) and Loegria (understood to be England, the portion of Brutus' kingdom he gave to his son Locrinus).

of the family in specific passages.[19] These passages, which take place in the continuation of the chronicle from 1377 to 1419, portray Mortimer men positively: they are brave, noble, wealthy, physically attractive, and always loyal to the king.[20] In particular, the copy of the *Brut* in CUL Kk.1.12 (s. xv[med], from central Herefordshire) describes the death of Roger, 4th earl of March, in 1398 in markedly laudatory terms:

> And the Erle of the March, at þat same parlement holdon at Westemynstre, yn playne parlement among al þe Lordeʒ and Comyns, was proclaymed Erle of the March, and heyre parant vnto þe croune of Engelonde aftir King Richarde. The which Erle of the Marche went ouyr see yn-to Irelond vnto his lordeschippeʒ and londeʒ, for the Erle of Marche is Erle of Vlcestre yn Irelonde, and by ryʒt lyne and heritage. And at a Castill of his he lay þat tyme; and þere come apon hym a grete multitude yn buschmentis of wilde Iryschmen, hym for to take and distroye, and he come out ffersly of his Castell with his peple, and manly ffauʒt with ham; and þere he was take, and hew al to pecis, and þere he deied; on whose soule God haue mercy! Amen![21]

> And the earl of March, at that same parliament held at Westminster, in full parliament among all the lords and common people, was proclaimed earl of the March, and heir apparent to the Crown of England after King Richard. The same earl of the March went over the sea to Ireland to his lordships and lands, for [he] is earl of Ulster in Ireland, by right lineage and inheritance. At that time, he lodged at a castle of his, and there a great multitude of wild Irishmen came upon him in ambush, intending to take and destroy him, and he came courageously out of his castle with his people, and vigorously fought with

---

[19] Rawlinson B. 173 and CUL Kk.1.12. Both of these versions of the English *Brut* are classified as the Common Version to 1419. They are a translation into English of the Long Version of the Anglo-Norman Prose *Brut* to the year 1333, plus a continuation composed in English from 1333 to 1419.

[20] There is no Herefordshire bias in the Middle English text before 1333, perhaps because it was a close translation of the French exemplar. In fact, it is critical of Roger Mortimer, 1st earl of March's ascension to the throne: see *The Brut: Or, The chronicles of England*, ed. Friedrich W. D. Brie, 2 vols, Early English Text Society, os 131, 136 (London, 1906–8; repr. 1960), i.254, 257–62, 264, 268–72. By comparison, the Wigmore Chronicle, the family chronicle of the Mortimers, declines to mention Roger's forfeiture of his lands in 1330 at all; see Given-Wilson, 'Chronicles of the Mortimer Family', 74.

[21] *Brut*, ed. Brie, ii.341.

them, and there he was taken, and hewn all to pieces, and there he died, on whose soul God have mercy! Amen!

The text is here describing Roger's tragic death in Ireland at the age of 24 during a battle with the Irish outside a castle in Kellistown (County Carlow) or perhaps Kells (County Meath). His death was particularly unfortunate for the family's political fortunes: he had been the purported successor to King Richard II, as mentioned above, but his 7-year-old son Edmund was passed over as a claimant to the throne, probably because of his youth. Had Roger lived to succeed Richard, the family's history might have been very different.

The text is careful to delineate Roger's right to the throne ('heyre parant vnto þe croune of Engelonde aftir King Richarde') and his right to the earldom of Ulster ('the Erle of Marche is Erle of Vlcestre yn Irelonde, and by ryȝt lyne and heritage'). It also emphasizes his bravery in defending the castle against the Irish ('he come out ffersly of his Castell with his peple, and manly ffauȝt with ham').[22]

This section of the Prose *Brut*, strikingly, shares close similarities to the story of his death in a Latin chronicle in Chicago 224 known as the *Fundationis et Fundatorum Historia*, a history of the Mortimer family written at Wigmore Abbey between c.1262 and 1413.[23] The Latin passage reads:

> Iste Rogerus, vir licet bellicosus et inclitus, ac negotiis fortunatus, pulcherque et formosus, ut praemittitur, fuerit; nimis tamen lascivus, et in divinis, heu! remissus; consilioque juvenum, antiquorum rejecto, abductus nimia animositate, immo verius ferocitate leonina, leonelli nepoti satis innata, sed (proh dolor!) non regulata, irruendo, exercitum praecedens, Hibernicali vestitus et equitatus apparatu, nec suos in succursum expectans, ac hostes invadens apud Kenles

---

[22] By comparison, the death of the comparably young nobleman John Hastings, 3rd earl of Pembroke, at a joust in 1389 is reported perfunctorily and without praise; *Brut*, ed. Brie, ii.344–5.

[23] Chicago 224 (fols. 48ʳ–60ᵛ), printed in *Monasticon Anglicanum: Or, The history of the ancient abbies, monasteries, hospitals, cathedral and collegiate churches, with their dependencies, in England and Wales*, ed. William Dugdale, 6 vols (London, 1718; repr. 1846), VI (i).348–55; discussed by Given-Wilson, 'Chronicles of the Mortimer Family', 68–76.

> in Hibernia per homines obrinque [*corr.* utrimque] invasus, belli eventu in animas suorum hostium, in festo St. Margaretae virginis, an. Dom. mcccxcviii. cecidit inde, quia hostibus ignotus quam dolenter trucidatus, et inde ad dictam abbathiam, juxta parentes suos transfertur tumulatus.[24]
>
> That Roger was a man who, although valorous and celebrated, and prosperous in his occupations, and handsome and beautiful, as mentioned above, was nevertheless too licentious, and in religion— woe!— too lax. And taking the advice of young men, and rejecting the advice of the old, he was carried off by excessive boldness, or rather, more truthfully, by a leonine fierceness, natural enough in the descendant of a little lion,[25] but (O, grief!) not undisciplined. Rushing in, going ahead of his army, clothed and mounted in the manner of an Irishman,[26] and not waiting for his men to help him, and charging the enemies at Kenles in Ireland, he was attacked by men on both sides. By the chance of war against the souls of his enemies, on St Margaret's Day [20 July], in the year 1398, he died there. Because he was unrecognized by his enemies, how sorrowfully was he slaughtered, and he was brought back from there to the aforesaid abbey to be interred next to his parents.

The similarities in the two accounts—praise of Roger's bravery, expressions of lamentation, and the precise details about his death in an ill-fated, ill-prepared battle—demonstrate that both chronicles, despite being written in different languages, emerged from the same general way of thinking about and portraying the Mortimer family.

The connection between these two chronicles, one in Middle English and one in Latin, raises an important point about the textual history of a very popular work like the Middle English Prose *Brut*. So many acts of recopying and continuing may have allowed for the 'customization' of *Brut* texts, with a pan-British history overlaying regional identities. The continuations may have absorbed local interests, perhaps drawn from regional chronicles like the ones produced at Wigmore Abbey in

---

[24] Chicago 224, fol. 59ᵛ; *Monasticon Anglicanum*, ed. Dugdale, VI (i).354–5. Preceding the account of his death, the *Fundationis et Fundatorum Historia* praises Roger as *ille inclitus leo, Hector secundus* 'that renowned lion, a second Hector', a laudatory phrase reminiscent of the elegy for Lord Rhys ap Gruffudd discussed in Chapter 5.

[25] Referring here to his descent from Llywelyn ab Iorwerth, whose name is *Leolinus* in Latin.

[26] i.e. without a saddle.

intended aggrandizement of the Mortimers, their right to the throne, and their rightful claim to Welsh and English lands. The promotion of the Mortimers in these versions of the *Brut*, which give extended time to Mortimer episodes, may have reinforced a sense of regional identity for a Herefordshire textual community, a particular iteration of marcher identity that emphasized their lords' proximity to the English Crown, fame, and importance. These expressions of identity took place in English-language texts in addition to Latin, French, and Welsh ones, attesting to the multilingual character of the March of Wales. The Welsh aspects of this identity come into focus in the documents produced for the Mortimers themselves.

The Mortimers and Welsh genealogies

The texts in Chicago 224 provide evidence for direct engagement with Geoffrey's *DGB* as well as Welsh genealogical sources, shedding light on the Mortimer family's attitudes towards its own history, lineage, and identity in a Galfridian context. The manuscript was written by at least six scribes in the fourteenth and fifteenth centuries.[27] It contains:

1. An account of the foundation of Wigmore Abbey, in French (fols. 1^v–5^r)[28]
   ○ 5^v–6^r blank
2. A genealogical note on Jupiter, king of Crete, in Latin (fol. 6^v)
3. A Latin version of the Prose *Brut*[29] (fols. 7^r–24^v), in which four genealogical lists are embedded:
   a. Scottish kings from Brutus and Albanactus to Malcolm (fols. 10^v–11^r)
   b. Dukes of Cornwall (fol. 11^v)

---

[27] It has been discussed in print in a series of articles by Mary Giffin: Giffin, 'The Wigmore Manuscript and the Mortimer Family'; Giffin, 'Cadwalader'; Mary E. Giffin, 'A Wigmore Manuscript at the University of Chicago', *NLWJ* 7/4 (1952), 316–25. The manuscript is digitized: University of Chicago Library, https://www.lib.uchicago.edu/e/scrc/findingaids/view.php?eadid=ICU.SPCL.MS224, accessed 7 March 2022.

[28] Printed in *Monasticon Anglicanum*, ed. Dugdale, VI (i).344–8, with the title *Fundationis eiusdem Historia*; J. C. Dickinson and P. T. Ricketts, 'The Anglo-Norman Chronicle of Wigmore Abbey', *Transactions of the Woolhope Naturalists' Field Club*, 39 (1967–9), 413–45.

[29] For discussion of the Latin Prose *Brut*, see Matheson, *Prose Brut*, 5–6, 15–16, 37–47.

c. Welsh king list beginning with Brutus, which splits into (i) rulers of South Wales down to Rhys ap Gruffudd and (ii) rulers of North Wales down to Llywelyn ab Iorwerth (fols. 12^r–13^r)[30]
d. British king list from Brutus to Cadwaladr, sourced from Geoffrey (fols. 20^r–23^v)
4. A series of royal pedigrees, illustrated with genealogical roundels in red and blue and accompanied by detailed prose explanations, in Latin:
   a. Early English, Anglo-Norman, and English kings to Edward III (fols. 25^r–35^r)
   b. French kings to Edward III (fols. 35^v–36^r)
   c. Edward III to Richard II (fols. 36^v–37^v)
   d. Descendants of Henry IV (fols. 38^v–39^r)
      ○ *40^r–47^v left blank or erased*[31]
5. An elaborate genealogy of the Mortimer family, decorated with illuminated shield roundels in gold, red, blue, and black, interwoven with a Mortimer family history, known as *Fundationis et Fundatorum Historia*, in Latin (fols. 48^r–60^v)[32]
   ○ *61^r–61^v unfinished*
6. Miscellaneous notes on marcher families affiliated with the Mortimers, in Latin and French (fols. 62r–67r)
7. Heraldic arms, unfinished (fols. 67v–69v)
8. Leaf of Latin sermon (fol. 70r–v)

The last full entry of item 5, the Mortimer genealogy, is for Roger, 4th earl of March (fol. 59^v). The genealogy was probably written into the

---

[30] The Welsh King List is edited and translated in Appendix A.
[31] These seven folia were left blank or erased, and they contain: ghostly pencil sketches of a knight (fol. 40^r) and angels (fol. 47^v), offsets of the genealogical roundels (fols. 41^r–42^r), an alphabetical list of names in a much later hand (fols. 43^v–44^r), an erased list of place names in England, Wales, and Ireland visible under UV light, possibly a list of towns and properties under Mortimer control (fols. 44^r–46^v), and a sketch of a knight and an ownership inscription (fol. 47^v).
[32] Printed in *Monasticon Anglicanum*, ed. Dugdale, VI (i).348–55, with the title *Fundationis et Fundatorum Historia* (not to be confused with *Fundationis eiusdem Historia* mentioned above). Given-Wilson, 'Chronicles of the Mortimer Family', 71 uses the title *Fundatorum Historia*. The pedigree of Gwladys Ddu is edited in Appendix B.

manuscript after he came of age in 1394 but before his death in Ireland in 1398.[33] Additions were made to the genealogy in the fifteenth century.[34]

In the pages below, I build upon Giffin's argument that the compilers of this manuscript use the ideology of Geoffrey's history to 'show that if Roger de Mortimer were to come to the throne, he would be, by direct line of descent, King of England, Scotland, and Wales.'[35] To Giffin's conclusions I add detailed evidence for the use of Welsh genealogical sources by the compilers, demonstrating how these texts combine a marcher understanding of Galfridian history with Welsh genealogies to present an elaborate, careful argument for the Mortimers' claim to the throne.

At the time of the manuscript's compilation, Roger was most likely alive, in his early twenties, just emerged from the guardianship of Thomas Holland, earl of Kent. He was granted control of his Irish estates in 1393 and his English and Welsh estates in 1394, and his claim to the throne was openly discussed.[36] It may have been necessary at this time to assert that claim and begin consolidating power and authority in preparation for potential succession. As others have observed, both the list of Welsh kings (item 3c) and the genealogy of the Mortimer family (item 5) emphasize Roger's descent from Gwladys Ddu ('dark-haired, dark-eyed'), the Welsh noblewoman and widow of Reginald de Braose who married Ralph de Mortimer in 1229. Gwladys is significant to the text's genealogical argument because she was, as mentioned above, the daughter of Llywelyn ab Iorwerth, ruler of Gwynedd (known as Llywelyn Fawr, 'Llywelyn the Great') and Joan, natural daughter of King John of England. Descent from Gwladys forms a key argument for the Mortimers' symbolic right to rule.[37]

---

[33] Argued by Given-Wilson, 'Chronicles of the Mortimer Family', 70.
[34] Chicago 224, fols. 37^v, 39^v–41^v.
[35] Giffin, 'Cadwalader', 119.
[36] R. R. Davies, 'Mortimer, Roger, fourth earl of March and sixth earl of Ulster', *ODNB*, accessed 29 December 2021. Roger is proclaimed as Richard's heir at the Parliament of 1385 in a version of the Prose *Brut* in a manuscript that might be from Ruthin, Denbighshire (Aberystwyth, NLW, 21608D); see *An English Chronicle, 1377–1461: Edited from Aberystwyth, National Library of Wales MS 21068 and Oxford, Bodleian Library MS Lyell 34*, ed. William Marx (Woodbridge, 2003), xxxix, 9.
[37] Llywelyn ab Iorwerth is known for unifying Wales, to the extent that it could be unified, in a series of diplomatic moves and military stand-offs with Kings John and Henry III. See J. Beverley Smith, *Llywelyn ap Gruffudd: Prince of Wales* (Oxford, 1998), 1–37;

In the Mortimer genealogy, Gwladys receives one of just two rubricated illuminations in the text: a large triangle of leaves in red, blue, and gold leaf with a rubricated letter 'H' that extends down the left-hand margin to form a border around her pedigree. The text begins: *Hic incipit genealogia domine Gwladuse filie et heredis Lewelini quondam principis Wallie uxoris nobilis uiri domini Radulphi de Mortuo Mari domini de Wyggemore* 'Here begins the genealogy of the lady Gwladys, daughter and heir of Llywelyn the former prince of Wales, wife of the noble man Lord Ralph de Mortimer, lord of Wigmore' (fol. 51^v; Figure 2.1).[38] This is the most decorated opening in the entire text, emphasizing her importance to the family lineage.

A retrograde pedigree of Gwladys follows. It traces her lineage backwards through the historical and legendary kings of North Wales, including Gruffudd ap Cynan, Rhodri Mawr, and Maelgwn Gwynedd; the Galfridian kings of Britain; and their Trojan and biblical ancestors, back to Adam (fols. 51^v–52ra). Tracing royal pedigrees back to Adam and/or God was not a common practice in Welsh genealogies, with the important exception of genealogies of princes of Gwynedd (North Wales) from the twelfth century onwards, which the Gwladys pedigree follows.[39] In fact, it follows extant Gwynedd genealogies so closely that the Mortimer compilers at Wigmore Abbey must have had access to a Welsh genealogical text—an important instance of textual transmission from Wales to the March, spurred by the interests of marcher

---

David Stephenson, 'Llywelyn Fawr, the Mortimers, and Cwmhir Abbey: The Politics of Monastic Rebuilding', *Transactions of the Radnorshire Society*, 80 (2010), 29–41.

[38] Chicago 224, fols. 51^v, 55^v; Giffin, 'Wigmore Manuscript at the University of Chicago', 319. Gwladys was not in fact Llywelyn's heir—the text is exaggerating her status. For the full text, see Appendix B. In this and other quotations from Chicago 224, I have expanded abbreviations and added punctuation and capitalization.

[39] The linking of the Gwynedd pedigree with the kings of Britain and Troy, back to Adam, became more common in late medieval Welsh genealogies owing to the influence of Geoffrey's history; for discussion, see *MWG* 233–64; David E. Thornton, 'A Neglected Genealogy of Llywelyn ap Gruffudd', *CMCS* 23 (1992), 9–23, at 11–12, 18–20; *Early Welsh Genealogical Tracts*, ed. Peter C. Bartrum (Cardiff, 1966), 38–9; *Vita Griffini Filii Conani: The Medieval Latin Life of Gruffudd ap Cynan*, ed. and trans. Paul Russell (Cardiff, 2005), §3, 52–5. The genealogy of Llywelyn ap Gruffudd in Exeter, Cathedral Library, 3514 (s. xiii^{ex}), the genealogy of Gruffudd ap Cynan in *Historia Gruffud vab Kenan*, and the genealogy of Llywelyn ap Gruffudd in Aberystwyth, NLW, 3036B (Mostyn 117, s. xiv^{in}) trace Welsh royal lineage in this way.

ROYAL ASPIRATIONS | 89

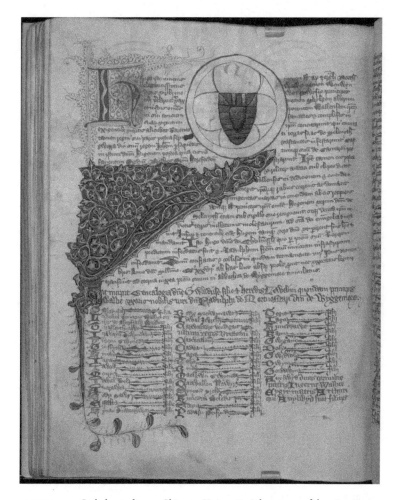

FIGURE 2.1   Gwladys pedigree, Chicago, University Library, 224, fols. 51^v–52^r.
By permission of the Hanna Holborn Gray Special Collections Research Center, University of Chicago Library

lords. As I demonstrate further below, the genealogies of Gwladys's father, Llywelyn ab Iorwerth, are the likely source for her pedigree in the Chicago manuscript.

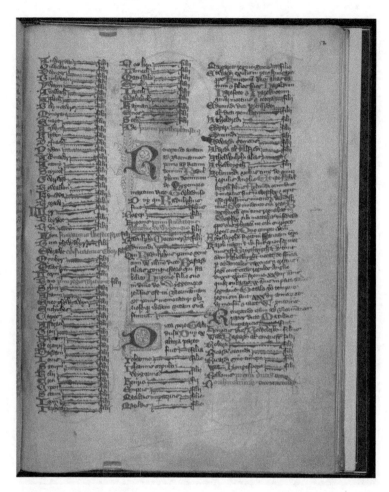

FIGURE 2.1   (*Continued*)

The compilers of this manuscript brought together texts that work together to present a complex argument about Mortimer lineage. The family's descent from Welsh, Galfridian, Trojan, and biblical ancestors is made explicit in the Gwladys pedigree and also in a list of North and South Welsh kings (item 3c), hereafter called the 'Welsh King List' (fols. 12ʳ–13ʳ).[40] Unlike the retrograde pedigree of Gwladys Ddu, the Welsh King List is not a genealogy, but a list of kings in order of succession, beginning with Brutus and ending with Rhys ap Gruffudd (d. 1197) in the south and Llywelyn ap Gruffudd (c.1233–82) in the north. The compilers embed several of these kinds of lists in the Latin Prose *Brut*. The Welsh King List follows a discussion of the different peoples of Britain (Norman, Flemish, Scottish, Cornish, and Welsh), and is followed by the Latin Prose *Brut* episode concerning Vortigern, who hands control of Britain to the Saxon brothers Hengist and Horsa and begins the Britons' slide into ruin. This placement in the *Brut* may not be an accident, as the beginning of the end of British–Welsh rule was typically marked in Welsh historical narrative by Vortigern's betrayal.[41] Therefore, it forms a natural thematic conclusion to the Welsh King List, which articulates the decline of two Welsh kingdoms. And yet, this text departs completely from Welsh historical tradition in the sense that king lists were not at all common in medieval Welsh genealogies or histories. In other words, though compiled from Welsh sources, the Welsh King List is unique to this marcher context, an innovation original to Wigmore. It is innovative in the English context as well, as there is no Welsh king list attested in medieval English historical sources, nor any English historical or genealogical text that makes such extensive use of Welsh textual sources. Its uniqueness is a result of the precise combination of royal and marcher aspirations held by the Mortimer family at this time.

The Welsh King List begins with the legendary founder Brutus and his son Camber, ruler of Cambria, the territory that eventually becomes Wales. It lists the standard line of Galfridian kings until Sisillius, at which point it turns to the pedigree of the sixth-century Welsh ruler Maelgwn Gwynedd.[42] After Maelgwn Gwynedd, it splits into two lines. First it names the *reges siue principes Southwallie* 'kings or princes of South Wales', from Maelgwn's son Arviragus to the Lord Rhys ap Gruffudd of Deheubarth. It states that, after Rhys's death, the kingdom of the Britons in South Wales collapsed. Second, it lists the *reges siue principes northwallie* 'kings or princes of North Wales', from Maelgwn's

---

[40] See Appendix A for text and translation.
[41] See Ch. 1, pp. 42–3, for further discussion.
[42] The genealogy of Gruffudd ap Cynan in *Historia Gruffud vab Kenan* and the genealogies of Llywelyn ab Iorwerth also do this.

son Rhun to Gwladys Ddu.[43] The original hand of the text does not, interestingly, conclude with Llywelyn ap Gruffudd (widely viewed as the last prince of Gwynedd), which would parallel its articulation of the end of Welsh rule in South Wales, but with Gwladys Ddu, a rather more successful end point for the Mortimers. This premature ending has been remedied by a different hand from the main text, which adds an extended note to the end of the list on Llywelyn ab Iorwerth's children, particularly Gwladys Ddu, as well as the death of Llywelyn ap Gruffudd. The note, which extends to the bottom of fol. 13^r in crowded lines, emphasizes Gwladys's marriage to Ralph de Mortimer, this time in the context of Gwynedd's dynastic politics.[44] It begins:

> Et quia reges siue principes Southwallie desierunt per mortem Resi ante dicti, principatus Southwallie remaneret Lewelino filio Ierwerth supradicto, qui quidem Lewelinus ex Johanna uxore sua filia regis \Johannis/ genuit filium nomine Dauid et vincam [*corr*: unicam] filiam nomine Gwladusam, uxorem domini Radulphi de Mortuomari domini de Wygemore vero.[45]

> And because the kings or princes of South Wales came to an end with the death of the aforementioned Rhys, the principality of South Wales was left to the above-mentioned Llywelyn ab Iorwerth. Llywelyn had a son named David [Dafydd] from his wife Johanna, daughter of King John, and an only daughter named Gwladys, wife of lord Ralph de Mortimer, the true lord of Wigmore.

A narrative of the battle for succession between Llywelyn ab Iorwerth's sons, Gruffudd and Dafydd, follows. It describes the succession of Gruffudd's son, Llywelyn, his marriage to Eleanor de Montfort, and his death at Buellt in 1282, marking the end of independent Gwynedd and the conquest of Wales by Edward I.

This extended note seems to have the overall goal of emphasizing Gwladys's noble ancestry, and, by implication, her descendants' right to rule over Wales through their descent from Llywelyn ab Iorwerth,

---

[43] This split at Maelgwn Gwynedd is unusual, as most Welsh genealogies split the line into northern and southern dynasties at the ninth-century ruler Rhodri Mawr, as in Gerald of Wales, *Descriptio Kambriae*, i.2, ed. J. F. Dimock, *Giraldi Cambrensis Opera*, 6 (London, 1868). I am grateful to Ben Guy for discussing this point with me.

[44] The hand of the main text is Hand B, with notes added by Hand D; see Giffin, 'Wigmore Manuscript at the University of Chicago', 318–19.

[45] Chicago 224, fol. 13^r.

whose direct line was extinguished. In the context of the rest of the manuscript, the implication of the final statement (*Et iste Lewelinus rex vel princeps Wallie tercio Idus Decembris a° domini m° .cc°. lxxxii°. in terra de Buolt occiditur et exercitus. Eadwardus rex filius regis Henrici cum herede suo optinuit principatum Wallie* 'And this Llywelyn, king or prince of Wales, and his army, was killed on 11 December 1282 in the land of Buellt. King Edward, son of King Henry, with his heir, obtained the principality of Wales') is that Roger Mortimer, 4th earl of March, direct descendant of Gwladys Ddu, is a new heir who will carry on the long line of northern Welsh kings.[46] This implication comes into full view when one considers the Gwladys Ddu pedigree later in the manuscript.

As previously mentioned, the retrograde pedigree of Gwladys displays her descent from the kings of North Wales as well as from the Galfridian kings of Britain, the Trojans, and Adam. The compilers went to such lengths to trace this descent in order to make a very specific argument in favour of Roger Mortimer's right to rule.[47] This genealogical argument relies fundamentally on Geoffrey of Monmouth. In *DGB*, Brutus, the eponymous founder of Britain, divides the island between his three sons upon his death.[48] Locrinus, the eldest son, inherits Loegria, which will eventually become England; Albanactus inherits Alba, or Scotland, and Camber inherits what will become Cambria, later Wales. Genealogies of medieval Welsh princes typically list royal descent through Locrinus, the eldest brother. This changed in the late thirteenth century with Llywelyn ap Gruffudd and his diplomatic dealings with Edward I. Llywelyn was always careful in his genealogies and in his correspondence with Edward I to acknowledge his descent from Camber, subordinate to Locrinus, and to acknowledge Locrinus' right to rule over his younger brothers.[49] By implication, he was acknowledging that

---

[46] Chicago 224, fol. 13ʳ. For Llywelyn's death, see Llinos Beverley Smith, 'The Death of Llywelyn ap Gruffudd: The Narratives Reconsidered', *WHR* 11 (1982–3), 200–13. An important subtext of this statement is that Edmund Mortimer, grandson of Gwladys Ddu, was rumoured to be responsible for Llywelyn's death. See Crump, 'Mortimer, Roger de, lord of Wigmore'.

[47] Giffin, 'Wigmore Manuscript and the Mortimer Family', 4.

[48] *DGB* ii.23.5–11, pp. 30–1.

[49] See *MWG* 246–7; J. Beverley Smith, *Llywelyn ap Gruffudd*, 278, 335; J. Beverley Smith, *Yr Ymwybod â Hanes yng Nghymru yn yr Oesoedd Canol: Darlith Agoriadol/The Sense of History in Medieval Wales: An Inaugural Lecture* (Aberystwyth, 1991).

he held Wales by Edward's permission. This use of Geoffrey's history in the conflict between Edward I and Llywelyn prompted new redactions of Welsh genealogies that traced Llywelyn's descent through Camber rather than Locrinus.[50] In contrast, Gwladys's retrograde pedigree follows the earlier models, with descent traced through Locrinus. What would have been a very dangerous move for Llywelyn ap Gruffudd during the delicate acts of diplomacy surrounding the conquest of Gwynedd in the late thirteenth century was perhaps less risky in this marcher environment: a late-fourteenth-century marcher lord could be descended from Welsh kings and from Locrinus without extreme symbolic threat to the English Crown (after all, Roger's claim to the throne was acknowledged). Descent from Locrinus was furthermore possible because Gwladys was the granddaughter of King John, a point that is driven home by the genealogy of English kings immediately following her pedigree in the manuscript.

In the Welsh King List, the ancestor figure Camber, not Locrinus, is listed after Brutus, following the newer Llywelyn ap Gruffudd genealogical tradition. Highlighting Gwladys's dual lines of descent from Camber and Locrinus (and, by extension, Roger's descent from two of Brutus' heirs) may have been a purposeful move on the compilers' part, a difference between sources that did not need to be reconciled because it was advantageous. Roger was in the unusual position of being able to claim descent from both Welsh and English rulers—he was descended from King Edward III on his mother's side, through whom he derived his strong claim to the English throne, but he was also descended from Llywelyn ab Iorwerth on his father's side, through Gwladys Ddu. Positioning himself as an heir to both English and Welsh lines of descent may have been intended to strengthen his ideological claim to the throne of England and, simultaneously, imply that he had the potential to bring the different regions together and rule over a once-again unified Britain, as Giffin suggests. In other words, descent from Brutus via both Camber and Locrinus would have linked Roger to a time when the island of Britain was unified, and by implication suggested that it was he who could unify the kingdoms of England, Scotland, and Wales.[51]

---

[50] *MWG* 246–9.

[51] A list of kings of Scotland from Brutus and Albanactus indicates that the compilers were interested in the full scope of Geoffrey's history (Chicago 224, fols. 10^v–11^r).

Closer to home, stressing his Welsh descent would have the additional outcome of strengthening the Mortimer claim to their Welsh lands, which had been contested in the past—not through military might, in this case, but through an articulation of Welsh descent.[52] Giffin notes how the Mortimer family seems to have been very aware of the symbolic utility of Geoffrey of Monmouth's history: they were known for holding various Round Table feasts invoking King Arthur and a nostalgic era of chivalry and unity: Roger Mortimer, lord of Wigmore (1231–82), held a Round Table at Kenilworth in 1279 and Roger Mortimer, 1st earl of March, held two, at Wigmore and Bedford, in 1328.[53] The manuscript's compilers, keenly interested in the family's Galfridian and Welsh ancestry, drive home this connection.

The 4th earl of March's ties to Welsh culture seem to have been celebrated in more than just this set of texts from Wigmore Abbey. He is the only 'English' marcher lord known to be the recipient of a Welsh praise poem, 'Moliant Syr Rosier Mortimer', composed by Iolo Goch between 1394 and 1398.[54] In this poem, Iolo Goch, like the compilers of Chicago 224, stresses Roger's descent from Gwladys Ddu and positions him as the heir to the kingdom of Wales:

> Ŵyr burffrwyth iôr Aberffraw,
> Draig ynysoedd yr eigiawn,
> Dragwn aer—darogan iawn
> Ydd wyf—madws it ddyfod
> Gymru lle rhyglyddy glod.[55]

Descendant of the pure-fruited lord of Aberffraw, dragon of the islands of the deep, dragon of battle—I prophesy truth—it is high time for you to come to Wales, where you deserve praise (ll. 14–18)

In suggesting that Roger is the true heir to Wales, Iolo Goch uses Roger's descent from Gwladys in a similar way as the compilers of the Chicago

---

[52] The text preceding the Welsh King List discusses the geography and rulers of Maelieyndd, a Welsh lordship controlled by the Mortimers in the thirteenth century.

[53] Giffin, 'Cadwalader', 111.

[54] It is difficult to say whether this poem is truly anomalous: one imagines poems in Welsh could have been written for other 'English' marcher lords, but do not survive. William Herbert, a Welsh marcher lord, was the recipient of several praise poems in Welsh.

[55] *Gwaith Iolo Goch*, ed. D. R. Johnston (Cardiff, 1988), 84–9.

manuscript, suggesting that his Welsh lineage was more widely known than one might assume. The poet specifically stresses Roger's connection to the kingdom of Gwynedd: *Darogan yw mae'n draig ni / A lunia'r gwaith eleni: / O ben y llew glew ei gledd / Coronir câr i Wynedd* 'There is a prophecy that our dragon / will accomplish the work this year; / from the head of a lion, his sword is brave; / Gwynedd's kinsman will be crowned' (ll. 53–6).[56] He also stresses Roger's descent from multiple peoples of Britain:

> Pa ryw ystyr, pâr osteg,
> Y rhoed i'r arfau tau teg
> Pedwarlliw? Pedair iarlleth
> Sy dau. Pwy piau pob peth?
> Asur sydd yn dy aesawr,
> Iarll Mars, gyda'r eurlliw mawr;
> Sinobr ac arian glân gloyw
> Im yw'r ysgwyd amrosgoyw;
> Pedair cenedl diedliw
> A ddeiryd it: Gwyndyd gwiw,
> Ffrancod, Saeson, wychion weilch,
> Gwyddyl, mam cynfyl, ceinfeilch.
> Gwaed Ffrainc, gwiw a da ei ffrwyth,
> Ydiw'r eurlliw diweirllwyth.

> For what reason, call for silence,
> were four colours put into
> your fair arms? Four earldoms
> are yours. To whom does each belong?
> Azure is your shield,
> Earl of March, with the great gold colour;
> cinnabar [*gules*] and pure bright silver [*argent*]
> to me is the diagonal shield;
> four blameless nations
> are kin to you: worthy Venedotians,[57]
> French, English, fine hawks,
> Irish, mother of contention, fine and proud.

---

[56] *Gwaith Iolo Goch*, ed. Johnston, 85. Here and above, 'dragon' is an epithet for 'hero, warrior'.

[57] Venedotians are the people of Gwynedd.

The blood of France, worthy and good its fruit,
is the gold colour of a pure tribe. (ll. 71–84)[58]

Helen Fulton argues that this poem positions Roger as the *mab darogan* 'son of prophecy', who will return to free the Welsh in their hour of need.[59] In addition, the poem indicates that Roger's Welsh ancestry, and the accompanying idea that he continued a line of Gwynedd kings that had been previously interrupted by the death of Llywelyn ap Gruffudd, were not concepts that were limited to the compilers and readers of Chicago 224, but were rather more widely known. The conquest of Gwynedd and the collapse of its line of kings is seen not as the end, in this case, but as a starting point. In addition, Iolo Goch describes Roger as an amalgamation of different peoples (North Welsh, French, English, and Irish), a praiseworthy feature of his identity that further situates him as inheritor of multiple kingdoms. This description of Roger's lineage forms a powerful expression of marcher identity. That it is written in Welsh is further evidence of the multifaceted character of marcher society.

The importance of Gwladys Ddu's pedigree to Mortimer lineage is also apparent in Adam Usk's chronicle (London, British Library, Add. 10104, fols. 155^r–176^v, s. xiv^4–s. xv^1).[60] Adam Usk, whose patron was Roger's father, Edmund Mortimer, 3rd earl of March, was involved in many of the southern Welsh, marcher, and English political events of his day. His chronicle covers the years 1377 to 1421, and is part Mortimer family history, part autobiography. He includes a pedigree of Gwladys Ddu very similar to the one described above, tracing the lineage of Roger through Gwladys and back to Adam:

---

[58] *Gwaith Iolo Goch*, ed. Johnston, 85; *Iolo Goch: Poems*, trans. Dafydd Johnston (Llandysul, 1993), 86.

[59] Helen Fulton, 'Class and Nation: Defining the English in Late-Medieval Welsh Poetry', in Ruth Kennedy and Simon Meecham-Jones (eds), *Authority and Subjugation in Writing of Medieval Wales* (New York, 2008), 191–212, at 196; see also Victoria Flood, *Prophecy, Politics and Place in Medieval England: From Geoffrey of Monmouth to Thomas of Erceldoune* (Woodbridge, 2016), 186–7; Dafydd Johnston, *Llên yr Uchelwyr: Hanes Beirniadol Llenyddiaeth Gymraeg, 1330–1525* (Cardiff, 2005), 351–2.

[60] See *The Chronicle of Adam Usk, 1377–1421*, ed. and trans. Chris Given-Wilson (Oxford, 1997).

Hec ipsius comitis genologia[61]: Rogerus, filius Edmundi, filii Rogeri, filii Edmundi, filii Rogeri primi comitis Marchie, filii **Cladus Thui** [Gwladys Ddu], filie Llewellyn ap Iorwerth Troynden principis NortheWalie, filii Oweyn, filii Griffith, filii Canaan, filii Yago, filii Idwall, filii Mauric, filii Ydwall Voyll, filii Anaraud, filii Rodry Vawr ex Essill filia Kynan, Filii Rodry Maylwynnog, filii Ydwall Yeorth, filii Cadualadre benedicti ultimi regis brytonum,[62] filii Cadwalonis, filii Caduani, filii Yiago, filii Beli, filii Rune, filii Mailgan Goynet, filii Caduallon Lawyr, filii Yvor Hyrth, filii Cunetha Wledik, filii Ederne, filii Padarne Peys Ruthe, filii Tegyt, filii Iago, filii Kunneddanc, filii Caynan, filii Borgayn, filii Doly, filii Gortholy, filii Gwyne, filii Corthewyn, filii Amleweth, filii Anweyrid, filii Cuweth, filii Donkere, filii Brychwane, filii Ymwane, filii Analathas, filii Affleth, filii Beli Vawre, filii Mynagan, filii Enaye, filii Gerwyt, filii Creden, filii Dyffnach, filii Pryden, filii Aedmawr, filii Antony, filii Sirioll, filii Garowest, filii Ruallon, filii Cunetha ex Regaw, filia Leyr qui fecit Licestriam,[63] filii Bladudd qui fecit balnea apud Bathoniam,[64] filii Rune, filii Llann, filii Bruti uiridis scuti, filii Eboracy qui fecit ciuitatem Eboracum,[65] filii Membryci, filii Madag, filii Locriny, filii Bruti primi regis britonum,[66] filii Siluy, filii Escannyi, filii Enee Scothewyn,[67] filii Enchiges, filii Capus, filii Asseraci, filii Troysse, filii Elicony, filii Mercurii, filii Dardani, filii Iouis, filii Saturni, filii Seluis, filii Creti, filii Ceprii, filii Ieuan, filii Iaseph, filii Noee, filii Lameth, filii Matusalem, filii Ennoc, filii Iaffeth, filii Malaleel, filii Caynan, filii Ennoc, filii Seth, filii Ade prothoplausti.[68]

This genealogy matches the Gwladys pedigree in the Chicago manuscript, though orthographical differences in the names suggest that the Chicago text was not the immediate exemplar—another copy

---

[61] *Hec ipsius comitis genologia* 'The genealogy of this earl is as follows'.
[62] *filii Cadualadre benedicti ultimi regis brytonum* 'son of the blessed Cadwaladr last king of the Britons'.
[63] *Leyr qui fecit Licestriam* 'Leir who built Leicester'.
[64] *Bladudd qui fecit balnea apud Bathoniam* 'Bladud who built the bathhouse at Bath'.
[65] *Eboracy qui fecit ciuitatem Eboracum* 'Ebraucus who built the city of York'.
[66] *Locriny, filii Bruti primi regis britonum* 'Locrinus, son of Brutus the first king of the Britons'.
[67] i.e. *Ysgwydwyn* 'white-shield', an epithet for Aeneas in Welsh.
[68] *filii Ade prothoplausti* 'son of Adam the first creature'; text from *Chronicle of Adam Usk*, ed. and trans. Given-Wilson, 40–3; I have expanded abbreviations. The genealogy is briefly discussed in *MWG* 257.

must have existed.[69] Adam Usk characterizes Roger as the true inheritor of British kingship, able to unite the various peoples that comprise the kingdom of Britain. Following the pedigree, in a sentiment that echoes Iolo Goch, he writes: *Vltra dictorum Brytanie, Ytalie, Troge, Anglie, Francie et Hispanie nobilium regum nobilissimum exortum, ut quid mora? ecce quanta comitum March[ie] florens regalis prosapia* 'Beyond this glorious descent from the noble kings of Britain, Italy, Troy, England, France, and Spain, need I say more? Harken to the way that the royal line of the earls of March has prospered'.[70] In other words, the earls of March are particularly royal, and particularly deserving of the mantle of kingship, because of their descent from so many royal lines; by implication, they are uniquely qualified to unite those lines.[71] In other words, the implicit argument made by the Wigmore compilers of the Chicago manuscript is taken a step further and made explicit by Adam Usk. His use of the Welsh pedigree underscores its ideological importance to the Mortimers even after Roger's death.

It is highly unusual before the Tudor period to see a prospective English monarch promoting his Welsh ancestry, but the Mortimers were happy to do so in a range of different literary contexts, and in fact this genealogical endeavour may have provided some precedent for the Yorkist kings of the fifteenth century and, later, the Tudors, to do so. This use of Geoffrey's history is calculated and very well could have been an indication of a more broadly effective political strategy had Roger not died prematurely in 1398.[72]

In any case, the house of York breathed new life into the strategy in the fifteenth century. The Mortimer genealogy had a significant afterlife in the lineage of Edward IV (1442–83) during the Wars of the Roses.

---

[69] e.g. Adam Usk's *Cladus Thui* for *Gwladys Ddu*, *Ennoc* for *Enos*, *Iaffeth* for *Iareth*, *Iaseph* for *Iapheth*, om. *Settim*, *Elicony* for *Herictonii*, *Troysse* for *Troii*, *Enchiges* for *Enchiches*, *Enee Scothewyn* for *Enee ysgwytwyn*, *Llann* for *Leon*. Cf. MWG 257, 257, n. 139.

[70] *Chronicle of Adam Usk*, ed. and trans. Given-Wilson, 42–3, perhaps echoing *Brut*, ed. Brie, i.220.

[71] And, indeed, the lines are already symbolically united in the Mortimers' descent from the Trojans through the Welsh and the Normans; see Penny Eley, 'The Myth of Trojan Descent and Perceptions of National Identity: The Case of *Eneas* and the *Roman de Troie*', *Nottingham Medieval Studies*, 35 (1991), 27–40.

[72] A poem attributed to Guto'r Glyn for Edward IV, 'Annog Edward IV i adfer trefn yng Nghymru' ('To Urge Edward IV to Restore Order in Wales') expresses a similar sentiment and references the Mortimer ancestry; see poem 29, ed. *Guto'r Glyn.net*, ed. Barry J. Lewis (Aberystwyth, 2013), http://www.gutorglyn.net/gutorglyn/poem/?poem-selection=029&first-line=%23, accessed 9 May 2022.

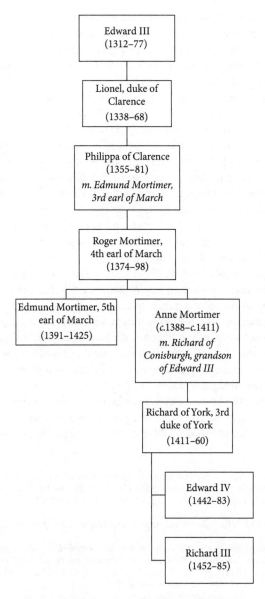

FIGURE 2.2 Mortimers and the House of York.

He was promoted in the Yorkist claim to the throne and became king in 1461 by overthrowing Henry VI.[73] The Mortimer family features in his genealogy because his strongest claim to the throne derived from his Mortimer ancestry (see Figure 2.2). The parents of Roger, 4th earl of March, were Edmund Mortimer, 3rd earl of March (1352–81), and Philippa, daughter of Lionel, duke of Clarence, and granddaughter of Edward III. It was through this line of descent that the Yorkist claim to the throne was made, for Edward IV was a direct descendant of Edward III through Philippa. Additionally, Edward IV's paternal grandfather was Richard of Conisburgh, earl of Cambridge (1385–1415), the youngest grandson of Edward III.[74] Remarkably, the Mortimers are important here not only because of their marriages to descendants of Edward III, but because of their descent from Welsh princes, as the genealogies of Edward IV show.

The Mortimer genealogy discussed previously in this chapter in the context of Chicago 224 also features in Cambridge, Corpus Christi College (hereafter CCCC), 98 (c.1470), a 39-foot-long genealogical roll written in French that traces a line of descent from Adam to Richard, duke of York (1411–60), father of Edward IV.[75] The original line of descent is updated to include two of the duke of York's children, Edward and Anne. Similar to the entwining of genealogy and narrative history in Chicago 224, the genealogical tree in CCCC 98 is interwoven with a French Prose *Brut* chronicle. The genealogical line begins with Adam and Eve, then Trojan royalty, then the Galfridian kings of Britain, with the line traced from Locrinus to Llywelyn ab Iorwerth. Three separate lines trace the pre-conquest English kings, ending with Edward the Confessor, the dukes of Normandy, and the Mortimer

---

[73] Discussed in *MWG* 257–8; Alison Allan, 'Yorkist Propaganda: Pedigree, Prophecy and the "British History" in the Reign of Edward IV', in Charles Ross (ed.), *Patronage, Pedigree, and Power in Later Medieval England* (Gloucester and Totowa, NJ, 1979), 171–92, at 175–8; Sydney Anglo, 'The *British History* in Early Tudor Propaganda: With an Appendix of Manuscript Pedigrees of the Kings of England, Henry VI to Henry VIII', *Bulletin of the John Rylands Library*, 44 (1961–2), 17–48.

[74] For discussion of these claims, and the genealogies that sought to prove them, see Laynesmith, 'Anne Mortimer's Legacy'.

[75] The roll is discussed in *MWG* 257–8; Siân Echard, 'Navigating Absence in the Digital Realm', in Benjamin Albritton, Georgia Henley, and Elaine Treharne (eds), *Medieval Manuscripts in the Digital Age* (London, 2020), 82–90; Diana B. Tyson, 'The Adam and Eve Roll: Corpus Christi College Cambridge MS 98', *Scriptorium*, 52/2 (1998), 301–16.

family. Additional lines trace the Plantagenets, Lacys, Marshals, and their marriages.[76]

Ben Guy observes that the CCCC 98 roll 'grants the most prominent central position to the British and latterly Welsh line of descent, up until the union of Gwladus Ddu and Ralph Mortimer'.[77] The roll, notably, records the marriage of Ralph de Mortimer and Gwladys Ddu (*Monnseignur Rauf qui espousa dame Gwladuse* 'Lord Ralph who married Lady Gwladys'), which unites the Mortimer line with the Welsh line of Gwynedd and the kings of Britain. Their marriage is illustrated in the roll with a large shield that combines the two family crests, with the shield of Llywelyn ab Iorwerth immediately above it. As in the Mortimer genealogies in Chicago 224 and the chronicle of Adam Usk, the line ends, not with Llywelyn ab Iorwerth's sons, but with Gwladys and Ralph's children.

J. L. Laynesmith suggests that Edward IV became 'aware of the legendary implications that this marriage had accrued for the Mortimers' while growing up at Ludlow Castle, a Mortimer family seat.[78] The Mortimers feature prominently in the roll, not only because they are key to Edward IV's descent from Edward III, but because their Welsh ancestry through Gwladys Ddu gives Edward further legitimacy by showing his descent from the kings of Britain and Gwynedd. By implication (as was the case with Roger Mortimer, 4th earl of March, several generations before), Edward is a figure who unites the various kingdoms of Britain into one. This roll shows the continued importance of British–Welsh ancestry to claimants to the throne of England, and the continued authority that Geoffrey's history provided during disputes of succession.

A similar genealogical argument is made in London, British Library, Add. 18268A (s. xv).[79] This roll depicts Welsh, English, and French lines of descent to Henry VI and Edward IV, with the Welsh line traced through Llywelyn ab Iorwerth, Gwladys Ddu, and the Mortimers. Once again, the Mortimers are positioned as inheritors of British–Welsh

---

[76] These lines depict some of the same marriages and female descendants as the genealogical compilations discussed in Chapter 3.

[77] *MWG* 257.

[78] Laynesmith, 'Anne Mortimer's Legacy', 223.

[79] *MWG* 256; Anglo, '*British History*', 23–4; Laynesmith, 'Anne Mortimer's Legacy', 236.

kingship. In a reference to Geoffrey of Monmouth's *Prophetiae Merlini*, the English line is labelled *Albus Draco* 'white dragon' and the Welsh line *Rubius Draco* 'red dragon'. Guy notes that the end of the roll depicts Henry VI as the white dragon, who has been defeated by Edward IV, the red dragon, 'clearly equat[ing] Edward IV's regality with his descent from British kings, through the Welsh line of Gwynedd'.[80] A rhetorical move made by the Wigmore compilers of the Chicago manuscript appears to have been repeated several generations later.

An additional genealogy of Edward IV is extant in Philadelphia, Free Library, Lewis E 201, a late-fifteenth-century roll, possibly commissioned for his coronation, that traces his descent from God with a chronicle based on Geoffrey's *DGB* alongside.[81] Laynesmith notes that this genealogy gives Edward's British–Welsh lineage pride of place on the right side of the roll, rather than its typical location in other rolls on the left side.[82] Finally, the *Genealogical Chronicle of the Kings of England*, a piece of 'Yorkist propaganda' from the 1460s, which is extant in Latin and English versions (eighteen manuscripts in total), depicts Edward IV's descent from the Welsh line of kings through Ralph de Mortimer and Gwladys Ddu.[83] Additional genealogies tracing Edward IV's Welsh ancestry through the Mortimers and Gwaldys Ddu are found in a late-fifteenth-century manuscript (London, British Library, Cotton Vespasian E. vii, fols. 69^v–72^r) and what is probably an eighteenth-century copy of a fifteenth-century genealogy (London, British Library, Egerton 1076, fols. 1^v–2^r).[84] In an indication that this aspect of Edward IV's lineage was also known to Welsh audiences, the Welsh poet Lewys Glyn Cothi (fl. 1447–86) mentions Edward IV's descent from Gwladys.

---

[80] *MWG* 257. A range of other genealogical rolls of Edward IV are surveyed in Anglo, 'British History', 22–3; Allan, 'Yorkist Propaganda', 179–82, 187–8.

[81] This manuscript is described by Laura Blanchard and digitized here: http://libwww.freelibrary.org/digital/feature/medieval-edward-index, accessed 29 June 2023; it is discussed by Laynesmith, 'Anne Mortimer's Legacy', 236–9 and can be seen on the cover of this book.

[82] Laynesmith, 'Anne Mortimer's Legacy', 237.

[83] E. D. Kennedy and Raluca Radulescu, 'Genealogical Chronicles in English and Latin', in Graeme Dunphy and Cristian Bratu (eds), *Brill Encyclopedia of the Medieval Chronicle* (Leiden, 2016), http://dx.doi.org/10.1163/2213-2139_emc_SIM_01076, accessed 7 March 2022.

[84] Laynesmith, 'Anne Mortimer's Legacy', 230.

Such a statement may have been used to rally Welsh Yorkists.[85] The Mortimer genealogies in Chicago 224, therefore, seem to have been part of a larger project that occupied writers of history and genealogy in the fourteenth and fifteenth centuries.

These royal genealogies, emphasizing the British and Welsh ancestry of prominent figures in late medieval England, show the wide impact of marcher literature and marcher culture. It was in the March of Wales that it became possible, through marcher lords' contact with Welsh history, genealogy, and intermarriage with Welsh nobility, to construct a sense of British kingship and identity that resolved the fragmentation and discontinuities that had been wrought by centuries of conquest. Margaret Lamont has analysed how the Middle English Prose *Brut* 'persistently calls up a "kynde [natural] bloode of Engeland" that arises, almost alchemically, out of a population it simultaneously describes as a mixture of Britons, Saxon, Danes, French, Normans, Spaniards, Romans, and others'.[86] One of the solutions to this fragmented mixture of different peoples was the unifying approach taken by the Mortimers: it is they, the earls of March, who are true inheritors of the various lines laid out in Geoffrey's history, and therefore ought to rule Britain. Through their descent from French, Welsh, and English peoples, the Mortimers resolve the ethnic fragmentation present in the Galfridian narrative of British history, in which the kingdom was split into three parts and ultimately conquered by the Saxons, mirroring later conquests and divisions of Wales and the March into smaller and smaller lordships. This expression of marcher identity, importantly, does not hide its multiplicity, but displays it as an asset. The Welsh, French, and English ancestry embedded in marcher identity gave the Mortimers a particular claim and authority over British kingship that

---

[85] Discussed by Anglo, 'British History', 20; cf. Allan, 'Yorkist Propaganda', 178–9. Lewys Glyn Cothi references Edward's descent from Gwladys Ddu in 'Moliant Harri VII' ('In Praise of Harry VII'), ll. 53–6: *Mil yw o Wynedd, ŵr moliannus, / a dar a tharw o waed Arthurus, / goludog frenin o gorff Gwladus—Du / a dderyw dynnu o Ddardanus* 'The beast is from Gwynedd, praiseworthy man, / a leader and a bull from the blood of Arthur, / wealthy king from the body of Gwladys Ddu / who happens to derive from Dardanus' and in 'Moliant Syr Wiliam Herbert' ('In Praise of Sir William Herbert'), ll. 73–4: *Ac o Wladus Du un o egin / yw llewpart Rhisiart drwy'r ddaear hon* 'And the leopard Richard is one of the descendants of Gwladys Ddu throughout this world' (*Gwaith Lewys Glyn Cothi*, ed. Dafydd Johnston (Cardiff, 1995), 43, 253); see also n. 72 above.

[86] Lamont, 'Becoming English', 285–6, quoting the Prose *Brut*, ed. Brie, i.220.

continued to be attractive as a political argument into the late fifteenth century, achieving wider prominence in the genealogies of Edward IV, as discussed above. In this sense, the marcher culture that gave rise to the Mortimers' Welsh connections was responsible for the continued symbolic prominence of Welsh identity and kingship beyond Wales. The importance of British–Welsh descent was further amplified for Henry Tudor (1457–1509), who could trace descent from the princes of Wales through his grandfather Owain Tudur (c.1400–61), and who highlighted this ancestry during his campaign against Richard III in 1485.[87]

The Chicago manuscript and textual transmission from Wales into the March

The Mortimers' Welsh genealogies, which underscore their right to rule over a unified Britain, also provide evidence for textual transmission of Welsh genealogies into a marcher context and demonstrate close contact between Welsh and marcher literary cultures. Below, I evaluate evidence for this transmission, showing that the source for the Gwladys Ddu pedigree in Chicago 224 is probably the Welsh genealogical tract known as the 'Llywelyn ab Iorwerth genealogies' compiled in the first half of the thirteenth century, probably between 1216 and c.1233, in Gwynedd.[88] I also show that the ultimate source for the Welsh King List in Chicago 224 is probably the *Vita Griffini filii Conani*, a biography of the North Welsh king Gruffudd ap Cynan (c.1055–1137) from twelfth-century Wales.[89] The two texts in Chicago 224, moreover, have different sources and were probably the product of different compilers.[90]

---

[87] See discussion in Anglo, '*British History*'.
[88] For the Llywelyn ab Iorwerth genealogies, see *MWG* 159–231.
[89] Because significant portions of the earliest copy of *Vita Griffini filii Conani* (*VGC*) and portions of the genealogy of Gruffudd ap Cynan are missing, it is not possible to give *VGC* readings. I have supplied them from the early thirteenth-century Welsh translation of *VGC*, the *Historia Gruffud vab Kenan* (*HGK*), in brackets. It is reasonable to assume that the genealogy in *HGK* matches the lost text in *VGC* (Paul Russell, personal communication). It is likely that Wigmore genealogists would have accessed a Latin text. *VGC* is edited in *Vita Griffini*, ed. and trans. Russell, 52–5; *HGK* in *Mediaeval Prince*, ed. and trans. Evans, 23.
[90] See Appendices for full texts.

First, the Welsh King List and the Gwladys pedigree both utilize a genealogical source that uses Welsh rather than Latin spellings for Galfridian names (see Table 2.2). These Welsh spellings are consistent with the Welsh versions of Geoffrey's history (*Brut y Brenhinedd*, 'History of the Kings') rather than Geoffrey's Latin Vulgate. This means not that the redactors were necessarily reading *Brut y Brenhinedd*, but that their Latin source used Welsh forms of the names. This source must have come from Wales or from a Welsh informant in the March.

Whatever those underlying sources were, they seem to have been influenced by the royal biography of Gruffudd ap Cynan, which existed in both Latin (*Vita Griffini filii Conani*) and Welsh (*Historia Gruffud vab Kenan*) (hereafter *VGC/HGK*). It is known that *VGC/HGK*

TABLE 2.2 Use of Welsh rather than Latinate names for Galfridian figures

Latinate names	Welsh names				
Geoffrey's Vulgate	*Brut y Brenhinedd*[a]	Llywelyn ab Iorwerth genealogies, §11.1[b]	*VGC/HGK*[c]	Gwladys pedigree	Welsh King List
Maddan	Mada6c	Madawg	Madauc	Madoc	Madocus
Mempricius	Membyr	Mymbyr	Membyr	Mymbyr	Membir
Ebraucus	Efra6c	Efrawg	-	Ewrawc	Euraucus
Brutus Viride Scutum	Brutus Daryan Las	Brutus Ysgwythir	Brutus Ysgwyt Ir	Bruti[d] ysgwydhyr	Brutus ysgwydhir
Bladud	Bleiddut	Bleidyd	Bleidud	Bleydvt	Bleyduth
Riuallo	Rywalla6n	Riwallawn	Riwallaun	Rywallon	Rywallun
Gurgustius	Gor6yst	Gwrwst	Gurust [Gurwsti]	Gwrrwst	Gorwst
Sisillius	Seissyll	Seirioel	Seiryoel [Seirioel]	Seyroel	Seyrioel

[a] I have used names from the Red Book of Hergest version of *Brut y Brenhinedd*.
[b] *MWG* 361–2.
[c] *Mediaeval Prince*, ed. and trans. Evans, 24; *Vita Griffini*, ed. and trans. Russell, 52.
[d] This is a genitive singular ending.

introduced variant names into the Welsh genealogical tradition.[91] As a result, some copies of the Llywelyn ab Iorwerth genealogies agree more closely with *VGC/HGK* against standard names in *Brut y Brenhinedd* and Geoffrey. The Gwladys pedigree and the Welsh King List also share these *VGC/HGK* variants, suggesting a source influenced by that set of texts (see Table 2.3). For example, they use the name *Brutus Ysgwydhir* for *Brutus Daryan Las* (Geoffrey's *Brutus Viride Scutum* 'Brutus Green-shield') and *Seiryoel* for *Seisyll* (Geoffrey's *Sisillius*).[92]

However, the Gwladys pedigree agrees with some names in the Llywelyn ab Iorwerth genealogies over *VGC/HGK*. For example, it makes Run the father of Bledud (ultimately following Geoffrey). The Welsh King List agrees instead with *VGC/HGK* against the main text of the Llywelyn ab Iorwerth genealogies; for example, it follows *VGC/HGK*'s error

TABLE 2.3 The influence of *Historia Gruffud vab Kenan* on the Llywelyn ab Iorwerth genealogies and the Welsh King List

Brut y Brenhinedd	*VGC/HGK*[a]	Llywelyn ab Iorwerth genealogies, main text, §11.1[b]	Welsh King List	Gwladys pedigree
Raga6	Regat	Regau	Regav	Regaw
Llyr	Lyr	Lyr	Llyr	Llyr
Bleiddut	Rud	Bleidyd	Ruth	Bleydvt
Run palatyruras	Bleidud	Run Baladyr Bras	Bleyduth	Rvn
Lleon	Lliwelyt	Lleon	Lewelinus	Leon
Brutus daryan las	Brutus Ysgwyt Ir	Brutus Ysgwythir	Brutus ysgwydhir	Bruti ysgwydhyr
Seisyll	Seiryoel [Seirioel]	Seirioel	Seyrioel	Seyroel

[a] *Mediaeval Prince*, ed. and trans. Evans, 24; *Vita Griffini*, ed. and trans. Russell, 52.
[b] *MWG* 361–2.

---

[91] *MWG* 121–2, 227–8, 320–1; also discussed by Brynley F. Roberts, 'The Treatment of Personal Names in the Early Welsh Versions of *Historia regum Britanniae*', *Bulletin of the Board of Celtic Studies*, 25 (1973), 274–90, at 282.
[92] See also *MWG* 316–17.

in making Run/Rud the son rather than the father of Bledud.[93] These variants suggest that the Welsh King List used a genealogical source that contained these variants from *VGC/HGK*, and the Gwladys pedigree did not.

The Gwladys pedigree instead consistently agrees with the Llywelyn ab Iorwerth genealogies over *VGC/HGK*. In addition to the Run/Bledud variant, it also shares the *Leon* reading with the Llywelyn ab Iorwerth genealogies rather than the reading in *VGC/HGK*. Therefore, the Gwladys pedigree used a version of the Llywelyn ab Iorwerth genealogies as a source.[94]

The Welsh King List, furthermore, offers some unusual innovations (marked in bold in Table 2.4). Table 2.4 presents an excerpt from both Chicago texts with side-by-side comparison to some key Welsh genealogical texts.[95] This table shows that the Gwladys pedigree is remarkably consistent with extant Gwynedd genealogies, particularly the Llywelyn ab Iorwerth genealogies, while the Welsh King List includes a number of extra names in its list. These extra names show that (i) it is a king list rather than a pedigree and (ii) it uses textual sources beyond a Welsh genealogical tract influenced by *VGC/HGK*.

Table 2.4 shows that the Gwladys pedigree follows Welsh genealogical tradition to the letter, while the Welsh King List has included a number of names that are not in the standard genealogical line of Gwynedd. These additional names in the Welsh King List are clustered in the Galfridian section of the list (the kings of Britain from Brutus to *Seyssel*) and in the final portion of the Llywelyn ab Iorwerth pedigree (from Cadwaladr to Llywelyn ab Iorwerth). They are probably taken from Welsh chronicles. The names are mostly real historical figures—for example, the compilers inserts three additional sons of Idwal Foel between Idwal Foel and Meurig, disrupting the line of descent in a typical Llywelyn

---

[93] Manuscript L of the Llywelyn ab Iorwerth genealogies does this as well.

[94] This was not its only source, however—the Gwladys pedigree has *Anylwyd* in the ancestry of Cunedda, a significant variant that does not appear in any of the extant genealogies; see *MWG* 275, 289. I am grateful to Ben Guy for discussing some of these points with me.

[95] The Welsh texts I have used for comparison are *VGC/HGK*, genealogies of Llywelyn ap Gruffudd in Exeter 3514 and Mostyn 117, and the Llywelyn ab Iorwerth genealogies; for discussion of the latter, see *MWG* 243–51.

TABLE 2.4 Comparison of texts in Chicago 224 with extant Welsh genealogies: The Gwynedd pedigree

Welsh King List	Gwladys pedigree	VGC/HGK[a]	Exeter 3514, p. 56	Mostyn 117[b]	Llywelyn ab Iorwerth genealogies, §11.1[c]
Mayelgyn Gwyned	Maelgwn Gwyned	Maelgun	Malgonus	Maelgwn Gwyned	Maelgwn Gwyned
Rvn	Run	Run	Run	Run	Run
[B]Ely	Bely	Beli	Beli	Beli	Beli
Iago	Iago	Yago	Iago	Iago	Iago
Cadvan	Cadvan	Catvan	Caduan	Katuan	Katfan
Cadwallon	Cadwallon	Catwallaun	Cadwallaun	Katwallawn	Katwallawn
Cadwaladre vendigayt	Cadwaladre vendigait	Catwalader Vendigeit	Cadwaladri Benedicti	Katwaladyr vendigeit	Katwaladyr Vendigait
Seyssel	—	—	—	—	—
Walgayenus	—	Idwaldere	—	—	—
Idwal Iwrth	Idwal Iwrch	Idwaldere	Itwal Iurch	Idwal iwrch	Idwal Ywrch
Rodry maelwynawt	Rodry maelwynawc	—	Rodri Maeluennauc	Rodri maelwynawc	Rodri Malwynnawg
Karadaucus	—	—	—	—	—
Kynan Dyndaethwy	Kynan dindaethwy	Kenan o gastell Dindaethue	Kanan Dyntelethoe	Kynan Tindaethwy	Kynan Dyndaethwy
Essillt filia Kynan	Essillt	Etill	Dethild	Esyllt	Essylt

Continued

Welsh King List	Gwladys pedigree	VGC/HGK[a]	Exeter 3514, p. 56	Mostyn 117[b]	Llywelyn ab Iorwerth genealogies, §11.1[c]
Meruymbricus rex	—	—	Meruen Wrech	Meruyn vrych, gwr priawt Esyllt	—
Gunonie causa					
Essilt uxoris sue					
Rodry mawr	Rodri mawre	Rodri	Rodri	Rodri	Rodri Mawr
Cadellus	—	—	—	—	—
Morwynus	—	—	—	—	—
Anarawt filius rodry	Anarawt	Anaraut	Anaraut	Anarawt	Anarawt
Howelus filius howeli	—	—	—	—	—
Idwal voel	Idwal voel	—	Idwal Voil	Idwal voel	Idwal Foel
Iago filius Idwal	—	—	—	—	—
Ionav [*corr*: Ieuav] filius secundus	—	—	—	—	—
Rodry filius tercius	—	—	—	—	—
Meuryt	Meuryc	Meuryc	Meuric	[Meuric]	Meurig

		Elissed				
—	Idwal	Idwal	Itwal	—	—	Idwal
—	Iago	Yago	Iago	[Idwal]	Iago	Iago
—	Kynan	Cynan	Kanan	Iago	Kynan	Kynan
Kynan	Gruffyth	Gruffudd	Griffud	Kynan	Gruffyd	Gruffyd
Griffinus	—		—	Gruffyd		
Owenus	—		—	—	—	—
Eyneon filius Oweni				—	—	—
Uweyn Gwyned	Yweyn Gwyned		Oweyn	Owein	Owein	Ywein
Ierwerth filius yweyn	Ierwerth		Ioruerth	Ioruerth	Ioruerth	Iorwerth
Lewelinus filius Ierwerth Drwyndwn[d]	Lewelini principis Wallie		Lewelini	Llywelyn	Llywelyn	Llywelyn
	Gwladus[a]		Griffini		Gruffyd	
			Lewelinus		Llywelyn	

[a] *Mediaeval Prince*, ed. and trans. Evans, 23.

[b] *MWG* 429–30; *Early Welsh Genealogical Tracts*, ed. Bartrum, 38.

[c] *MWG* 361.

[d] The text ends here, followed by an extended note on Gwladys and the other descendants of Llywelyn ab Iorwerth.

pedigree from Idwal Foel directly to Meurig.[96] The text takes particular interest in the sons of Idwal Foel and their fights for succession with the sons of Hywel, and uses additional chronicle sources in order to accomplish this.[97] Some of the extra names seem to be taken from Latin chronicles from Wales (known in scholarship as *Annales Cambriae*), indicating the range of sources that were available to the Wigmore compilers.[98] In fact, the names are so consistent with the Welsh annals that it is very possible that the compilers had access to a Welsh chronicle, most likely in Latin.

The extra names are significant because they show that the compilers of the Welsh King List were writing not a pedigree of the kings of Gwynedd, tracing genealogical lines down to the present day, but a

---

[96] See the Llywelyn ab Iorwerth genealogies §28.1.1, ed. in *MWG* 370. Idwal Foel had at least six sons, Anarawd, Ieuaf, Iago, Meurig, Cynan, and Idwal Fychan. It was Meurig from whom Gruffudd ap Cynan was descended, so the North Welsh pedigrees logically list only Meurig. The Welsh King List adds *Iago, Ionav*, and *Rodry*, possibly by reading the Welsh Latin annals, which mention all three of these sons in the same order; see *Annales Cambriae* B-text, items b972; b974; b975.

[97] Similarly, the Deheubarth (South Wales) portion of the Welsh King List does not follow the typical pedigree of Rhys ap Gruffudd, as one would expect. Instead, it is a list of succession. While extant pedigrees of Rhys ap Gruffudd and his son Rhys Gryg in Welsh genealogical tracts go back only as far as Rhodri Mawr or Merfyn Frych, this list extends the line of kings further back to Maelgwn Gwynedd. It is a mixture of names from different sources, including the *Historia Brittonum*, *DGB*, and dukes of Brittany from the Carolingian era (such as *Nvmeneus, Horispois, Salomon*, and *Pasceuth*, and known in Breton cartulary sources as *Nomeneo, Erispoe, Salomon*, and *Pascuethen*. I am grateful to Ben Guy for pointing out these names to me; see also discussion in Wendy Davies, *Small Worlds: The Village Community in Early Medieval Brittany* (London, 1988), 19, 21).

[98] The added name *Seyssel* probably refers to a person in the Welsh Latin annals who dies in a battle with Iago son of Beli: 'bellum Kairlion in quo Seysil filius chinan et Iago felius [*corr*: filius] beli moriuntur cum multis aliis' (b641). *Eyneon filius Oweni* is a tenth-century prince of Deheubarth and descendant of Rhodri Mawr who lays waste to Gower; see *MWG* 370; 'Einion filius oweyn uastauit goer' (b992); 'Eyniaun filius owein pugnauit contra saxones' (c308). *Karadaucus, Morwynus, Cadellus*, and *Arthen* are also external to the line of Llywelyn ab Iorwerth, but appear in the annals: *Karadaucus* refers to a king of Gwynedd (b829, c124), *Morwynus* is in the B-text and the C-text (b928, c228), *Cadellus* appears in both (b934, c234), and *Arthen* appears in both (b838, c133). *Howelus filius howeli* is probably Hywel Dda and an error for *Howel filius cadell*: 'hoelus da filius cacel romam iuit' (b.952); 'Howel rex filius cadell romam perrexit' (c252). *Cadellus* (Cadell) is indeed a son of Rhodri Mawr; see *MWG* 370. *Owenus* is an erroneous repetition of Owain Gwynedd. References in this footnote are to *Annales Cambriae* B text and *Annales Cambriae* C text.

list of succession.[99] They suggest that the compilers were engaged in a more active type of compilation than simply copying a genealogy. As the genealogies of Llywelyn ab Iorwerth do not include the complex succession patterns of the kingdom of Gwynedd, the compilers of the Welsh King List seem to be trying to restore the names of kings who had been left out.

By contrast, the Gwladys pedigree follows the Llywelyn ab Iorwerth genealogies so closely in the Gwynedd portion that it must have used them as a source. This source was a different one from that used by the compilers of the Welsh King List, which follows *VGC/HGK* over the Llywelyn genealogies, as discussed above.[100] This evidence indicates that these two texts in the Chicago manuscript are not the product of the same phase of compilation. Instead, they are separate texts.

Overall, this analysis reveals intriguing textual connections between the texts in Chicago 224 and extant Welsh genealogical tracts. It suggests that the Wigmore compilers were able to access exemplars ultimately reliant on Welsh genealogical tracts and on *VGC/HGK*. Ben Guy has argued that a large collection of Welsh genealogies (Oxford, Jesus College, 20) was compiled in Glamorgan at the end of the fourteenth century by the same group of scribes and patrons who were responsible for the Red Book of Hergest and several other important Welsh manuscripts.[101] One can imagine Welsh genealogical sources like those

---

[99] The following evidence suggests that the Welsh King List is very likely to be a copy of an underlying exemplar: it lists *Meruymbricus rex Gunonie causa* 'Merfyn Frych king of Gwynedd by cause' and *Essilt uxoris sue* 'Essillt his wife' on separate lines—phrases that would have been joined in a previous exemplar (*Meruymbricus rex Gunonie causa Essilt uxoris sue* 'Merfyn Frych king of Gwynedd by cause of Essillt his wife'), as is the case in Mostyn 117 (*Meruyn vrych, gwr priawt Esyllt* 'Merfyn Frych, husband/man married to Essillt'). I am grateful to Ben Guy for pointing this out to me. Other errors (*Iredyn* for *Prydein*, *Grychewayn* for *Brychwayn*) are corrected by a later hand. Interestingly, the name *Meruymbricius* (Merfyn Frych), absent in the Gwladys pedigree and the Llywelyn ab Iorwerth genealogies, is present in the Welsh genealogies in Exeter 3514 and Mostyn 117, suggesting that the Welsh King List compilers looked at a genealogical source that shares these variants.

[100] This is a conclusion based on variants: as mentioned above, pp. 107–8, the Gwladys pedigree has *Leon* and *Bledud/Run*, where the Welsh King List and *VGC/HGK* have *Lewelinus* and *Run/Bledud*, and *Kunedda* and *Antony*, where those names are omitted in the Welsh King List and *VGC/HGK*, as well as *Anylwyd*, which does not appear in the Welsh King List, *VGC/HGK*, or the Llywelyn ab Iorwerth genealogies.

[101] *MWG* 101–6.

used in the compilation of Jesus 20 travelling from Glamorgan to Wigmore for inclusion in Chicago 224 in the late fourteenth century. A similar transmission pattern from Glamorgan to Ludlow is, after all, demonstrated in Chapter 1. That said, proximity is not always the primary determining factor for which texts are transmitted between Wales and the March, and one could just as easily imagine a Welsh genealogical source coming to Wigmore from a monastic house in North Wales, particularly as the Chicago 224 texts have close connections to northern Welsh genealogies such as *VGC* and *HGK*. The relationship with Welsh annals suggests further that Wigmore may have possessed a copy of a Welsh chronicle.

Conclusion

The genealogies in Chicago 224 exemplify the unique, nuanced ways that Geoffrey's history was read and understood in a marcher environment. To return to the example of the Mortimers in the Middle English Prose *Brut* with which this chapter began: it is quite possibly the Mortimers' interest in the history of Britain that allowed adaptations of Geoffrey like the Prose *Brut* to germinate in western Herefordshire and other areas of the March. The treatment of Galfridian history by the Mortimers shows how local adapters of Geoffrey's widely disseminated narrative bridged a gap between regional and national history: through the provision of localizing details that anchored the story of British history within regional family structures, in this case a family with royal ambitions. As inhabitants of a borderland, marcher readers may have taken particular interest in a history that articulated a kingdom's divisions, disputes, unifications, and alliances over a long period of time, given their own familiarity with those dynamics in the ever-evolving March of Wales.

A further attraction of Geoffrey's history was the ideological framework it provided for marcher aristocrats who viewed themselves as a fusion of the different peoples of Britain. In their aspiration to kingship, the Mortimer family produced a strong articulation of marcher identity, which was not exclusively English, Welsh, or Norman/French, but an idealized combination of all of these, a 'third category' of identity that was more than the sum of its parts. Moreover, their interest in articulating this identity resulted in Welsh texts reaching wider audiences outside Wales. Marcher genealogists and historians working at Wigmore forged a line of transmission with a Welsh centre of learning because their impetus for obtaining Welsh material was so strong. These instances of transmission were not passive acts happening in the background of literary cultural production, but deliberate moves for specific reasons, and they resulted in a uniquely marcher text, the Welsh King List, which innovated beyond what is extant in Welsh and English historical traditions.

The Mortimer argument for primacy based on their Welsh roots is an important precursor to Yorkist and Tudor arguments for the English throne. In addition to Edward IV's display of his Welsh ancestry, via the Mortimers, in the genealogical rolls discussed previously, during Henry Tudor's campaign for the throne at the conclusion of the Wars of the Roses, his royal Welsh descent through his paternal grandfather Owain Tudur was emphasized in pageants, pedigrees, and heraldic symbols. He bore a battle standard with a red dragon when he landed in Pembrokeshire and marched to battle against Richard III with an army that included Welsh soldiers in 1485. Additionally, he used Geoffrey's history—in particular the figure of Arthur and the genre of prophecy—as political propaganda during his reign.[102] The Mortimer promotion of their Welsh ancestry was a significant antecedent to the efforts of Edward IV and Henry Tudor, exhibiting the long reach of the marcher environment that gave birth to these ideas. The Mortimers' position in the March as colonizers and antagonists gave them access to ideas of Welsh kingship and ancestry, which they adopted and refashioned to great effect, and brought those ideas to a wider audience and higher level of significance outside Wales than they might have had otherwise. In fact, the idea that Welsh ancestry or association with Wales is in some way at the core of British kingship survives to this day, even as the contemporary inheritor of British kingship, the English monarchy, maintains a colonial relationship with Wales.

---

[102] For discussion of these points, see John Morgan-Guy, 'Arthur, Harri Tudor and the Iconography of Loyalty', in Steven Gunn and Linda Monckton (eds), *Arthur Tudor, Prince of Wales: Life, Death and Commemoration* (Woodbridge, 2009), 50–63; Russell Rutter, 'Printing, Prophecy, and the Foundation of the Tudor Dynasty: Caxton's *Morte Darthur* and Henry Tudor's Road to Bosworth', in E. L. Risden, Karen Moranski, and Stephen Yardell (eds), *Prophet Margins: The Medieval Vatic Impulse and Social Stability* (New York, 2004), 123–47; Gruffydd Aled Williams, 'The Bardic Road to Bosworth: A Welsh View of Henry Tudor', *Transactions of the Honourable Society of Cymmrodorion* (1986), 7–31; Anglo, 'British History'.

| 3 |

Ancestral Memory

Overall, this book reveals the ways in which baronial families in the March of Wales used Welsh texts to imagine, construct, and record their family histories, employing narratives about the British–Welsh past to fashion distinct family and regional identities as well as political arguments in their favour. The texts discussed here have a common origin in the March of Wales, but they are not uniform: they span several centuries, audiences, and genres, and have different goals. However, they all tend to do several things: promote a marcher family, establish their line of succession, and assert ownership over the family's lands—which are, in the marcher context, typically conquest territories taken over from native Welsh princes and/or territories under English administrative governance. They articulate expressions of marcher identity as multifaceted, multilingual, and characterized by a close ideological connection to Wales and the Welsh past. Whereas Chapter 1 discussed the adaptation of Geoffrey of Monmouth's *De gestis Britonum* (*Historia regum Britanniae*)—a vital aspect of marcher reimagining of the past—in various marcher contexts, and Chapter 2 discussed the use of Welsh genealogies to articulate a vision of marcher identity that staked a claim to the English throne, this chapter takes a closer look at the underlying patronage relationships between marcher families and local monastic houses that laid the foundation for the production of these texts. Together, these three chapters establish that the March of Wales was inhabited by a distinct textual community that relied on networks of transmission to fulfil a common goal: establishing a sense of identity and belonging in the March of Wales by integrating family history with legendary history and producing a new vision of the past that wrote marcher families into the previously recorded histories of Britain and Wales. It is therefore important to take a more detailed look at the mechanisms of textual production underlying these broad efforts, chiefly addressing questions of authorship, audience, patronage, and manuscript production, in a study of several overlooked marcher family genealogies.

Increasingly in the twelfth and thirteenth centuries, professional scribes working in households were involved in the making of books.[1] But in cases where a manuscript's place of origin was monastic, historical materials written about specific baronial families offer clues about the relationships between the producers of a manuscript (scribes, authors, compilers, chroniclers) and the families depicted. In these cases, questions about the nature of that relationship arise: are the texts aspirational—trying to attract patronage—or the result of commission? If the latter, how closely is production supervised by a patron? Is language choice significant to determining audience? These questions are of paramount importance because they help us determine how influential a text is, how closely its contents resemble the views of the baronial subjects, and whether their identities were constructed to appeal to a broader public as well as to their own descendants and immediate contemporaries.

In some ways, the relationship between marcher lords and the monasteries they patronized was typical of medieval Europe overall. As elsewhere in Europe, marcher lords established and supported monasteries for their own benefit: a family house was a good place in which to deposit younger sons who were not going to inherit; it was also 'a retirement home and family necropolis, a refuge for extraordinarily

---

[1] Jaakko Tahkokallio, *The Anglo-Norman Historical Canon: Publishing and Manuscript Culture*, Cambridge Elements: Elements in Publishing and Book Culture (Cambridge, 2019), 14–16; Michael Gullick, 'Professional Scribes in Eleventh- and Twelfth-Century England', *English Manuscript Studies*, 7 (1998), 1–24. Unless otherwise noted, transcriptions and translations are my own. I am grateful to Joshua Byron Smith, Hannah Weaver, and Ben Guy for checking various translations in this chapter; any errors are mine.

pious or unmarriageable kinsfolk'.[2] Family houses aided the consolidation of territory and economic production and served as important status symbols for nobility.[3] The relationship between family and monastery was, overall, a mutually beneficial contract that allowed not only for the preservation of memory in the form of prayers for souls of the deceased, monuments, and epitaphs, but also for the writing of family histories. Family memory was a collective effort, relying on recorded events beyond an individual lifespan and therefore dependent on other people's acts of preservation in the form of textual production.

In other ways, the relationship between family and monastery was specific to the political and economic circumstances of the March of Wales. Genealogies and family histories such as those discussed in this chapter seem to have been generated because of disputes over how inheritance should be divided, usually in situations where a lord died without a male heir.[4] Such disputes led to the creation of voluminous written materials recording divisions of inheritance and transfers of power from one generation to the next. As is the case in the next chapter's focus on romances, failures of male heirs led to a marked focus on inheritance through women, as inheritance was typically divided among surviving female children and their husbands.[5] Such documentation, in turn, sheds light on how marcher families conceived of and

[2] C. Warren Hollister, 'Anglo-Norman Political Culture and the Twelfth-Century Renaissance', in C. Warren Hollister (ed.), *Anglo-Norman Political Culture and the Twelfth-Century Renaissance* (Woodbridge, 1997), 1–16, at 3; Brock W. Holden, *Lords of the Central Marches: English Aristocracy and Frontier Society, 1087–1265* (Oxford, 2008), 81–4.

[3] Hollister, 'Anglo-Norman Political Culture', 3.

[4] The failure of a number of prominent marcher families owing to a lack of a male heir is discussed by R. R. Davies, *The Age of Conquest: Wales, 1063–1415* (Oxford, 2000), 83–5. He notes that the marcher lordships that changed hands for this reason in the twelfth century include Glamorgan, Gwynllŵg, Brecon, Abergavenny, Ewyas Lacy, Oswestry, Chepstow, Usk, and Ceredigion. As a result, a new baronage was 'created or promoted in the March in each generation' (*Age of Conquest*, 84).

[5] For women in the March of Wales, see Emma Cavell, 'Intelligence and Intrigue in the March of Wales: Noblewomen and the Fall of Llywelyn ap Gruffudd, 1274–82', *Historical Research*, 88/239 (2015), 1–19; Emma Cavell, 'Aristocratic Widows and the Medieval Welsh Frontier: The Shropshire Evidence', *TRHS*, 17 (2007), 57–82. Marriage is discussed by David Stephenson, *Medieval Wales, c.1050–1332: Centuries of Ambiguity* (Cardiff, 2019), 72–6; Brock Holden, 'The Making of the Middle March of Wales, 1066–1250', *WHR* 20/2 (2000), 207–26, at 219–23. Women are also a focus in the genealogical rolls discussed in Chapter 2; see Diana B. Tyson, 'The Adam and Eve Roll: Corpus Christi College Cambridge MS 98', *Scriptorium*, 52/2 (1998), 301–16, at 315–16, though cf. *MWG* 257–8.

presented their own histories in the broader context of the history of Britain.[6] Monastic textual productions helped marcher barons solidify their territorial gains through the production of new family histories that placed families in the geographical and historical context in which they now found themselves. In this borderland context, issues related to diocesan boundaries, jurisdiction, lordship boundaries, and/or ancestral rights to territory in Wales required investigations into the Welsh past, and it is this need for investigation that stirred marcher houses to acquire Welsh documents, copy them, and use them as sources for new texts. My analysis establishes a broad picture of marcher identity and textual production by way of some of the major themes of marcher literature outlined previously—family triumph, clear succession line, and ownership of land—as well as the role of monasteries and monastic manuscript production in preserving family memory.

In this chapter, I analyse several sets of marcher genealogies from the thirteenth and potentially the fourteenth centuries, written in French and Latin, in order to shed light on these broader questions of patronage, audience, and circumstances of production.[7] I focus on (1) a set of historical texts produced at Llanthony Priory for the lords of Brecon and (2) short histories of the earldoms of Gloucester and Hereford, all of which delineate complicated lines of succession in families that persistently lacked male heirs. Lords of Brecon, earls of Hereford, and lords of Abergavenny were all involved in first conquering, and then governing, Welsh kingdoms that became marcher lordships.[8] These texts make implicit arguments about rights to land and title by establishing clear lines of succession, particularly in circumstances when the reality was

---

[6] For general discussion of Anglo-Norman genealogies, see John Spence, 'Genealogies of Noble Families in Anglo-Norman', in Raluca L. Radulescu and Edward Donald Kennedy (eds), *Broken Lines: Genealogical Literature in Medieval Britain and France*, Medieval Texts and Cultures of Northern Europe, 16 (Turnhout, 2008), 63–78, at 64, 77.

[7] For the broader scope of Anglo-Norman genealogies, see John Spence, *Reimagining History in Anglo-Norman Prose Chronicles* (Woodbridge and Rochester, 2013); Spence, 'Genealogies'.

[8] See David Crouch, 'The Transformation of Medieval Gwent', in Ralph A. Griffiths, Tony Hopkins, and Ray Howell (eds), *The Gwent County History*, volume 2. *The Age of the Marcher Lords, c.1070–1536* (Cardiff, 2008), 1–45; Jeremy K. Knight, 'The Anglo-Norman Conquest of Gwent and Glamorgan', in N. J. G. Pounds (ed.), *The Cardiff Area: Proceedings of the 139th Summer Meeting of the Royal Archaeological Institute, 1993*, Supplement to the Archaeological Journal, 150 (London, 1993), 8–14; Paul Courtney, 'The Norman Invasion of Gwent: A Reassessment', *JMH* 12/4 (1986), 297–313.

much more tenuous. I focus on the dependence of the French-language *Genealogy of the Lords of Brecknock* (probably written for the Bohun earls of Hereford) on Gerald of Wales as a source, and its manuscript's relationship to Llanthony Priory as it relates to patronage. I discuss the genealogy's attitudes towards memory and the lordship's complicated relationship with its own history, which may have led to the writing of the text. Then, I discuss this genealogy's intertextual relationship with two genealogies extant in early modern transcripts, known as the 'genealogies of the earls of Hereford', which broaden our view of the function of genealogies for the marcher families involved, and establish the probable patrons of these texts. The *Genealogy of the Lords of Brecknock* has been discussed by Diana Tyson and John Spence, but has not been very well covered by scholarship otherwise.[9] The other genealogies have not, to my knowledge, been mentioned more than in passing by scholars, and none has been the subject of an extended contextual study.

The *Genealogy of the Lords of Brecknock*

The *Genealogy of the Lords of Brecknock* offers a complex picture of Brecon (formerly the Welsh kingdom of Brycheiniog), an important marcher lordship in South Wales, and the twists and turns of its line of succession. Detailed study reveals a close relationship between the lords of Brecon and the monastery that was probably responsible for producing the text and its manuscript (Llanthony Secunda Priory in Gloucestershire), as well as a complicated set of patronage relationships that worked to preserve family memory. Before discussing these broader themes, however, it is necessary to introduce the text, its manuscript context, and sources.

---

[9] Diana B. Tyson, 'A Medieval Genealogy of the Lords of Brecknock', *Nottingham Medieval Studies*, 48 (2004), 1–14; Spence, *Reimagining History*, 144–7; Spence, 'Genealogies'. I discuss the *Genealogy* and the *History of Llanthony Priory* further in 'The Reception of Gerald of Wales in Welsh Historical Texts', in Sadie Jarrett, Katharine Olson, and Rebecca Thomas (eds), *Memory and Nation: Writing the History of Wales* (Cardiff, forthcoming).

The *Genealogy of the Lords of Brecknock* is a mid-thirteenth-century French-language genealogy of the marcher lords of Brecon, covering events and individuals from the 1090s to c.1246.[10] It is extant in London, British Library, Cotton Julius D. x (s. xiii), a small manuscript (171 mm × 128 mm) bound by the Cotton Library and containing three texts. The *Genealogy of the Lords of Brecknock* is preceded in the manuscript by a Latin 'Life of Robert of Bethune', bishop of Hereford (1131–48) and former prior of Llanthony Secunda Priory, written by William of Wycombe, who succeeded him as prior.[11] It is followed by the *History of Llanthony Priory*, which recounts Llanthony's initial foundation in Monmouthshire in the early twelfth century by William, a pious knight in the service of Hugh de Lacy; the displacement of the monks to Hereford in 1135 owing to the disruptive behaviour of Welsh people; and the establishment of Llanthony Secunda Priory in Gloucestershire shortly thereafter from grants of land by Miles fitz Walter, lord of Brecon and earl of Hereford (d. 1143).[12] Llanthony Secunda quickly superseded its mother house, Llanthony Prima, in wealth and rank.

Robert Bartlett has recently attributed authorship of the *History of Llanthony Priory* to Gerald of Wales.[13] The author is most sympathetic to Llanthony Prima, lamenting the sacking of its treasures by the monks of Llanthony Secunda and its use as a pasture for elderly monks who are no longer productive members of the daughter community. This manuscript is usually given a Llanthony Secunda provenance, because of the *History* and the 'Life of Robert of Bethune' in it. Supporting this connection is the fact that several people mentioned in the *Genealogy*

---

[10] The text is transcribed in Tyson, 'Medieval Genealogy', 8–13. For continuity's sake I follow her in using 'Brecknock' rather than 'Brecon' in the title of the work.

[11] William of Wycombe became prior of Llanthony in 1137, after it had moved from Wales to its new site in Gloucestershire. This life is translated by B. J. Parkinson, 'The Life of Robert de Bethune by William de Wycombe: Translation with Introduction and Notes' (unpublished B.Litt. dissertation, University of Oxford, 1951).

[12] *The History of Llanthony Priory*, ed. and trans. Robert Bartlett (Oxford, 2022).

[13] Robert Bartlett, 'Gerald of Wales and the *History of Llanthony Priory*', in Georgia Henley and A. Joseph McMullen (eds), *Gerald of Wales: New Perspectives on a Medieval Writer and Critic* (Cardiff, 2018), 81–96; repr. in *History of Llanthony Priory*, ed. and trans. Bartlett, pp. xxvii–xxxvi.

of the Lords of Brecknock were patrons of Llanthony Secunda and are buried there.[14] Bartlett has recently suggested Prima is more likely.[15]

The *Genealogy of the Lords of Brecknock* is typically referred to in scholarship and in its title as a single genealogy, but it is important to note that it consists of two components: a narrative genealogy (Cotton Julius D. x, fols. 28^r–29^v) as well as a family tree diagram (fol. 30^r; see Figure 3.1).[16] The first item, the narrative genealogy, discusses the descent of the lords of Brecon from Bernard de Neufmarché (who conquered Brycheiniog from Rhys ap Tewdwr c.1088–93, and died 1121 × 5?) to the death of Isabel de Braose after 1246. During this span of time, the lordship passed through various hands, from Bernard to Miles fitz Walter, to the Braose family, and finally to the Bohuns. Owing to a lack of male heirs in the family line, the lordship frequently passed to a daughter, then to her husband or son. This is presumably why the line of succession, lacking straightforward inheritance through a male line, was so important to delineate in writing. The second component of the text is a family-tree diagram that functions as a visual aid to the individuals mentioned in the narrative.

The text is most supportive of Eleanor de Braose and her husband, Humphrey V de Bohun (d. 1265); they may have been its intended audience. For example, it characterizes the claim of Peter fitz Herbert (grandson of Miles fitz Walter through his daughter Lucy) to a third of the inheritance of Brecon as unfounded, instead supporting Giles de Braose (c.1170–1215), who reclaimed that land for his brother Reginald (d. 1227/8), grandfather of Eleanor (see Figure 3.2 for family tree). It is persistently interested in tracking the ownership of Brecon, not the family's other lordships, which included Abergavenny, Radnor, and many others.

---

[14] These benefactors include Miles fitz Walter and his daughter Margaret de Bohun, Miles's descendant Eleanor de Braose, and her husband Humphrey V de Bohun.

[15] Spence, 'Genealogies', 66; Neil R. Ker, *Medieval Libraries of Great Britain: A List of Surviving Books*, 2nd edn (London, 1964), 108; *History of Llanthony Priory*, ed. and trans. Bartlett, p. xii.

[16] Owing to its placement in the manuscript (the genealogy is written on the first leaf of a new quire, fol. 30^{r-v}, and the diagram is written on the second leaf of that quire, fol. 31^r), Tyson has argued that the text was integral to the codex at the time of production, and not added onto empty leaves in later years; see 'Medieval Genealogy', 5.

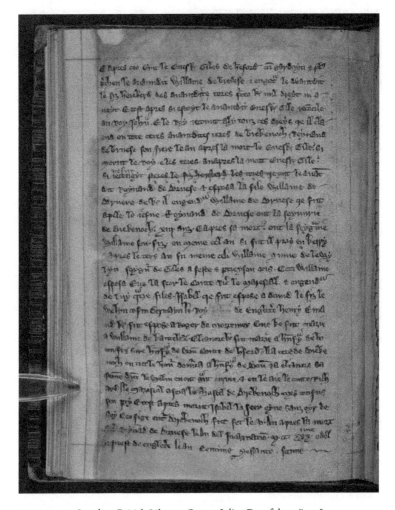

FIGURE 3.1 London, British Library, Cotton Julius D. x, fols. 29ᵛ–30ʳ.
© The British Library Board. The second page of the narrative genealogy (verso) and the genealogical diagram of the lords of Brecknock (recto)

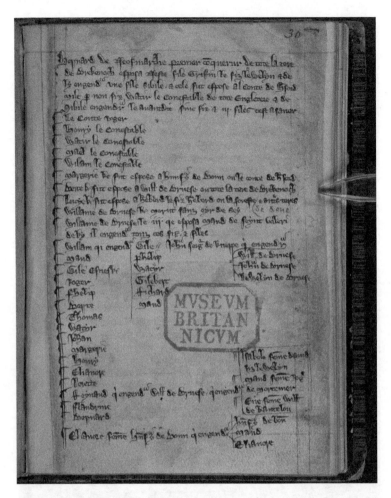

FIGURE 3.1 (*Continued*)

The first part of the narrative genealogy is substantively a translation into French of Gerald of Wales's *Itinerarium Kambriae* 1.2.[17] It describes Bernard de Neufmarché's conquest of Brycheiniog and his

[17] Gerald of Wales, *Itinerarium Kambriae,* i.2, ed. J. F. Dimock, *Giraldi Cambrensis Opera,* 6 (London, 1868), 29.

marriage to Nest, daughter of a *cruel tirant de Gales* 'cruel tyrant of Wales', Gruffudd ap Llywelyn (d. 1064).[18] Following Gerald, the text describes the dramatic saga of their son Mahel's disinheritance:

> Sa mere Neste sus son baron ama un chivalir, e a partir de sa mere le baty e ledement le defela, dunt sa mere grevement a ly se corusa; e apres la mort Bernard de Nefmarche, son baron, a la curt Henry le veyl s'en ala e devant le roy e tut son baronage apertement iura qe ceti Mael n'estoy pas le fiz Bernard de Nefmarche mes de un autre chivalir, qe ele pro ama, le aueyt consu. Dunt le rey Henry, plus par volunte qe par dreyture, a l'auantdit Mael le heritage de Brekenoch tolist e le dona a la file l'auantdite Neste, Sibile par nun apele, pur ceo qe la mere temonia qe ele fut de son baron Bernard de Nefmarche engendre.[19]

> The mother Nest loved a knight more than her husband, and upon the knight's departure from his mother, [Mahel] beat him and wounded him horribly, for which reason his mother became grievously angry with him. And after the death of her husband Bernard de Neufmarché, she went to Henry [the elder]'s court, and in the presence of the king and all his nobility she publicly swore an oath that this Mahel was not the son of Bernard de Neufmarché, but that she had conceived him by another knight, whom she loved very much. Then the King Henry, more from wilfulness than from righteousness, took the inheritance of Brecknock away from the aforementioned Mahel and gave it to the daughter of the aforementioned Nest, called by the name Sibyl (because the mother testified that she was begat from her baron Bernard de Neufmarché).

The text labours to explain that Mahel's disinheritance results in the lordship passing to his sister Sibyl, whose paternity is not in question. King Henry gives Sibyl in marriage to Miles fitz Walter, constable of

---

[18] In fact, Bernard de Neufmarché married Gruffudd ap Llywelyn's granddaughter, Nest. The compiler is probably confusing this Nest with her mother, Gruffudd's daughter, who was also called Nest. The source, Gerald of Wales, gets this detail right.

[19] Cotton Julius D. x, fols. 28[r–v]. This text is also transcribed in Tyson, 'Medieval Genealogy', 8–12, at 8–9. K. L. Maund suggests that Mahel, a figure who is only recorded by Gerald of Wales, was an illegitimate son of Bernard's; see 'Neufmarché, Bernard de (d. 1121×5?)', *ODNB*, accessed 2 February 2022.

Gloucester and later earl of Hereford, with *tut le honur de Brekenoch* 'all the honour of Brecknock' and the Forest of Dean. Miles and Sibyl have a number of children, and the lordship passes to their son Roger (d. 1155). As is typical of marcher family histories, the family's origin story begins with the successful conquest of territory in Wales, but, interestingly, dwells not on defending rights to that territory against the Welsh as one might expect, but rather on the continuity of the lordship's line of succession. It is determined to show that ownership of the lordship passes seamlessly from Bernard, Norman conqueror of Brycheiniog, whose legitimacy was sealed through marriage to a Welsh princess, down to the Bohun earls of Hereford in the thirteenth century.

The next episode in the genealogy is also taken from Gerald's *Itinerarium Kambriae* 1.2.[20] It concerns William Constable, a son of Miles and Sibyl, who wrongfully persecutes David fitz Gerald, bishop of St Davids (1148–76) and Gerald of Wales's uncle. In an incident of divine punishment, young William is mortally wounded in a fire at Bronllys Castle in Powys.[21] As he dies, he sends a message to David fitz Gerald recognizing his error:

> Mentenant enveia il ses messagirs la ou le eueske de Seynt Dauid estoyt e hastiuement le fist a ly venir e pitusement ly dist: 'E ben, pere esueske, cruelement se venge de mey Nostre Seynur, e ne atent pas la conuersion al pecheur mes haste la mort a perdition.' Entre cete paroles, le premer an de sa seynurie ne mye del tut finy, le esperit de sa qualete rendi.[22]

> He immediately sent his messengers to where the bishop of St Davids was, and he had him come to him and pitiably he said to him, 'Truly, Father Bishop, cruelly Our Lord takes revenge on me, and conversion does not wait for the sinner, but death hurries to destruction.' During these words, [with] the first year of his lordship not at all ended, he handed over the spirit from his being [i.e., died].

These two stories are recognizably Giraldian: the themes of revenge, divine retribution, and salacious family turmoil are all characteristic of

---

[20] Gerald of Wales, *Itinerarium Kambriae*, i.2, 30–1.
[21] In some sources, this son is called Mahel; see Emma Cavell, 'Bohun, Margaret de [*née* Margaret of Gloucester] (*c*.121–1196/7)', *ODNB*, accessed 2 February 2022.
[22] Cotton Julius D. x, fols. 28ᵛ–29ʳ; Tyson, 'Medieval Genealogy', 9.

his writing, and they are preserved in full by the author–translator of the French text.

As Gerald's *Itinerarium Kambriae* then moves on to discuss other matters, the French text here departs from him as a source.[23] It then relates the marriages of Miles fitz Walter's daughters, Margaret, Bertha, and Lucy (see Figure 3.2 for family tree). Their marriages are important, because their brothers die without heirs and the family's lands are split between them instead. The eldest daughter Margaret (*c*.1121–96/7) marries Humphrey II de Bohun (d. 1164/5), who receives Miles's lands in England. Bertha marries William II de Braose, who receives the lordship of Brecon, and Lucy marries Herbert fitz Herbert, who receives the Forest of Dean.[24] The lordship's line of succession would continue through Bertha's descendants.

Following the division of Miles fitz Walter's inheritance between his daughters, the text notes that Braoses hold the lordship of Brecon through the reigns of Kings Henry, Richard, and John, until King John throws William III de Braose (d. 1211) and his heirs out of England *saunz acheson e par sa volunte e sanz iugement* 'without reason and by his wilfulness and without official decree'. The text omits the fact that William III died in Paris and that his wife Maud de Saint Valéry and eldest son William IV were allegedly starved to death in prison at Windsor or Corfe Castle in 1210, with his other sons also imprisoned by King John. It chooses not to discuss such details, though it alludes to them in its criticism of John's reprehensible actions.

It is up to William III's son Giles, bishop of Hereford from 1200 to 1215, to restore the lordship to the family by making peace with King John and reclaiming a third of the lordship from Peter fitz Herbert. Following Giles's peace with John and the restoration of Brecon to Giles's brother Reginald, the lordship passes to Reginald's son, William V, who is then executed by Llywelyn ab Iorwerth in 1230 (*Willame conuie de Lewylyn, seygnur de Gales, a feste, e par treyson ocis* 'William was invited by Llywelyn, lord of Wales, to a feast, and for treason he was killed').[25] In fact, William V de Braose was hanged for being caught in the bedchamber of

---

[23] For further discussion, see Henley, 'The Reception of Gerald of Wales in Welsh Historical Texts'.
[24] The roman numerals after the names are not in the text; they are added for ease of comprehension.
[25] Cotton Julius D. x, fol. 29^v; Tyson, 'Medieval Genealogy', 11.

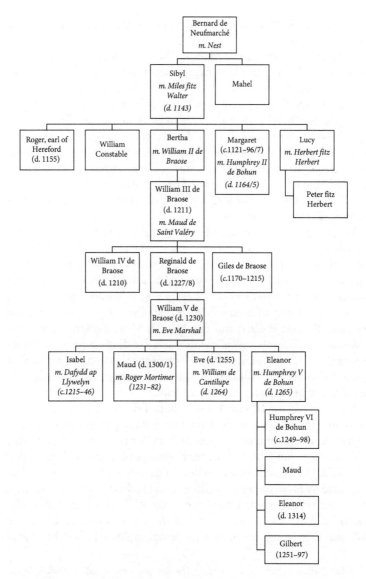

FIGURE 3.2 The lords of Brecon according to the *Genealogy of the Lords of Brecknock*.

Note: To these and other genealogical diagrams, I have added birth and death dates where available from the *ODNB*.

Llywelyn's wife Joan, but the text does not mention this indiscretion.[26] After his execution, Laura Cleaver argues, 'the division of his lands became a significant political issue'.[27] Once again, disputed inheritance spurred an instance of textual production.

The text is particularly interested in William V de Braose's children and their marriages: it notes that he married Eve, sister of the powerful Richard Marshal,[28] and that together they had four daughters: Isabel, who marries Dafydd ap Llywelyn (c.1215–46); Maud (d. 1300/1), who marries Roger Mortimer (1231–82); Eve (d. 1255), who marries William de Cantilupe (d. 1254), and Eleanor, who marries Humphrey V de Bohun. Once again, daughters are the heiresses. This final daughter, Eleanor, is most important because in 1241 the lordship of Brecon passed to her son, Humphrey VI de Bohun (c.1249–98). The narrative genealogy concludes with an account of Llywelyn ab Iorwerth becoming jealous of Humphrey V and besieging Brecon Castle *en out grant envie* 'out of great envy', which according to Welsh annals occurred in either 1231 or 1233.[29] The latest event mentioned in the text is the death of Isabel de Braose, wife of Dafydd ap Llywelyn, which occurred sometime after 1246, as mentioned previously.[30]

The narrative genealogy concludes on fol. 29^v. On the following, facing-page folio (fol. 30^r), the scribe includes a diagram of the lords of Brecon that corresponds to the genealogy just outlined (see Figure 3.1 above). The diagram functions as a visual reference to the individuals and family relationships discussed in the preceding text. The last people mentioned are Eleanor de Braose, her husband Humphrey V de

---

[26] For discussion, see J. Beverley Smith, 'Dafydd ap Llywelyn (c.1215–1246)', *ODNB*, accessed 2 February 2022.

[27] Laura Cleaver, 'Past, Present and Future for Thirteenth-Century Wales: Two Diagrams in British Library, Cotton Roll XIV.12', *Electronic British Library Journal* (2013), 1–26, at 5.

[28] Eve and Richard's father was William Marshal (c.1146–1219), whose biography is discussed at length in Ch.4, pp. 177–84.

[29] Several others who have written about this text cite 1232 as its final event recorded, when Llywelyn ab Iorwerth besieged Brecon Castle. In fact, the siege happened in 1231 or 1233; see *The Inventory of Historic Battlefields in Wales* (Aberystwyth, 2017), http://battlefields.rcahmw.gov.uk/, accessed 12 October 2022; also noted by Spence, 'Genealogies', 68, n. 24.

[30] An exact death date is not secured by external sources, but she was still alive in 1246 as recorded in an order; see *Calendar of Patent Rolls, Henry III*, volume 3. 1232–1247 (London, 1906), 485; J. E. Lloyd, *A History of Wales from the Earliest Times to the Edwardian Conquest*, 2 vols, 2nd edn (London, 1912), ii.705, n. 69.

Bohun, and their children Maud, Eleanor, and Humphrey VI (c.1249–98), suggesting a mid- to late-thirteenth-century composition date for the text. John Spence suggests that it was written during Eleanor and Humphrey V's lifetimes in the mid-thirteenth century, possibly for them or their son Humphrey VI.[31] Eleanor and Humphrey were patrons of Llanthony Secunda Priory, a possible place of origin of Cotton Julius D. x, and Eleanor was buried there after her death.[32] Llanthony Secunda had long-standing associations with the lords of Brecon, having been founded by Miles fitz Walter, and the *Genealogy of the Lords of Brecknock* serves as a secular complement to the history of the priory in the same manuscript.

One potential circumstance that could have necessitated this recording of the lordship's history for the Bohuns at the time was the fact that from 1265 until 1270 the lordship of Brecon was in the custody of Gilbert de Clare, earl of Gloucester, while Eleanor and Humphrey V's son, Humphrey VI, was a minor. During his minority, Brecon was de facto controlled by Llywelyn ap Gruffudd, prince of Wales (c.1233–82), who was in a phase of expansion in South Wales at the time.[33] These destabilizing events could have instigated a desire to demonstrate the continuity of succession on the part of the Bohuns, who were relative newcomers to the March by comparison to older families such as the Braoses and Lacys, and who effectively did not have control of the lordship they had inherited through marriage.

In the genealogical roll London, British Library, Cotton Roll XIV 12 (s. xii$^{2/4}$), related materials, including genealogical roundels, discuss Bernard de Neufmarché's family and the division of his inheritance among the children of Miles fitz Walter.[34] The roll, written in Latin, may

---

[31] Spence, *Reimagining History*, 28; Spence, 'Genealogies', 68. This does not negate the possibility that the section of the narrative genealogy derived from Gerald was translated sometime earlier. These portions of the *Itinerarium Kambriae* could have been translated into French at any time between their publication by Gerald and their appearance in this genealogical context. I am grateful to Paul Russell for suggesting this point to me.

[32] Spence, 'Genealogies', 68.

[33] Scott L. Waugh, 'Bohun, Humphrey de, third earl of Hereford and eighth earl of Essex (c.1249–1298)', *ODNB*, accessed 22 October 2021; J. Beverley Smith, *Llywelyn ap Gruffudd: Prince of Wales* (Oxford, 1998), 142.

[34] For discussion, see Cleaver, 'Past, Present and Future', 4–7.

have been created at Battle Abbey for its dependency, Brecon Priory.[35] The relevant text is embedded in a universal chronicle. It describes Bernard's gift of Brecon Priory to Battle Abbey as well as the splitting of his inheritance between Miles and Sibyl's daughters, though it gets their names wrong (fol. 33ʳ).[36] Though it is not immediately textually related to the *Genealogy of the Lords of Brecknock*, Cleaver suggests a similar context for the roll's delineation of the line of succession of the lordship of Brecon, noting that Humphrey V's claims to Brecon were contested by Dafydd ap Llywelyn, resulting in 'hostilities' in 1244: 'the marriages and contemporary politics might thus have revived interest in the founding family of Brecon Priory and claims to Brecon lands.'[37] This circumstantial evidence for the creation of genealogical and historical materials on behalf of a marcher lord attests to the role that monastic textual production played in the long-term preservation of power in a family. Knowledge and presentation of historical information were essential to maintaining political power over generations.

Following the *Genealogy of the Lords of Brecknock* in the manuscript is the *History of Llanthony Priory*, which, as mentioned previously, may have been written by Gerald of Wales.[38] These two texts in Cotton Julius D. x have notable similarities and overlapping events, and give further clues to the strong relationship between the priory and the lords of Brecon. Placed next to each other in the manuscript, they work together to demonstrate the religious dedication of the rulers of the lordship and the centrality of Llanthony Priory to the family's displays of piety.[39] Transmitting a message that is not uncommon in church histories, the *History of Llanthony Priory* takes pains to highlight the strong relationships between both priories of Llanthony and their noble benefactors.

---

[35] Cleaver, 'Past, Present and Future', 4, citing W. H. Monroe, 'Thirteenth- and Early Fourteenth-Century Illustrated Genealogical Manuscripts in Roll and Codex: Peter of Poitiers' *Compendium, Universal Histories* and *Chronicles of the Kings of England*' (unpublished Ph.D. thesis, University of London, 1989), 519.

[36] Cleaver, 'Past, Present and Future', 4–5. Margaret marries Humphrey de Bohun, who inherits the earldom of Hereford; Lucy [*corr.* Bertha] marries William de Braose, and Joanna [*corr.* Lucy] marries Herbert fitz Herbert.

[37] Cleaver, 'Past, Present and Future', 7.

[38] *History of Llanthony Priory*, ed. and trans. Bartlett; Bartlett, 'Gerald of Wales'; Michael Richter, 'Giraldus Cambrensis and Llanthony Priory', *SC* 12–13 (1977–8), 118–32.

[39] I discuss this matter further in 'The Reception of Gerald of Wales in Welsh Historical Texts'.

It is this close relationship that strengthens the case for the provenance of the manuscript at Llanthony Secunda and shows how mutually beneficial a relationship between a noble family and a monastery could be.

One of the patronage relationships reinforced by the *History* is the strong link between Miles fitz Walter and Llanthony Secunda. During Miles's lifetime, the monks of Llanthony Prima flee from their home because of the unruly behaviour of a Welsh family who seeks refuge from warfare at the priory, but whose female members disrupt the community. The monks appeal to Robert of Bethune (d. 1148), bishop of Hereford and former prior of Llanthony Prima.[40] Further disrupted by the war between Stephen and Matilda, the monks realize they cannot return to the Vale of Ewyas, and, upon Robert of Bethune's request, Miles fitz Walter grants them a new foundation in Gloucestershire.[41] Miles is thus framed as the patron who makes the foundation of Llanthony Secunda Priory possible.

The church is consecrated in 1136, but with the stipulation that the monks will eventually return to the mother house, where thirteen of the best monks have been left behind. The generosity of the patronage of Miles and his children is emphasized in the *History*:

> Cernens itaque uir illustris Milo comes, regis constabularius, ecclesie illius fundator et aduocatus, religiosam ipsorum conuersacionem, et quanti essent apud Deum meriti, et quam grate in impetrando efficacie per experienciam satis eruditus, una cum egregia sobole sua, militibus uidelicet opinatissimis et matronis famosissimis, ecclesiam illam uariis donariis et possessionibus non minus large quam uoluntarie ditare adiecit.

> So, that illustrious man, Earl Miles, constable of the king, founder and advocate of that church, observing their religious way of life, and how great was their merit before God, and learning well by experience how graciously efficacious they were in seeking things, turned his mind to endowing the church both abundantly and willingly with various gifts and possessions, joined in this by his remarkable lineage, that is, renowned knights and famous ladies.[42]

---

[40] As mentioned above, William of Wycombe's 'Life of Robert of Bethune' survives in the same manuscript.
[41] *History of Llanthony Priory* ii.2, ed. and trans. Bartlett, 56–7.
[42] Ibid., 58–9.

The text celebrates the generosity and piety of the patron endowing the monastery. This sentiment may have been motivated by a broader desire to encourage nobility to tend to the church.

In this case, praise is followed by a sharp critique of the monks of Llanthony Secunda, who squander Miles's gifts by turning to vice and refusing to visit Llanthony Prima. As others have observed, the author of the *History*, who may be Gerald of Wales, is very critical of the community at Llanthony Secunda, and takes pains to underscore its status as a dependency of the original monastery. He laments the fact that the monks have been weakened and corrupted by Gloucestershire's gentle, fertile climate. Roger, earl of Hereford, son of Miles, is greatly displeased by the monks' theft of goods from Llanthony Prima, to the extent that he forces William of Wycombe (prior of Llanthony Secunda from 1137 to 1147) from office.[43] In this episode, Roger is depicted as an agent of justice for the community, an example of how a patron can offer moral direction.

The *History of Llanthony Priory* and the *Genealogy of the Lords of Brecknock* display thematic parallels that tie them together in the manuscript. Both texts are interested in noblemen's relationships to monasteries as routes to either salvation or damnation. The *History*, for its part, focuses on pious acts by nobility, particularly that of Walter Constable, who retires to Llanthony Prima with great humility:

> Walterus constabularius, princeps milicie domus regie, uir magnus et potens et inter primos regni precipue honoratus, audito tam celebris sanctitatis, tamque religiose conuersacionis preconio, uniuersis seculi pompis grataque sobolis fecunditate et numerose cognacionis turba relictis, pre cunctis Anglie tam egregiis cenobiis, inter pauperes Christi apud Llanthoniam residuum uite sub habitu canonici transigere.

> Walter the constable, commander of the knights of the royal household, a great and powerful man and especially honoured among the chief men of the kingdom, hearing praise of such famous sanctity and such a religious way of life, abandoning the pomp of the world and the happy fecundity of his family and his numerous kindred, decided,

---

[43] *History of Llanthony Priory* ii.5, ed. and trans. Bartlett, 70–3. In this, he follows in the footsteps of his father Miles, who was violently at odds with William's friend Robert of Bethune.

by a most firm resolution, to spend the rest of his life in the habit of a canon among the poor of Christ at Llanthony.[44]

The *Genealogy of the Lords of Brecknock* instead highlights the immorality of Walter Constable's grandson William, *le plus felons des autres* 'the most wicked of all of them'. As discussed above, he is mortally wounded in a fire at Bronllys Castle as divine punishment for persecuting David fitz Gerald. Taken together, the two texts teach a lesson about the benefits of a moral life.

Both texts also begin with legendary origins, a central feature of Anglo-Norman genealogies of this period.[45] Both origin stories are sourced from Gerald of Wales's *Itinerarium Kambriae*: the *Genealogy of the Lords of Brecknock* with the story of Mahel's disinheritance after scorning his mother Nest's lover, and the *History of Llanthony Priory* with William the pious knight's discovery of the beautiful, rugged Vale of Ewyas. Both depict the Welsh as antagonists: the *Genealogy of the Lords of Brecknock* mentions Llywelyn's jealous siege of Brecon Castle, and the *History of Llanthony Priory* offers frequent commentary about the ignorant, ungodly habits of the local Welsh people. These similarities suggest that, when read together, these two texts in Cotton Julius D. x present a harmonized picture of the lords of Brecon and their relationship with Llanthony Priory in its broader social and geographical context.[46]

Much like other manuscripts containing marcher family histories, the languages of these texts are Latin or French. It is often assumed that vernacular indicates a lay audience, and Latin indicates a clerical audience, but the fact that so many books from this era contain both languages (or indeed multiple vernaculars), and the fact that secular aristocrats were educated in Latin (often second or third sons trained as clerics), complicates the matter significantly.[47] There is no reason to assume that members of noble families could not read Latin, given that younger sons were trained for the church. Therefore, one should not assume that

---

[44] *History of Llanthony Priory* i.8, ed. and trans. Bartlett, 42–5.

[45] Spence, 'Genealogies', 77.

[46] Additional seventeenth-century transcripts printed by William Dugdale corroborate the information in the *Genealogy of the Lords of Brecknock* and suggest that more versions or copies of this text circulated in the medieval period.

[47] Discussed by Tahkokallio, *Anglo-Norman Historical Canon*, 11, citing M. T. Clanchy, *From Memory to Written Record: England 1066–1307*, 2nd edn (Oxford, 1993), 224–52; Martin Aurell, *Le Chevalier lettré: Savoir et conduite de l'aristocratie aux XIIe et XIIIe siècles* (Paris, 2011).

only the French texts were for noble patrons, and only the Latin texts for the monks of Llanthony. Perhaps *all* the texts in this manuscript were intended to elicit family pride and highlight the strength of the relationship between the lordship, the diocese of Herefordshire, and Llanthony Priory. In any case, Latin functioned as the language of authority and record-keeping in this era, regardless of whether readers could understand it.

It is common to attribute the composition of texts for noble patrons to particular political circumstances. It is less clear how, exactly, the patronage relationship between compiler and noble patron worked. Were compilers at Llanthony Secunda working to solicit benefaction, or are the texts in Cotton Julius D. x an affirmation of an already solicitous relationship between the priory and the family, a sort of contract that was being followed to ensure the preservation of memory? Given the family members' burials there, the second is more likely. This matter will become clearer in the discussion below.

Genealogies of the earls of Hereford transcribed by William Dugdale

A similar genealogical account of the lords of Brecon and earls of Hereford is extant in Oxford, Bodleian Library, Dugdale 18 (AD 1670). The texts in this manuscript provide further information about the role that textual production played in the preservation of family land rights and titles over several rocky generations of dynastic succession. As above, it is first necessary to introduce this relatively unknown text before discussing the evidence it provides for the relationship between family and monastery, as well as textual production and family memory, in the March of Wales.

Dugdale 18 is a paper manuscript written by the seventeenth-century antiquarian Sir William Dugdale (1605–86) consisting of transcripts of medieval historical and genealogical texts from the Duchy of Lancaster Office, the manuscript collections of Robert Glover, and other sources.[48] Dugdale was an antiquary and herald from north Warwickshire who was particularly interested in Warwickshire history,

---

[48] *A Summary Catalogue of Western Manuscripts in the Bodleian Library at Oxford*, ed. Falconer Madan and H. H. E. Craster, vol. ii, part 2 (Oxford, 1937), 1079–80, number 6508.

the foundation documents of monasteries, and the English legal system. He wrote over forty manuscripts now in the Bodleian Library and published some sixteen printed works, the most famous of which are the *Monasticon Anglicanum* (3 vols, 1655, 1661, 1673) and *The Baronage of England* (3 vols, 1676, 1677). Throughout his career, he worked in the London exchequer, the Office of Arms, the Tower of London, and the Cotton Library, and travelled to visit gentry families, cathedrals, and churches to read manuscripts.[49]

Dugdale 18 includes a short Latin chronicle about the Lacys and Mortimers that he says he copied from the Register of Wigmore Abbey (fols. 15^r–18^r) and a set of genealogies and prose histories (fols. 29^r–30^v) copied from an unnamed source.[50] This latter set of texts is interested in a constellation of marcher families descended from Miles fitz Walter, including the Braoses, Marshals, Clares, and their minor descendants, all the way down to the Hastings family, who were lords of Abergavenny in the late thirteenth and early fourteenth centuries. This set of genealogies and prose histories, henceforth referred to as the 'genealogies of the earls of Hereford', is in French and Latin. It consists of:

1a. Family tree diagram from single ancestor Dru, lord of Ballon, to Reginald de Braose (d. 1227/8), fol. 29^r (Latin)
1b. Genealogy explaining diagram in 1a, fol. 29^r–29^v (Latin)
2a. Family tree diagram from William V de Braose to William Hastings (1282–1311) and his siblings, fol. 29^v (French)
2b. Genealogy explaining diagram in 2a, down to John Hastings (1262–1313), fol. 29^v (French)
3. Family tree diagram of ancestry of Ada of Huntingdon, a Hastings ancestor, fol. 30^r (French)
4. Family tree diagram of children of William Brewer (d. 1226), fol. 30^r (French)
5. Family tree diagram of descendants of William Marshal (1146/7–1219) to John II Hastings (1287–1325) and his siblings, fol. 30^r–30^v (French)
6. Charters recording grants of land to members of Hastings family, fol. 30^v (Latin)

---

[49] Graham Parry, 'Dugdale, Sir William (1605–1686)', *ODNB*, accessed 22 October 2021.
[50] The Register of Wigmore Abbey he is referring to is probably the *Liber Niger de Wigmore*, London, British Library, Harley 1240 (personal communication, Chris Given-Wilson).

Transcribed in 1670 from unrecorded sources,[51] these texts probably formed the basis for details about the earls of Hereford, the Braoses, and the Hastings printed in *The Baronage of England*.[52] To my knowledge, they have not been studied by modern scholars.

Although it is impossible to date these texts securely, given that they are extant in a 1670 transcript of medieval exemplar(s) that do not survive, some clues are available. Item 5, for example, ends with the statement *Humfrey Conte de Hereford qui ore est* 'Humphrey earl of Hereford who lives presently', referring to Humphrey VII de Bohun, suggesting that item 5 was written during his lifetime, between c.1276 and 1322 (see Figure 3.6 at the end of this chapter for his family tree).[53] The pedigrees in items 2a and 2b, similarly, end with Hastings men who died in 1311 and 1313, suggesting a similar time frame for them (see Figure 3.3). It is not possible to determine with certainty whether all six of the texts listed above came from the same original source (and medieval manuscript studies would teach us to doubt that they did), or from multiple manuscript exemplars used by Dugdale, but their interrelatedness would suggest they came from one or more sources interested in the noble ancestry of the Hastings lords of Abergavenny in the late thirteenth and early fourteenth centuries.[54] These lords are the most likely patrons of this collection of texts, if it was indeed a coherent collection before Dugdale's time. The Hastings lords of Abergavenny were based in Warwickshire (Allesley and Coventry), a county Dugdale knew well.

The overall aim of these genealogies is to show that the Hastings lords of Abergavenny—namely, John I Hastings, 1st baron Hastings and lord of Abergavenny (1262–1313), and his son John II, 2nd baron Hastings and lord of Abergavenny (1287–1325)—are descended from the

---

[51] Dugdale's diary for 1670 leaves no clues as to where Dugdale 18 was written; it is unclear whether he would have travelled to a location, like a gentry house, to copy the texts, or whether they were sent to him at his residence, Blyth Hall; see the entries for 1670 in *The Life, Diary, and Correspondence of Sir William Dugdale*, ed. William Hamper (London, 1827), 132–3.

[52] *The Baronage of England* uses information from Dugdale 18, pp. 414–21 (Braose), 536–8 (earls of Hereford), and 574 (Hastings).

[53] Dugdale 18, fol. 30ᵛ; J. S. Hamilton, 'Bohun, Humphrey de, fourth earl of Hereford and ninth earl of Essex (c.1276–1322)', *ODNB*, accessed 22 October 2021.

[54] They are distant relations of the line of Theophilus Hastings, 7th earl of Huntingdon, whom Dugdale visited and corresponded with from 1673 onwards. Dugdale 18 predates Dugdale's relationship and correspondence with Lord Hastings, which began in 1673; F. M. Powicke, 'Notes on Hastings Manuscripts', *Huntington Library Quarterly*, 3 (1938), 247–76.

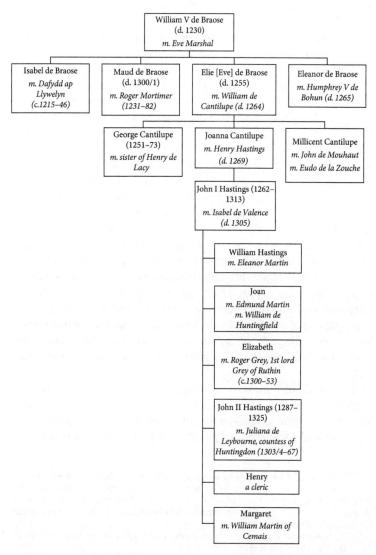

FIGURE 3.3 The ancestry of John II Hastings according to Dugdale 18, items 2a and 2b.

Marshals and the Braoses through John I's mother, Joanna Cantilupe, and that, through her, the family holds the wealthy Cantilupe lands and titles, including the lordship of Abergavenny (see Figure 3.3).[55] One might speculate that it was the political insecurity of John I's father, Sir Henry Hastings, dying in 1269 when his son was just 7 years old—with the result that his lands were held by William de Valence, earl of Pembroke (d. 1296) until John reached adulthood, and John's aunt Millicent came knocking for a share of the Cantilupe inheritance—that precipitated a desire to record the family inheritance in semi-permanent records.[56] This minor gentry family in the March of Wales would later marry into the English royal family at various points and play noteworthy roles in the Hundred Years' War and the Wars of the Roses.

There are striking similarities between passages in the genealogies in Dugdale 18 and the *Genealogy of the Lords of Brecknock* discussed above. These similarities occur after the latter departs from Gerald of Wales as a source, and they suggest that this account of the lordship of Brecon's inheritance circulated in multiple copies and languages. The events in the latter section of the *Genealogy of the Lords of Brecknock*, describing the division of Brecon lands between Miles fitz Walter's daughters Margaret, Bertha, and Lucy; their marriages; Peter fitz Herbert's unjust claim to part of the inheritance rightfully belonging to Reginald de Braose; the death of William V de Braose at the hands of Llywelyn ab Iorwerth; and the division of William's inheritance between his four daughters, are also recorded in Dugdale items 1a, 1b, 2a, 2b, using strikingly similar wording, even as they are in Latin instead of French (refer back to Figure 3.2 above for the lineage of this family). For example, they describe the division of inheritance between the three daughters of Miles fitz Walter in parallel terms. The *Genealogy of the Lords of Brecknock* states:

---

[55] For an argument that the fourteenth-century wooden effigy in Abergavenny Priory depicts John II Hastings, and that John reformed the church in 1319 and was eventually buried there, see Claude Blair, 'The Wooden Knight at Abergavenny', *Church Monuments: Journal of the Church Monuments Society*, 9 (1994), 33–52. Blair shows that John Hastings had a presence in Abergavenny and did not rule the lordship entirely from Coventry, as one might assume. For the lives of both John Hastings, see Fiona Watson, 'Hastings, John, first Lord Hastings (1262–1313)', *ODNB*, accessed 2 February 2022.

[56] This is discussed further below in the light of passages in item 2b.

> Margerie se esposa a Hunfry de Boun, ou sa partie qe estoyt le conte de Hereford. Berte se marie a Willame de Brewes, ou tote sa tere de Brekenoch. Lucie se maria a Hereberd le fiz Hereberd, ou tote la foreste de Dene e autres teres. Mes cesti Hereberd, pur trespass qe fet aueyt au roy de Engletere Henry le secund, fiz le emperice, le an cely roy quart tote la foreste le rendi e quite clama.[57]
>
> Margaret married Humphrey de Bohun, whose share was the earldom of Hereford. Bertha married William de Braose, who held the whole land of Brecon. Lucy married Herbert fitz Herbert, who held the whole Forest of Dean and other lands. But, because of a transgression that was committed against the King of England (Henry II, son of the Empress), this Herbert gave up, to this same king, a quarter of the whole forest and released his claim.

Similarly, item 1a of the genealogies of the earls of Hereford lists the three daughters of Miles:

> Margeria uxor Humfr. de Bohun Comitis Herefordiae. Berta uxor Philippi[58] de Breosa. Lucia nupta Herberto filio Herberti, cum foresta de Dene; qui, in brevi, forisfecit eam, et reddidit et quietum clamavit regi.[59]
>
> Margaret, wife of Humphrey de Bohun, earl of Hereford; Bertha, wife of [William] de Braose; Lucy was married to Herbert fitz Herbert, with the Forest of Dean, who, in short, forfeited it, and handed it over and gave up his claim to the king.

Comparison of these passages reveals a very similar account of events. Both texts describe Peter fitz Herbert's dispute over the Braose inheritance in similar wording, though in different languages.

As discussed previously, Peter fitz Herbert was the son of Lucy, daughter of Miles fitz Walter, and her husband, Herbert fitz Herbert. Peter claimed to have inherited one-third of Brecon through his mother Lucy, but the claim was disputed by the Braose descendants of his aunt Bertha. The *Genealogy of the Lords of Brecknock* supports the Braose side of the dispute:

---

[57] Cotton Julius D. x, fol. 29ʳ; Tyson, 'Medieval Genealogy', 9–10.
[58] This name is incorrect; Bertha married William II de Braose.
[59] Dugdale 18, fol. 29ʳ.

Le an del incarnation Nostre Seygnur .m.cc.viii. esteyt tote Engletere entredite e Gales la nomme kalende de Aueril. E la secunde kalend de May apres, si prist le roy Johan les teres e les chateus le auantdit Willame de Brewse par sa volunte demeyne, e le engeta de Engletere ou les seus. E quant il estoyt engete en exil, Pareres le fiz Hereberd pria le roy Johan qe il le grantast la terce partie de la tere de Brekenoch, ceo est a sauer Blenteueny[60] e Talgar e la Walecherie ou les apurtenances a sa volunte. E apres ceo, vint le eueske Giles de Hereford cum gardayn e plus prechen le auaundit Willame de Brewse, e engeta le avantdit le fiz Hereberd des auantdite teres pur ceo, ke nul dreyt n'i aueyt. E tost apres si estoyt le auantdit Eueske Gile reconcile au roy Johan. E le roy reconut a ly touz ces dreys qe il clama en tote cetes auantdites teres de Brekenoch, Reynaud de Bruese son frere.[61]

The year of Our Lord 1208, all England and Wales was placed under an interdict on the 9th Kalends of April [24 March]. And on the 2nd Kalends of May [30 April] thereupon, King John took the lands and the castles of the aforementioned William de Braose for himself, by his own command, and threw him out of England with his men. And when [William de Braose] had been cast out in exile, Peter fitz Herbert asked King John to grant him one-third of the part of the land of Brecon, that which is known as Blaenllyfni and Talgarth, including the Welshry, with its appurtenances, by his command. And after that, Giles, bishop of Hereford, came with a guard and the next of kin of the aforementioned William de Braose, and he threw out the aforementioned son of Herbert from the aforementioned lands because he had no right there. And soon after, the aforementioned Bishop Giles reconciled with King John. And the king returned to him all those rights which he had claimed, and all those aforementioned lands of Brecon, to Reginald de Braose his brother.

By comparison, item 1b in Dugdale 18 describes a very similar sequence of events in parallel wording, including beginning with the interdict—this time in Latin, but with more detail about Peter fitz Herbert's lands:

Anno igitur ab incarnatione domini MCCVIII° interdicta fuit tota Anglia, et Wallia, nouo kal. Aprilis. Sexto verò Kal. Maii coepit Rex

---

[60] The word 'Blenteueny' has been crossed out with a lead tip that has left a deep groove.
[61] Cotton Julius D. x, fol. 29[r–v]; Tyson, 'Medieval Genealogy', 10–11. I am grateful to Paul Russell for suggesting a translation for 'Walecherie'.

Iohannes terras et castella Willielmi de Breousa, ipso Willielmo annuente, et eiecit eum, cum suis, ut supradictum est. Cum autem eiecti essens in exilio, Petrus filius Herberti impetravit à domino Iohanne Rege, quod ipse ei concessit tertiam partem terrae Breconiae, scilicet: Bleynleveny, Talgarde, et Walensuam, cum suis pertinentiis; et sic impetravit ad voluntatem ipsius domini Regis.

Postea dominus Egidius, filius praedicti Willielmi de Breousa, qui tunc erat Episcopus Herefordiae, ut propinquior haeres praedicti Willielmi, eiecit praedictum Petrum filium Herberti de dictis terris, eo quod in eis nullum ius habuit: Et statim postquam praedictus Egidius reconciliatus fuit domino Regi, idem Rex recognovit praedicto Episcopo, totum ius suum quod clamavit in illis terris: et ipse Egidius Episcopus praedictas terras tota vita sua possedit et obtinuit sicut ius suum. Obiit autem ipse Egidius Episcopus anno ab incarnatione domini 1215 tenente post eum terras et opida Reginaldo fratre suo.[62]

Then in the year after the Incarnation of the Lord 1208, an interdict was placed over all England and Wales on the 9th Kalends of April [24 March]. On the 6th Kalends of May [26 April], King John captured lands and castles of William de Braose, with the same William assenting to it, and expelled him with his family, as is mentioned above. But when they had been cast out, Peter fitz Herbert, who was living in exile, requested from the lord King John that he grant to him a third part of the land of Brecon, namely, Blaenllyfni, Talgarth, and the Welshry, with their appurtenances, and thus he obtained them at the will of the lord king.

Afterwards Lord Giles, son of the aforementioned William de Braose, who was then bishop of Hereford, and therefore the closest heir of the aforementioned William, expelled the aforementioned Peter fitz Herbert from said lands, because he had no right to them. And, as soon as the aforementioned Giles had been reconciled with the lord king, the same king acknowledged to the aforementioned bishop his entire right which he claimed in those lands. And the same aforementioned Bishop Giles possessed and held the aforementioned lands for his whole life, as was his right. Bishop Giles died in AD 1215, with his brother Reginald holding his lands and towns after him.

The fact that items 1a and 1b are written in Latin could suggest that the French-language *Genealogy of the Lords of Brecknock* relied on a Latin source for its post-Gerald section that bore some relationship to the

---

[62] Dugdale 18, fol. 29ᵛ.

texts copied by Dugdale. One can imagine the compiler of the *Genealogy* working with more than one Latin source. But, without a medieval copy of the genealogies of the earls of Hereford, it is impossible to make conclusions about their exact relationship. Nevertheless, their existence suggests that several versions of this family history circulated and were significant to more than one branch of the family. Both the Bohuns and the Hastings seem to have needed this information recorded.

Apart from these textual parallels, the genealogies of the earls of Hereford and the *Genealogy of the Lords of Brecknock* differ in some important respects. Though they have a common interest in the splitting of the Braose inheritance among female descendants, the genealogies of the earls of Hereford in Dugdale 18 are less interested in the fate of the lordship of Brecon in the hands of the Bohuns (the suspected patrons of *Genealogy of the Lords of Brecknock*) than the passing of the lordship of Abergavenny to the Hastings family. Item 2b, for example, labours to explain how Abergavenny and Cilgerran passed to John I Hastings (1262–1313). The lordship passed from Eve de Braose (d. 1255) and her husband William III de Cantilupe (d. 1254) to her son George Cantilupe (1251–73). George died young, at the age of 22, which meant the inheritance passed to his sister Joanna Cantilupe, wife of Henry Hastings (d. 1269), and then to her son John I Hastings (see Figure 3.3). This was a tricky moment of succession, and it occurred because, as is typical in these texts, William V de Braose had no sons, and neither did George Cantilupe. Additionally, John I Hastings, which item 2b explains, was 7 years old when his father died. He was a ward of the king until he reached the age of majority, and, as mentioned above, his eventual father-in-law, William de Valence, earl of Pembroke (d. 1296), cared for his lands during his minority. John held onto his lands despite his aunt Millicent's attempt to claim the Abergavenny portion of the inheritance.[63] When he came of age, he did homage to the king for his possessions *par sa lettre qu'est enrolle apres* 'according to the charter that was recorded afterwards' and married William de Valence's daughter Isabel (d. 1305).[64] As stated previously, the tenuousness of the inheritance during John's minority would have been a strong motivator for delineating this complicated line of succession.

---

[63] While Joanna inherited the lordship of Abergavenny, her sister Millicent, wife of Eudo de la Zouche from 1268–79, inherited their brother's other estates; see Nicholas Vincent, 'Cantilupe, Sir George de (1251–1273)', *ODNB*, accessed 2 February 2022.

[64] Dugdale 18, fol. 30ʳ.

Items 3, 4, and 5 are interested in the Hastings's past—namely, the bigger picture of several Hastings ancestors, including William Marshal, earl of Pembroke (relevant because he was the great-grandfather of Isabel de Valence), Ada of Huntingdon (daughter of David of Scotland, and mother of Henry Hastings, who married Joanna Cantilupe), and William Brewer (d. 1226, father of Griselle, wife of Reginald de Braose). The overall intent seems to be to show that the Hastings have illustrious ancestry (see Figures 3.4, 3.5, and 3.6).

In terms of date, the most recent living people described in item 3, which delineates the many families descending from William Marshal and Isabel de Clare's ten adult children, are the children of Isabel de Valence and John I Hastings.[65] These children's birth and death dates provide approximate date ranges for the writing of item 3, placing it in the first half of the fourteenth century—that is, during the lifetime of John II Hastings (1287–1325). Out of all the descendants of William Marshal, the Hastings family line is described in the most detail in this group of texts. Most of the other families are described only to the second or third generation, suggesting again that a Hastings family member was the intended audience.

Collectively, these genealogies from Dugdale 18, as well as the *Genealogy of the Lords of Brecknock*, its associated Llanthony Priory histories, and the genealogical diagram of the lords of Brecon in Cotton Roll XIV 12, exhibit a keen focus on the complexities of succession and inheritance through generations of marcher families. Amidst marriages, premature deaths, conquests, and a lack of male heirs in a system of primogeniture, it was necessary to record family histories to ensure that present conditions—lands, titles, and other major currencies of power in the March of Wales—were justified, maintained, and handed down to the next generation in a stable manner. The *Genealogy of the Lords of Brecknock* attests to a close relationship between family and priory, providing important clues about the relationship between literary production and the preservation of family memory and, with it,

---

[65] These children are William, who marries Eleanor, daughter of William Martin; Joan, who marries Edmund Martin and then William de Huntingfield; Elizabeth, who marries Roger Grey, 1st Lord Grey of Ruthin (*c.*1300–53); John II (1287–1325), who marries Juliana de Leybourne, countess of Huntingdon (1303/4–67); Henry, a cleric; and Margaret, who marries William, son of William Martin of Cemais. See Figure 3.3.

ANCESTRAL MEMORY | 145

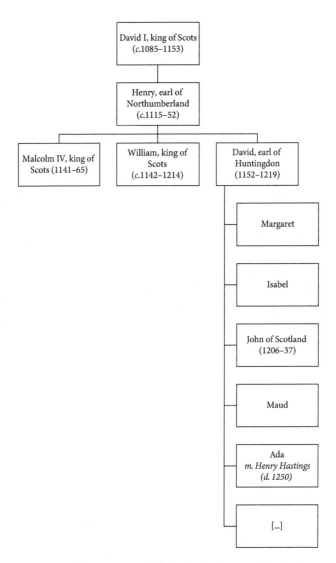

FIGURE 3.4 The ancestry of Ada of Huntingdon according to Dugdale 18, item 3.

146 | REIMAGINING THE PAST IN THE BORDERLANDS

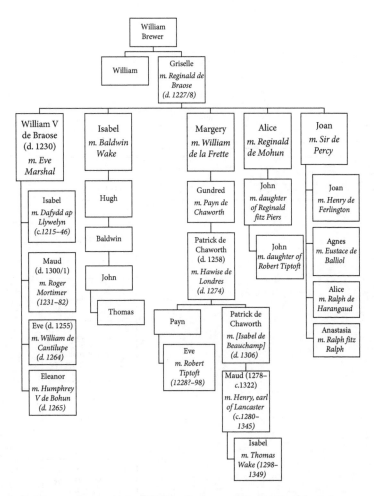

FIGURE 3.5 Descendants of William Brewer according to Dugdale 18, item 4.

lasting power. Texts like these genealogies were probably commissioned by families seeking to define their family's line of succession at moments in time when it was uncertain or tenuous; texts like the *History of Llanthony Priory* were, on the other hand, probably intended to solicit benefaction and encourage piety and gifts on the part of the nobility. The texts discussed in this chapter shaped readers' impressions of the past and provided families with information about their ancestors in a manner that encoded their rights to valuable lordships. This was particularly important in the shifting political arena of the March of Wales, where regional power was dependent on the actions and ambitions of individuals, and rulership of Welsh conquest territories required ideological justification and defence.

For these patrons and readers, family memory was in a sense indistinguishable from hereditary right, succession, and political power. It relied on recollecting details that were not actually one's own memories, but instead depended on other people to preserve and pass down information in the form of textual production: information that was stored, compiled from disparate sources, and available for recollection when necessary. Owing to the skill and expense of producing manuscript books, for a noble family this process necessitated a good relationship with an abbey and the economic conditions necessary for creating such

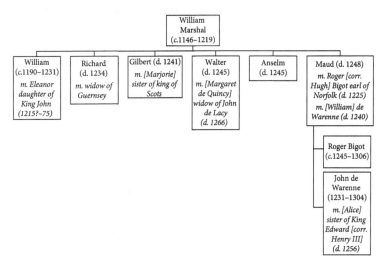

FIGURE 3.6   Descendants of William Marshal according to Dugdale 18, item 5.

148 | REIMAGINING THE PAST IN THE BORDERLANDS

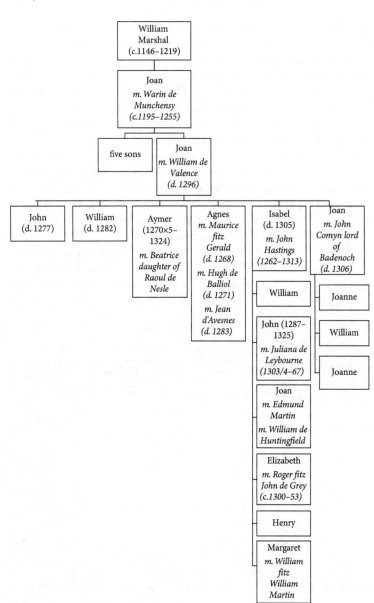

FIGURE 3.6 (*Continued*)

ANCESTRAL MEMORY | 149

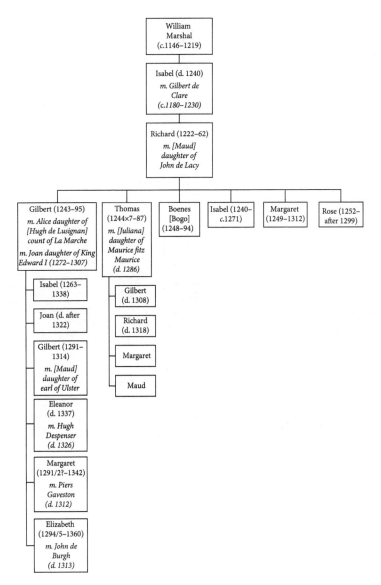

FIGURE 3.6   (Continued)

150 | REIMAGINING THE PAST IN THE BORDERLANDS

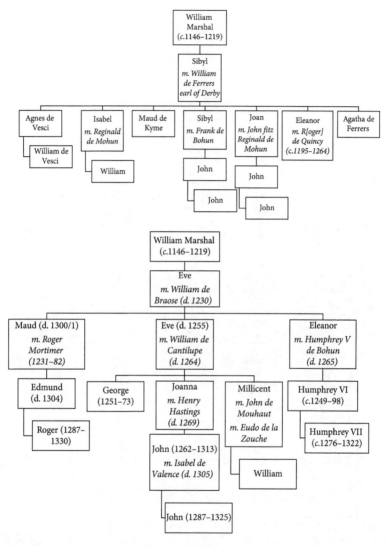

FIGURE 3.6 (Continued)

expensive objects—the relationship between abbey and patron that was so mutually beneficial in the Middle Ages. For a noble patron, relying on one's ancestors to store, process, and hand down information was a practice that reinforced the line of succession—a family had to be wealthy and privileged enough to employ people to preserve their history, which then helped reinforce their wealth and privilege. A written family history was a display of the wealth, achievement, and success of that family. The preservation of family memory also came in the form of prayers for the soul of deceased family members, monuments, gravestones, epitaphs, and elegies, all of which would be preserved by a monastery, sustaining the legacies of individuals for future members of the family. The relationship between patron and monastery was thus focused on planning for the future: the nobility ensured their entry into heaven after death by making sure that monks would pray for them, while the preservation of information in books helped ensure that land and title would stay in the hands of the family's heirs.

In the case of the March of Wales, and the texts detailed in this chapter, one can discern further motivations for writing down family histories. It was a collective effort that encoded colonization into the family's past.[66] The beginning of the *Genealogy of the Lords of Brecknock* depicts the early conquest period, during the 'land grab' of Welsh conquest territories by Norman elites. During this period, it was necessary to establish claims to land, when those lands were won by right of conquest and were disputed by Welsh princes or by English administrative jurisdiction—a major theme of marcher baronial literature. The recording of such information was a mutual effort between monastery and patron that benefited both parties, as ecclesiastical institutions were also participating in the acquisition and consolidation of Welsh lands, and used textual production to do so, as John Reuben Davies has shown.[67] This practice evolved, after the Edwardian conquest of Wales, to one focused on the continuities of dynastic succession, as seen in the genealogies discussed in this chapter, and another key theme of marcher baronial literature. The relationship between monastery and patron remained mutually beneficial, but the motivation for writing family history was not only about ensuring ownership of conquered land, but also about solidifying memory of the family as a successful

[66] Mary Carruthers, *The Book of Memory: A Study of Memory in Medieval Culture*, 2nd edn (Cambridge, 2008).
[67] John Reuben Davies, 'The Saints of South Wales and the Welsh Church', in Alan Thacker and Richard Sharpe (eds), *Local Saints and Local Churches in the Early Medieval West* (Oxford, 2002), 361–95.

entity that was enduring, virtuous, and able to maintain continuous control over land and title over a long period of time. Monasteries wrote their own histories for the same reasons, recording their long-standing rights to certain lands and the benefits they received from various rulers. In several manuscripts and texts discussed in this book, these practices were intertwined. This practice of textual production consolidated legends and myths about a family that initially would have been told orally into something that could be preserved for the future on durable parchment.

As part of this process of defining a line of succession in writing, in its historical context, a particular sense of marcher identity was articulated: families were anchored in the March; their presence in the region (which was the result of conquest and colonization efforts, initially) was shown to be long-standing and justified. Marcher family histories made sense of a family's establishment of its dynasty in the March as well as the continuity of that dynasty over time. This was particularly important when their presence in the region was disputed, either by Welsh princes or by the English Crown, which would have heightened the significance of any issues of succession. Efforts to place themselves in the historical and geographical context of the March of Wales through the writing of history was an important part of the negotiation of identity and ethnic difference that is characteristic of a border culture. As seen in the previous chapter of this book, which discussed the Mortimer family genealogies, in some cases the writing of marcher family history could raise families from obscure beginnings to the highest reaches of political power. In the following chapter, which discusses the romance of *Fouke le fitz Waryn*, we will see how such efforts could be aided by a further adorning of marcher family history in the trappings of Galfridian and Arthurian romance.

4

Romance and Identity

While previous chapters have dealt with historical and genealogical writing associated with marcher families and monasteries, Chapters 4 and 5 turn to literary texts, specifically romance literature and poetry, directed at vernacular readerships in the March of Wales. These texts are avenues through which the use and impact of ideas of the legendary British past in the March of Wales can be evaluated. Romances provide a teleological scope through which now-familiar marcher themes are articulated. They are a useful counterpoint to the marcher histories and genealogies discussed in previous chapters, offering a broader imaginative context in which Geoffrey's vision of the British past was explored and reframed by a marcher baronial readership.[1]

In this chapter, I discuss three romances that originated in a borderland context, evaluating each in turn for the interests that convey the lived experiences of a border culture and its negotiation of identity and belonging in a border context. The French-language romance of *Fouke le Fitz Waryn*, set initially in Shropshire and redacted by the fourteenth-century Harley scribe of Herefordshire, depicts the disinheritance of Fouke III de Warin (d. 1258) and his subsequent adventures during exile

---

[1] This readership would have been multilingual in character, active in reading English, Welsh, and French vernaculars, as well as Latin. Unless otherwise noted, translations are my own.

on the continent and in Wales, where he is assisted by Welsh princes Llywelyn ab Iorwerth (c.1173–1240) and Gwenwynwyn ab Owain Cyfeiliog (d. 1216). This romance offers a key articulation of marcher identity that draws upon proximity to and knowledge of Wales and Welsh culture to underscore a rejection of English political control. This chapter argues that the themes of marcher literature discussed throughout this book (particularly defensive ownership of and claim to land in Wales and the March of Wales, involvement with Welsh princes and the Welsh past, the idea of women as key players in lines of succession of lordships, and a firm grounding in the legendary history of Geoffrey of Monmouth's *De gestis Britonum*) are central to the romance of *Fouke le Fitz Waryn*, and aid the articulation of a particular kind of marcher identity that emerged from a border culture that was preoccupied with issues of seeking and maintaining political power and autonomy. By contrast, the thirteenth-century French-language *History of William Marshal* portrays the exceptional life of William Marshal, 1st earl of Pembroke (c.1146–1219) as praiseworthy and virtuous. It puts forward an example of an aristocrat whose relationship with his marcher lands was primarily exploitative rather than immersive or identity-forming. In other words, this text depicts a different marcher perspective, that of the colonial outsider using marcher lands and titles to consolidate power, not in the local region of the March of Wales, but in the arena of the English royal court and its interests in France. It offers a counterpoint to *Fouke* in its indifference—even cruelty—towards the predicaments of borderland inhabitants, and thus highlights the potency of *Fouke*'s articulation of the marcher culture defined in this book. The chapter concludes with discussion of the Anglo-Scottish borderlands romance *The Awntyrs off Arthure at the Terne Wathelyn* (c.1430), written in Middle English, which displays similar anxieties about land rights and political authority, but in a different border context.

For clarification of marcher identity as discussed in this chapter, it would be useful to refer to the definitions of the identity terms 'Welsh', 'marcher', and 'English' in the Introduction and the accompanying discussion of the inescapable binaries present in a border culture, which is, by definition, sandwiched between two or more other cultures.[2] I define 'marcher' identity as a third category of identity that was

[2] See pp. 17–23 for further discussion.

both/and/neither English nor Welsh, with fluid boundaries and multiple opportunities for 'code-switching' as part of identity performance. The romance of *Fouke le Fitz Waryn* does a great deal to articulate this marcher identity and to demonstrate how border figures like Fouke were able to blur the boundaries between 'English' and 'Welsh' identities in their articulation of the third category. However, the existence of marcher identity as defined in this book does not preclude the existence of 'English' or 'Welsh' identities that existed within or indeed beyond the March of Wales. There were aspects of English, Welsh, marcher, and other cultures in the March of Wales, all at the same time, and inhabitants of the March would have been aware of cultural differences and, in some cases, able to perform different identities depending on the social context. In addition, contemporary sources document localized awareness of what it meant to be 'English' or 'Welsh' at the time, making it difficult to escape a binary definition of 'English vs Welsh'. One hopes that the present discussion of marcher literature, in staking claim to a third category of identity in the region, complicates the traditional binary.

The romance of *Fouke le Fitz Waryn*

The Anglo-French romance *Fouke le Fitz Waryn* (henceforth *Fouke*) was originally written in the mid-thirteenth century. It is extant in one manuscript copy (London, British Library, Royal 12 C. xii, s. xiv[in]), a trilingual miscellany of Ludlow provenance written by the well-known Harley scribe.[3] It has been called an 'ancestral romance', a 'family romance', a 'legalistic romance of the outlaw type', and an 'exilic narrative'.[4] These terms reflect the difficulty of categorizing the text, which lies somewhere between the two poles of romance and history (which

---

[3] For Ludlow provenance, see Carter Revard, 'Scribe and Provenance', in Susanna Fein (ed.), *Studies in the Harley Manuscript: The Scribes, Contents, and Social Contexts of British Library MS Harley 2253* (Kalamazoo, 2000), 21–110, at 24. For the scribe, see Revard, 'Scribe and Provenance', 58–61, 69–73; *FFW*, pp. xxxviii–xliv. For related discussion in Chapter 1, see pp. 61–3.

[4] Ralph Hanna, 'The Matter of Fulk: Romance and History in the Marches', *Journal of English and Germanic Philology*, 110/3 (2011), 337–58, at 337; M. Dominica Legge, *Anglo-Norman Literature and its Background* (Oxford, 1963), 139, 171–5; Catherine Rock, 'Fouke le Fitz Waryn and King John: Rebellion and Reconciliation', in Alexander L. Kaufman

indeed were not necessarily separate genres for medieval audiences). Its subject is the real-life marcher baron Fouke (Fulk) III of Whittington (d. 1258).[5] In a flagrant display of royal overreach, Fouke is dispossessed of his lands by King John, who gives Whittington to Moris, son of Roger de Powys. Fouke kills Moris and goes into exile, where he has many adventures involving robbery, tournaments, disguises, marriage proposals, and battles with giants and dragons. He journeys to Wales, Scotland, Ireland, Brittany, Norway, Gotland, Barbary, and Spain. He has many helpers, including a nobleman called Robert fitz Sampson in the march of Scotland and Llywelyn ab Iorwerth, prince of Gwynedd (c.1173–1240).[6] Eventually he is pardoned by King John and regains his inheritance. He founds a priory near the river Severn called Alberbury, has children with Clarice d'Auberville, and is buried at New Abbey. The tale is framed by Galfridian historical context: an extensive prologue describes the arrival of Brutus and the overthrow of giants in the region of Whittington, and a Merlinic prophecy prefaces Fouke's death.

Many of the characters in the romance are real historical figures. Roger de Powys did indeed hold the castle of Whittington, and it was granted to his son Moris (Meurig) by King John.[7] The real Fouke (III) was outlawed from 1200–3 following a rebellion against King John, and he took possession of Whittington Castle in 1203 (for the Fitz Warin

(ed.), *British Outlaws of Literature and History: Essays on Medieval and Early Modern Figures from Robin Hood to Twm Shon Catty* (Jefferson, NC, 2011), 67–96, at 67; Susan Crane, 'Anglo-Norman Romances of English Heroes: "Ancestral Romance"?' *Romance Philology*, 35/4 (1982), 601–8.

[5] For background, see Max Lieberman, *The Medieval March of Wales: The Creation and Perception of a Frontier, 1066–1283*, Cambridge Studies in Medieval Life and Thought, 78 (Cambridge, 2010), 86–7, 94–5, 98–9; Janet Meisel, *Barons of the Welsh Frontier: The Corbut, Pantulf, and Fitz Warin Families, 1066–1272* (Lincoln, 1980), 34–54, 87–100, 112–17, 121–2.

[6] Llywelyn ab Iorwerth is widely viewed as the dominant political power in Wales from c.1210 to 1240, ruling over a greater swathe of territory than any Welsh ruler since the early Middle Ages. He was married to Joan (d. 1237), natural daughter of King John, and was sometimes allied and sometimes in conflict with English kings and marcher lords. His father was Iorwerth Drwyndwn (Iorwerth 'flat- or broken-nosed'), also mentioned in *Fouke*.

[7] David Stephenson, '*Fouke le Fitz Waryn* and Llywelyn ap Gruffudd's Claim to Whittington', *Transactions of the Shropshire Historical and Archaeological Society*, 78 (2002), 26–31, at 26.

family line, see Figure 4.1).[8] The Fitz Warins held Whittington until at least 1264; it was granted to Llywelyn ap Gruffudd (d. 1282) in the Treaty of Montgomery in 1267.[9] The Welsh characters Iorwerth Drwyndwn (*Yervard Droyndoun*), Gwenwynwyn ab Owain (*Guenonwyn le fitz Yweyn*), and Llywelyn ab Iorwerth (*Lewys/Lowis le prince de Walys*) are also historical figures.[10] Other characters, like Sir Ernalt de Lyls, are fictitious.

The extant manuscript copy, which dates to c.1325–30, represents a French-language prose adaptation of an earlier, non-extant verse romance in French, with some of the verse surviving embedded in the prose.[11] The original verse romance, written in octosyllabic couplets, was probably composed for a wealthy household in the borough of Ludlow.[12] Linguistically it dates to the end of the thirteenth century.[13] Though it does not survive, John Leland saw a version in French octosyllabic couplets in the 1530s or 1540s.[14] He saw an additional version in fourteenth-century English alliterative verse that also does not survive.[15] Given that Fouke is referenced in a number of fourteenth-century Welsh court poems, it has also been suggested that a Welsh-language romance circulated, though it is more likely that Welsh poets accessed the French version. In any case, the extant text represents 'a popular medieval narrative tradition that reverberated in all three of the March's

---

[8] See Stephenson, '*Fouke*', 26–8; Frederick Suppe, *Military Institutions on the Welsh Marches: Shropshire, AD 1066–1300*, Studies in Celtic History, 14 (Woodbridge, 1994), 166–9; Meisel, *Barons*, 36–40, 132–8.

[9] Stephenson, '*Fouke*', 26.

[10] See Max Lieberman, 'The English and the Welsh in Fouke le Fitz Waryn', *Thirteenth-Century England*, 12 (2009), 1–11, at 4; Stephenson, '*Fouke*', 27; *FFW* 27.

[11] See Hanna, 'Matter of Fulk', 337; *FFW*, pp. xix–xx.

[12] *FFW*, pp. ix, xxi; Meisel, *Barons*, 53.

[13] For the language of the text, see *FFW*, pp. xxi, liii–cxvi. Stephenson suggests it was written soon after the death of Fouke IV (the son of the Fouke depicted in the story) while fighting the Battle of Lewes in 1264, and certainly after the titular character Fouke died in 1258; see '*Fouke*', 28–9. Legge suggests this rewriting was done for Fouke V, grandson of the Fouke in the tale; see *Anglo-Norman Literature*, 171. See Figure 4.1 for family tree.

[14] *FFW*, pp. xxi–xxvi.

[15] Hanna, 'Matter of Fulk', 355.

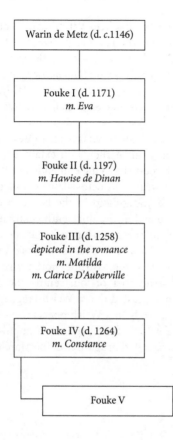

FIGURE 4.1 The Fitz Warin family.

vernaculars'.[16] The text's multiple forms suggest ongoing relevance to the Fitz Warin family over time.[17]

The Harley scribe, who wrote Royal 12 C. xii, is also known for writing two other important compilations of literature in English, French, and Latin: London, British Library, Harley 2253, and parts of London,

---

[16] Joshua Byron Smith, 'Fouke le Fitz Waryn', in Jocelyn Wogan-Browne, Thelma Fenster, and Delbert W. Russell (eds), *Vernacular Literary Theory from the French of Medieval England: Texts and Translations, c.1120–c.1450* (Cambridge, 2016), 293–302, at 294–5; for the Welsh poems, see pp. 175–6.

[17] Hanna, 'Matter of Fulk', 358.

British Library, Harley 273, all most likely written in or near Ludlow.[18] There is general agreement that the Harley scribe adapted the original verse text into its current prose form.[19] He put Royal 12 C. xii together over a period of years in the manner of a commonplace book.[20] *Fouke* is copied in two stints, the first between 1325 and 1327, and the second in the mid-1330s, in a one-column layout rather than the two-column layout that is typical of French verse romance.[21] A historicist reading places the prose romance in the context of the unpopular, short-lived efforts by Hugh Despenser the Younger (d. 1326) to disrupt the hereditary descent of property in the March of Wales in the 1320s.[22]

Fouke's classification as an 'ancestral romance' places it in the milieu of *Bevis of Hampton*, *Guy of Warwick*, *King Horn*, *Havelok the Dane*, *Gamelyn*, *Waldef*, and *Athelston*, stories in which young nobles are exiled and go on adventures before returning to claim their inheritance in England, or with *Les Quatre Fils Aymoun*, a *chanson de geste* in which nobles outlawed from Charlemagne's court take control of royal land.[23] The term 'ancestral romance' refers to these texts' preoccupation with baronial interests, such as land tenure, legality, seigneurial rights, honour, idealized leadership qualities, and family security.[24] This generic context is important, but, in the regional context of the March, *Fouke* must also be compared to texts similarly interested in the lands and livelihoods of marcher lords, such as those discussed in this book: the genealogy of the earls of Hereford, chronicles and genealogies

---

[18] For discussion, see Ch. 1, pp. 61–3.
[19] Revard, 'Scribe and Provenance', 29–30; *FFW*, p. xxxvii.
[20] Revard, 'Scribe and Provenance', 60–1.
[21] There has been speculation about the reasons for this ten-year break; see Revard, 'Scribe and Provenance', 71; Jason O'Rourke, 'Imagining Book Production in Fourteenth-Century Herefordshire: The Scribe of British Library, MS Harley 2253 and his "Organizing Principles"', in Stephen Kelly and John J. Thompson (eds), *Imagining the Book* (Turnhout, 2005), 45–69, at 55; Matthew Fisher, *Scribal Authorship and the Writing of History in Medieval England* (Columbus, 2012), 144.
[22] Hanna, 'Matter of Fulk', 357; for context, see David Stephenson, *Medieval Wales, c.1050–1332: Centuries of Ambiguity* (Cardiff, 2019), 150.
[23] For discussion, see Hanna, 'Matter of Fulk', 337–8, 350–1; Roger Pensom, 'Inside and Outside: Fact and Fiction in *Fouke le Fitz Waryn*', *Medium Ævum*, 63 (1994), 53–60; Timothy Jones, 'Geoffrey of Monmouth, "Fouke le Fitz Waryn", and National Mythology', *Studies in Philology*, 91/3 (1994), 233–49, at 247; Crane, 'Anglo-Norman Romances'.
[24] For a critique of this label as too narrow, see Crane, 'Anglo-Norman Romances'.

associated with the Mortimers and the de Braoses, and the *Epitome historiae Britanniae*.[25] Its marcher context has been attended to in various historicist readings, but not with regard to this body of marcher baronial literature and its attendant themes.

There is little scholarly consensus, furthermore, about the positioning of the March in *Fouke*. Ralph Hanna sees Shropshire as self-aware of its position on a periphery, 'looking back into England from the edge', and *Fouke* as depicting the foundation of 'a second Britain' in an 'otherwise savage and/or unoccupied territory in the West'.[26] In other words, Shropshire is operating on a periphery at the edges of known civilization. Conversely, Matthew Lampitt emphasizes a non-Anglocentric, 'global world-view' in *Fouke*, in which marcher culture 'present[s] itself not as the western periphery of an English power to which it is assimilable, but [located] ... in a global geography'.[27] Similarly, Emily Dolmans sees *Fouke* as imagining the March to be borderless, and a central part of Britain, and 'the border between England and Wales ... merely semiotic'.[28] These contrasting views exemplify the scholarly tension between viewing marcher literature as self-consciously peripheral and as confidently destabilizing Anglophone culture (typically seen as the centre in the centre/periphery model) by presenting itself as globally connected.

The text's attitude towards the Welsh is also unresolved. Recent studies have emphasized its lack of separate ethnic descriptors and labels for Welsh and English, which challenges our expectations of perceived ethnic difference. Dolmans and Lampitt, for example, point out that Fouke and Llywelyn ab Iorwerth share a class identity and a language that transcends ethnic or cultural differences.[29] Elsewhere, Dolmans notes

[25] For discussion of French marcher literature, particularly Hue de Roteland's *Ipomedon*, see Matthew Siôn Lampitt, 'Networking the March: The Literature of the Welsh Marches, c.1180–c.1410' (unpublished Ph.D. dissertation, King's College London, 2019).
[26] Hanna, 'Matter of Fulk', 355, 338, 341.
[27] Lampitt, 'Networking the March: Literature', 104.
[28] Emily Dolmans, 'Locating the Border: Britain and the Welsh Marches in *Fouke le Fitz Waryn*', *New Medieval Literatures*, 16 (2016), 109–34, at 110, 133, 126; Emily Dolmans, *Writing Regional Identities in Medieval England: From the Gesta Herwardi to Richard Coer de Lyon* (Cambridge, 2020), 97–132, at 102.
[29] Dolmans, 'Locating the Border', 124; Dolmans, *Writing Regional Identities*, 117–20; Lampitt, 'Networking the March: Literature', 154–5.

that the romance presents 'a Marcher identity that connects, rather than divides, the English and the Welsh'.[30] Max Lieberman similarly observes only an implicit distinction between English and Welsh: 'This was probably because there was just nothing very alien about the Welsh as far as the intended audience was concerned'.[31] On the other hand, Timothy Jones argues that the story justifies the Edwardian conquest of Wales, and Hanna emphasizes the March as a wasteland ready for conquest.[32] These various interpretations attest to the slipperiness of marcher identity's relationship to Wales, as the marchers are both conquerors of and assimilators to Welsh culture.

This chapter examines *Fouke* as a marcher text, demonstrating that it is anchored in particularly marcher interests (which are not exclusively English nor Welsh interests) that emerge only when one considers the greater context of the marcher literature discussed in this book. Marcher interests were variable and depended on the particular circumstances of the family or individual under discussion; in this case, we see how a Shropshire family of Norman origins negotiated its presence in the region by performing Welshness in sometimes surprising ways. In the marcher context, it becomes apparent that *Fouke* adheres to three key themes of marcher literature: first, a keen interest in the Welsh past, particularly the strain of British history and prophecy indebted to Geoffrey of Monmouth; second, a focus on lordships' lines of succession, particularly as marcher women were often key inheritors of lordships; and, three, defensive ownership of and claim to lands in Wales and the borderlands. These themes are characteristic of a marcher family situating itself in the history of the March of Wales and Britain more broadly. In addition, the unusual legal and social status of the marcher lords, as discussed in the Introduction, gave rise to a particular strain of independence from English royal control that plays out in this text, both through the outlaw narrative and through an affinity with the Welsh princes' independence from the English Crown.[33]

---

[30] Dolmans, *Writing Regional Identities*, 102.
[31] Lieberman, 'The English and the Welsh', 7.
[32] Timothy Jones, 'Geoffrey of Monmouth', 235; Hanna, 'Matter of Fulk', 346.
[33] Similar observations are made by Hanna, 'Matter of Fulk', 338–9; Dolmans, 'Locating the Border', 123–4.

The Galfridian framework of the romance of *Fouke le Fitz Waryn*

First, *Fouke* takes particular inspiration from Galfridian history and prophecy, apparent in both its manuscript context and the plot. In Royal 12 C. xii, *Fouke* appears alongside extracts from the *Prophetiae Merlini*, other Merlinic prophecies,[34] a chronicle of English history from Brutus called the *Short English Metrical Chronicle* (which the Harley scribe had a hand in modifying[35]), and various prognostications, scientific verses, fortunes, and medical diagrams (see Table 4.1). The prophecies and the chronicle, both reliant on Geoffrey, place the romance in the broader context of the ancient British past and bring broader historical significance to Fouke's fight for his inheritance. Matthew Fisher notes that the *Short English Metrical Chronicle* 'narrates the history of the island of Britain, divided into the three conventional periods of *translatio imperii* as constructed by insular historiography: legendary British history (Galfridian), Anglo-Saxon history... and post-Conquest history'.[36] The Harley scribe and any readers of his miscellany would have been aware that *Fouke* fit into this larger scheme.

Galfridian connections are also explicit within the romance, which opens with a foundation legend about Fouke's ancestral home, *Blanche Launde* in Shropshire. The castle is founded on the very place where Corineus, companion of Brutus and founder of Cornwall, fought with the giant Goemagog and tossed him off the island:

---

[34] The prophecies in Royal 12 C. xii are: a prophecy for 1325 (fol. 6^r), a prophecy for 1293 (fol. 6^v), a prophecy and explanation beginning 'Quia antiqui mistice loqui cupientes' (fols. 14^r–15^r), a prophecy attributed to Methodius (fol. 15^r), a prophecy beginning 'Ni pax formetur' (fol. 15^r), the *Prophecy of Merlin Silvester* beginning 'Catulus linxius' (fol. 15^v), the prophecy of the lily and lion beginning 'Hermerus deus sapientum' (fol. 16^r), and 'The Holy Oil of St Thomas' (fol. 16^v). The prophecy beginning 'Catulus linxius' is discussed by Lesley A. Coote, *Prophecy and Public Affairs in Later Medieval England* (Woodbridge, 2000), 78–82, though not in relation to this manuscript.

[35] For an edition of this chronicle, see *The Abridged English Metrical Brut edited from London, British Library MS Royal 12 C. XII*, ed. Una O'Farrell-Tate (Heidelberg, 2002), 46–50; for discussion, see Fisher, *Scribal Authorship*, 116–41; Thorlac Turville-Petre, *England the Nation: Language, Literature, and National Identity, 1290–1340* (Oxford, 1996), 75, 108–11, 174–5, 180.

[36] Fisher, *Scribal Authorship*, 117.

TABLE 4.1 The contents of Royal 12 C. xii

Unit 1

1^{r-v}	office in honour of Thomas of Lancaster
2^r–3^v	charters of Edward I and Henry III
4^r–6^v	hymns, prayers, verses, proverbs
7^{r-v}	satirical verses in Latin, French, and English; medical notes in Latin and French

Unit 2

8^r–10^v	arithmetical and other puzzles in Latin
11^r–13^r	cooking recipes in Latin and French
13^r–16^v	**prophecies, including extracts from Geoffrey of Monmouth's *Prophetiae Merlini***

Unit 3

17^r–32^v	*Merour d'eglise* by Edmund Rich, archbishop of Canterbury (1234–40)

Unit 4

33^r–60^v	***Fouke le Fitz Waryn***
61^r	chant hymn from the Corpus Christi office
61^v	blank
62^r–68^v	***Brut* Chronicle to 1312 in English (*Short English Metrical Chronicle*)**

Unit 5

69^r–76^r	*Amys and Amylion* [not written by the Harley scribe]
76^v	hymn to Mary and poem on the vanity of life

Unit 6

77r–91^v	Treatises, medical notes, prognostications
91^v–94^r	*Secret des secrets*
94^r–105^v	scientific verses and fortune-telling
105^v–107^v	medical, chiromantic texts and diagrams

Unit 7

108^r–123^v	*Liber experimentarius* of astrological verses translated from Arabic into Latin [not written by the Harley scribe]

Source: The contents of this table are taken from the British Library Archives and Manuscripts online catalogue, http://searcharchives.bl.uk/IAMS_VU2:LSCOP_BL:IAMS040-002106725, accessed 27 October 2022.

Jadys vindrent en cest pays Brutus, un chevalier mout vaylaunt, e Coryneus, de qy Cornewayle ad uncore le noun, e plusours autres, estretz du lignage troyene, e nul n'y habita ces parties, estre tre[s] lede gentz, grantz geans, dount lur roy fust apelee Geomagog. Cyl oyerent de la venue Brutus, e se mistrent en la voye a l'encountre, e al dreyn furent tous lé geantz occys, estre Geomagog, qe fust mervilous grant. Coryneus, le valyant, dist que volenters luttreyt ou Geomagog, pur esprover la force Geomagog. Le geant, a la premere venue, embraça Coryneus si estroitement qu'il debrusa ces trois costes. Coryneus se coroça, si fery Geomagog del pee qu'il chay de un grant roche en la mer, e si fust Geomagog neyé.

Once upon a time, Brutus, a very valiant knight, came to this country, as did Corineus, from whom Cornwall gets its name, and many others originating from the lineage of Troy. No one lived in these parts except for a vile race of people, great giants, whose king was called Geomagog. They heard of the arrival of Brutus and set out to confront him. In the end all the giants were killed except for Geomagog, who was astonishingly tall. Corineus, the valiant, said he would gladly do combat with Geomagog in order to test the latter's strength. At the first onset the giant grasped Corineus so tightly that he broke three of his ribs. Corineus became angry and gave Geomagog such a hard kick that he fell into the sea from a great rock. Thus Geomagog was drowned.[37]

The author is here drawing from Geoffrey of Monmouth's *De gestis Britonum* I.21 (hereafter *DGB*).[38] The story of the giants who inhabited Britain before Brutus and the Trojans arrived was particularly popular in fourteenth-century England, and is extant in several embellished retellings, including the Anglo-French poem *Des grantz geanz*, the Latin text *De origine gigantum*, and the Latin Prose *Brut* discussed in Chapter 2.[39] In *Fouke*, Geomagog's corpse is possessed by an evil

---

[37] *FFW* 4; trans. Burgess, 133. It should be said that the sea is nowhere near Shropshire, and the fight between Corineus and Geomagog at *Blanche Launde* is imagined.

[38] *DGB* i.21, pp. 26–9.

[39] See pp. 77, 85; Hélène Bellon-Méguelle, 'Une œuvre protéiforme: Mises en prose et dérimage des Grantz Geanz', in Paola Cifarelli, Maria Colombo Timelli, Matteo Milani, and Anne Schoysman (eds), *Raconter en prose, xive-xvie siècle*, Encounters 279, Medieval Civilization, 21 (Paris, 2017), 355–66; James P. Carley and Julia Crick, 'Constructing Albion's Past: An Annotated Edition of *De origine gigantum*', *Arthurian Literature*, 13 (1995), 41–114.

spirit who returns to the site of the battle and haunts the countryside.[40] The local King Bran's attempt to rebuild the city is thwarted by the devil stealing everything that was in the city and frightening away its people, rendering the land an uninhabitable waste.[41] By implication, Corineus' defeat of the giants—and the Britons' claim to the island—is incomplete.

Fouke then departs from Geoffrey as a source, though maintaining thematic similarities. Centuries later, William the Conqueror's cousin Payn Peverel hears of the haunted castle and decides to seek out the possessed giant. He defeats the giant with the help of divine intercession:

> Se cocha a la terre, e ou bone devocioun pria Dieu e sa mere Marie que ly defendreynt cele nuyt del poer de deble. A peyne out fyny sa preere, vynt le malfee en semblance Geomagog, e si porta un grant masue en sa mayn, e de sa bouche geta fu e femee ... Le deble, par vertu de la croys, fust tut enpoury e perdy force, quar yl ne poeit adeser la croys. Payn le pursywy, qui'l ly fery de l'espee, qu'il comença crier, e chey tut plat a terre, e se rendy mat.

> [Payn] lay down on the ground and with true devotion prayed to God and his mother Mary, asking them to defend him that night from the power of the Devil. Scarcely was [Payn's] prayer finished when the Devil arrived in the likeness of Geomagog. He carried a huge club in his hand, and from his mouth spewed fire and flame ... The Devil, through the power of the cross, became frightened and lost his strength, for he could not approach the cross. Payn pursued him, striking him with his sword in such a way that he began to cry out and fell flat on the ground in surrender.[42]

Following its defeat, the devil utters a verse prophecy, using animal imagery akin to Geoffrey's *Prophetiae Merlini*. It foresees that Payn's descendants will hold the land *ou grant estrif e guere* 'with great strife

---

[40] FFW 4.

[41] It is possible that King Bran is an eponym for Dinas Brân, an Iron Age hillfort and medieval castle site located some ten miles north-west of Whittington near Llangollen, Denbighshire. The name may have evoked the figure of an ancient Briton to the audience of the romance. I am grateful to Ben Guy for suggesting this point.

[42] FFW 5; trans. Burgess, 134.

and war'.[43] The prophecy comes true: William the Conqueror, astonished by the sight of Geomagog's body and his large club, gives Payn *Blanche Launde*, in which *Blancheville* (Whittington) is located. This episode sets the scene for Fouke's ancestral right to these lands, which extends back to this ancient time. Payn's actions run parallel to the events of *DGB* Book 1. He earns his land by defeating its devilish inhabitant, just as Brutus and Corineus conquered Britain by vanquishing the giants of Albion.

Lumbley reads Geoffrey's giants as 'racialized Others' whose monstrous bodies are racially marked.[44] They are an indigenous race conquered by the Britons, and their purpose in the narrative is to cement the settlers' imperial might.[45] By implication, Payn, who conquers *Blanche Launde*, establishes his own empire in the March of Wales. Dolmans observes, following Monika Otter, that the March is '*gaainable tere*, territory that can be taken, which has the potential to be cultivated and revitalized. The destruction of the March provides a blank slate upon which the Norman conquerors can inscribe their identities and where Marcher lords can create their own society.'[46] This civic foundation is explicitly Christian: Payn defeats the devil with God's help, implying a divine right to *Blanche Launde*.[47] His descendants' rights to this land are unquestioned, but they must wrest them from other claimants again and again, offering multiple opportunities to show bravery and worth in the face of injustice and royal overreach: William the Conqueror retakes Whittington, but offers Fouke's father a chance to regain it, and when Fouke himself is dispossessed of the land, he must regain it using his own skill, wit, and courage. All the while, Merlinic prophecies guide the family towards success, indicating that their ownership of *Blanche Launde* is predestined and inevitable. In this sense, the Payn Peverel episode folds eleventh-century events into the ancient

---

[43] *FFW* 6; trans. Burgess, 135.
[44] Coral Lumbley, 'Geoffrey of Monmouth and Race', in Georgia Henley and Joshua Byron Smith (eds), *A Companion to Geoffrey of Monmouth*, Brill's Companions to European History, 22 (Leiden, 2020), 369–96, at 384.
[45] Lumbley, 'Geoffrey of Monmouth and Race', 385.
[46] Dolmans, 'Locating the Border', 115.
[47] Timothy Jones suggests the author is implying that Brutus and Corineus failed to stamp out evil in Britain because they were pagan, and the conquest is complete only once it is a Christian one; see 'Geoffrey of Monmouth', 239.

British past and anchors it to a prophetic future, aligning it with a politics of empire that would have been familiar to a marcher baronial audience.

Related to this, it has been noted that the text uses the identity term 'Briton' rather than 'Welsh' to refer to the Welsh prince Maredudd ap Bleddyn of Powys (d. 1132), thus locating Welsh identity in an era before the Britons had lost the island to the English and became Welsh (according to Geoffrey of Monmouth).[48] While William the Conqueror lived well after the shift from Briton to Welsh described at the end of *DGB*, the use of the term 'Briton' elides the temporal distance between the eleventh century, when the Normans were overrunning parts of South Wales, and an earlier, legendary time when the Britons ruled the entire island. Payn's defeat of Geomagog has the same effect: by reframing the eleventh century in a Galfridian context, the text implies that Fouke's family has held *Blanche Launde* since ancient times and has a predestined right to do so.

Galfridian overtones are also present in several Merlinic prophecies uttered about Fouke.[49] In the Payn Peverel episode, the devil tells Payn of a wolf that will drive a boar out of *Blanche Launde*. The wolf will be challenged by a leopard, and he will eventually defeat the leopard and settle in his home.[50] Prophecy in the form of heraldic animals standing in as symbols for people recalls the *Prophetiae Merlini*, and the prophecy seems to foretell how Fouke (the wolf) will regain his inheritance from King John (the leopard). A version of this prophecy is uttered again towards the end of the romance, when Fouke is an old man. In this prophecy (one of the few sections of the text to preserve the verse exemplar), Merlin and Arthur are mentioned explicitly by name:

> Merlyn dit que
> En Bretaigne la Graunde
> Un lou vendra de la Blaunche Launde.
> .xii. dentz avera aguz,
> Sys desouz e sis desus.

---

[48] *DGB* xi.207, pp. 280–1; Lieberman, 'The English and the Welsh', 4–5; Dolmans, 'Locating the Border', 117.

[49] These are briefly discussed in Victoria Flood, *Prophecy, Politics and Place in Medieval England: From Geoffrey of Monmouth to Thomas of Erceldoune* (Woodbridge, 2016), 58–65.

[50] *FFW* 6.

> Cely avera si fer regard
> Qu'il enchacera le leopard
> Hors de la Blaunche Launde,
> Tant avera force e vertue graunde.
>
> Mes nous le savom qe Merlyn
> Le dit par Fouke le fitz Waryn,
> Quar chescun de vous deit estre ensur
> Qe en le temps le roy Arthur
> La Blaunche Launde fust appelee
> Qe ore est Blauncheville nomee.

Merlin says that in Britain the Great a wolf will come from Blanche Lande. It will have twelve sharp teeth, six below and six above. It will have such a fierce look that it will chase the leopard away from Blanche Lande, such strength and power will it have. But we know that Merlin said this about Fouke Fitz Waryn. For each of you can be sure that in the time of King Arthur what is now called Blancheville [Whittington] was called Blanche Lande.[51]

Once again imitating the *Prophetiae Merlini*, this prophecy fits the very specific circumstances of Fouke's dispossession. The leopard (King John) chases the wolf (Fouke) away from his territory, but Fouke is in the right because his ancestral claim to the land dates from the time of Arthur. Fouke's life trajectory is thus linked to that of Geoffrey's historical and legendary figures (detailed elsewhere in the manuscript's *Short English Metrical Chronicle*). The scribe and any readers of the manuscript would have recognized these parallels, which strengthen Fouke's claim to his land and emphasize the injustice of King John.[52]

Female succession

The second major theme of marcher literature discussed in this book is a focus on succession through the female line, important to marcher

---

[51] *FFW* 59–61; trans. Burgess, 182.
[52] The Harley scribe may have selected these texts to include in the miscellany because of their similarities. They occur in the same section of the manuscript (Unit 4). Revard argues that the *Short English Metrical Chronicle* was the first item the scribe copied c.1316–17, while the copying of *Fouke* was begun in the mid-1320s; see 'Scribe and Provenance', 58–60.

families because they often did not produce male heirs, or because their male heirs died young, resulting in lordships passing through sisters and daughters.[53] For example, the Braose genealogy discussed in Chapter 3 focuses on the passing of the lordship of Brecon through female descendants, ultimately to Humphrey VI de Bohun (c.1249–98); similarly, the genealogy of the earls of Hereford remarks *morust sans heir de say* 'he died without an heir' so often that it reads like a formula. The Mortimers go so far as to legitimize Roger Mortimer's claim to the throne of Britain by way of Gwladys Ddu, daughter of Llywelyn ab Iorwerth, as discussed in Chapter 2. Such genealogies were protective measures, intended to dispel confusion, thwart disputes, and justify why a lordship belonged to the family in the present day. Straightforward, undisputed inheritance would not generate nearly as much documentation. As discussed in the previous chapter of this book, present-day families—the presumed patrons of these texts—had a vested interest in having the complexities of succession written down and followed.

This theme is expressed in the romance of *Fouke le Fitz Waryn*. When Payn Peverel dies without a male heir, ownership of Whittington and its lands passes to his sister's son William. William has two daughters and no sons, so the lands go to his daughter Mellet and any man who can win her hand in a tournament.[54] Later, the text dwells on the titular Fouke's daughter, Eve. It makes a careful record of her marital life:

> Quant dame Johane, la femme Lowis, le prince de Walys, que fust la file le roy Henri de Engleterre, fust devyee, pur le grant renoun de prowesse e de bounté que sire Fouke aveit, yl maunda a ly pur Eve, sa file, e il la graunta, e a grant honour e solempneté fuerent esposee. Mes Lowis ne vesqui que un an e demi aprés; morust, e fust ensevely a Aberconewey, saunz heir engendré de Eve, e pus fust ele esposé a ly sire de Blancmostiers.

> When Lady Joan, wife of Llywelyn, Prince of Wales, who was the daughter of King Henry of England, was dead, [Llywelyn] asked Sir Fouke, because of his great reputation for prowess and bravery, for his daughter Eve. Fouke granted her to him and with great honour and solemnity they were married. But Llywelyn lived for only a year and

---

[53] For discussion of marcher widows, see Emma Cavell, 'Aristocratic Widows and the Medieval Welsh Frontier: The Shropshire Evidence', *TRHS* 17 (2007), 57–82; see also pp. 61, 118.
[54] *FFW* 8.

a half afterwards. He died and was buried in Conway [Aberconwy], without having produced an heir by Eve. Afterwards she was married to the Lord of Blancminster [either Oswestry or Whitchurch in Shropshire].[55]

This excerpt is very similar to the genealogies of the lords of Brecknock and Hereford discussed in Chapter 3, carefully recording women's multiple marriages and children. In this case, Eve's marriage brings the family an alliance with Welsh royalty.[56] Eve takes the place of Llywelyn's previous wife, the highly regarded Joan, daughter of King John (mistakenly called the daughter of King Henry here). This match implies that the Fitz Warin family is equal in social status to English and Welsh royalty. Eve's marriage to Llywelyn is a tribute to Fouke's bravery and reputation, as it is Fouke who has elevated the family through his deeds. This episode also suggests that a significant degree of class mobility was acceptable to the author and to readers of this romance.[57] Fouke's deeds, not his birth, elevate him to this status.

Land rights and Welsh princes

Additional major themes of marcher literature that *Fouke* adheres to are a focus on legitimate possession of land and, relatedly, a particular relationship to Wales and the Welsh that stems from *Fouke*'s borderland position. A major goal of baronial marcher literature (and, indeed, baronial literature more generally) was to legitimize control over territory, in this case, especially conquest territories in Wales. Like the hagiographical revival of early twelfth-century South Wales analysed by John Reuben Davies and others, in which diocesan control over

---

[55] *FFW* 59; trans. Burgess, 182.

[56] There is no Welsh genealogical or chronicle record of this marriage, though it is mentioned in the Annals of Chester; for discussion, see Stephenson, '*Fouke*', 27; Emma Cavell, '*Fouke le Fitz Waryn*: Literary Space for Real Women?' *Parergon*, 27/2 (2010), 89–109, at 101–2.

[57] Dolmans, 'Locating the Border', 125, reads these two characters as sharing the same class identity, in part due to shared language, whereas I am assuming a Welsh prince would have implicitly higher status than Fouke. This is reflected in the fact that Welsh princes and their offspring married English royalty or members of powerful baronial families in the March of Wales who were of higher status than the Fitz Warins of Whittington. I am grateful to Ben Guy for suggesting this last point.

particular localities was written into the historical past by hagiographers plotting out the presence of local Welsh saints in the landscape, marcher baronial literature imagines a past in which marcher ownership of Welsh lands is backdated: it is predetermined, ancient, and divinely designed.[58] It is also free of English royal control. The theme of landownership is central to the plot of *Fouke*, explored through Fouke's dispossession of his lands by King John and his quest to regain his inheritance.

This central conflict in the romance sets up an affinity between Fouke and the Welsh princes, who are also dispossessed of land by English kings. David Stephenson argues that *Fouke*'s respect for Welsh princes is a sign of increasing acculturation in the March in the thirteenth century.[59] The romance imagines a past in which Welsh princes and marcher lords were not at odds fighting over the same lands, as medieval Welsh chronicles so often describe, but aligned in their desire for independence from the English Crown. Fouke's affinity with Welsh princes is not only political but social, apparent in the marriage of his daughter, Eve, to the most powerful Welsh ruler of the thirteenth century. Their similar desires for independence and the right to possess their ancestral lands are underscored in the romance. Fouke's relationships with the Welsh princes, as well as his performance of recognizable aspects of Welsh culture and identity, legitimize his claims to independence and increase his standing as an outlaw. This attitude towards the Welsh sets *Fouke* apart from other 'ancestral romances' of its type. The affinity between, and parallel experiences of, Fouke and the Welsh princes is sustained in several episodes in the text.

Both Fouke and the Welsh princes Llywelyn ab Iorwerth and Gwenwynwyn ab Owain Cyfeiliog are at odds with King John, the villain of the story. The conflict between Fouke and the English Crown is set up at the beginning of Fouke's life, when he is fostered at court and plays with young Prince John. When John strikes Fouke with a chessboard,

---

[58] John Reuben Davies, 'The Saints of South Wales and the Welsh Church', in Alan Thacker and Richard Sharpe (eds), *Local Saints and Local Churches in the Early Medieval West* (Oxford, 2002), 361–95; Wendy Davies, 'Property Rights and Property Claims in Welsh "Vitae" of the Eleventh Century', in Evelyne Patlagean and Pierre Riché (eds), *Hagiographie, cultures et sociétés IVe–VIIe siècles: Actes du colloque organisé à Nanterre et à Paris (2–5 mai 1979)* (Paris, 1981), 515–33.

[59] Stephenson, *Medieval Wales*, 78.

Fouke hits him back, and John goes to his father and tattles. King Henry beats John, and John hates Fouke forever afterwards. When they come of age, John takes his revenge by giving Fouke's inheritance to the wrong person, thus setting off the action of the romance. King John's well-known conflicts with Welsh princes, particularly Llywelyn ab Iorwerth, with whom he went to war in 1215, form an implicit backdrop to this characterization of Fouke.

When Fouke is first exiled by King John after killing Moris, he goes straight to Llywelyn in Rhuddlan as a supplicant. He confesses to killing Moris, Llywelyn's cousin by marriage, which angers the prince. But Llywelyn soon recovers, because he grew up with Fouke and recognizes the similarities in their situations:

> Le prince e sire Fouke e ces freres fuerent norys ensemble en la court le roy Henri. Le prince fust molt lee de la venue sire Fouke, e ly demanda quel accord fust entre le roy e ly. 'Sire', fet Fouke, 'nul, quar je ne pus aver pees pur nulle chose, e, pur ce, sire, su je venuz a vous e a ma bone dame pur vostre pees aver'. 'Certes', fet le prince, 'ma pees je vous grant e doynz, e de moy bon resut averez. Le roy d'Engletere ne pees ou vous ne moy ne autre siet aver.'

> The prince, Sir Fouke, and his brothers had been brought up together at King Henry's court. The prince was very glad that Sir Fouke had come, and he asked him what sort of agreement there had been between himself and the king. 'Lord,' said Fouke, 'none, for I am unable to gain peace under any circumstances. For this reason, lord, I have come to you and my good lady in order to have your peace.' 'Certainly,' said the prince. 'I grant and give you my peace and you will receive a good welcome from me. The King of England is incapable of having peace with you or me or anyone else.'[60]

This passage emphasizes the close relationship between Fouke and Llywelyn from an early age, creating an affinity between Fouke's exile and dispossession and the experience of Welsh princes, who also suffer alienation from their inheritance. Llywelyn's comment about King John's inability to make peace puts the two men in league with one another and initiates the circumstances for a powerful alliance. Furthermore, Fouke's appeal to Llywelyn as a ruler who can grant peace puts Llywelyn on an equal footing with King John. Dolmans interprets their

---

[60] *FFW* 33; trans. Burgess, 159.

alliance as a mark of shared class identity, but their alliance is more subversive than that.[61] Llywelyn's ability to overrule King John's authority and dole out land in Shropshire delegitimizes the king's authority over the March and reinforces the independence of Wales and the March. In this, the text is pro-marcher, in the sense that it supports marcher rights over those of the Angevin kings.[62]

Fouke's relationship with Gwenwynwyn ab Owain Cyfeiliog, prince of Powys, furthers the association between Fouke and the Welsh. While he is resident at Llywelyn's court, Fouke gives Llywelyn advice about a conflict with Gwenwynwyn, who is Llywelyn's enemy:

> En icel temps grant descord fust entre le prince Lewys e Guenonwyn le fitz Yweyn Keveyloc, e a cely Guenonwyn grant partie de le pays de Powys apendeit, e si fust molt orgylous, hauteyn e fer, e ne vodra rien deporter le prince, mes fist grant destruxion en sa terre. Le prince a force avoit tot abatu le chastiel Metheyn, e avoit pris en sa meyn Mochnant, Lannerth e autres terres qe furent a Guenonwyn. Le prince comaunda la mestrie de tote sa terre a Fouke, e ly comaunda coure sur Guenonwyn, e destruere totes ces terres ... Tant precha Fouke au prince e parla qe le prince e Guenonwyn furent entreacordeez, e le prince ly rendy totes ces terres qe de ly eynz furent prises.

> At that time there was great discord between Prince Llywelyn and Gwenwynwyn, son of Owain Cyfeiliog. A large part of the territory of Powys belonged to this Gwenwynwyn and he was very arrogant, haughty and proud. He was not willing to submit in any way to the prince, rather did he cause a great deal of destruction in his land. The prince had destroyed Mechain castle by force and he had captured Mochnant, Llannerch and other lands which belonged to Gwenwynwyn. The prince assigned the ownership of all his lands to Fouke and commanded him to attack Gwenwynwyn and destroy all his lands ... Fouke spoke so earnestly to the prince that he and Gwenwynwyn were reconciled, and the prince gave him back all his lands, which had previously been taken from him.[63]

---

[61] Dolmans, 'Locating the Border', 125.

[62] Cf. Timothy Jones, 'Geoffrey of Monmouth'; Dolmans, 'Locating the Border', 110, n. 6.

[63] *FFW* 34; trans. Burgess, 159–60. For the historical Gwenwynwyn and the basis of this quarrel, see Burgess, 189, n. 31; David Stephenson, *Medieval Powys: Kingdom, Principality and Lordships, 1132–1293* (Woodbridge, 2016), 75–96; David Stephenson, 'The Politics of Powys Wenwynwyn in the Thirteenth Century', *CMCS* 7 (1984), 39–61.

Both Fouke and Gwenwynwyn are dispossessed of their lands by a more powerful rival, and Fouke immediately sympathizes with Gwenwynwyn when he hears of his plight. In a demonstration of how conflicts about land ought to be handled, Fouke convinces Llywelyn not to attack the rival prince—by implication criticizing King John's rash behaviour.[64] The episode creates further parallels between Fouke's experience and that of the Welsh princes.

Fouke's affinity with Gwenwynwyn is strengthened when they join together to ambush their mutual enemy, King John, in a mountain pass near Castle Bala in Gwynedd. This episode further places Fouke in league with the Welsh, whose military tactics are emphasized:

> Fouke fist assembler al chastel Balaham, en Pentlyn, .xxx. mil de bons honmes, e Guenonwyn le fitz Yweyn vynt ou ces gentz, qe fortz e hardys fuerent. Fouke fust assez sage de guere, e conust bien tous les passages par ont le roy Johan covenist passer; e le passage fust mout escars, enclos de boys e marreis, issi qu'il ne poeit passer si noun le haut chemyn, e le passage est apelé le Gué Gymele.

> Fouke assembled at the castle of Bala in Penllyn thirty thousand fine men, and Gwenwynwyn, son of Owain, came with his men, who were strong and bold. Fouke was very skilled in war, and he knew all the defiles through which John would have to pass. The pass was very narrow and surrounded by woods and marshes so that he could pass only by the highway. The pass is called the Ffordd Gam Elen.[65]

Matching Gwenwynwyn, Fouke engages in the guerrilla military tactics the Welsh were known for, as described by Gerald of Wales in his *Descriptio Kambriae*.[66] In this episode, Fouke is more like the Welsh than the Normans or English, displaying recognizable Welsh identity markers. With Fouke's help, Gwenwynwyn sends King John packing to Shrewsbury. He is rewarded for his service by Llywelyn, who grants him

---

[64] Here, *Fouke* embodies one of the essential themes of 'ancestral romance': idealized portrayal of leadership; Crane, 'Anglo-Norman Romances', 602.

[65] *FFW* 35; trans. Burgess, 160.

[66] Gerald of Wales, *Descriptio Kambriae*, i.8, ed. J. F. Dimock, *Giraldi Cambrensis Opera*, 6 (London, 1868), 179–82. For the exploits of Powysian princes in the March of Wales, see Gruffydd Aled Williams, 'Welsh Raiding in the Twelfth-Century Shropshire/Cheshire March: The Case of Owain Cyfeiliog', *SC* 40 (2006), 89–115. This episode is also discussed as an example of Fouke adopting elements of Welsh culture in Dolmans, *Writing Regional Identities*, 120–1.

Ystrad Marchell (*Estrat*) in Powys and Dinorben (*Dynorben*) in Rhos, as well as his rightful inheritance in Whittington (*Blanchevyle*).[67] Fouke's deeds and his association with Llywelyn and Gwenwynwyn increase his wealth and standing, and highlight his leadership abilities and military skills. The episode also emphasizes King John's lack of power and authority—it is Llywelyn, not John, who has the power to return Blancheville to Fouke, even though it was John who took Blancheville in the first place. Llywelyn has authority to grant Fouke land not only in Wales, but in Shropshire, overruling King John's decisions.

Fouke's quest to have his lands returned to him can be read as a conflict between him and the king for marcher liberties, as discussed in the Introduction in relation to Gower, wherein the king overextends his administrative authority over the March and the marcher lord pushes back.[68] Real anxieties over marcher independence very well could have bled over into literature about and for marcher families. In this tale, an affinity is recognized between marcher lords' and Welsh princes' mutual struggle for independence from the English Crown. Unlike what was often the case in reality, when marcher lords and Welsh princes were at war with each other, this romance imagines an ideal reality, in which the two united against a common threat. Perhaps the author was influenced by impressions of these Welsh princes and modelled the character of Fouke on them, or perhaps this affinity is a sign of cultural unity among the Welsh and English populations in the region of Shropshire, the increasing acculturation of the thirteenth century that Stephenson describes.

Strikingly, the feeling appears to have been reciprocated: Fouke sparked the interest of Welsh poets Iolo Goch (*c*.1320–98), Dafydd ap Gwilym (fl. 1340–70), Guto'r Glyn (fl. 1430–90), and Tudur Aled (fl. 1480–1526), who mention Fouke (*Syr Ffwg, Ffwg ap Gwarin*) in eulogies and praise poetry as a stock figure of chivalry and hospitality.[69]

---

[67] FFW 36.
[68] For discussion of marcher liberties, see Introduction, pp. 25–9.
[69] These poems include Iolo Goch poem 3, 'I Ieuan ab Einion' ('To Ieuan ab Einion'), and poem 33, 'Cywydd y Llong' ('Cywydd to a Ship'), in *Gwaith Iolo Goch*, ed. D. R. Johnston (Cardiff, 1988), 13–14, 147–8; Dafydd ap Gwilym poem 12, 'Englynion i Ifor Hael' ('In Praise of Ifor Hael'), ed. Dafydd Johnston, *DafyddapGwilym.net*, http://www.dafyddapgwilym.net/eng/3win.htm, accessed 18 March 2022; Guto'r Glyn poem 80, 'Moliant i Syr Siôn Bwrch ap Huw Bwrch o'r Drefrudd' ('In Praise of Sir John

Adam Price downplays these references, arguing that '*Syr Ffwg* for them is merely a symbol of knightly prowess and gracious hospitality', while Dolmans suggests that it was his marcher identity, his ability to 'dismiss the boundaries between Welsh and English', that appealed to poets of the Welsh gentry.[70] Other critics have taken these references as evidence of the story's longevity in Shropshire, particularly Oswestry.[71] But, perhaps even more interestingly, the references suggest that the figure of Fouke—with his trappings of Merlinic prophecy and acts of resistance to Angevin control—provided an appealing and recognizable symbol, for Welsh poets, of the post-conquest world. He joined the ranks of romantic figures to be quoted in poetry because he was culturally recognizable and appropriate. As mentioned above, these references could indicate that a Middle Welsh version of the romance circulated, though it is perhaps more likely that Welsh readers accessed the French version.

In conclusion, when *Fouke* is considered in a marcher context rather than an English literary context, the added resonances of Galfridian history, marcher identity, and an alignment with Welsh princes as assertions of marcher independence become apparent. While previous critics have identified *Fouke* as a pro-Norman text, justifying Norman conquest and the politics of empire, this analysis has shown that its allegiances are rather more sympathetic to the Welsh than previously appreciated.[72] Fouke's battle for his inheritance aligns with Welsh princes' desire for autonomy and to other marcher lords' interest in legal (marcher) liberties, demonstrating a spirit of independence from the English Crown and a strong marcher identity in medieval Shropshire

---

Burgh ap Huw Burgh of Wattlesborough'), ed. R. Iestyn Daniel, *GutorGlyn.net*, http://www.gutorglyn.net/gutorglyn/poem/?poem-selection=080&first-line=%23, accessed 18 March 2022; Tudur Aled poem 67, 'Cyngor i Anturiwr: Cywydd i Robert Salbri o Ial' ('Advice to the Adventurer: Cywydd to Robert Salisbury of Yale'), in *Gwaith Tudur Aled*, ed. T. Gwynn Jones, 2 vols (Cardiff, 1926), i.272–5. For discussion, see Alison Williams, 'Stories within Stories: Writing History in *Fouke le Fitz Waryn*', *Medium Ævum*, 81/1 (2012), 70–87, at 77.

[70] Adrian Price, 'Welsh Bandits', in Helen Phillips (ed.), *Bandit Territories: British Outlaw Traditions* (Cardiff, 2008), 58–72, at 61; Dolmans, *Writing Regional Identities*, 130.

[71] A. Williams, 'Stories', 77; Helen Fulton, 'Literature of the Welsh Gentry: Uses of the Vernacular in Medieval Wales', in Elizabeth Salter and Helen Wicker (eds), *Vernacularity in England and Wales, c.1300–1550*, Utrecht Studies in Medieval Literacy, 17 (Turnhout, 2011), 199–223, at 220.

[72] Timothy Jones, 'Geoffrey of Monmouth', 235; Dolmans, 'Locating the Border', 115.

that adopted aspects of Welsh identity as needed. Combined with the use of Galfridian prophecy and history to strengthen ideologically the Fitz Warin family's right to their ancestral lands, this text shows the degree to which the themes of Welsh history, literature, and culture worked to the advantage of a marcher family.

The History of William Marshal

The thirteenth-century French verse text *The History of William Marshal* (*L'Histoire de Guillaume le Maréchal*) offers a useful counterpoint to *Fouke*. This depiction of the illustrious life of a far more prominent marcher lord than Fouke, William Marshal, 1st earl of Pembroke (*c.*1146–1219), demonstrates the qualities of a different kind of marcher ruler: the absentee colonial aggressor whose power and authority stemmed entirely from the lands he controlled in the March, but whose life was culturally embedded in the francophone culture of the English royal family and its involvement in France. His dealings with Welsh princes, by contrast with Fouke, are entirely negative, and he does not use aspects of Welsh identity or ancestry to shore up his position. The *History*'s main geographical focus is not the March of Wales, but France and sometimes Ireland, where the Marshal spent the majority of his time. Nevertheless, this text was probably written in the southern March, possibly Lower Gwent, and it demonstrates the broad range of audiences, interests, and characters that could be produced by a writer working in the March of Wales, but whose attention was for the most part focused eastward.[73]

Like *Fouke*, the audience of the *History* was the subject's direct descendants. Commissioned *c.*1224 by the Marshal's son William (*c.*1190–1231) and his long-time associate John of Earley (*c.*1173–1229), it

---

[73] David Crouch, 'Marshal, William [*called* the Marshal], fourth earl of Pembroke', *ODNB*, accessed 2 February 2022; David Crouch, 'Writing a Biography in the Thirteenth Century: The Construction and Composition of the "History of William Marshal"', in David Bates, Julia Crick, and Sarah Hamilton (eds), *Writing Medieval Biography, 750–1250: Essays in Honour of Professor Frank Barlow* (Woodbridge, 2006), 221–35, at 225.

was written by a self-described *trouvère*, Jean, using a range of sources.[74] It was probably completed by 1226.[75] It consists of over 19,000 lines of rhyming couplets, and is extant in a single manuscript that contains no other texts (New York, Pierpont Morgan Library, M.888, s. xiii).

The *History* offers a positive portrayal of William Marshal and his descendants, particularly his military achievements and the good marriages of his children. Its focus on landownership, succession, and marriage is a result of its primary aim: to solidify the family's legacy and defend the Marshal's loyalty to the kings he served against vocal posthumous detractors.[76] In contrast to *Fouke*, it is focused on the Marshal's loyalty to the Crown of England and his moral character. Most often in scholarship, it is discussed in terms of its themes (of war, violence, and chivalry) and its generic classification (aristocratic biography or *roman d'aventure*).[77] But it also contains some distinctive marcher elements that have not been discussed, particularly its references to Galfridian history, a key aspect of marcher baronial literature. It is further interested in the themes of landownership and succession that preoccupied the baronial class in general, in a manner that is not specific to the March of Wales. Analysis of this text alongside the romance of *Fouke le Fitz Waryn* highlights the exceptional features of the latter text, particularly its positive portrayal of Welsh princes, and helps us understand how history writing was used in the March of Wales to encode rights of land and inheritance in different ways.

The Marshal's consolidation of power in the March was the result of his marriage in 1189 to the very wealthy heiress Isabel de Clare (1171×6–1220), daughter of Richard de Clare, lord of Striguil, known as Strongbow (*c*.1130–76), and Aoife, daughter of Diarmait Mac Murchada, king

---

[74] These sources consisted of Marshal household records, correspondence, the Gloucester continuation to the chronicle of John of Worcester, and eyewitness accounts as sources; for discussion, see Crouch, 'Writing a Biography', 223, 227–8.

[75] Crouch, 'Writing a Biography', 226.

[76] Ibid., 223–4.

[77] Richard W. Kaeuper, 'William Marshal, Lancelot, and the Issue of Chivalric Identity', in Christopher Guyol (ed.), *Kings, Knights and Bankers: The Collected Articles of Richard W. Kaeuper* (Leiden, 2016), 221–42; Laura Ashe, 'William Marshal, Lancelot, and Arthur: Chivalry and Kingship', *Anglo-Norman Studies*, 30 (2008), 19–40; John Gillingham, 'War and Chivalry in the *History of William the Marshal*', *Thirteenth Century England*, 2 (1998), 1–13; David Crouch, *William Marshal: Court, Career, and Chivalry in the Angevin Empire, 1147–1219* (London, 1990).

of Leinster (c.1110–71). Through her, William gained vast lands in Ireland, Wales, and the March of Wales, including the Forest of Dean, the shrievalty of Gloucester, the earldom of Striguil (Chepstow) in Monmouthshire, the earldom of Pembroke, and the lordship of Leinster in Ireland.[78] In 1213, he was granted the lordships of Carmarthen, Gower, and Haverford.[79] Despite spending most of his life in France on military campaigns for the Angevin kings, in his adulthood he drew nearly all his influence and power from his lands in the southern March and Leinster. His career illustrates the absentee character of many Anglo-Norman earls of the Marches and the substantial political and economic advantages that came with controlling marcher land.[80]

Given that his power, in the form of lands and titles, came entirely from his marriage, the text is keenly focused on legitimacy and succession, highlighted in two key moments of power transfer in the Marshal's life—his marriage and his death. His marriage to Isabel is brokered by King Richard after the death of King Henry II, whom the Marshal loyally served, and the *History* takes time to discuss the lands and titles that the Marshal gains from the marriage.[81] While the text is quick to add what he will bring to the marriage in return, it focuses primarily on how quickly and authoritatively he secures her lands.

The marriage continues to be important to the Marshal's control of his lands. Later, when he and his wife are in Leinster, he must quickly return to England. He gives a series of speeches to his barons, implicitly asking them not to go to war with one another in his absence in a manner that emphasizes the symbolic presence of his wife:

> Vostre dame naturalment,
> Fille al conte qui bonement
> Vos fefa tuz par sa franchise

---

[78] For discussion, see David Crouch, 'The Transformation of Medieval Gwent', in Ralph A. Griffiths, Tony Hopkins, and Ray Howell (eds), *The Gwent County History*, volume 2. *The Age of the Marcher Lords, c.1070–1536* (Cardiff, 2008), 1–45, at 32–5.

[79] It should be noted that some of these lands and titles came and went depending on King John's favour.

[80] The Marshal was also involved in several military campaigns against the Welsh. In 1204 he recaptured Cilgerran in Ceredigion from the princes of Deheubarth; in 1215, in the war between Llywelyn ab Iorwerth and King John, he led campaigns in the March against the Welsh; and in 1217 he warred with Morgan ap Hywel over Caerleon, discussed in more detail below.

[81] *HWM* i.476–7, ll. 9369–71.

> Quant il out la terre conquise. Entre vos enceinte remaint;
> Dusqu'a tant que Dex me remaint,
> Vos pri a toz que bonement
> La gardez e naturalment,
> Que vostre dame est, ce savon;
> Ge n'i ai rien si par lui non.
>
> She is your lady by birth,
> the daughter of the earl who graciously,
> in his generosity, enfieffed you all,
> once he had conquered the land.
> She stays behind here with you as a pregnant woman.
> Until such time as God brings me back here,
> I ask you all to give her unreservedly
> the protection she deserves by birthright,
> for she is your lady, as we well know;
> I have no claim to anything here save through her.
> (ll. 13,535–44)[82]

In this passage, Isabel functions as a symbol of power for the barons in Ireland. Her presence in Leinster, independent of her husband, serves as a reminder of the family's position and status and helps protect the Marshal's claim to the lordship in his absence. Indeed, Meilyr fitz Henry is forced to make peace with her, not the Marshal, following his failed rebellion at Kilkenny during the Marshal's absence.[83]

Similarly, the Marshal's deathbed scenes focus on the rightful inheritance of his children, as he divides up his estate and wealth among his sons and unmarried daughter (*Lors se porvit de ses enfanz / E parti sa terre e dona, / Si com sis cuers li adona* 'He then provided for his children, / dividing up his lands and bequeathing them, / as his heart prompted him').[84] This focus on landownership and succession is characteristic of a number of the marcher texts discussed in this book, and suggests a similar focus on succession on the part of his son William II, the poem's patron. These qualities alone, however, are not unique qualities of marcher literature, as a great many family-oriented medieval romances were interested in land rights and inheritance. The most intriguingly

---

[82] *HWM* ii.176–9.
[83] Ibid., ii.194–5, ll. 13871–82.
[84] Ibid., ii.408–11, ll. 18136–70; ii.408–9, ll. 18136–8.

marcher aspects of the text are instead William's interactions with Welsh princes and the references to Geoffrey of Monmouth.

Unlike Fouke, the Marshal, as Justiciar of the March, was not an ally of Welsh princes, but a staunch enemy. Welsh princes are mentioned several times in the text, particularly in conjunction with King John's clashes with Llywelyn ab Iorwerth in 1215, in which the Marshal was responsible for several military campaigns in the March against the Welsh.[85] These episodes are a major point of difference between the *History* and *Fouke*. The Marshal is very loyal to King John and allied with him against Llywelyn. These episodes betray diverse aspects of marcher attitudes towards the Welsh, who were sometimes allies and sometimes enemies of marcher lords.

One important, extended moment of conflict between the Marshal and the Welsh is his clash with Morgan ap Hywel in 1217. He takes Caerleon and its appurtenances from Morgan, using a combination of military might and legal judgment. When Louis VIII of France makes a truce with the English following his failed invasion in the First Barons' War, Morgan refuses to observe the truce, and wages war against the Marshal, despite Llywelyn ab Iorwerth's clear instructions to desist.[86] With Morgan as aggressor, the war takes on a moral dimension, with Morgan portrayed as characteristically wicked for breaking the truce: *Guerreia Morganz tot adés, / C'onques nul jor ne tint le pes, / Car en son cuer ert tot dis feil* 'Morgan never stopped fighting; / not for a single day did he observe the peace, / for he was ever a wicked man at heart' (ll. 17777–9).[87] Morgan refuses to give up, even after William Marshal has taken Caerleon, choosing instead to prolong the fighting: *Aprés si dura cele guere / Grant piece e empeira la terre; / Sin fu noaz a plusors genz* 'After that event the fighting still continued / for a long time, devastating the land / and bringing disaster to many people' (ll. 17785–7).[88] By implication, it is Morgan's fault that the people suffer continued hardship and devastation.[89]

---

[85] *HWM* ii.224–25, ll. 14473–90. Another reference to the Marshal's conflicts with the Welsh in Gwent comes when he expresses fear that his men in Netherwent will be attacked after his death; see ibid., ii.410–11, ll. 18169–78.
[86] Ibid., ii.390–1, ll. 17748–62.
[87] Ibid., ii.390–1.
[88] Ibid., ii.390–1.
[89] A rather different view is expressed in the Middle Welsh chronicle *Brut y Tywysogion* ('History of the Princes'), which reads, *Yg kyfrwg hynny yd ymladawd Willym Marscal a*

In an episode that provides harsh insight into the realities of marcher–Welsh political relations, peace talks are eventually arranged with Llywelyn ab Iorwerth and the papal legate. Llywelyn asks for Morgan's lands to be returned to Morgan.[90] But William Marshal emerges as the rightful owner of Caerleon, because Morgan forfeited his rights when he broke the truce.[91] The Marshal argues successfully that, because of Morgan's wicked deeds—including the burning of churches—his lands should remain under the Marshal's control.[92] This episode displays the ruthless methods, both legal and military, that a marcher lord could use to hold onto Welsh territory. In contrast to the positive relationship with Welsh princes in the romance of *Fouke le fitz Waryn*, this episode shows that not all marcher lords were interested in positive dealings with the Welsh. Marcher lordship in Wales was highly variable, and dealings with Welsh princes–whether positive or negative–were ultimately motivated by gaining power.

Despite its distinction from the acculturation between marchers and Welsh described in *Fouke*, the *History* exhibits another common aspect of marcher literature in its references to Arthurian legend and Galfridian history. Two out of three of these occur in passages about the Young King Henry, who is being ruined by his largesse and overspending. The poet laments the decline of chivalry in his age, and refers back to the age of the *Brut*, when chivalry flourished and acts of generosity were rewarded:

> E Dex nos doint al tens venir
> Que nos veions ce avenir
> Que Merlins en profetiza,
> Quant des reis dist e devisa
> Ce que en est avenu puis,
> Esi comme el Brute le truis.

Chaer Llion ac y goressgynnawd, cany chytsynnyassei y Kymry a'r tagneued vchot gann tebygu y hebyrgoui yn y kymot neu y dielwi 'In the meantime William Marshal laid siege to Caerleon and gained possession of it; for the Welsh had not agreed to the above peace, thinking that they had been scorned or ignored in the pact'. In other words, the Welsh did not obey the treaty because they were not part of it. See *Brut y Tywysogyon, or The Chronicle of the Princes, Red Book of Hergest Version*, ed. and trans. Thomas Jones (Cardiff, 1955), 216–17.

[90] *HWM* ii.392–3, ll. 17807–14.
[91] Ibid., ii.390–1.
[92] Ibid., ii.394–7, ll. 17831–71.

> Dex en tel point mete la terre
> A fei que li reis d'Engletere
> Recovre ce qu'il deit aveir,
> Qui par coveitise d'aveir
> E par traïson fu vendue!
>
> And may God grant that in days to come
> we shall see come to pass
> what Merlin prophesied,
> when he spoke of our kings and described
> what subsequently happened to them,
> as I find it written in the *Brut*.
> May God bring our land to its true allegiance
> so that the King of England
> regains what is rightfully his,
> which was sold off through acquisitiveness
> and treachery! (ll. 2701–11)[93]

In an interesting reversal of Merlin's prophecy, which, as discussed in Chapter 1, was interpreted by Welsh readers as predicting the eventual renewal of the Welsh, this poet seems to think that a fulfilment of Merlin's prophecy will result in an English king's lands being returned to him. The second reference to the age of Arthur comes in the form of a stock phrase praising the Young King, comparing him to Arthur and Alexander, and the third is a reference in passing to the town name *Chinon* from the name of Sir Kei.[94] Previous critics have argued rightly that these references to Arthurian legend, conventional in the romance genre, indicate that the poet was educated in the vernacular literature of his day.[95] They also create an impression that Arthurian-era chivalric values were alive and well in the Marshal's lifetime, forging a sense of continuity between the ancient British past and the present day. Strikingly, the prophecies are not directed at the life of the Marshal specifically (as they are in *Fouke*) but at the Young King, a tragic figure full of unfulfilled potential whose time is already past. In other words,

---

[93] *HWM* i.138–9. This reference to the written *Brut* could be to Geoffrey's *DGB* or to Wace.
[94] *HWM* i.182–3; i.400–1.
[95] Crouch, 'Writing a Biography', 222.

though the poet is interested in couching his story in subtly Arthurian terms, the Marshal himself needs no mythologizing.

In these passages, the *History* exhibits its strongest moments of adherence to a major theme of marcher literature: placement of the story of a family in the broader contextual world fashioned by Geoffrey of Monmouth. These references to the British past bring with them a sense of continuity in unified rule across time, which, as we have seen in Chapter 3, was a key political argument for marcher families. But, unlike *Fouke*, which depicts a man wholly embedded in the local region of Shropshire and its concerns, specifically concerns about marcher liberties, the *History of William Marshal*'s interests are focused on France, Ireland, and the English royal court. William Marshal is a colonial aggressor whose involvement in the March is entirely due to its ability to provide him with wealth and power.

Conquest and dispossession in marcher family literature

The literature discussed so far reveals a border society keenly interested in succession, continuity of rule, and rights to land. The inhabitants of this border society, aware of the ethnic differences in the region in which they lived as well as the fact that they were, in many cases, descended from both local Welsh families and Norman/English conquerors and settlers, were interested in defining and negotiating their position in the March, politically, economically, and culturally, and they accomplished this in part through written expression. When the typical baronial preoccupations of succession and inheritance are taken together with disputes with the Welsh and the use of Geoffrey's history as part of the narrative framing of a story, a distinctly marcher type of literature becomes visible. This literature is interested in defining the place of its subjects in the March of Wales using Galfridian history and Welsh ancestry and identity. The counterexample of the *History of William Marshal* shows that some barons with lands in the March of Wales chose not to assimilate to the hybrid culture of the March of Wales to the extent that the Fitz Waryns or the Mortimers did; they gained extraordinary power and wealth through their lands in the March of Wales but did not obtain or flaunt connections to Wales or Welsh culture.

In this final section of the chapter, I broaden the discussion to include marcher romances from a different region of Britain, the Anglo-Scottish borderlands. This final piece of the discussion places the literature of the March of Wales and its themes in a broader insular context, and points forward to the sort of comparative work that marcher literary studies would benefit from in future scholarship.[96] In particular, the early fifteenth-century alliterative Arthurian romance *The Awntyrs off Arthure at the Terne Wathelyn* (*The Adventures of Arthur at the Tarn Wadling*), written in a northern or northern Midlands Middle English dialect and originally from northern England or southern Scotland, exhibits similar concerns as Welsh marcher literature with conquest, dispossession, and land rights.[97] These are themes that are characteristic of a colonized borderland environment. It offers a useful counterpoint for an episode in the *History of William Marshal* in its treatment of issues of disinheritance and justice for unlawful possession of land. These concerns reflect a militarized society in which ownership of land shifted rapidly and legal recourse for the conquest and colonization of land was often fleeting or unobtainable.

The Awntyrs off Arthure survives in four fifteenth-century manuscripts.[98] It can be divided into two distinct sections, *Awntyrs* A and *Awntyrs* B, separated by episode as well as by style. While they may represent two separate poems that were joined together, the two

---

[96] For the Anglo-Scottish borderland, see Mark P. Bruce and Katherine H. Terrell, 'Introduction: Writing Across the Borders', in Mark P. Bruce and Katherine H. Terrell (eds), *The Anglo-Scottish Border and the Shaping of Identity, 1300–1600* (New York, 2012), 1–14, at 2–7; Anthony Goodman, 'The Anglo-Scottish Marches in the Fifteenth-Century: A Frontier Society?' in Roger A. Mason (ed.), *Scotland and England: 1286–1815* (Edinburgh, 1987), 18–33; Andy King, 'Best of Enemies: Were the Fourteenth-Century Anglo-Scottish Marches a "Frontier Society"?', in Andy King and Michel Penman (eds), *England and Scotland in the Fourteenth Century: New Perspectives* (Woodbridge, 2007), 116–35.

[97] This text bears important similarities to the thirteenth-century French-language Arthurian romance *Roman de Fergus*, whose titular hero is from Galloway; see *The Romance of Fergus*, ed. Wilson Frescoln (Philadelphia, 1983). The Scottish borderlands are in fact mentioned briefly in *Fouke*, when Fouke helps Piers de Bruvyle regain lands there. The episode reiterates the concept of borderlands as contested spaces. For discussion, see Dolmans, *Writing Regional Identities*, 123–4.

[98] See *The Awntyrs off Arthure at the Terne Wathelyn: An Edition Based on Bodleian Library MS. Douce 324*, ed. Ralph Hanna III (Manchester, 1974), 1–11, at 48–50, 143–54.

sections were read together by contemporary audiences.[99] In the A section, Arthur's court goes on a hunt in Inglewood Forest in Cumbria outside Carlisle. At a lake called Tarn Wadling, Guinevere and Gawain have a supernatural encounter with the ghost of Guinevere's mother, who describes the pains of Purgatory in the manner of a dream vision, and warns them that they must embrace Christian piety and charity lest the Round Table decline into corruption. The B section describes Sir Galeron of Galloway's attempt to win back his lands, which have been conquered by Sir Gawain, in a tournament at Arthur's court in Carlisle. While the section dubbed *Awntyrs* A—and the degree to which the two sections are structurally and thematically linked—has been the subject of most of the scholarship on the poem, this chapter will discuss *Awntyrs* B.

The central conflict of *Awntyrs* B is Galeron's dispossession of his lands by Gawain, an episode that reveals the centrality of themes of conquest, inheritance, dispossession, and legal justice to a border society. Critics have coalesced around a hypothesis that the text reproaches Arthur's policy of imperial expansion, in implicit criticism of English expansionism in the Anglo-Scottish borderlands under Edward I and III.[100] The text's interest in 'dispossession and repossession ... stages the centrality of land to power plays in the Anglo-Scottish marches ... in which the "currency" of power was land'.[101] Galfridian ideology was in fact a key component of Edward I's own policy of expansion: for example, in a 1301 letter to Pope Boniface VIII, Edward I cited Scotland's acceptance of Arthur's sovereignty as precedent for his own right to rule over Scotland.[102] This ideology bled over into the embrace of Arthur as an imperialist English king in fourteenth-century Middle

---

[99] *Awntyrs*, ed. Hanna, 17–24; cf. Randy P. Schiff, 'Borderland Subversions: Anti-Imperial Energies in *The Awntyrs off Arthure* and *Golagros and Gawane*', *Speculum*, 84 (2009), 613–32, at 616, n. 15; A. C. Spearing, '*The Awntyrs off Arthure*', in Bernard S. Levy and Paul E. Szarmach (eds), *The Alliterative Tradition in the Fourteenth Century* (Kent, OH, 1981), 183–200.

[100] Schiff, 'Borderland Subversions', 612, 621; *The Awntyrs off Arthure at the Terne Wathelyne: Modern Spelling Edition*, ed. Helen Phillips (Lancaster, 1988), 9.

[101] Schiff, 'Borderland Subversions', 613, 621.

[102] Lee Manion, 'Sovereign Recognition: Contesting Political Claims in the *Alliterative Morte Arthure* and *The Awntyrs off Arthur*', in Robert S. Sturges (ed.), *Law and Sovereignty in the Middle Ages and the Renaissance* (Turnhout, 2011), 69–91, at 69–70; Matthew Fisher, 'Genealogy Rewritten: Inheriting the Legendary in Insular Historiography', in

English Arthurian romances, in which Arthur stood for the 'centralizing power of the English crown'.[103] Fifteenth-century readers of *Awntyrs* in the Anglo-Scottish borderlands would probably have recognized that this was the English (not the Welsh) Arthur, as claimed by Edward.[104] For anti-English readers, Arthur is as an aggressor who needs to be curbed.

Arthur is described as a *conquerour kydde* 'famous conqueror' in the opening lines of the poem.[105] This is not a flattering description, but a critique of imperialist activity.[106] In one passage, the ghost of Guinevere's mother warns Gawain that Arthur's conquests are weakening the Round Table. In another, Gawain paints the court's imperial activity in a negative light, describing himself and his fellow warriors as *we ... þat fonden to fight, / and þus defoulen þe folke on fele kings londes, / And riches ouer reymes withouten eny right, / Wynnen worshipp and wele þorgh wightnesse of hondes* 'we who undertake to fight, / and thus trample upon the people in many of the kings' lands, / and enter realms without any right, / and win renown in war through prowess of arms'.[107] With this statement, Gawain recognizes the destructive power of imperial expansion, confirmed by the ghost who warns him of the consequences of expanding too greedily.[108] From the *Morte Arthure* (the only extant copy of which is in Lincoln, Lincoln Cathedral, 91, an *Awntyrs* manuscript), it was known that Arthur's empire collapsed once he tried to conquer Rome and was thwarted by Mordred at home. Within this Arthurian framing, the morality of King Edward's real-life imperial project could be critiqued and questioned.

In *Awntyrs* B, the text is concerned with the politics of royal expansion from a particularly marcher point of view, expressed through Galeron

---

Raluca L. Radulescu and Edward Donald Kennedy (eds), *Broken Lines: Genealogical Literature in Medieval Britain and France*, Medieval Texts and Cultures of Northern Europe, 16 (Turnhout, 2008), 123–42.

[103] Schiff, 'Borderland Subversions', 620.

[104] Schiff notes that Carlisle, the location of Arthur's court in *Awntyrs*, is where English soldiers garrisoned for centuries. For this reason, they would be read as English; see ibid., 627.

[105] *Awntyrs*, ed. Hanna, 64, ll. 1–3. Translations are from *Sir Gawain: Eleven Romances and Tales*, ed. Thomas Hahn (Kalamazoo, 1995), with some modifications.

[106] Schiff, 'Borderland Subversions', 618–19.

[107] *Awntyrs*, ed. Hanna, 76, ll. 261–4.

[108] Ibid., ll. 265–8. This episode is also discussed in Patricia Clare Ingham, *Sovereign Fantasies: Arthurian Romance and the Making of Britain* (Philadelphia, 2001), 184–9.

of Galloway's attempt to regain his patrimonial lands, which were taken from him by Gawain, by means of single combat.[109] In the borderland context, the conflict between the two men, which puts Arthur's greatest knight in danger, is a direct consequence of the politics of conquest critiqued in *Awntyrs* A. In the years leading up to the events of the tournament, Arthur had pursued a policy of conquest, not only uniting England, Wales, and Scotland, but also conquering Ireland and nearly Rome. As a result, he must bear out the consequence of dispossessed marcher lords seeking justice. In this case, the mannered chivalric context of the tournament is juxtaposed against the violent military expansionism in which Arthur and his knights have previously engaged. To begin the episode, the splendidly armoured Galeron rides into Arthur's court. Arthur asks him who he is, and Galeron states his purpose:

> Mi name is Sir Galaron, withouten eny gile,
> Þe grettest of Galwey of greues and gylles,
> Of Connok, of Carrak, of Conyngham, of Kyle,
> Of Lonrik, of Lennex, of Loudan Hilles.
> Þou has wonen hem in werre with a wrange wile
> And geuen hen to Sir Gawayn—þat my hert grylles.
> But he shal wring his honed and warry þe wyle,
> Er he weld hem, ywis, again myn vnwylles.
> Bi al þe welth of þe worlde, he shal hem neuer welde,
>
> While I þe hede may bere,
> But if he wyn hem in were,
> With a shelde and a spere,
> On a fair felde.[110]

My name is Sir Galeron, without any guile, the greatest knight of Galloway, of thickets and ravines, of Connok, of Conyngham, and also Kyle, of Lomond, of Losex, of Loyan Hills. You have taken these lands in war with an unjust trick and given them to Sir Gawain. That angers my heart. But he shall wring his hands and curse the time before he

---

[109] Because Galloway was a contested border zone, Christine Chism argues that the choice to make Galeron a character from Galloway 'implicat[es]' Arthur in the imperial ambitions of later medieval kings'; see *Alliterative Revivals* (Philadelphia, 2002), 253. She characterizes Galloway as contested territory because Edward I pillaged the region in 1298 but ultimately could not take it over.

[110] *Awntyrs*, ed. Hanna, 83–4, ll. 417–29.

took control of them, certainly, against my will. By all the wealth of
the world, he shall never hold them while I have a head on my shoulders, unless he wins them in combat, with a shield and a spear, on a
fair [equitable] field.

Like Fouke, Galeron has been dispossessed of his inheritance. In this
passage, he emphasizes the range of territories that have been taken
from him. In particular, he objects to the manner in which they have
been taken: he would not object if they were won fairly, in single combat on a field with a nobleman, but they were taken by trickery during a
war.[111] In other words, imperial warfare is unfair and deceptive, pitching
unequal armies against each other without formal public agreement or
courtesy.

A bitter, ritualized fight commences between Gawain and Galeron,
and the men fight nearly to the death before Arthur has them stop. At
this moment, Galeron recognizes Gawain's courage and cedes his lands
to him:

> Her I make þe releyse, renke, by þe rode,
> And, byfore thiese ryalle, resynge the my ryghte;
> And siþen make the monraden with a mylde mode
> As man of medlert makeles of might.[112]

> Here I grant you quit-claim, sir, by the Cross, and before these royal
> persons, I resign to you my right [claims to lands and entitlements],
> and afterwards do homage with good will, insofar as you are a man
> of middle earth, matchless in strength.

Arthur rewards the knights by granting Gawain lands in Wales, Ireland,
and Brittany. In turn, Gawain returns Galeron's lands in the Scottish
borderlands, provided that Galeron becomes a member of the Round
Table. With this clever twist, Galeron regains his own lands, but only by
permission of Arthur's court. This rebalancing of territories by formal
decree reaffirms Arthur's (and perhaps by implication King Edward's)
jurisdiction over the Scottish Marches.[113] And, unlike Morgan ap Hywel

---

[111] *Awntyrs*, ed. Hanna, 84, ll. 430–1.
[112] Ibid., 93, ll. 639–43.
[113] Manion, 'Sovereign Recognition', 86.

in the *History of William Marshal*, Galeron acknowledges Arthur's jurisdiction and lordship, allowing peace to commence. This reading of the text as motivated by themes of imperial expansion speaks to key border anxieties that animated authors and readers at the time: fear of collapse of empire on the one side (Arthur), and of conquest and dispossession on the other (Galeron).

Several details in this episode are worth discussing further for what they tell us about attitudes towards conquest and colonization in the text. First, Galeron is depicted as churlish and discourteous. Hanna observes: 'He shows fulsome arrogance in his habitually contemptuous use of the familiar pronoun to address Arthur ... His insistence upon the first person pronoun in his speeches is similarly discourteous, as well as somewhat amusing because he has forgotten to announce his name and status,'[114] which would have been the proper thing for a knight to do. Arthur is instead forced ask his name.[115] These missteps would have indicated a lack of familiarity with courtly customs. In a colonial context, this lack of chivalric etiquette displays Galeron's otherness. He also behaves boorishly during the battle with Gawain, slashing at Gawain, laughing at him, and butchering his horse.[116] A mantle of civility and gentility can be granted only by Arthur's court, when Galeron joins the Round Table.[117] In this manner, Galeron is similar to other colonized subjects in transcultural contexts such as Peredur in the Middle Welsh romance *Peredur vab Efrawc*, loosely based on Chrétien de Troyes's *Perceval*. Peredur, a young knight from Wales who joins Arthur's court, is a country bumpkin, similarly uncouth and unmannered; he does not recognize knights as knights when he sees them, uses withes instead of a harness on his horse, and arrives at Arthur's court wearing the wrong clothing.[118] In *Perceval*, similar markers of barbarity convey Perceval's Welshness. Despite Galeron's recognition of and participation in the

[114] Ralph Hanna III, '*The Awntyrs off Arthure*: An Interpretation', *Modern Language Quarterly*, 31 (1970), 275–97, at 294.
[115] *Awntyrs*, ed. Hanna, 83, ll. 414–16.
[116] Ibid., 89, ll. 540–1.
[117] Schiff, 'Borderland Subversions', 620.
[118] See Susan Aronstein, 'Becoming Welsh: Counter-Colonialism and the Negotiation of Native Identity in *Peredur vab Efrawc*', *Exemplaria*, 17/1 (2005), 135–68; Kristen Lee Over, 'Transcultural Change: Romance to *Rhamant*', in Helen Fulton (ed.), *Medieval Celtic Literature and Society* (Dublin, 2005), 183–204, at 196–9; Stephen Knight, 'Resemblance and Menace: A Post-Colonial Reading of *Peredur*', in Sioned Davies and Peter

values of chivalric behaviour (such as the honour inherent in participating in ritualized single combat), he cannot assimilate into Arthur's court until he has conceded his loss and is no longer a threat to Arthur's empire.

As mentioned above, the curious detail of Arthur rewarding Gawain for his bravery in the tournament with lands in Glamorgan, Ulster, and Waterford provides further clues to the text's attitudes towards land rights in a borderland context. Arthur says,

> Here I gif Sir Gawayn, with gerson and golde,
> Al þe Glamergan londe with greues so grene,
> Þe worship of Wales at wil and at wolde,
> With Criffones Castelles curnelled ful clene;
> Eke Vlster Halle to hafe and to holde,
> Wayford and Waterforde, walled I wene;
> Two baronrées in Bretayne with burghes so bolde,
> Þat arn batailed abouȝt and bigged ful bene.[119]

Here I give Sir Gawain, together with treasure, all the land of Glamorgan with groves so green, the lordship of Wales at his command, with Criffones Castle crenellated so cleanly; also Ulster Hall to have and to hold, Wayford and Waterford, walled towns I guess; two baronies in Brittany with fortified cities, that have surrounding battlements and have been very well built.

These are, of course, not lands in England, but territories brought into the remit of English rule by conquest: Glamorgan, 'Criffones Castelles' (probably Caerphilly Castle in Glamorgan), 'Vlster Halle' (probably Ulster in Ireland or Oysterlow in South Wales), Wayford (Wexford), Waterford, and Brittany.[120] It is striking that he is giving away conquest

---

Wynn Thomas (eds), *Canhwyll Marchogyon: Cyd-destunoli Peredur* (Cardiff, 2000), 128–47.

[119] *Awntyrs*, ed. Hanna, 94–5, ll. 664–71.

[120] Rosamund Allen and Andrew Breeze argue that 'Criffones Castelles' refers to Caerphilly Castle in Glamorgan. Allen argues that 'Vlster Halle' refers to Ulster in Ireland, while Breeze suggests Oysterlow (*Ystlwyf*) Castle in South Wales. Wayford refers to Wexford in Ireland; see Rosamund Allen, '*The Awntyrs off Arthure*: Jests and Jousts', in Jennifer Fellows et al. (eds), *Romance Reading on the Book: Essays on Medieval Narrative Presented to Maldwyn Mills* (Cardiff, 1996), 129–42; Andrew Breeze, '"The Awntyrs off Arthure", Caerphilly, Oysterlow, and Wexford', *Arthuriana*, 9/4 (1999), 63–8. The place names are slightly different in the other copies of the text. For discussion of this episode, see

territories that would have been recognized as such by contemporary audiences.[121] In *Awntyrs*, the list of territories displays the breadth of Arthur's empire and reaffirm his power over Britain and Ireland. It also places the romance firmly in the political realities of medieval Britain, when these territories were highly valuable, wealthy lordships under marcher control. By implication, this English Arthur, a symbol of Edwardian conquest, can give land to his barons in Ireland and Wales because he has the authority to do so. This was not at all the reality for English kings at the time: they did not have the authority to grant lands in the March. In this, the text reinscribes and affirms the paradigm of colonization and conquest beyond what was actually politically possible.

The Arthurian tournament in *Awntyrs* as a means of resolving colonial-era conflicts of land dispossession strikes an interesting parallel with the themes of conquest, morality, and justice that play out in the conflict between William Marshal and Morgan ap Hywel in the *History of William Marshal*. Similar to the fictional character Galeron, Morgan is dispossessed of his lands by war. However, as discussed previously, he makes no formal petition for their return, instead illegally harrying the countryside and breaking Louis VIII's treaty of peace.[122] He forfeits his right to his lands by behaving wickedly. In his argument against Morgan, the Marshal uses the etiquette of chivalry and the concept of 'fair fight' to place a moral judgement on Morgan's military actions, and there is no recourse, military or legal, for Morgan to regain his lands. This is a rather different case from the politics of dispossession depicted in *Awntyrs* or in *Fouke*, in which both heroes successfully regain their property by displaying knightly virtues in battle. In the world of romance, a path to regaining one's inheritance is made possible by *reson and riʒt* 'consideration and justice', a legalistic phrase repeated several times in *Awntyrs* that refers to Arthur's formal recognition of Galeron's demands and his ability to create circumstances in

---

A. C. Spearing, 'Central and Displaced Sovereignty in Three Medieval Poems', *Review of English Studies*, 33/131 (1982), 247–61, at 251.

[121] Wales, specifically, has already been identified as 'the storehouse or reserve supply of foreign kings' in Chrétien de Troyes's *Cligés*, in which Arthur gives a kingdom in Wales to Alexander; Over, 'Transcultural Change', 190–1.

[122] *HWM* ii.390–1, ll. 17777–9.

which those demands can be rightfully met.[123] The tournament and its attendant pageantry of chivalric behaviour generates the circumstances of a fair, equal fight whose outcome is divinely determined.[124] In other words, Galeron plays by the conqueror's rules and regains his lands on the conqueror's terms. In contrast, Morgan's fate in the *History of William Marshal* demonstrates the impossibility of retaking land, legally or militarily, when a charge of immorality was attached to unsanctioned violence.[125] The *History* articulates the control of Welsh princes by legal and moral means and demonstrates that the only sanctioned violence is that which is condoned by English kings. In the formalized world of Arthurian romance, the poet imagines a world in which chivalric honour solves military conflicts, while, in the *History of William Marshal*, we see how rarely this was actually the case.[126]

We return finally to *Fouke*, which offers another portrayal of land dispossession in a borderland context. As argued above, Fouke's dispossession of his inheritance by King John and subsequent battles align him politically and culturally with contemporary Welsh princes. In Fouke's case, open warfare against King John is sanctioned, coded as Welsh, and portrayed as admirable and heroic. Gwenwynwyn and Fouke's ambush of King John reveals a much more favourable attitude towards Welsh warfare tactics than in the *History of William Marshal*, wherein Fouke displays recognizable markers of Welsh culture and identity as positive traits. As seen in the *History* and in a range of contemporary chronicles, harsh consequences followed for Welsh princes who assaulted King John and his marcher barons, and this portrayal of Gwenwynwyn and Fouke's attack of John is highly romanticized, an expression of a particular family's marcher identity.

The romances discussed in this chapter use ideas of chivalry, fair fight, and virtue to determine disputed ownership of land, when the reality

[123] *Awntyrs*, ed. Hanna, 80, 81, ll. 350, 362.
[124] When Arthur laments the possibility of Gawain's death in the fight, Gawain says, *God stond with þe riȝt* 'May the best man win'; ibid., 86, l. 471; discussed by Hanna, '*Awntyrs off Arthure*: An Interpretation', 294–5.
[125] This occurs despite the fact that Morgan's harrying of the countryside is precisely the strategy that William Marshal adopted in wars in France; see Gillingham, 'War and Chivalry'.
[126] Similar themes of land dispossession play out in the Middle Scots Arthurian poem *Golagros and Gawain*, which for reasons of space I cannot discuss here.

was much more violent and difficult to resolve cleanly. All three of these texts betray considerable anxieties about how to resolve protracted disputes over land in a conquest environment—whether resolution was moral, legal, or military—and how to determine which individuals had greater authority and jurisdiction to mete out justice and repatriation. Though each land dispute in these three texts is settled at the end and the rightful parties retire happily, in reality, disputes over land in the March of Wales or Scotland could last generations without clear resolution. These were very real concerns for inhabitants of the unstable, shifting territories of a borderland society. The present discussion shows how central land disputes were to marcher identity, and how the framework of Geoffrey's history offered a suitable means to discuss these issues in alternative contexts like romance. The next chapter features another aspect of the negotiation of power relationships between Welsh princes and their neighbours in the form of a study of external perceptions of their lives and deaths. It will return to the topic that began this book: the role that marcher literary culture (with its attendant interest in renegotiating the legendary and historical past in Britain) played in the transmission of texts from Wales to locations further afield.

| 5 |

Elegies for Welsh Princes

This chapter turns from romance to elegy, a mode of historical writing deeply rooted in memory and affective experience, to examine further attitudes towards Welsh princes that are grounded in marcher literary culture, this time by English as well as by marcher readers. It focuses on the inclusion of elegies and epitaphs to important Welsh princes of the twelfth and thirteenth centuries, Rhys ap Gruffudd (d. 1197) and Llywelyn ap Gruffudd (c.1233–82), in chronicles from the March of Wales, particularly Chester, as well as England, and the effect of such elegies on non-Welsh readers. While this chapter moves beyond the focused remit of the March of Wales that occupies much of this book to discuss the broader context of the literary and historical relationship between Wales and England, a relationship that was undergirded by a system of colonization in Wales and the March of Wales, it must be noted that the transmission of historical materials from Wales to England, and perhaps even the nature of English interest in Wales as displayed by the materials discussed herein, could not have happened without the March of Wales functioning as mediator between the two. Chester, in particular, emerges as a linchpin of transmission of and interest in Welsh texts; this is not an accident, as Chester is/was a border town that functioned in the medieval period as a mediator between different worlds. This chapter therefore departs from the previous chapters of this book in its movement away from the tightly focused baronial literature of the March of Wales to a broader view on the Welsh 'penumbra' and its reverberations in marcher, and later English, historical writing.[1] Most of this chapter focuses on elegies for Rhys ap Gruffudd, with brief discussion of epitaphs for Llywelyn ap Gruffudd towards the end.

Elegies are in fact a feature of many prose chronicles from the medieval insular world and can be constituted as part of a broader tradition in the writing of history in the medieval period.[2] When they appear in chronicles, poems that eulogize fallen leaders are typically couched in the busy happenings that otherwise concern chronicle writers: elections of bishops, changes in royal succession, famine, and climate events. They punctuate a steady stream of economic and political details with their finality. Commemorating the deaths of important figures, and simultaneously acting as prayers for entry into Heaven, elegies in chronicles emphasize the passage of time that underlies every medieval chronicle, while also elevating the tone to a higher rhetorical register than the simple language of the surrounding prose. They are also intended to have an emotional effect on the reader, and they provide important clues, in the case of elegies for Welsh princes appearing in marcher and English contexts, about how the Welsh past was imagined and framed outside Wales.[3] The presence of these elegies in English and marcher chronicles is a result of Latin textual transmission spurred on by marcher activities, as discussed throughout this book, and attests to the complexity of the literary relationships interlinking the March of Wales, England, and Wales.

---

[1] For the Welsh 'penumbra', see Simon Meecham-Jones, 'Where Was Wales? The Erasure of Wales in Medieval English Culture', in Ruth Kennedy and Simon Meecham-Jones (eds), *Authority and Subjugation in Writing of Medieval Wales* (New York, 2008), 27–56. Unless otherwise noted, translations are my own. For definitions of 'Welsh' and 'English' as identity terms, see the Introduction, pp. 17–18, 21–2.

[2] These include Irish chronicles (the Annals of Ulster, the Annals of Tigernach, the Annals of the Four Masters, *Lebor Gabála Érenn*), later versions of the *Anglo-Saxon Chronicle*, and the Middle Welsh chronicle *Brut y Tywysogion* ('History of the Princes').

[3] I assume that Welsh and English audiences were part of the same emotional community, sharing 'important norms concerning the emotions that they value and deplore and the modes of expressing them' and a shared emotional vocabulary (Barbara H. Rosenwein, *Generations of Feeling: A History of Emotions, 600–1700* (Cambridge, 2016), 3, 6).

Within this context, I take particular interest in the affective experiences of chronicle readers as enabled by elegiac poetry in chronicles.[4] In memorializing fallen leaders, chroniclers enacted an elevation of rhetoric that heightened the immediacy of the past and created a sense of immersion and continuity across historical time, particularly through references to Greek and Latin heroes. The elevated rhetoric of the elegy made the past feel more immediate by evoking *pathos* in the reader, while also accentuating its finality by offering a stark reminder of death and the mutability of human life. An elegy appearing in a chronicle placed a local ruler's deeds on a continuum with all the other great deeds of past rulers. In this sense, the purpose of elegy and chronicle coincide: both record lives and deaths for posterity and instruction, the *digna memoria* 'things worthy of memory' that instruct, through example, how readers might lead a Christian life.[5]

The reader was meant to identify with the Welsh people and experience the deep sense of loss and fragmentation that the deaths of their princes represented, perhaps surprising in the context of an English or marcher chronicle, given that the view of Wales by its neighbours in England and the March of Wales was so frequently negative. At the same time, the elegy provided a crucial sense of distance from the difficult colonial relationship between England and Wales, and the March and Wales, by portraying threatening Welsh leaders as unequivocally living in the past. For thirteenth- and fourteenth-century English and/or marcher readers, elegies for Welsh princes existed in the context of continued efforts to pacify Wales after its conquest by Edward I in 1282–4 and the continued threat of Welsh rebellion in the decades following. This threat would have been especially significant for non-Welsh settlers living in South Wales and the March in the early years of the fifteenth century, as the idea of Welsh independence coalesced around Owain Glyndŵr.[6] The elegiac mode provided a sense of remove,

---

[4] For emotion in poetry, see Antonina Harbus, 'Embodied Emotion, Conceptual Metaphor, and the Aesthetics of Reading Old English Poetry', in Michael Champion and Andrew Lynch (eds), *Understanding Emotions in Early Europe*, Early European Research, 8 (Turnhout, 2015), 127–49; for emotion in chronicles' accounts of death, see Alicia Marchant, 'Narratives of Death and Emotional Affect in Late Medieval Chronicles', *Parergon*, 31/2 (2015), 81–98.

[5] For discussion, see Roger D. Ray, 'Medieval Historiography through the Twelfth Century: Problems and Progress of Research', *Viator*, 5 (1974), 33–60, at 49–52, 44–8.

[6] See Ch. 1, pp. 48–53.

memorializing Welsh princes as if they were classical heroes: evocative, but no longer a threat. These chronicles' recollections of Welsh loss attest to the ability of elegiac verse to transgress and to break down boundaries of culture through affective experience while still protecting cultural dominance. Furthermore, this study of Welsh elegies in specifically English contexts demonstrates a key outcome of marcher baronial interest in Wales and the Welsh past: the transmission of Welsh texts beyond the borderlands and into regions of England that did not border Wales at all.

Elegies for the Lord Rhys ap Gruffudd in Welsh contexts

The Lord Rhys ap Gruffudd ruled over the Welsh kingdom of Deheubarth in South Wales from 1155 until his death in 1197. He enjoyed an uneasy diplomatic relationship with King Henry II of England and was a cousin of the marcher cleric and writer Gerald of Wales.[7] Though a number of poems written for Rhys in Welsh have survived as part of the professional bardic tradition of praise poetry in Wales, none of them is an elegy.[8] The only extant elegies written for him are, remarkably, in Latin. One is in prose, and one is in verse, and they survive in chronicles, not in compilations of poetry. I begin with a discussion of the elegies for Rhys in their original, Welsh contexts before discussing their transmission beyond Wales.

A Latin prose elegy for Rhys appears in a Latin chronicle from Wales, *Cronica de Wallia*, that was probably compiled at the Cistercian abbey of Whitland (in Carmarthenshire) in the late thirteenth century using sources from Strata Florida Abbey and elsewhere.[9] Strata

---

[7] For biography, see Roger Turvey, *The Lord Rhys: Prince of Deheubarth* (Llandysul, 1997); Huw Pryce and Nerys Ann Jones (eds), *Yr Arglwydd Rhys* (Cardiff, 1996).

[8] Nerys Ann Jones 'Canu Mawl Beirdd y Tywysogion i'r Arglwydd Rhys', in Pryce and Jones (eds), *Yr Arglwydd Rhys*, 129–44.

[9] For text, see Thomas Jones, '"Cronica de Wallia" and Other Documents from Exeter Cathedral Library MS 3514', *Bulletin of the Board of Celtic Studies*, 12 (1946), 27–44; for discussion, see Ben Guy, 'Historical Scholars and Dishonest Charlatans: Studying the Chronicles of Medieval Wales', in Ben Guy, Georgia Henley, Nia Wyn Jones (published under Owain Wyn Jones), and Rebecca Thomas (eds), *The Chronicles of Medieval Wales*

Florida, a Cistercian house in Ceredigion, was patronized by Rhys and his descendants throughout the twelfth and thirteenth centuries.[10] This extended elegy displays a wide-ranging knowledge of classical heroes and Latin rhetorical tropes, including tricolon, auxesis, metaphor, and climax. In an echo of Boethius, it describes how Fortuna has cast Rhys from her wheel. An excerpt reads:

> [4] Hic namque nobilissima regum ortus prosapia, uerum ipse clarus genearcha, mentis probitatem generi coequauit, et sic geminans animum nobilitate generis, consolator procerum, forcium debellator, subditorum benignus tutator, urbium ualidus expugnator, bella mouens,[11] turmas instaurans, hostiles cateruas obruens, [h]aut secus quam aper frendens audacia, seu leo rugiens caude uerbere stimulatus in iras, ferritate deseuiebat in hostes. O belli gloria, milicie decus ac clipeus, nobile tutamen patriae, armorum decus, brachium fortitudinis, largitatis manus, rationis occulus, honestatis splendor, animositatis apex,
>
> [5] probitatis Hercule, secundus Achillis asperitatem pectore gerens, Nestoris modestiam, Tidei audaciam, Sampsonis fortitudinem, Hectoris grauitatem, Euriali agilitatem, Paridis formam, Vlixis facundiam, Salomonis sapienciam, Aiacis animositatem, iniurie dampna morte recompensantem!
>
> [6] O miserorum tutum refugium, nudorum indumentum, esuriencium morsus, siciencium potus! O omnium postulancium prompta satisfactio donorum!
>
> [7] O dulcis eloquio, comis obsequio, morum honestus, sermone modestus, uultu hilaris, facie decorus, cunctis benignus, omnibus equus, simplicitatis [h]aut ficte pietas, humilitatis [h]aut fabricate sublimitas! Heu! heu! iam Wallia uiduata dolet ruitura dolore.

[4] For this man, descended from the most noble line of kings, himself indeed a leader of his race, the honesty of his mind was equal to that of his ancestors, and thus doubling his spirit by the nobility of his lineage, a consoler of nobles, a fighter against the brave, a

---

and the March: New Contexts, Studies and Texts, Medieval Texts and Cultures of Northern Europe, 31 (Turnhout, 2020), 69–106, at 88–92.

[10] For patronage, see Jemma Bezant, 'The Medieval Grants to Strata Florida Abbey: Mapping the Agency of Lordship', in Janet Burton and Karen Stöber (eds), *Monastic Wales: New Approaches* (Cardiff, 2013), 73–88.

[11] 'bella mouens' is a phrase from Virgil's *Aeneid* xii.333.

kindly protector of the subjected, a powerful destroyer of cities, starting wars, preparing battalions, destroying enemy columns, snarling with courage like a boar, or a roaring lion lashing its tail roused to anger, he would rage with ferocity at the enemy. O glory of war, honour and shield of soldiers, noble protector of his country, honour of arms, arm of bravery, hand of generosity, eye of reason, splendour of honour, peak of fierceness,

[5] a Hercules of honesty, a second Achilles bearing harshness in his heart, the modesty of Nestor, the daring of Tydeus, the strength of Samson, the dignity of Hector, the agility of Euryalus, the beauty of Paris, the eloquence of Ulysses, the wisdom of Solomon, the spirit of Ajax, repaying the damage of insult with death!

[6] O safe refuge for the wretched, clothing for the naked, food for the hungry, drink for the thirsty. O ready provider of gifts for all who petition!

[7] O sweet in speech, agreeable in behaviour, honourable in his customs, modest of speech, cheerful of expression, decorous of appearance, kind in all things, fair to all, a dutifulness of unfeigned simplicity, a loftiness of genuine humility! Alas! Alas! Wales mourns, now widowed and doomed to be destroyed by grief.[12]

Classical and pseudohistorical comparanda are situated in a sophisticated, highly rhetorical Latinity that is unexpected in the context of a monastic chronicle, which one would expect to be rather simple in style.[13] The elegy, which has been called a 'great howl of grief' that stands out from the other sections of the chronicle, praises Rhys's virtues and compares him to Trojan, Greek, Egyptian, and biblical heroes.[14]

---

[12] Thomas Jones, 'Cronica de Wallia', 31; trans. Paul Russell, '"Go and Look in the Latin Books": Latin and the Vernacular in Medieval Wales', in Richard Ashdowne and Carolinne White (eds), *Latin in Medieval Britain*, Proceedings of the British Academy, 206 (Oxford, 2017), 213–46, at 218; see also discussion in Georgia Henley, 'Rhetoric, Translation and Historiography: The Literary Qualities of Brut y Tywysogyon', *Quaestio Insularis*, 13 (2012), 78–103, at 109–15.

[13] For further discussion, see Russell, 'Go and Look in the Latin Books'; at 219–20 he notes that this higher register is also used in the entry for 1201 describing the deaths of Rhys's sons Maredudd and Gruffudd. For medieval historians' simple style, see Ray, 'Medieval Historiography', 49–52.

[14] Russell, 'Go and Look in the Latin Books', 216. Comparisons with Homeric heroes are common in medieval literature, including Welsh poetry; see Marged Haycock, 'Some Talk of Alexander and Some of Hercules', *CMCS* 13 (1987), 7–38; Helen Fulton, 'Translating Europe in Medieval Wales', in Aidan Conti, Orietta Da Rold, and Philip Shaw (eds), *Writing Europe, 500–1450: Texts and Contexts*, Essays and Studies, 68 (Cambridge, 2015),

The author conforms to several tropes of Latin panegyric, including what Ernst Curtius calls the inexpressibility topos, an 'emphasis on inability to cope with the subject',[15] wherein the author conveys the impossibility of voicing his sorrow for the deceased:

> Ad tanti ergo obitum uiri accedens [h]aut sine lacrimis enarrandum, utpote planctu dignum, [h]aut cuique sine dolore recordandum, quia omnibus dampnosum, [h]aut sine merore audiendum, quia cunctis lugubrem, deficio, uox silet, lingua stupet.
>
> Therefore, to approach the death of so great a man, which is not to be narrated without tears, as is worthy of a lament, not to be remembered by each person without sorrow, because it caused the loss of all things, not to be heard without grief, because it is mournful for all, I am insufficient; the voice is silent; the tongue is numb.[16]

As others have noted, the author also uses the modesty topos, saying that Statius would have been able to praise Rhys properly had he been alive in the twelfth century.[17] Further, the author's hyperbolic use of 'all people' mourning Rhys's death (*iam Wallia uiduata dolet ruitura dolore* 'Wales mourns, now widowed and doomed to be destroyed by grief') is common in Latin panegyric.[18] These examples show how well versed the author was in Latin rhetoric.

The elegy also fits a Welsh context. Poets in medieval Wales commemorating fallen leaders often conveyed the very real political consequences of their deaths, as the political order that Welsh princes maintained in their lifetimes was rarely carried forward by their immediate descendants.[19] The comparison of Rhys to Homeric heroes, particularly the Trojan brothers Hector and Paris, would have reinforced Rhys's

---

159–74, at 164. In the marcher context, Roger Mortimer is praised as *ille inclitus leo, Hector secundus* 'that renowned lion, a second Hector' in the *Fundationis et Fundatorum Historia* in Chicago, University Library, 224, discussed in Ch. 2, pp. 83–4.

[15] Ernst Robert Curtius, *European Literature and the Latin Middle Ages*, trans. Willard R. Trask, Bollingen Series, 36 (Princeton and Oxford, 1953; repr. 2013), 159–60.

[16] Thomas Jones, 'Cronica de Wallia', 30–1; trans. Russell, 'Go and Look in the Latin Books', 217.

[17] Russell, 'Go and Look in the Latin Books', 218.

[18] Curtius, *European Literature*, 160.

[19] Such sentiment surfaces in Higden's notice of Rhys ap Tewdwr's death in 1093: *Rees rex Walliae occisus est in pugna juxta Breknot, et sic reges ibi desiere* 'Rhys king of Wales was killed in a battle near Brecon, and thus kings ceased [in Wales]'; see Ranulph Higden, *Polychronicon*, and John Trevisa, *Polychronicon*, ed. Churchill Babington and Joseph Rawson

link to Troy by blood as well as by repute. As discussed in Chapter 1, the standard narrative of Welsh history in the late twelfth century was that the Welsh were descended from the Trojans, who fled to Britain in the generations after the fall of Troy and founded a line of kings that survived until the Saxon conquest of the early medieval period.[20] Genealogies of Rhys ap Gruffudd trace his lineage back to legendary figures Rhodri Mawr, Beli Mawr, and ultimately Brutus, legendary descendant of Aeneas and eponymous founder of Britain.[21] The elegy places Rhys in the context of the standard narrative of Welsh history and genealogy.

Another elegy for Rhys, this one in verse, appears in a Welsh vernacular chronicle from the fourteenth century. This chronicle is known as the Peniarth 20 version of *Brut y Tywysogion* ('History of the Princes'), so named after its earliest surviving manuscript.[22] This version of the chronicle offers a narrative of Welsh history from 682 (where Geoffrey of Monmouth's *De gestis Britonum* leaves off with the death of Cadwaladr, last king of Britain) to 1332, detailing the activities of Welsh princes.[23] The chronicle is dependent on sources from St Davids, Llanbadarn Fawr, and Strata Florida Abbey—all significant sites of textual production in medieval Wales. The verse elegy consists of thirty-six lines of leonine hexameter, excerpted here:

Lumby, *Polychronicon Ranulphi Higden monachi Cestrensis*, 9 vols (London, 1865–86) (hereafter, *Polychronicon*). This sentiment is probably sourced from the chronicle of John of Worcester, which uses Welsh sources; see a similar passage in the Middle Welsh chronicle *Brut y Tywysogyon, or The Chronicle of the Princes, Red Book of Hergest Version*, ed. and trans. Thomas Jones (Cardiff, 1955), 32–3. For Worcester chronicles' Welsh sources, see Georgia Henley, 'Networks of Chronicle Writing in Western Britain: The Case of Worcester and Wales', in Francesca Tinti and David Woodman (eds), *Constructing History through the Conquest: Worcester c.1050–c.1150* (Woodbridge, 2022), 227–70.

[20] See pp. 50–3.
[21] For discussion, see *MWG* 33, 240–9.
[22] Peniarth 20 is one of the three versions of *Brut y Tywysogion*. For edition, see *Brut y Tywysogion, Peniarth MS 20*, ed. Thomas Jones (Cardiff, 1941), 140–1; for translation, see *Brut y Tywysogion, or, the Chronicle of the Princes: Peniarth MS 20 Version*, ed. Thomas Jones (Cardiff, 1952), 77–8. For a translation into Modern Welsh, see Huw Pryce, 'Y Canu Lladin', in Pryce and Jones (eds), *Yr Arglwydd Rhys*, 212–23, at 217–19; for translations into Modern English, see Russell, 'Go and Look in the Latin Books', 223–4; Henley, 'Rhetoric', 101; Turvey, *Lord Rhys*, 117–18.
[23] For discussion, see, e.g., Huw Pryce, 'Chronicling and its Contexts in Medieval Wales', in Guy et al. (eds), *Chronicles of Medieval Wales*, 1–32, at 11–15.

Nobile Cambrensis cecidit dyadema decoris
    Hoc est Resus obit, Cambria tota gemit.
Resus obit; non fama perit sed gloria transit.
    Cambrensis transit gloria, Resus obit.
Resus obit, decus orbis abit, laus quoque tepescit.   5
    In gemitum viuit Cambria, Resus obit.

[...]

Resus obit; ferrugo tegit galeam, tegit ensem,
    Arma rubigo tegit Cambria, Resus obit.
Resus abest, inimicus adest, Resus quia non est
    Iam tibi nil prodest Cambria, Resus abest.
Resus obit, populi plorant, gaudent inimici.   15
    Anglia stat, cecidit Cambria, Resus obit.
Ora rigant elegi cunctis mea fletibus isti.
    Cor ferit omne ducis dira fagitta necis.

[...]

Camber Locrinus Reso rex Albaque nactus   25
    Nominis et laudis inferioris erant.
Cesar et Arthurus leo fortis vterque sub armis,
    Vel par vel similis Resus vtrique fuit.
Resus Alexander in velle pari fuit alter
    Mundum substerni gliscit vterque sibi.   30
Occasus solis tritus esi fuit armis
    Sensit Alexandri solis in orbe manum.
Laus canitur cineri sancto; cantetur ab omni
    Celi laus regi debita spiritui
Penna madet lacrimis quod scribit thema doloris,   35
    Ne careat forma, littera cesset ea.

The noble crown of Welsh honour has fallen
    This is to say, Rhys is dead, the whole of Wales mourns.
Rhys is dead; his fame has not perished but his glory has passed away.
    The glory of Wales has passed away, Rhys is dead.
Rhys is dead, the glory of the world has gone, his praises too grow cold.   5
    Wales lives on in her grief, Rhys is dead.
[...]

> Rhys is dead; rust covers his helmet and his sword;
>> Rust covers his armour, Wales, [for] Rhys is dead.
> Rhys is gone, the enemy closes in, for Rhys is no more.
>> Nothing avails you now, Wales, Rhys is gone.
> Rhys is dead, the people weep, our enemies rejoice.   15
>> England stands, Wales has fallen, Rhys is dead.
> My face is wet with all the tears of his elegy.
>> The dire arrow of the ruler's death strikes every heart.
>
> [...]
>
> King Camber, Locrinus, and Albanactus   25
>> Were inferior in name and repute to Rhys.
> Caesar and Arthur, both brave [as] lions in arms,
>> Rhys was their equal or similar to both.
> Rhys was a second Alexander of similar desire,
>> Both yearned for the world to stretch out beneath them   30
> The west was beaten down by the arms of Rhys;
>> He felt the hand of Alexander in the sun's orbit.
> Praise is sung to holy ashes; let due
>> Praises be sung by everyone to the king of heaven [and] the holy spirit.
> My pen grows wet with tears for it writes on a theme of grief,   35
>> Let the writing cease, lest it lose its form.[24]

In this verse elegy, Rhys is compared to geographically and lineally proximate heroes from Geoffrey's *De gestis Britonum* (Camber, Locrinus, Albanactus, Arthur, and Caesar) as well as to heroes from further afield like Alexander the Great. Rhys's Trojan ancestry is implied in the references to Camber, Locrinus, and Albanactus, the sons of Brutus who carry on the Trojan line by founding what will become the kingdoms of Wales, England, and Scotland.[25] Praise of ancestors is common in Latin panegyric, and these references would have reminded readers of the line of British kings who ruled before the English, and whose deeds Rhys ap Gruffudd emulated. Immediately following the poem is an epitaph in Latin, introduced to the reader in Welsh:

---

[24] *Brut y Tywysogion: Peniarth MS 20 Version*, ed. Thomas Jones, 140–1. A digital facsimile is available on the NLW Digital Gallery site, http://hdl.handle.net/10107/4754463, accessed 11 October 2022. The translation is mine, with the exception of the last line, which is from Russell, 'Go and Look in the Latin Books', 224; cf. Henley, 'Rhetoric', 101.

[25] *DGB* ii.23, pp. 30–1.

Llyma wedy hyny y gwerseu mydyr o Ladin ysyd yn volyant ar y ved ef ac a wnaethpwyt wedy darvot y gladu ef.

Grande decus tenet iste locus, si cernitur ortus
Si quis sit finis queritur ecce cinis
Laudis amator honoris odor dulcedinis auctor.
Resus in hoc tumulo conditur exiguo
Cesaries quasi congeries solis radiorum
Principis et facies vertitur in cineres Hic tegitur sed detegitur quia fama perhennis.
Non finit illustrem voce latere ducem
Colligitur tumba cinis hac sed transuolat ultra
Nobilitas claudi nescia fune breui
Wallia iam viduata dolet ruitura dolore.

After that, these are metrical verses of Latin that are a eulogy on his sepulchre and that were composed after he had been buried.

If its origin is sought, that place has great majesty;
If one asks what is his end, here are his ashes:
One who loved a fair name, one fragrant with distinction, a fount of gentleness,
Rhys is buried in this small tomb;
The prince's hair, like a mass of the sun's rays,
And his face are turned to ashes
Here he lies hidden, but he is revealed, for his eternal fame
Does not allow the ruler, famed for his words, to lie concealed.
His ashes are collected in this tomb but his nobility flies beyond it
Refusing to be confined by a short rope.
Wales mourns, now widowed and doomed to be destroyed by grief.[26]

The epitaph is linked to the prose lament in *Cronica de Wallia* through the shared concluding phrase *iam Wallia uiduata dolet ruitura dolore* 'Wales mourns, now widowed and doomed to be destroyed by grief'. It has been suggested that the Latin exemplar on which the prose version

---

[26] *Brut y Tywysogion: Peniarth MS 20 Version*, ed. Thomas Jones, 141; translation adapted from Turvey, *Lord Rhys*, 118.

is based also contained the poem, and the prose copyist of *Cronica de Wallia* omitted it except for the final line.[27]

Though there are a number of bilingual Welsh–Latin manuscripts from medieval Wales, code-switching in the middle of a text is rare in medieval Welsh chronicle writing and signals an author and intended audience comfortable in both languages.[28] Moreover, these elegies were written by authors comfortable with not only Latin panegyric, as discussed above, but with Welsh poetic conventions. Paul Russell has discussed the repetition of *Heu! heu! iam Wallia uiduata dolet ruitura dolore* as an echo of patterns of repetition that emphasize grief in medieval Welsh vernacular elegies, or *marwnadau* ('death poems'), such as that written by Gruffudd ab yr Ynad Coch for Prince Llywelyn ap Gruffudd after his death in 1282: *Gwae fi am arglwydd, gwalch diwaradwydd! / Gwae fi o'r aflwydd ei dramgwyddaw! / Gwae fi o'r golled, Gwae fi o'r dynged! / Gwae fi o'r clywed fod clwyf arnaw!* 'Woe is me for a prince, a hawk beyond reproach! / Woe is me for the ill that overcame him! / Woe is me for the loss. Woe is me for the fate! / Woe is me to hear that he was wounded!' (ll. 7–10).[29] This poet adheres to additional conventions of Welsh poetry: the lines *ferrugo tegit galeam, tegit ensem, / Arma rubigo tegit* 'rust covers his helmet and his sword; / Rust covers his armour' (ll. 11–12) echo conventional descriptions of the passage of time and decline of a prince's worldly belongings in the *Canu Urien* saga poems of early medieval Wales. Written before the mid-twelfth century, these poems commemorate the death of a late-sixth-century king, Urien of Rheged. The poem *Aelwyd Rheged* ('Rheged's Hall') describes the death of Urien in terms of the decline of his hall, which is given back to nature and wild plants after he dies. Each three-line *englyn* stanza describes wild plants growing over the hearth: *Yr aelwyt honn, neus kud dynat* 'this hearth, nettles cover it'; *Yr aelwyt honn, neus cud glessin* 'this hearth, borage covers it'; *Yr aelwyt*

---

[27] Russell, 'Go and Look in the Latin Books', 226.
[28] Examples of bilingual manuscripts from Wales include paired Welsh and Latin texts in the Book of Llandaf, Ieuan ap Sulien's Welsh-language poem on St Padarn in the *Llanbadarn Augustine* (CCCC 199, fol. 11ʳ), and the Latin manuscripts of the Welsh laws. For Latinity in Wales, see Russell, 'Go and Look in the Latin Books'; Georgia Henley, 'From "The Matter of Britain" to "The Matter of Rome": Latin Literary Culture and the Reception of Geoffrey of Monmouth in Wales', *Arthurian Literature*, 33 (2016), 1–28.
[29] *Gwaith Bleddyn Fardd a beirdd eraill ail hanner y drydedd ganrif ar ddeg*, ed. Rhian M. Andrews and Catherine McKenna, Cyfres Beirdd y Tywysogion, 7 (Cardiff, 1996), 414–33, at 423; trans. Russell, 'Go and Look in the Latin Books', 225.

honn, neus cud kallawdyr llwyt 'this hearth, grey lichen covers it'.[30] The hearth is also covered by brambles, thorns, and dock leaves, and wild pigs and chickens root in it. These lines are echoed in the elegy to the Lord Rhys. To a Welsh reader, the location of an elegiac poem at Rhys's grave would have marked his status among the ranks of Welsh heroes and reaffirmed the ability of poetry to spread fame after death.

The elegies for Rhys also conform to Latin poetic conventions. Describing Rhys as *esuriencium morsus, siciencium potus* 'food for the hungry, drink for the thirsty' recalls Augustine of Hippo, who describes Christ's teachings as nourishing meals for young children, beginning with milk and progressing to solid food.[31] The elegy's food metaphors would have strengthened an association between Rhys's generosity and the bodily sacrifice of Christ. In addition, the prose elegy in particular is characterized by the building-up of successive sets of short epithets: in §4, Rhys is an *urbium ualidus expugnator, bella mouens, turmas instaurans, hostiles cateruas obruens, [h]aut secus quam aper frendens audacia, seu leo rugiens caude uerbere stimulatus in iras* 'a powerful destroyer of cities, starting wars, preparing battalions, destroying enemy columns, snarling with courage like a boar, or a roaring lion lashing its tail'. This build-up of noun pairs and noun–adjective pairs, with animal imagery emphasizing Rhys's strength and bravery, concludes in a climax in §7 that proclaims the grief experienced by the entire country after his death. The poem's last phrase, an outcry of mourning over the death of Rhys (*Wallia iam viduata dolet ruitura dolore* 'Wales mourns, now widowed and doomed to be destroyed by grief'), was surely intended to invoke an affective response in the reader.[32] The pain and grief in this lament are universally intelligible.

For a Welsh audience, these texts may have reaffirmed cultural pride in South Wales's ability to resist English conquest during Rhys's lifetime. The poem's comparison of Rhys to Alexander the Great invokes ideas of conquest and empire: *Resus Alexander in velle pari fuit alter / Mundum substerni gliscit vterque sibi. / Occasus solis tritus esi fuit armis / Sensit Alexandri solis in orbe manum* 'Rhys was a second Alexander of similar desire; / both yearned for the world to stretch out beneath them.

---

[30] For general discussion, see *Early Welsh Saga Poetry: A Study and Edition of the Englynion*, ed. and trans. Jenny Rowland (Cambridge, 1990), 75–119.
[31] Curtius, *European Literature*, 134–6.
[32] For an argument that emotion in pre-modern literature is intelligible to the modern reader, see Harbus, 'Embodied Emotion', 129, 137–8.

/ The West was beaten down by the arms of Rhys; / he felt the hand of Alexander in the orbit of the sun'.[33] This hyperbolic comparison to Alexander points to Rhys's ability to unite and rule over considerable portions of South Wales, much as Alexander had conquered and ruled over his empire. The phrase *occasus solis* deliberately points to the western portion of the island of Britain where the sun sets—in other words, Rhys's territory, stretching to the coast of West Wales. The comparison to Alexander also highlights Wales's downfall upon Rhys's death, as no ruler after him was able to maintain sole political control over Deheubarth. Following his death, the region was split between his descendants, and was later brought under marcher and English political control. Later, a savvy fourteenth-century reader of the chronicle surely would have recognized the parallels between Rhys and the predicament of Llywelyn ap Gruffudd, last prince of Wales, whose death at the hands of marcher soldiers in 1282 marked the end of Welsh independence and the beginning of a colonial relationship that continues to the present day.

Elegies for the Lord Rhys ap Gruffudd in marcher and English contexts

These two elegies exemplify a pattern of literary transmission that defined contact between cultures in the March of Wales. Like the journey of the *Epitome historiae Britanniae* detailed in Chapter 1, these elegies for the Lord Rhys moved from Welsh to marcher to English audiences in the fourteenth century. This movement was made possible by Ranulph Higden (d. 1363), a Benedictine monk and historian working at the abbey of St Werburgh in Chester in the early to mid-fourteenth century, because he included excerpts of the elegies in his *Polychronicon*.[34] The *Polychronicon* offers a universal history of the world with particular focus on Britain, Wales, and Chester.

---

[33] For medieval interpretations of Alexander the Great, see Venetia Bridges, *Medieval Narratives of Alexander the Great: Transnational Texts in England and France*, Studies in Medieval Romance, 20 (Cambridge, 2018); Markus Stock (ed.), *Alexander the Great in the Middle Ages: Transcultural Perspectives* (Toronto, 2015); Hildegard L. C. Tristram, 'More Talk of Alexander', *Celtica*, 21 (1990), 658–63.

[34] *Polychronicon*, i.11. For discussion, see Emily Steiner, 'Compendious Genres: Higden, Trevisa, and the Medieval Encyclopedia', *Exemplaria*, 27/1–2 (2015), 73–92; Kathy

Perhaps because he came from Chester, a border town, and understood Chester to have been part of Wales historically, Higden gives more focus to Wales than some of his English contemporaries.[35] He was aware of the proximity of Chester to Wales in the greater context of British history: concerning the town's geographical position, he writes:

> Urbs quidem in confinio Angliae ad prospectum Cambriae, inter duo marina brachia, Dee et Mercee, situata; quae tempore Britonum caput fuit et metropolis Venedotiae, id est, Norwalliae; cujus fundator ignoratur.[36]
>
> The city is situated on the border of England in sight of Wales, between two marine arms, the Dee and the Mersey. In the time of the Britons it was the capital and chief city of Venedotia, that is, North Wales; its founder is unknown.

Through his long historical view of Chester, including its name changes throughout history, Higden signals awareness that he resides in a borderland whose political geography, borders, and structures of power fluctuate over time. Though Chester is no longer part of North Wales, the city links the two peoples together in shared admiration: *Anglis et Cambris nunc manet urbs celebris* 'Now the city is celebrated by

---

Lavezzo, *Angels on the Edge of the World: Geography, Literature, and English Community, 1000–1534* (Ithaca, NY, 2006), 71–92; John Taylor, *English Historical Literature in the Fourteenth Century* (Oxford, 1987), 90–109.

[35] For Higden and Chester, see Jane Beal, 'Mapping Identity in John Trevisa's English *Polychronicon*: Chester, Cornwall and the Translation of English National History', *Fourteenth Century England*, 3 (2004), 67–82. For medieval Chester, see Catherine A. M. Clarke (ed.), *Mapping the Medieval City: Space, Place and Identity in Chester c.1200–1600* (Cardiff, 2011); Elizabeth Danbury, 'The Intellectual Life of the Abbey of St Werburgh, Chester in the Middle Ages', in Alan T. Thacker (ed.), *Medieval Archaeology, Art and Architecture at Chester*, The British Archaeological Association Conference Transactions, 22 (Leeds, 2000), 107–20. Higden's chapter on Wales (i.38) is his only chapter written in verse; it is based mostly on Gerald of Wales's *Itinerarium Kambriae* and *Descriptio Kambriae*; see *Polychronicon*, i.394–430; Ronald Waldron, 'Trevisa's Translation of Higden's *Polychronicon*, Book I, Chapter 38, *De Wallia*: An Edition', in Ruth Kennedy and Simon Meecham-Jones (eds), *Authority and Subjugation in Writing of Medieval Wales* (New York, 2008), 99–135.

[36] *Polychronicon*, ii.76–8; Beal, 'Mapping Identity', 69. Trevisa translates *in confinio Angliae ad prospectum Cambria* as *in þe marche of Engelond toward Wales*, locating Chester specifically in the March; *Polychronicon*, ii.79. Several times Trevisa uses the word 'march' where Higden does not.

the English and the Welsh.[37] Recent work on medieval Chester has demonstrated a permeable rather than fixed boundary between the two cultures within the city and its environs, with Welsh people engaging in trade and religious worship within the city and viewing the city as part of a 'larger political whole' of English colonization.[38]

Among the number of short poems Higden includes in his chronicle are sixteen lines of the verse elegy to Rhys, a variant form of what is printed above, as well as a short, pithy excerpt of the prose lament from *Cronica de Wallia*. His excerpt, in book VII.31, reads:

> Hoc anno obiit Resus princeps Walliae, de quo quidam sic cecinit: O belli gloria, militiae clipeus, patriae tutamen, armorum decus, brachium fortitudinis, largitatis manus, rationis oculus, honestatis splendor, pectore gerens Herculis, Achillis asperitatem, Nestoris modestiam, Tydei audaciam, Samsonis fortitudinem, Hectoris gravitatem, Eurialii agilitatem, Paridis formam, Ulixis facundiam, Salamonis sapientiam, Ajacis animositatem. O nudorum vestis, famelicorum morsus, omnium denique postulantium plena satisfactio. O dulcis eloquio, comes obsequio, actu honestus, sermone modestus, vultus hilaris, facie decorus, singulis benignus, omnibus aequus.

> Versus de Reso principe Walliae.
>
> Nobile Cambrensis cecidit diadema decoris
>   Hoc est Resus obit, Cambria tota gemit.
> Resus obit; non fama perit sed gloria transit.
>   Cambrensis transit gloria, Resus obit.
> Resus obit, decus orbis abit, laus quaeque tepescit.   5
>   In gemitu vivit Cambria, Resus obit.
> Resus abest, inimicus adest, Resus quia non est
>   Iam sibi nil prodest Cambria, Resus obit.
> Non moritur sed subtrahitur, quia semper habetur
>   Ipsius egregium nomen in orbe nouum.   10
> Grande decus, tenet iste locus, sed cernitur ortus
>   Si quis sit finis quaeritur ecce cinis.
> Hic tegitur, sed detegitur, quia fama perennis
>   Non fuit illustrem, voce latere ducem.

---

[37] *Polychronicon*, ii.80. For Chester as a social space shared by Welsh and English people, see Helen Fulton, 'The Outside Within: Medieval Chester and North Wales as a Social Space', in Clarke (ed.), *Mapping the Medieval City*, 149–68.

[38] Fulton, 'Outside Within', 164.

> Excessit probitate modum, sensu probitatem, 15
> Eloquio sensum, moribus eloquium.[39]

In this year Rhys prince of Wales died, of whom the following was sung: O glory of war, honour of soldiers, protector of his country, honour of arms, arm of bravery, hand of generosity, eye of reason, splendour of honour, bearing Hercules in his heart, the harshness of Achilles, the modesty of Nestor, the daring of Tydeus, the strength of Sampson, the dignity of Hector, the agility of Euralius, the beauty of Paris, the eloquence of Ulysses, the wisdom of Solomon, the spirit of Ajax. O clothing for the naked, morsel for the famished, laden provider for all who petition. O sweet in speech, agreeable in behaviour, honourable in deed, modest of speech, cheerful of expression, decorous of appearance, kind in each thing, fair to all.

> Verses on Rhys prince of Wales:

> The noble crown of Welsh honour has fallen
>   This is to say, Rhys is dead, the whole of Wales mourns.
> Rhys is dead; his fame has not perished but his glory has passed away.
>   The glory of Wales has passed away, Rhys is dead.
> Rhys is dead, the glory of the world has gone, his praises too grow cold. 5
>   Wales lives on in her grief, Rhys is dead.
> Rhys is gone, the enemy closes in, for Rhys is no more.

> Nothing avails you now, Wales, Rhys is gone.
> He does not die but is removed, for his fair name
>   Is held ever fresh throughout the world. 10
> If its origin is sought, that place has great majesty;
>   If one asks what is his end, here are his ashes.
> Here he lies hidden, but he is revealed, for his eternal fame
>   Does not [allow] the ruler, famed for his words, to lie concealed.
> He surpasses measure with his honesty, honesty with his affection, 15
>   affection with his eloquence, eloquence with his virtue.

---

[39] *Polychronicon*, viii.158–60. The appearance of both poem and prose lament in the *Polychronicon* heightens the possibility raised by Russell that the *Cronica de Wallia*'s exemplar at some level included both prose passage and poem, suggested by the leftover last line embedded at the end of the prose passage in *Cronica de Wallia*. Higden's possession of both prose and poem, and in the same order, is strong evidence that a Latin text of both prose and poem circulated. See discussion above, pp. 205–6.

How exactly Higden obtained these texts is unknown, but their presence in the *Polychronicon* suggests a transmission link between Valle Crucis Abbey in Powys (where Peniarth 20 was produced) and Chester on the Welsh border, through a monastic network that connected Cistercian, Benedictine, and Augustinian abbeys in the borderlands. Written in a language he knew, and containing common cultural touchpoints such as the Latin and British heroic epithets discussed above, the elegies had enough currency with Higden's view of Wales (a country once great, but now needing to be brought in line with English cultural norms) to be worthy of inclusion.[40] John Taylor attributes the popularity of Higden's chronicle to interest in the classical world at the time, inspiring various writers to connect 'the origin of their societies with those of the ancient world'.[41] The lament for Rhys, with its extended comparisons to classical heroes, may have appealed to Higden's tastes for this reason.

English readers in Chester and beyond would have been attracted to the idea of English exceptionalism put forth in the *Polychronicon*.[42] Higden's prefaces 'define England as the most special place described in the chronicle ... a land of divine wonders and natural plenty'.[43] Kathy Lavezzo sees this desire for English exceptionalism as the author's natural reaction to his position in Cheshire: 'As a resident of a county on the edge of his nation, Higden may well have been more inclined to invoke in his writing the positioning of his nation on the edge of the world'.[44] This place of 'geographic alterity', in Lavezzo's view, encouraged a sense of isolation and marginality that charged Higden with a desire to embrace England, an exceptional country with a continuous history that was not substantially interrupted despite successive waves of conquest. In her reading of Higden, it is the presence of Wales and the Welsh that provides Cheshire, and its 'marginal' position, with 'the threat of wildness and regression [that offers] the potential for [English] independence and sovereignty' and, even more significantly in the

---

[40] For discussion, see Tim Thornton, 'Wales in Late Medieval and Early Modern English Histories: Neglect, Rediscovery, and their Implications', *Historical Research*, 90/250 (2017), 663–858, at 685.

[41] Taylor, *English Historical Literature*, 98.

[42] For my definition of English identity in this context, see the Introduction, pp. 17–22.

[43] Lavezzo, *Angels on the Edge*, 73.

[44] Ibid., 74.

colonial context of the Marches, with the 'uncivil and even the savage'.[45] In other words, Cheshire's marginality is due to its proximity to Wales. The portrayal of England as exceptional because of its abundant farmland implicates Wales as comparatively wild and uncultivated—not because it is infertile, which it is not, according to Higden, but because the inhabitants do not know how to harness its agricultural potential.[46] Higden's narrative of British history thus traces the decline of Wales and the rise of England and puts forward a negative image of the Welsh. In this colonial context, the death of Rhys ap Gruffudd acquires new meaning for the generation of chronicle readers that lived immediately after the conquest of Wales, a meaning I address further below.

Higden's decision to include the elegies brought them to a much larger audience than they would otherwise have enjoyed. Given that the *Polychronicon* circulated widely in England, surviving in an extraordinary 118 manuscripts and fragments, his inclusion of the elegies to Rhys meant that many Latinate English readers came into contact with them, including John Wyclif, Thomas Usk, and, later, antiquarians such as Stephen Batman and William Cecil.[47] Furthermore, the *Polychronicon* was translated into English by John Trevisa between 1378 and 1382, printed by Caxton in 1482, and reprinted by Wynkyn de Worde in 1496, duly exposing the elegies for Rhys to a vernacular English readership that included John Lydgate and possibly Geoffrey Chaucer.[48] From

---

[45] Lavezzo, *Angels on the Edge*, 74.

[46] Monika Otter terms this *gaainable tere*, land that can be conquered from those who are not using it properly and cultivated as farmland; see Otter, *Inventiones: Fiction and Referentiality in Twelfth-Century English Historical Writing* (Chapel Hill, NC, 1996), 59–60.

[47] A. S. G. Edwards, 'The Influence and Audience of the *Polychronicon*: Some Observations', *Proceedings of the Leeds Philosophical and Literary Society*, 17/6 (1980), 113–19, at 114–16.

[48] Richard A. Dwyer, 'Some Readers of John Trevisa', *Notes & Queries*, 212 (1967), 291–2. A second English translation by an anonymous translator was produced between 1432 and 1450. For the text of John Trevisa's English translation, see *Polychronicon*, with updates in Kazutaka Karasawa, 'John Trevisa's Middle English Translation of Ranulph Higden's *Polychronicon* Based on Senshu University Library, MS 1—A Diplomatic Edition', *Journal of the Faculty of Letters, Komazawa University*, 69 (2011), 23–59; 70 (2012), 1–85; 71 (2013), 21–101; 72 (2014), 1–97; 75 (2017), 29–89; 76 (2018), 29–90; Ronald Waldron, *John Trevisa's Translation of the Polychronicon of Ranulph Higden, Book VI: An Edition Based on British Library MS Cotton Tiberius D. VII*, Middle English Texts, 35 (Heidelberg, 2004). For discussion, see Jane Beal, *John Trevisa and the English Polychronicon*,

Caxton they came to be included in Camden's *Britannia* in 1586. No other Welsh elegy has enjoyed such wide circulation. And yet their fragmentary form and emphasis on the passing of a Welsh leader as if he is some distant classical hero is indicative of the attitude towards Welsh history exhibited by English chroniclers and readers. The elegy is moving, perhaps even inspiring of sympathy, but it places the heroic age of Wales firmly in the past. Welsh exceptionalism, bravery, and military prowess have faded into historical memory.

It is useful to take a closer look at contemporary English readers of Higden to imagine how the laments for Welsh princes would have been received. John Trevisa was an Oxford-educated cleric possibly from Trevessa in St Enoder, Cornwall.[49] He completed the translation of *Polychronicon* between 1378 and 1382, and it survives in fourteen manuscripts.[50] The translation was commissioned by his patron, the young Thomas, Lord Berkeley (1352–1417) of Gloucestershire. Trevisa translates the prose of Higden and omits most of the verse elegy to Rhys, including only the last line.[51]

Thomas Berkeley and other English readers of Trevisa living in Gloucestershire, separated from Wales by the Severn River, may have been particularly interested in the historical princes of Wales.

Arizona Studies in the Middle Ages and Renaissance, 37 (Turnhout, 2013); Emily Steiner, 'Radical Historiography: Langland, Trevisa, and the *Polychronicon*', *Studies in the Age of Chaucer*, 27 (2005), 171–211.

[49] Trevisa is a Cornish place name most often identified with Trevessa in St Enoder, Cornwall. The evidence that John Trevisa was Cornish is based on his Cornish surname, his addition to the *Polychronicon* of information about Cornwall, and his admission to Exeter College, Oxford, which catered to students from Cornwall; see Beal, 'Mapping Identity', 71–4; Ronald A. Waldron, 'Trevisa's "Celtic Complex" Revisited', *Notes & Queries*, 36/3 (1989), 303–7.

[50] David C. Fowler, *John Trevisa* (Aldershot, 1993), 14–17.

[51] The text reads: *Þis ȝere deide Ree prince of Wales; of him oon seid in þis manere: O blis of bataille, child of chivalrie, defens of contray, worschippe of armes, arme of strengþe, hond of largenes, yȝe of resoun, briȝtnes of honoste, berynge in breest Ector his proves, Achilles his scharpues, Nestor his soburnes, Tydeus his hardynesse, Sampson his strengþe, Ector his worþynesse, Eurialus his swiftnes, Parys his fairnes, Ulix his faire speche, Salomon his wisdom, Ajax his hardynes. O cloþing of þe naked, þe hungry his mete, fulfillynge alle men bone þat hym wolde ouȝt bidde. O faire of speche, felowȝ in service, honest of dede and sobre in word. Glad of semblaunt and loveliche of face. Goodliche to everiche man, and riȝtful to alle; þe noble dyademe of þe fairnes of Wales is now afalle* (*Polychronicon*, viii.159–60). The final line is a rendition of the first line of the poem, *Nobile Cambrensis cecidit diadema decoris* 'The noble crown of Welsh honour has fallen'. It is possible that Trevisa was accessing a Latin version that did not have the whole verse elegy in it, as in the *Cronica de Wallia*, or he cut it on purpose.

Gloucestershire nobility had a vested interest in maintaining its colonial relationship with South Wales, where the earls of Gloucester (the Despensers in the fourteenth century) controlled significant conquest territories. The colonial hierarchy established by the mid-fourteenth century, several generations after the 1282 conquest of Wales, would have been ideologically reinforced by a historical narrative of Welsh royal decline as detailed in Higden and Trevisa. Moreover, Thomas Berkeley served as the admiral of the south and west in the wars against Owain Glyndŵr, fighting against the rebel leader in a naval battle in 1405.[52] With this backdrop of Trevisa's patron's military engagement with the Welsh in mind, it is not difficult to detect a colonial ideology present in the translation. Readers like Thomas Berkeley would have read Trevisa's account of British history as a narrative of decline, with the Welsh people, though descended from the legendary Britons and Trojans, no longer deserving of independent rule.[53] A few examples from the *Polychronicon* bear this out.

At the heart of the *Polychronicon* is the narrative arc, taken ultimately from Geoffrey of Monmouth, of successive waves of invasion that displaced Britain's rulers. First the Britons, led by Brutus from Troy, land on Britain's shores and displace its resident giants; then the Britons are themselves conquered by the Romans, Scots, and Picts. As a consequence, the Saxons take over; later they are nearly conquered by the Danes and fully conquered by the Normans. At the centre of this thematic emphasis on waves of conquest is the Britons' loss of control of the kingdom. Trevisa explains that the kingdom of Britain stood strong as one kingdom from Brutus to Julius Caesar, after which point it was taken over by the Romans, who ruled it by proxy: *successoures of Bretouns faillede, and Romaynes reignede in Bretayne*.[54] The Romans' departure from Britain is the death knell for the Britons' independent rule:

---

[52] *Chronica Monasterii S. Albani. Thomæ Walsingham, quondam monachi S. Albani, Historia Anglicana*, ed. Henry Thomas Riley, 2 vols (London, 1863–4), ii.272, discussed by Ralph Hanna, 'Sir Thomas Berkeley and his Patronage', *Speculum*, 64/4 (1989), 878–916, at 891.

[53] These readers were probably for the most part baronial, and included the Beauchamp and Warwick families; see Ronald Waldron, 'The Manuscripts of Trevisa's Translation of the *Polychronicon*: Towards a New Edition', *Modern Language Quarterly*, 51/3 (1990), 281–317, at 282–3.

[54] *Polychronicon*, ii.97–9.

> Þanne Scottes and Pictes by mysledynge of Maximus þe tyraunt pursued Bretayne, and werred þerynne wiþ greet strengþe of men of armes long tyme, for to þe Saxones come at þe prayenge of [þe] Britouns aȝenst þe Pictes, and putte out Gurmund the Irische king wiþ his Pictes, and þe Britouns also wiþ here kyng, þat heet Careticus, and drof hem out of Engelond in to Wales. And so þe Saxons were victors, and eueriche prouince, as he was strengere, made hem kynges.[55]

The Britons lose their kingdom and are driven into Wales because they cannot defend it, and the Saxons take over because they are stronger. In a more detailed retelling later, Trevisa describes Gurmundus and the Saxons driving Careticus and the Britons across the Severn into Wales, *and from þat tyme forward þe Britouns loste þe hole kingdom of Bretayne*.[56] These actions are repeated by the early West Saxon king Ceaulinus, son of Kinricus, *who droof þe Britouns out of þe citees of Gloucestre, [of Surcetre], and of Baþe, into þe hilles and mountaynes and wildernesse of Wales*.[57] This loss of the right to rule over Britain so long ago would have reinforced, for English readers like Thomas Berkeley, why the status quo of early fifteenth-century English dominance over Wales ought to be maintained militarily—it was long-standing, with a precedent dating back to the Roman and Saxon invasions.

Other moments in Trevisa's translation subtly promote the superiority of England and English culture. First, though he knows that the Britons were, historically, converted to Christianity long before the English, Trevisa says that *Englische men ... torned first to riȝtful byleue*, implying that the Britons' early Christianity, corrupted by Pelagianism, was not true Christianity.[58] Second, while Higden describes the circumference of Wales as smaller than that of England (*...ujus circumferentia, / quamvis sit minor Anglia*), Trevisa goes further and elides the mention of circumference to say that Wales is *well lasse*, smaller in size or inferior: *And þey þat this londe / Be well lasse þan Engelonde, / As good glebe is oon as other, / In þe douȝter and in þe moder*.[59] Here, Trevisa

---

[55] *Polychronicon*, ii.99.
[56] Ibid., v.341–3.
[57] Ibid., v.349.
[58] *Polychronicon*, ii.29. For the conversion of the English, which comments on the failures of the Britons, see ibid., v.405–9.
[59] Ibid., i.396–7.

subordinates Wales to England by describing their relationship as one between mother and child, implying that England is a parent that nurtures and cares for—but also controls—its offspring. Third, embedded in the description of Wales's political structure is a transfer of power to England:

> I Wales how it be
> Were somtyme contrees þre;
> At Karmarthyn was þat oon,
> An þat oþer was in Moon;
> The þridde was in Powisy
> In Pengwern, þat now is Schroysbury.
> There were bisshopes seuen,
> And now beeþ foure euene,
> Vnder Saxons al at honde;
> Somtyme vnder princes of þat lond.[60]

Trevisa, following Higden, explains that there were three provinces (*contrees*) in Wales, centred in Carmarthen, Anglesey (Môn in Welsh, hence *Moon*), and Powys. These roughly map onto the twelfth-century Welsh polities of Deheubarth, Gwynedd, and Powys. But they have been transferred to English control: a former Welsh court is now an English town, Shrewsbury, and the number of bishoprics is reduced from seven to four. Formerly under the control of Welsh princes, they now answer to the English.[61]

Lastly, the rest of the chapter describes the cultural differences of the Welsh, sourced ultimately from Gerald of Wales's *Descriptio Kambriae*. Using a discourse of colonialism, Trevisa emphasizes the lack of civility of the Welsh people: they wear their legs bare and take refuge in the woods; they seldom eat baked wheat bread, and prefer potage, butter, milk, and cheese. Civilizing influence results in a change in their cultural practices:

> Best in maneres of Bretouns,
> For companye of Saxouns,
> Beeþ i-tourned to beter riȝt;
> Þat is knowe as clere as liȝt.

---

[60] *Polychronicon*, i.400–1.
[61] This process is described in further detail in ibid., ii.113–15.

> Thei tilieþ gardyns, feeld, and downes,
> And draweþ hem to gone townes;
> They rideþ i-armed, as wolde God,
> And gooþ i-hosed and i-schod;
> And sitteþ faire at hir mele,
> And slepeþ in beddes faire and wele.
> So þey semeþ now in mynde
> More Englische men þan Walsche kynd.[62]

Compared to their ancestors, the present-day Welsh have become more civilized by adopting the cultural practices of the English.[63] Instead of eating dairy, leeks, and potage meat, they have adopted agriculture; instead of running through the woods to battle, they ride horses. Where before they went barefoot and barelegged, now they wear shoes and hose; they sit at meals and sleep in beds. These cultural changes stemming from English influence alter their very mindset, to the extent that they seem more English than Welsh. To Trevisa's English readers, this cultural assimilation would have been a positive development. The elegy for the Lord Rhys is in this manner couched in anti-Welsh colonial sentiment.

An additional instance of transmission of the elegy from Wales to England provides another example of this combination of historical memory and anti-Welsh rhetoric. A paragraph of the prose lament to Rhys appears in a fourteenth-century manuscript from Norwich Priory (Cambridge, Corpus Christi College (hereafter CCCC) 264), underscoring how far the text travelled beyond Wales.[64] This manuscript contains Roger of Wendover's *Flores historiarum*, Bede's *Historia ecclesiastica gentis Anglorum*, and documents relating to Norwich Priory. The paragraph lamenting Rhys is written at the end of a quire on a blank verso (fol. 64^v) following the end of *Flores historiarum* (fol.

---

[62] *Polychronicon*, i.411.

[63] Later, the Flemings are described as becoming more like the English after keeping the company of Englishmen, underscoring the strength of their influence; see *Polychronicon*, ii.165. For general discussion of these tropes, see R. R. Davies, *The First English Empire: Power and Identities in the British Isles, 1093–1343* (Oxford, 2000).

[64] Provenance is secured to Norwich Priory by an *ex libris* note on fol. 1^r, *liber fratris Symonis Bozoun*, by Simon Bozoun.

64ʳ).[65] On the page facing the lament is the beginning of Bede's *Historica ecclesiastica* and the start of a new quire (fol. 65ʳ). The passage is written in a different hand from the main text, though it is contemporary. It was most likely added to this space after the initial plan for the manuscript was executed. The elegy probably travelled to Norwich Priory via a copy of Higden's *Polychronicon*, a copy of which was in fact in Norwich's library at the same time (London, British Library, Royal 14 C. xiii, *c.*1320–50). *Ex libris* and book list notes indicate that both of these books were owned by Simon Bozoun, prior of Norwich (1344–52). Simon's copy of the *Polychronicon* contains the Rhys elegy and, importantly, shares readings and spelling errors with the copy of the passage in CCCC 264, indicating that one was probably copied from the other. Finding the immediate exemplar for a manuscript copy is exceedingly rare in manuscript studies, but this appears to be the case with these two manuscripts. Monastic libraries, with many books collected under one roof, seem to have offered unprecedented opportunities for textual transmission spurred by individual readership.

It is very likely the noteworthy rhetorical complexity of the passage that made it so attractive for excerption on an otherwise blank folio of CCCC 264. But why was it added in this particular spot, between the excerpt of Roger of Wendover's *Flores historiarum* and Bede's *Historia ecclesiastica*? Towards the end of his chronicle, near the copied passage, Roger of Wendover includes a great deal of detailed information about Henry III and the Poitevin conflict in the 1230s, with attention given to the alliance between Richard Marshal (d. 1234) and the Welsh prince Llywelyn ab Iorwerth (*c.*1173–1240) against King Henry III, the capture of Richard's castle in Wales (presumably Pembroke), and Llywelyn's actions against Henry.[66] It is possible that the scribe who added the Rhys elegy felt inspired to do so because there was so much information about Welsh politics in the preceding pages. It is an excerpt that

---

[65] The end of the text in this copy is not actually the end of *Flores historiarum*; the copy in CCCC 264 is incomplete and ends in 1229.

[66] Roger of Wendover, *Flores historiarum*, ed. Henry Richards Luard, *Flores Historiarum*, 3 vols (London, 1890), ii.203, 210, 221; *Roger of Wendover's Flowers of History: Comprising the history of England from the descent of the Saxons to* AD *1235, Formerly ascribed to Matthew Paris*, trans. J. A. Giles, 2 vols (London, 1849), ii.569–71.

certainly would have piqued the interest of readers engaged in Welsh history and the activities of Welsh princes.

The lament for Rhys exists in tension with Roger of Wendover's markedly negative, bitter treatment of the Welsh in *Flores historiarum*. For example, when he describes the Saxon takeover of the island of Britain, and the flight of the Britons to Wales, Roger writes:

> Residebant igitur miserrimae Britonum reliquiae in tribus provinciis … semper gentem Anglorum, et etiam usque in hodiernum diem, quasi per eos propriis finibus proscripti, odio mortali perstringunt, nec illis libentius quam canibus communicare volunt. Sunt autem provinciae illorum inexpugnabiles … unde saepissime quasi mures de cavernis erumpentes, gentem Anglorum nequiter infestant, nec aliud ab eis in bello nisi capita solum pro redemptione requirunt.
>
> The miserable remnant of the Britons therefore settled in three provinces … they always blame the English people with relentless hatred, even now in the present day, as if the particular boundaries had been proscribed by them; nor are they willing to communicate with them more willingly than they would with dogs. These provinces are, moreover, impregnable … from where, bursting forth frequently as if mice from their holes, they wickedly harass the English people, and they seek nothing from them in war except their heads alone, as redemption.[67]

This anti-Welsh sentiment is quite typical of English chroniclers of the period, depicting the Welsh as animal-like and violent, residing in impregnable mountain fortresses (in implicit contrast to safe, civilized agricultural lowlands), and emerging from the mountains to harass the English. Popular resistance to conquest and colonization is characterized as vindictive, animalistic, and motivated by hatred for the English. It is in the light of this kind of rhetoric that the elegies for twelfth- and thirteenth-century princes of independent Wales in English manuscripts become all the more striking. Reading the elegies for Rhys gave post-conquest English audiences an unusual opportunity to empathize with the Welsh predicament without threatening their political dominance.

---

[67] Roger of Wendover, *Flores historiarum*, ed. Luard, i.280–1; translation adapted from *Roger of Wendover's Flowers of History,* trans. Giles, i.52–3. Thanks to Paul Russell for his comments on this translation.

Imagine an English reader (most likely a reader at a monastery, such as St Augustine's Canterbury, where a continuation was written, or a secular college) perusing Higden.[68] The elegy for Rhys in Higden builds up expectations with a cascade of star-studded praise epithets, with the metaphors and comparisons to Homeric heroes brought over from the original Welsh chronicle.[69] Then the English reader encounters the verse elegy. The first half of the poem laments his death and its consequences, with the glory and independence of Wales gone with him to his grave. The second half shifts to comfort, lessening the sorrow of his passing by declaring that his name will be remembered throughout the world and that one can seek comfort at the site of his grave.[70] Rhys's physical grave is contrasted with the endurance of his fame. Though his body is concealed beneath the earth, his fame shines eternally throughout the world.[71] The repeated refrain *Resus obit* 'Rhys is dead', a statement that befits the poem's chronicle context, builds throughout the poem. It adds constant reminders of death's finality, ultimately overpowering the poet's reassurance that he will live on. The elegies convey, surprisingly in the context of a non-Welsh chronicle, the deep sense of loss and fragmentation experienced by the Welsh after his death.[72] The language of lament is universal, 'in which human emotional pain of a recognizable nature is encapsulated in language'.[73] For English readers like Thomas Berkeley residing in the Welsh borderlands in the 1380s and 1390s, the years immediately leading up to the uprising of Owain Glyndŵr, the Welsh threat to their livelihood was a real one. But, by reading this poem, they would have been able to adopt a Welsh perspective temporarily and experience the emotion behind the death of an important, beloved leader. This experience of affective reading, of identifying with the poet and understanding and imagining the true impact of Rhys's death, closed a gap that otherwise yawned across distant geographies and cultural experiences. Any reader can understand

---

[68] Possible audiences, attested by manuscript provenance, are monastic or secular colleges. There are over 100 manuscripts of Higden's *Polychronicon* and for reasons of space I do not list their provenances here.
[69] See above, pp. 199–200.
[70] See above, p. 203, ll. 9-12.
[71] See above, p. 203, ll. 13-14.
[72] See above, p. 203, ll. 4-8.
[73] Harbus, 'Embodied Emotion', 140.

the pain of loss; it transcends language and nationality. Indeed, this poem may have resonated with an English reader especially during the fractured politics of the fifteenth century.

But the emotion in the poem also has a political function. The heightened rhetoric of the passage creates distance, as well as proximity, held in tension by the reader. While the poem inspires empathy, the repeated references to classical heroes have a different effect, firmly memorializing Rhys in the past, at a safe distance from the present day. This referential aspect of the elegiac mode, placing Rhys firmly in memory, provides a crucial sense of remove: he is memorialized as if he were a classical hero, evocative, but no longer truly a threat. The English reader can enjoy the aesthetic, perhaps personal experience of emotional feeling, but the subject is cast in the heroic light of Hercules and Alexander. He is long past, hardly real, and no longer a threat to the English state. This simultaneous honouring of Welsh loss and placing it at a safely defused remove attests to the ability of elegiac verse to transgress and to break down boundaries of culture and politics through affective experience, while still protecting the cultural dominance of the English in a colonial environment. The reader adopts the Welsh perspective in a manner that is almost exploitative. Trevisa in fact adds a phrase to his prose translation: *Now Wales helpeþ nouȝt it self*, perhaps referring to Wales's hand in its own demise.

Laments for Llywelyn ap Gruffudd

This chapter closes with brief discussion of another poem about a Welsh prince's death, a Latin epitaph for Llywelyn ap Gruffudd (d. 1282). This epitaph was read in medieval England and further illustrates the English affective experience of memorials to Welsh princes. Through a series of diplomatic manoeuvres and protracted military moves, Llywelyn ap Gruffudd was able to control the independent principality of North Wales during his lifetime. But his death at the hands of Edward I's soldiers in 1282, and the final annexation of Gwynedd by the English government afterwards, was widely lamented by Welsh poets and chroniclers as marking the end of Welsh independent rule.

Given the significance of his death to the landscape of Welsh–English politics, it is not surprising that several English chronicles include a set of epitaphs for Llywelyn in their entries for the year 1282. These are found in the *Polychronicon* and the Annals of Chester in Latin, and in Trevisa and a copy of the Middle English Prose *Brut* from Denbighshire in English.[74] The *Polychronicon* is probably the ultimate source for the others. The epitaphs appear in the *Polychronicon* immediately following Llywelyn's death by beheading and his younger brother Dafydd's death by drawing and quartering.[75] Strikingly, the epitaphs acknowledge two contrary perspectives on Llywelyn's legacy, one English and one Welsh:

> De Lewelino praedicto scripserunt duo religiosi metrice in hunc modum. Wallicus sic:
>
> Hic jacet Anglorum tortor, tutor Venedorum,
> Princeps Wallorum Lewelinus, regula morum,
> Gemma coevorum, flos regum praeteritorum,
> Forma futurorum, dux, laus, lex, lux populorum.
>
> Anglicus sic:
>
> Hic jacet errorum princeps et praedo virorum,
> Proditor Anglorum, fax livida, secta reorum,
> Numen Wallorum, trux, dux, homicida piorum,
> Fæx Trojanorum, stirps mendax, causa malorum.
>
> Concerning the aforementioned Llywelyn, two religious men wrote metres in this manner. The Welshman said:
>
> Here lies the tormentor of the English, protector of the men of Gwynedd,
> a prince of the Welsh, Llywelyn, a model of good character,

---

[74] *Polychronicon*, viii.266–8; *Annales Cestrienses: Or, Chronicle of the Abbey of S. Werburg at Chester*, ed. and trans. R. C. Christie (London, 1887), 108–10. The copy is Aberystwyth, NLW, 21608, fol. 88^v; discussed in *An English Chronicle, 1377–1461: Edited from Aberystwyth, National Library of Wales MS 21068 and Oxford, Bodleian Library MS Lyell 34*, ed. William Marx (Woodbridge, 2003), pp. xvi–xix; William Marx, 'Aberystwyth, National Library of Wales, MS 21608 and the Middle English Prose Brut', *Journal of the Early Book Society*, 1/1 (1997), 1–16, at 6. Another manuscript that includes the epitaph for Llywelyn ap Gruffudd (omitting the Englishman's response) is CCCC 281 (s. xii$^{med/2}$), fol. 79^r, in an early modern humanist hand. The same hand copies a poem by Madog of Edeirnion, discussed by Joshua Byron Smith, 'Madog of Edeirnion's *Strenua cunctorum*: A Welsh-Latin Poem in Praise of Geoffrey of Monmouth', *North American Journal of Celtic Studies*, 6/1 (2022), 1–14; he suggests a Welsh readership for CCCC 281.

[75] *Polychronicon*, viii.266.

> a jewel among his contemporaries, flower of the kings of the
>   past,
> a model for those in the future, the leader, praise, law, and light
>   of the people.

The Englishman replied:

> Here lies the prince of errors and robber of men,
> a betrayer of the English, a malicious firebrand, an adherent of
>   criminals,
> a deity of the Welsh, a savage leader, a murderer of the pious,
> [sprung from] the dregs of the Trojans, a deceitful race, a
>   source of evil things.[76]

These competing epitaphs, one in the voice of an Englishman and one in the voice of a Welshman, offer contrasting perspectives on Llywelyn's character and significance. The Welshman describes a figure beloved by the Welsh people. He eulogizes Llywelyn in standardized panegyric language and revels in his destruction of the English, invoking other important Welsh laments about the English presence in their lands.[77] In contrast, Llywelyn is vilified by the English. The Englishman's disparagement is heightened by the repetitive use of hard consonants (*fax, trux, dux, fex, mendax*). He insults Llywelyn's Trojan heritage, with the phrase 'deceitful/lying race' (*stirps mendax*), drawing attention to the Trojans' reputation as deceitful betrayers owing to Paris's kidnapping of Helen of Sparta.[78]

Staging the two epitaphs as a conversation between a Welshman and an Englishman humanizes these opposite extremes, rendering them into an exchange of two voices. The Englishman acknowledges the two

---

[76] *Polychronicon*, viii.266–8. I have adapted Christie's translation; see *Annales Cestrienses*, ed. and trans. Christie, 108–10.

[77] These include the poem *Armes Prydein Vawr* ('The Great Prophecy of Britain'), a tenth-century call to arms against the English, or the late-eleventh-century *Planctus* by Rhygyfarch ap Sulien; see Helen Fulton, 'Tenth-Century Wales and *Armes Prydein*', *Transactions of the Honourable Society of Cymmrodorion*, 7 (2001), 5–18; Sarah Zeiser, 'Latinity, Manuscripts, and the Rhetoric of Conquest in Late-Eleventh-Century Wales' (unpublished Ph.D. dissertation, Harvard University, 2012), 264–71; Michael Lapidge, 'The Welsh–Latin Poetry of Sulien's Family', *SC* 8 (1973), 68–106.

[78] In doing so, the poet echoes the sentiment of John Peckham, archbishop of Canterbury at the time of the Edwardian conquest of Wales, who also turned the esteemed legend of the Britons' Trojan origins on its head by attributing Welsh treachery to their origins in Paris's deceit. See the Introduction, pp. 1–2.

perspectives from which Llywelyn is considered, naming him *numen Wallorum* 'deity of the Welsh' while still castigating him for wickedness. The fact that these competing voices are reading epitaphs—figuratively standing at the grave of Llywelyn and reading the inscriptions on his gravestone—makes the sentiment all the more profound.

The Welsh vernacular *marwnad* ('death poem') for Llywelyn ap Gruffudd composed by Gruffudd ab yr Ynad Coch shortly after his death—one of the most deeply sorrowful and moving pieces of literature in Middle Welsh—offers a point of comparison with this epitaph. As mentioned previously, the poet builds up a succession of repetitive clauses for emotional effect:

> Poni welwch chwi hynt y gwynt a'r glaw?
> Poni welwch chwi'r deri'n ymdaraw?
> Poni welwch chwi'r môr yn merwinaw—'r tir?
> Poni welwch chwi'r gwir yn ymgyweiraw?
> Poni welwch chwi'r haul yn hwylaw—'r awyr?
> Poni welwch chwi'r sŷr wedi r'syrthiaw?[79]

> Do you not see the path of wind and rain?
> Do you not see the oaks clashing together?
> Do you not see the sea gnawing the land?
> Do you not see the truth in rebuke?
> Do you not see the sun traversing the sky?
> Do you not see that the stars have fallen? (ll. 63–8)

The repetition of phrases underscores how the very land cries out after Llywelyn's death. In these lines, Ann Matonis notes that the classical *topos* of nature mourning the death of a king 'universalizes the scope of the disaster which thus far had been presented as personal and local or national'.[80] The poet follows with a sentiment similar to that expressed in the Latin lament for Rhys ap Gruffudd—after the prince's death, there is nowhere to go; the speaker is lordless and stateless, and can find no comfort or resolution.

---

[79] *Gwaith Bleddyn Fardd*, ed. Andrews and McKenna, 414–33, at 424.
[80] Ann Matonis, 'The Rhetorical Patterns in *Marwnad Llywelyn ap Gruffudd* by Gruffudd ab yr Ynad Coch', *Studia Celtica*, 14/1 (1979), 188–92, at 191; see similar discussion in Llinos Beverley Smith, 'Llywelyn ap Gruffudd and the Welsh Historical Consciousness', *WHR* 12/1 (1984), 1–28, at 2.

Like the elegies for Rhys, these epitaphs cross the linguistic boundary from Latin to vernacular. Trevisa presents both speeches bilingually, first in Latin and then in English. The Welshman says, in English:

> Here lieþ þe tormentour of Englische men, wardeyn and tutor of Englishe [sic] men, prince of Walsche men, Lewelyn, rule of good dedes and þewes, cheef precious stoon of hem þat were in his tyme, floure of kynges þat were toforehonde, ensample of hem þat schal be after þis tyme, leder, preysinge, lawe, liȝt of peple.[81]

By translating this speech into English, Trevisa comments implicitly on the consequences of the death of Llywelyn, which brought about the annexation of North Wales by Edward I. Latin, a language known to both Welsh and English religious men, had no colonial overtones, but the Welshman speaking the English vernacular subtly signals that English culture has become dominant. The Englishman states:

> Here liþe þe prince of erroures, [þeef] and robber of men, traytour of Englische men; a dymme brond, and seete of evil dedes and doers; god of Walsche men, a cruel duke, sleere of god men; draftes of Trojanes, a false roote, cause of evel dedes.[82]

Trevisa's own narrative voice resumes immediately afterward to note that King Edward brought English law and sheriffs to Wales and arranged for his son to be born at Caernarfon Castle, while John Peckham, archbishop of Canterbury, came to Wales by way of Chester to reform the church.[83] While the Welsh perspective is acknowledged, it is clear which people has won out in the end. Moreover, the contrasting perspective of Welsh and English was one of the last moments that such a striking difference was possible: both Higden and Trevisa stress the increasing assimilation of Welsh people to English cultural customs, particularly following the suppression of the revolt of Madog ap Llywelyn in 1294, after which point war ceases *and Walsche men lyven as Englische men, and gadreþ tresoure, and dredeþ losse of catell*.[84] Rather than stealing treasure and cattle, the Welsh learn methods of agriculture

---

[81] *Polychronicon*, viii.267.
[82] Ibid., viii.269.
[83] Ibid., viii.269.
[84] Ibid., viii.283.

and other markers of civilization. The competing epitaphs represent the moment before cultural assimilation.

Conclusion

The laments to Rhys ap Gruffudd, appearing first in a Latin chronicle of borderland origin before being transmitted to contexts further afield, including Norwich Priory and the early printed copies of John Trevisa's chronicle by London printers, attest to the considerable geographical distances covered by monastic networks of textual exchange. The inclusion of the epitaphs for Llywelyn ap Gruffudd in the *Polychronicon* and Trevisa's chronicle further attests to a degree of interest in and exposure to literature about Welsh princes on the part of English readers. These items indicate English interest in Welsh figures, an interest that extends beyond attention to Wales as an exotic place, as in Arthurian romances, or as a place of danger and treachery, as in Roger of Wendover's *Flores historiarum*. They also demonstrate the important role that authors in the March of Wales (in this case, Higden) played in the transmission of Welsh texts from Wales to contexts further afield.

The presence of elegiac poetry in monastic chronicles is a testament to the elegy's capacity to transform textual record into personal affective experience. Through the affective reading of elegiac verse, personal and historical memory are joined: heightened rhetoric immerses the reader in the past, while references to Greek, Trojan, and biblical heroes create a sense of continuity across historical time. At the same time, the elegiac form provides a crucial sense of distance when discussing difficult political situations by portraying politically dangerous Welsh leaders as unequivocally past. In doing so, the poems, for English readers and English-leaning readers in the March of Wales, maintain English colonial dominance in a vision of history that honours Welsh leaders from a navigable distance.

Conclusion

Literary Borderlands

By the end of the fifteenth century, Geoffrey's history and its various iterations had eclipsed the popularity of all but a few other major works in the manuscript record. The concepts mined from the history by inhabitants of the author's birthplace, the March of Wales, reached new audiences and found renewed meanings among key players in the Wars of the Roses, which, like other conflicts of succession, sought answers in narratives of history and found recourse in political uses of the past. Ideas about Welsh history, identity, and culture did not fade into obscurity following the conquest of 1282, as is so often assumed, but continued to play an active role in the English literary and historical imagination. This influence is felt in the use of Welsh genealogies by Yorkist and Tudor kings; portrayals of Welsh people, particularly Welsh princes, in English chronicles; and the overall popularity, beyond Wales, of the vision of the British past and future articulated by Geoffrey of Monmouth.

The active role that Wales and the Welsh past played in the historical imagination of late medieval Britain was often mediated through the literature of the March of Wales, written for the baronial families of the marcher lordships, whose sprawling ties to different families and ecclesiastical institutions both within and beyond the March led to the transmission of ideas of the British–Welsh past into new contexts. Within the March of Wales, baronial literature comes into focus as a coherent archive defined by several central concerns: a fierce defence and justification of ownership of marcher lands; a focus on family inheritance and succession, incidentally often through a female line; an intimate but often fraught relationship with Wales, Welsh princes, culture, and customs; and an unprecedented degree of access to Welsh texts, including genealogies, chronicles, and prophecies, that allowed for condensed articulations of marcher identity. Expressions of marcher identity in this archive made concerted use of Geoffrey's *De gestis Britonum* (*Historia regum Britanniae*) as a framework, with its attendant themes of conquest, divine right to rule, prophecy, cyclical loss, and renewal.

Marcher concerns, borne out in the literature discussed in this book, stem from the particular circumstances in which marcher baronial families of the thirteenth and fourteenth centuries found themselves: typically in power by right of conquest and settlement of what would have been, for their Norman and Anglo-Norman ancestors, a foreign land; independent from English royal authority by right of customary law; self-aware of descent from English, Welsh, Norman, and other peoples; and buffeted by challenges to power and authority from all sides. These circumstances, combined with the heightened awareness of ethnic difference and the ability to negotiate such differences across cultures that is characteristic of inhabitants of any border society, precipitated a concerted effort by marchers to define themselves and their place in the region. In many cases, they used their Welsh ancestry to assert their dominance and authority in the borderlands, as well as in contexts further afield. The materials required to assert this regional power and sense of identity were found in previously existing texts, mainly histories and genealogies, written by and for Welsh people.[1] Marchers were well positioned to access such texts and reimagine them for new purposes and in new contexts. The development of marcher literature, which articulated a specific sense of marcher identity and authority, occurred alongside and was due to an unusual degree of access to narratives of British–Welsh history and its attendant prophecies, poetry, and genealogies. Marcher families adapted these narratives in their efforts at self-definition, reimagining the British–Welsh past for their own purposes.

Such acts of 'reimagining' were motivated by the predicament of the marcher family, animated by a need to defend authority and landownership in a contested region, and determined to show that a people descended from Welsh, English, and Norman ancestors was more than the sum of its parts. While some of what marchers wrote about the

---

[1] For a definition of 'Welsh' as an identity term, see the Introduction, pp. 17–23.

British–Welsh past was indeed 'imagined', the contents of these texts were just as real, for marcher readers, as the materials they borrowed from Welsh contexts had been for Welsh readers. The articulation of a British–Welsh past for marcher literature was therefore an act not of 'imagination', but of 'reimagination', an engagement in the truth-adjacent rhetoric of medieval historical writing that grounded historical fact in literary style.

In some instances, such as in the case of the Mortimer family discussed in Chapter 2, the process of rooting a marcher family in Geoffrey's richly developed British–Welsh past had high-reaching political ambitions, wherein a marcher lord's Welsh ancestry strengthened his claim to the English throne; in other cases, such as the lords of Brecon in Chapter 3 or the Fitz Warin family in Chapter 4, the same historical grounding exposed instead a rather more localized effort to solidify land rights, inheritance, and legal independence from English royal authority without the same degree of national ambition, but with nevertheless strong ties to a regional heritage that was grounded in the historical past. Such families were united in their use of creative, politically relevant reimaginings of the British–Welsh past for familial gain, and their activities stand in contrast to, for example, a marcher lord such as William Marshal, discussed in Chapter 4, whose relationship with the March of Wales and the Welsh people was wholly antagonistic and exploitative, and therefore exposes the degree of acculturation to the English–Welsh borderlands taking place among other families. Marcher families were united by the changeable political landscape of the March of Wales and the chaotic circumstances of colonization and conquest that brought them to rule the lordships of the region with characteristic inconsistency and individual ambition. It is perhaps this degree of chaos, ambiguity, power struggle, and multicultural mixing that led to a need for precise self-definition and self-promotion, and marcher articulations of the British–Welsh past were part and parcel of these efforts.

The literature studied in this book exposes the emergence of a coherent marcher identity in the medieval period. The articulation of this identity required awareness, on the part of marcher people, of the customs, languages, and behaviours that were marked as distinctly English, Welsh, Norman, or otherwise, when to use them, and when to recognize or deny their value. This mixed border culture gave rise to a 'third category' of identity that was recognizably not just English, nor Welsh, nor Norman, but a new identity immersed in the customs of several cultures and adept at fitting into different contexts—the *marchiones* that Gerald of Wales champions in his *Expugnatio Hibernica*.[2] Some marchers seem to have envisioned themselves as ideally bringing together the different cultural strands of the different people of Britain into one, while others maintained more of a binary awareness of English and Welsh peoples and 'code-switched' between them depending on the context. Other inhabitants of the borderlands would, of course, have self-identified as English or Welsh alone, but one can imagine a proliferation of all sorts of degrees of multicultural identity along a spectrum, such as exists in modern borderlands today. It also must be said that aristocratic families in other regions of Britain, beyond the March of Wales, were also engaged in literary activities that explored issues of identity, but what sets the families of the March of Wales apart is a particularly intense negotiation with Wales, the Welsh people, and the Welsh past as a vital part of their articulations of self. Marcher families highlighted their Welsh ancestry, not only in defence of their rulership over former Welsh kingdoms, but also to show that they were the ideological inheritors of British rulership overall. Their efforts show that Wales and Welsh culture had a strong political currency in medieval Britain that it is not usually afforded in modern scholarship.

'Marchers' were therefore a distinct group of people dwelling in the March of Wales, who did not strongly identify as either 'English', 'Welsh', or 'Norman' in that context, but as a hybrid of one or more of the cultures of the borderlands, in a manner that served their interests. This group found meaning in the historical framework provided by Geoffrey's *De gestis Britonum* (hereafter *DGB*) and its afterlives, and found some degree of purchase in understanding, aligning itself with, and/or adopting aspects of Welsh identity and culture. It is visible at certain moments in literary texts produced in the borderlands and becomes even more visible when the literature of the borderlands is taken as

---

[2] Gerald of Wales, *Expugnatio Hibernica*, ii.38, ed. and trans. A. B. Scott and F. X. Martin, *Expugnatio Hibernica: The Conquest of Ireland by Giraldus Cambrensis*, A New History of Ireland, Ancillary Publications, 3 (Dublin, 1978), 246; Gerald of Wales, *Descriptio Kambriae,* ii.8, ed. J. F. Dimock, *Giraldi Cambrensis Opera*, 6 (London, 1868), 220.

a whole. Marcher identity and culture would, of course, have been as variable as the geography and history of the March itself, composed of myriad lordships, counties, and the variable fortunes of marcher lords, and I anticipate that future studies will continue to uncover further nuances in its articulation.

A major and perhaps unexpected outcome of these marcher efforts at self-definition, self-promotion, and assertion of authority was the transmission of Welsh historical texts and ideas of the past into broader contexts, reaching readerships beyond Wales and the March. There, they had a considerable impact, rooting royal power in England in the ideologies of the British–Welsh past that had first emerged in the borderlands. In these circumstances, conquest did not impede the flow of essential historical ideas from a conquered people to their colonizers, as one might expect. Instead, these ideas worked in service to colonization. Geoffrey's ideology of a unified kingdom of Britain, and his story of the degeneration of the Britons into the Welsh, gave birth to the idea that Welsh ancestry or Welsh association is in some way at the core of British kingship, even as the inheritors of British kingship (the English Crown) maintain colonial ownership over Wales today.

Another outcome of the interface between the different cultures of the March of Wales was a flourishing of literature in the marcher lordships, particularly Arthurian romances and other Galfridian afterlives, written in English, French, Welsh, and Latin. Moving forward, it will be essential to take a closer look at other genres of medieval literature— in areas other than history-writing—produced in the March of Wales in order to evaluate the impact of marcher culture on the shaping of medieval British literature at large. Given that so much of canonical Middle English literature was produced and/or set in the borderlands, particularly the West Midlands (including *Piers Plowman*, *Sir Gawain and the Green Knight*, the Middle English Prose *Brut*, and the texts recorded by the Harley scribe), and that so much of canonical Middle Welsh literature (particularly the *Mabinogion*) survives in manuscripts from the conquest lordships of South Wales under the rule of marcher lords, it will be essential in the future for English, Welsh, and francophone literary studies to take this marcher context into account, further teasing out how the ideologies of a supposedly peripheral culture influenced the centre, and further examining the effect of cross-cultural contact and exchange on the development of national literatures in the region.

The findings of this book therefore encourage new readings of canonical texts that come from the English–Welsh borderlands, such as *Sir Gawain and the Green Knight*, from Cheshire and written in a north-west Midlands dialect of Middle English, or William Langland's *Piers Plowman*, from the West Midlands and written in a Herefordshire dialect. One might also consider minor works such as the *Seege of Troye* (thought to have been composed in the West Midlands), *Syre Gawene and the Carle of Carelyle* (thought to have been composed in the West Midlands, but extant in a manuscript from Shropshire or Caernarfonshire), or the alliterative *William of Palerne* (from Gloucester, composed for Humphrey VIII de Bohun (1309–61).[3]

In the following pages, a brief exploration of marcher themes in *Sir Gawain and the Green Knight* illustrates the potential impact of the marcher context as one moves away from the political, geographic borderlands evaluated in the historical literature discussed in this book to rather more abstract representations of borderlands and border-crossings that find expression in literary texts. A new reading of *Sir Gawain and the Green Knight* in the light of this book's findings helps resolve some ambiguities about the geography and the landscape through which Gawain travels on his way to meet the Green Knight. *Sir Gawain and the Green Knight* exhibits some of the now familiar characteristics of marcher baronial literature, particularly the vein of interest in Geoffrey of Monmouth's legendary past and an emphasis on the warlike character of the Britons. These were thematic elements that would have resonated particularly with a marcher audience, and I take each of these points in turn.

The opening passage of the poem frames the action of the Arthurian court as occurring in a legendary, Galfridian past, after the siege of Troy and Brutus' foundation of Britain, but before the takeover of Britain by the English. This framing places Gawain, Arthur, the Green Knight, and other figures of Arthurian romance in a mythical British past that would have—as this book has demonstrated—functioned as a richly relevant,

---

[3] For discussion, see Alison Wiggins, 'Middle English Romance and the West Midlands', in Wendy Scase (ed.), *Essays in Manuscript Geography: Vernacular Manuscripts of the English West Midlands from the Conquest to the Sixteenth Century*, Medieval Texts and Cultures of Northern Europe, 10 (Turnhout, 2007), 239–56.

intimate, and praiseworthy past that had been inherited by baronial marcher readers. The opening stanza reads,

> Sithen the sege and the assaut was sesed at Troye,
> The burgh brittened and brent to brondes and askes,
> The tulk that the trammes of tresoun there wroghte
> Was tried for his trecherye, the truest on erthe:
> Hit was Ennias the athel and his highe kynde
> That sithen depresed provinces and patrounes become
> Wel negh of all the wele in the west iles.
> Fro riche Romulus to Rome riches him swythe,
> With gret bobaunce that burgh he bigges upon firste
> And nevenes hit his owne name, as hit now hatte;
> Ticius to Tuskan and teldes begines,
> Langaberde in Lumbardie lyftes up homes;
> And fer over the French flod Felix Brutus
> On mony bonkes ful brode Bretayn he settes
> Wyth wynne,
> Where werre and wrake and wonder
> By sythes has wont thereinne,
> And oft both blisse and blunder
> Ful skete has skyfted synne.

Once the siege and assault of Troy had ceased,
with the city a smoke-heap of cinders and ash,
the traitor who conceived such betrayal there
was tried for his treachery, the truest on earth;
Aeneas, it was, with his noble warriors
who went conquering abroad, laying claim to the crowns
of the wealthiest kingdoms in the western world.
Mighty Romulus quickly careered towards Rome
and conceived a city in magnificent style
which from then until now has been known by his name.
Ticius constructed townships in Tuscany
and Langobard did likewise building homes in Lombardy.
And further afield, over the sea of France,
Felix Brutus founds Britain on broad banks
most grand.
And wonder, dread and war
have lingered in that land

> where loss and love in turn
> have held the upper hand. (ll. 1–19)[4]

Any reader of Middle English poetry familiar with Geoffrey's *DGB* (and we can assume literate readers would be familiar with this text in some form, through the medium of the *Brut* tradition, if not the Latin history itself) would have understood this setting to be the ancient Britain of Geoffrey.[5] The foundation of Britain by Brutus provides the backdrop for the action of the poem, linking Arthur and his Round Table to the long line of British kings set out in Geoffrey and in Welsh genealogies.

But the setting and characterization take on a particular valence in the marcher context. Though the medium of English has implicitly encouraged most modern critics to assume that readers of the poem were English, lived in England, and had an 'English' identity, the dialect and provenance of the poem complicate these assumptions. The poem is thought to have originated in the north-west Midlands—that is, Cheshire—and it is appropriate to consider Cheshire readerships for the poem, whose identities were not necessarily nationally linked to their knowledge of the English language.[6] For these hypothetical borderland readers, whose ethnic and cultural identities were complex and multivalent, the characters of Arthurian romance would have been recognizably Britons, the ancestors of the Welsh princes and the marcher lords, who were descendants of Brutus and his bold warriors:

> And when this Bretayn was bigged   by this burn riche,
> Bolde bredden thereinne   baret that lofden,
> In mony turned tyme   tene that wroghten.
> Mo ferlyes on this folde   haf fallen here ofte
> Then in any other that I wot   syn that ilk tyme.
> Bot of all that here bult,   of Bretaygne kynges,
> Aye was Arthur the hendest,   as I have herde telle.

---

[4] *WGP* 259–60, trans. Armitage, 21.

[5] And, indeed, the Pearl Poet is willing to engage in the idea of Trojan inheritance and the British past more directly than his famous compatriot, Geoffrey Chaucer; for discussion, see Georgia Henley, 'Chaucer's Vision of the British Past: Literary Inheritance and Historical Memory in Chaucer's *Canterbury Tales*', *Neophilologus*, 106 (2022), 331–47.

[6] Joshua Byron Smith, '"Til þat he neȝed ful neghe into þe Norþe Walez": Gawain's Postcolonial Turn', *Chaucer Review*, 51/3 (2016), 295–309, at 300.

> After Britain was built by this founding father
> a bold race bred there, battle-happy men
> causing trouble and torment in turbulent times,
> and through history more strangeness has happened here
> than anywhere else I know of on Earth.
> But most regal of rulers in the royal line
> was Arthur, who I heard is honored above all. (ll. 20–6)[7]

Some marcher readers would recognize Arthur as their ancestor, as expressed, for example, in the genealogies of the Mortimer family in Chapter 2, which present Roger Mortimer as an ideal descendant of Geoffrey's line of British kings. If we put any negative attitudes towards the present-day Welsh to the side, the figure of Arthur reflects marcher independence and rightful rule over the land that was so often contested in the borderland context, with marchers positioned as the inheritors of Arthur's imperial legacy.

Additionally, the opening stanza characterizes the Britons' rule as turbulent and warlike, another theme that runs through marcher baronial literature. Its focus on warlike kings striving for power, and the acquisition and settlement of land, would be recognized by marcher readers as a familiar predicament that linked the present to the past and brought continuity to present circumstances. Later, the Pearl Poet emphasizes the warlike, military character of Arthurian society when the Green Knight calls the knights of Arthur's court *the wyghtest and the worthyest of the worldes kynde / Preue for to play with in other pure laykes* (translated by Armitage as 'the worthiest knights ever known to the world, / both in competition and true combat' (ll. 261–2)).[8] Arthur will not eat until he has heard a tale *of alderes, of armes, of other aventures* 'the action-packed epics of men-at-arms' (l. 95) or watched a challenge between knights, who are dared *in joparde to laye, / Lede, lif for lif, leve uchon other, / As fortune wolde fylsen hem, the fayrer to have* 'to lay life on the line, / to stare death face-to-face and accept defeat / should fortune or fate smile more favorably on his foe' (ll. 97–9).[9] While this characterization of Arthur is sometimes interpreted negatively or as farce—he is childlike, impulsive, and therefore an ineffectual ruler—it in fact fits the

---

[7] *WGP* 260; trans. Armitage, 21–2.
[8] *WGP* 275; trans. Armitage, 37.
[9] *WGP* 265; trans. Armitage, 27.

interests of a marcher baronial society, which functioned on individual military strength and therefore valued and encouraged individual male ambition. The poem's subtle focus on the individual knight and how he holds up to tests and embodies idealized knighthood reflects the values of a militarized marcher society. In the romantic space of the poem, Gawain protects the reputation of Arthur's court, but could just as easily be protecting family land and title in a work of baronial marcher romance such as *Fouke le fitz Waryn*. The poem is therefore thematically aligned with other works of marcher literature discussed in this book.

Additionally, the borderland context is reflected, in a more literary sense, in the ambiguity of Gawain's journey to Hautdesert through the wilderness of the Wirral peninsula, a passage that previous critics have puzzled over. In this passage, Gawain travels from Logres (from Geoffrey's Loegria, the name for the territory granted to Brutus' son Locrinus that later becomes England), through North Wales, to the Wirral peninsula:

> Now rides this renk thurgh the ryalme of Logres—
> Sir Gawan on Godes halve, thagh him no game thoghte:
> Oft ledeles alone he lenges on nightes,
> There he fonde not him before the fare that he liked;
> Had he no fere bot his fole by frithes and downes,
> Ne no gome bot God by gate with to carpe,
> Till that he neghed ful negh into the north Wales.
> All the iles of Anglesay on lyft half he holdes,
> And fares over the fordes by the forlondes,
> Over at the Holy Hed, til he had eft bonke
> In the wyldrenesse of Wyrale; woned there bot lyte
> That other God other gome with good herte loved.

> Now through England's realm he rides and rides,
> Sir Gawain, God's servant, on his grim quest,
> passing long dark nights unloved and alone,
> foraging to feed, finding little to call food,
> with no friend but his horse through forests and hills
> and only our Lord in heaven to hear him.
> He wanders near to the north of Wales
> with the Isles of Anglesey off to the left.
> He keeps to the coast, fording each course,

> crossing at Holy Head and coming ashore
> in the wilds of the Wirral, whose wayward people
> both God and good men have quite given up on. (ll. 691–702)[10]

Gawain journeys through both real and mythical places at this point in the poem. When he departs Arthur's court, beginning his search for the Green Chapel, he makes a circuit from the realm of Logres to coastal North Wales with Anglesey on the left, into the Wirral forest in Cheshire. Joshua Byron Smith calls this passage a moment of clarity in a poem in which geography is often 'frustratingly indistinct'.[11] Overthrowing the common assumption that Gawain's journey through the wilderness of North Wales is an entry into a particularly Celtic brand of fairyland, Smith argues that coastal North Wales in the Pearl Poet's lifetime was a string of English colonial settlements in the form of garrisoned castles along the coastline, and would not have seemed wild at all, especially not to a Cheshire reader.[12] In this period, North Wales was not a wild, fantastical site of romance, but a civilized English colony, friendly to Gawain's visits. The wild place, occupied by giants and beasts that threaten Gawain's physical safety, is instead the Wirral forest, which was 'disafforested' by the Crown in 1376, around the time the poem was written.[13] Edward III's charter changed the forest's legal status and stripped outlaws within the forest of their legal protections. In other words, the strange land into which Gawain travels, home to unchristian or non-Christian people, has an uncertain legal status bestowed by the Crown, a problem that would be legible to marcher readers, given their demonstrated resentment of royal legal control in other contexts.

In fact, the ambiguity of Gawain's journey to Hautdesert can be read as a literary reflection of the ambiguous marcher space, in which territories and their boundaries were too often indefinite and indistinct. Gawain's passage from Camelot (presumably located, in the Galfridian framework, in South Wales, though possibly in Logres, legendary precursor to England) to the Wirral peninsula marks a journey through

---

[10] *WGP* 302–3; trans. Armitage, 67–8.
[11] Joshua Byron Smith, 'Til þat he neȝed', 296.
[12] Ibid.
[13] Gillian Rudd, '"The Wilderness of Wirral" in *Sir Gawain and the Green Knight*', *Arthuriana*, 23/1 (2013), 52–65, at 56.

a series of borders and borderlands that must be traversed to reach the Green Knight. Gawain's point of origin and location are always obscured, a familiar predicament for a marcher subject.

Curiously, the detailed description of the pentangle on Gawain's shield places England outside the field of action of the poem. Providing further clues as to Gawain's location of origin, the pentangle is *a figure that holdes five poyntes, / And uch lyne umbe-lappes and loukes in other, / And anywhere hit is endeles, and Englych hit callen / Overal, as I here, the endeles knotte* 'a five-pointed star / and each line overlaps and links with the last / so is ever eternal, and when spoken of in England / is known by the name of the endless knot' (ll. 627-30).[14] The poet's reference to the pentangle's name in English, 'endless knot', versus *the pure pentangle with the pepel called / with lore* 'the pure pentangle as people with learning have called it' (ll. 664-5), makes a distinction between different peoples and languages.[15] In other words, it is called an 'endless knot' in England, by people who speak the English vernacular, but a 'pentangle' by people, perhaps those of Gawain's homeland, who have book learning (*lore*)—that is, knowledge of Latin. This comment by the Pearl Poet could point to an awareness of the multilingualism of the March of Wales and its location outside England. It could also perhaps point to knowledge of the difference between legendary and contemporary England—the poem takes place in legendary Britain, as noted by the opening stanza and the use of the placename Logres, but it also comments on modern places such as North Wales and England, where distinct vernacular languages are spoken. This keen awareness of contemporary versus legendary/historical political geography and its bearing on linguistic difference is characteristic of the literature of a borderland.

Gawain's passage between legendary and literal geographic locations to reach the Green Knight could be an expression of the Otherworld, as in *Sir Orfeo*, as Gillian Rudd suggests, but the territorial ambiguity takes on further contemporary meaning in the context of the poem's Cheshire readership.[16] In this borderland between North Wales, the Wirral, and Hautdesert, somewhere in the wilds of Chester, Gawain

---

[14] *WGP* 297-8; trans. Armitage, 63.
[15] *WGP* 300.
[16] Rudd, 'Wilderness of Wirral', 59-60.

traverses a wild and desolate place home to wolves, wild men, and giants—the characteristics (in the Galfridian universe) of an unsettled and uncivilized land. This is not how the borderland would be understood by outsiders, but how it would be understood by local readers, as in *Fouke le Fitz Waryn*, as others have discussed.[17] In other words, the 'contrayes straunge' (l. 713) that Gawain traverses would be recognized by Cheshire readers as the unsafe areas outside garrisoned towns, operating on a civilization/wilderness binary, or a law/lawless binary, rather than an English/Welsh binary, as we so often expect.[18] The territory Gawain wanders through before finding Bertilak's castle is undefined and ambiguous, as so much marcher territory was, politically and socially, in the medieval period. Poorly defined land boundaries outside the confines of the castles and towns of English North Wales, the lawlessness of the Wirral forest (or, at least, governed by laws that were confusing and ill-defined, with jurisdictions under debate) would have been recognizable issues for a marcher audience. This wilderness at the edges of the Wales–Cheshire border becomes an ideal space for romance because it is ill-defined and ambiguous. When exported to non-borderland English readers, it would have been read as fantastical, surreal, and befitting of romance, but, for marcher readers, it was a daily reality of life.

In sum, though most critics read *Sir Gawain and the Green Knight* as an English poem, and evaluate it in an English cultural context, when we consider it in the light of other works of marcher literature, we see that it behaves according to that corpus's dominant themes, in line with its origins in the borderlands. This reading adds to the complexity of the Pearl Poet's expression.

This brief exploration of passages from a canonical work of Middle English literature reveals the added meanings that are possible when the marcher context is considered. Further exploration of the Welsh context of, in particular, *Piers Plowman* would also be fruitful, as would discussion of the marcher origins and readings possible in the minor literary

---

[17] In fact, the poet uses local dialect words to describe the landscape in this passage, which would be recognizable to Cheshire readers; see discussion in Ralph Elliott, 'The Materials of Culture: Landscape and Geography', in Derek Brewer and Jonathan Gibson (eds), *A Companion to the Gawain-Poet*, Arthurian Studies, 38 (Cambridge, 1997), 104–17, at 105.

[18] *WGP* 303; trans. Armitage, 69.

works mentioned above, and of canonical works of Welsh literature that were consumed by readers living in the marcher lordships, such as the *Mabinogion*.[19]

In addition to these literary valences, this book has also shown the outsized influence that narratives of Welsh–British history had on the political geography of fourteenth- and fifteenth-century England. As shown in Chapter 2, the efforts on the part of Edward IV and Henry VII's genealogists to demonstrate their Welsh ancestry through Gwladys Ddu and Ralph de Mortimer exemplify the legacy left behind by Mortimer genealogists of the late fourteenth century. The efforts of genealogists at Wigmore, using Welsh genealogical sources to defend Roger Mortimer's claim to the throne of England, epitomize the political advantages of access to Welsh textual sources in this period. They prove that networks of textual transmission were not only active between England and Wales, but politically advantageous. These genealogists display a keen understanding of the political utility of Geoffrey's *DGB*, a thematic thread that runs throughout marcher baronial literature. The many echoes of these genealogies in the poetry, history, and rolls of the Wars of the Roses in the next century further indicate that the Welsh ancestry of the Yorkist and Tudor kings was meaningful and politically advantageous. These materials played on long-established prophecies and ideologies of kingship originally rooted in Geoffrey and show the value that Welsh history had for political power in Britain in several different temporal and generic contexts. Undergirding any literary awareness of the relationships between Wales, England, and the March of Wales was a political and historical understanding of their common Galfridian heritage, a function of the networks of literary and political contact that linked England and Wales by way of the March. These relationships and networks were primarily motivated by the activities of marcher gentry patrons and ecclesiastical institutions whose efforts to understand and—more significantly—to reimagine British and Welsh history for their own purposes drew Welsh texts out of Wales, where they had a long afterlife in Britain's political and literary landscapes.

---

[19] Ceridwen Lloyd-Morgan suggests that the copy of the C-Text of *Piers Plowman* in Dublin, Trinity College, 212 might be of Welsh provenance, hence the suggestion to consider a Welsh readership for the poem: 'Lancelot in Wales', in Karen Pratt (ed.), *Shifts and Transpositions in Medieval Narrative: A Festschrift for Dr. Elspeth Kennedy* (Cambridge, 1994), 169–79, at 177.

Appendix A

Welsh King List

Chicago, University Library, 224, fols. 12^r–13^r

Incipit genealogia regum siue principium Wallie post mortem gigancium exceptio subregulis.[1]

Brutus

Camber

Madocus

Rudaucus

Membir

Morwynus

Gwalaes filia Ebrauci a qua Wallia nomen accepit.[2]

Euraucus[3]

Brutus Ysgwydhir

Lewelinus

Bleyduth[4]

---

[1] Suspensions, abbreviations, ligatures, and brevigraphs have been expanded and marked by italics. Letters supplied by scribes are in brackets. Interlinear glosses and superscript letters are marked by back slash and forward slash. Errors are corrected, with the manuscript reading included in the footnotes, and modern capitalization is introduced. Rubricated text is reproduced in bold. Translations in footnotes are my own. 'Here begins the genealogy of the kings or princes of Wales after the death of the giants, with the exception of the subordinate kings.'

[2] 'From whom Wales takes its name.'

[3] -u- for /v/, i.e. *Efrawg*.

[4] -th- for /θ/, i.e. *Bledydd*.

Ruth
Regav filia Llyr filii Ruth
Kvnedda filia Regav
Rywallun filius Kvnedde
Gorwst
Seyrioel
Aedmavr filius Antonii[5]
[P]Iredyn[6]
Difnache
[R]Cryden[7]
Kerwyth
Enayth
Mynogan
Bely
Afflech[8]
Avallagh
Ywayn
[B]Grychewayn[9]
Dwnger
Onwed
Anweyryd[10]
Gorddewyn
Dwyn
Gwrdoly

---

[5] The text departs from Geoffrey's line of kings here, and henceforth follows a source consistent with the Llywelyn ab Iorwerth genealogies.

[6] A later hand adds 'P' to the margin immediately preceding the initial letter 'I', correcting to *Predyn*.

[7] A later hand adds 'R' to the margin immediately preceding the initial letter 'C', correcting to *Ryden*, which is incorrect; the name here is indeed *Cryden*.

[8] The text seems to be using a Rhodri Mawr pedigree from here. Spellings are consistent with *Vita Griffini filii Conani* and *Historia Gruffud vab Kenan*.

[9] A later hand adds 'B' to the margin immediately preceding the initial letter 'G', correcting the text to *Brychewayn*.

[10] A marginal gloss in later hand adds 'Anwrvud dux cornub*ie* fil*ius* anweyryd'.

Doly
Gwrgayn
Kayn
Kvneddawt
Iago
Tegyt
Padarn Peisrvd[11]
Edern
Kvnedda Weledyc
Eynyon Yrth
Cadwallon Llawyr

Mayelgvn Gwyned ultimus tenens totam Walliam qui h*ab*uit duos filios *et* diuisit Walliam in duo regna scil*ice*t Southwalliam *et* Northwalliam ut su*per*dictum est. Dedit eciam Southwalliam Arvirago primogenito suo et Northwalliam Rvn secundo nato, de quor*um* successorib*us* respice subsequen*te* de genealogia regum siue principium Southwallie ob Northwallie.[12]

Reges siue principes Southwallie

Aruiragus
Bowus
Yaul
Cranlon
Bryecath
Mepryth

---

[11] Written in the lower margin is an extended gloss that is too abraded to read without the aid of UV light.

[12] 'Maelgwn Gwynedd, the last to hold all Wales, who had two sons and divided Wales into two kingdoms, namely, South Wales and North Wales, which was mentioned before. Indeed he gave South Wales to his firstborn, Arviragus, and North Wales to his second son, Rhun. Concerning their successors, turn your gaze subsequently to the genealogy of the kings or princes of South Wales, and then North Wales.' I have regularized punctuation in this paragraph.

Yaul
Eldoc
Morwyth
Eldac
Pasceuth
Aelmayl
Pasceuth
Gortegu
Gordenon
Gwythaul
Stater
Margadud
Cadwaldus
Walganus
Malgo
Cadwanus
Rodrus Valuanhauc
Chenclern
Mareducus
Owenus
Reyn
Gweythfynauc
Nvmeneus
Horispois
Salomon
Howelus
Cadwallon
Catercus
Idwallon
Cvstenen
Guehic
Eynyon

Mareducus
Ridercus
Iago
Gruffinus
Gruffinus
Bleyduth
Kynwynus
Kynacus
Rywallon
Mareducus
Idwallus
Bledynus
Resus
Traharon
Ridercus
Caradocus
Lewelinus
Resus
Gruffinus

Resus ultimus tocius Southwallie capud, qui quidem Resus in pugna iuxta Breghnoc obiit. Post anno obitum [*erasure*: reges dextralium][13] reges dextralium Brittonum, id est Demecie quod est Southwallie, desierunt, et regnum Britonum dehinc cecidit in Southwalliam, subregulis exceptis, nam Arthen subregulus de Cardygan et Guethfynauc subregulus Breconie, et sic de aliis.[14]

---

[13] The scribe appears to have written 'reges dextralium', rubbed it out, and written it again.

[14] 'Rhys, the last ruler of all of South Wales, who in fact died in battle near Brycheiniog. After the year of his death, the kings of the southern Britons (that is, Demetia, which is South Wales) ceased. And the kingdom of the Britons collapsed in South Wales after that, with the exception of the subordinate kings, namely Arthen, the sub-king of Cardigan, and Gweithfynawg, the sub-king of Brycheiniog, and the same concerning others.' I have regularized capitalization and punctuation in this paragraph.

Reges siue principes northwallie.

Rvn filius *secundus* Maelgvn Gwyned
[B]Ely[15]
Iago
Cadvan
Cadwallon
Cadwaladre Vendigayt
Seyssel
Walgayenus
Idwal Iwrth
Rodry Maelwynawt
Karadaucus
Kynan Dyndaethwy
Essillt filia Kynan
Meruymbricus rex Gunonie causa Essilt uxoris sue
Rodry Mawr
Cadellus
Morwynus
Anarawt filius Rodry
Howelus filius howeli
Idwal Voel
Iago filius Idwal
Ionav filius *secundus*
Rodry filius tercius
Meuryt
Kynan
Griffinus
Owenus
Eyneon filius Oweni qui vi et armis totam tenuit Walliam

---

[15] Marginal glosses in a later hand add: a capital B before 'Ely', correcting *Ely* to *Bely*; after 'Ely', a gloss: 'filius Enyau' frat*ris* senioris Run.'

Yweyn Gwyned
Ierwerth filius Yweyn
Lewelinus filius Ierwerth Drwydwn[16]

Et quia reges siue principes Southwallie desierunt per mortem Resi ante dicti, principatus Southwallie remaneret Lewelino filio Ierwerth supradicto, qui quidem Lewelinus ex Johanna uxore sua filia regis \Johannis[17] / genuit filium nomine Dauid, et vincam filiam nomine Gwladusam uxorem domini Radulphi de Mortuomari domini de Wygemore vero. Et ex Tanglosta, uxore sua secunda filia Lloirch ap Brian de Anglesia, genuit dictus Lewelinus filium nomine Gruffinum. Qui quid Gruffinus ex Cenina vxore sua filia regis Sovorie .i. regis insularum, scilicet Ovceyles, genuit .iiii^{or}. filios, scilicet Rodrinum, Lewelinum, Owenum Rufum, et Dauid Avenwen. Dauid vero Lewelini ap Ierwerth cepit Griffinum fratrem suum et eum incarcerauit a^o .ii^o. ante mortem Lewelini patris eorum, primo in carcere suo, postea in carcere regis Londoniam. Unde eium Gruffinus in prisona regis Londoniam teneretur, obiit Lewelinus eorum pater, quo mortuo, Dauid filius eius supradictus Griffino fratre suo sic in prisona existente, fecit occisis Northwalliam sibi, iurare et fidelitatem sibi facere, qui sic se tenuit pro rege siue principe Northwallie et regnauit sex annis. Medioque tempore obiit Gruffinus in prisona regis. Sex uero annis elapsis obiit idem Dauid frater Gruffini sine herede dicto corpore suo legitime procreato. Cui successit in regnum siue principatum Wallie Lewelinus filius Gruffini et Cenine.[18] Iste Lewelinus duxit in uxorem Alianoram filiam Symonis de Monteforti comitis Leicestre, ex qua genuit heredem non diu viuentem. Medioque tempore obiit Owenus Rufus sine liberis anno Domini m^o .cc^o. lxvii^o. Et Dauid frater eius anno sequenti apud Salop' occiditur. Et iste Lewelinus rex vel princeps Wallie tercio Idus Decembris a^o Domini

---

[16] 'Lewelinus filius Ierwerth Drwydwn' is written in the main hand of the text. The remainder of the text is in a smaller, different hand; this paragraph extends to the very edge of the lower margin of the page.
[17] This name is added by a rubricator; the name is in red ink.
[18] Rubricated capital 'I'.

m⁰ .cc⁰. lxxxii⁰. in terra de Buolt occiditur. Et exercitus Eadwardus rex filius regis Henrici cum herede suo optinuit principatum Wallie.¹⁹

---

¹⁹ 'And because the kings or princes of South Wales ceased with the death of the aforementioned Rhys, the principality of South Wales would remain with the above-mentioned Llywelyn ab Iorwerth. Llywelyn had a son named Dafydd from his wife Johanna, daughter of King John, and an only daughter named Gwladys, wife of lord Ralph de Mortimer, the true lord of Wigmore. And from his wife Tangwystl, second daughter of Llywarch ap Brân of Anglesey, said Llywelyn bore a son named Gruffudd. Gruffudd, from his wife Cenina, daughter of the king of Sovoria—that is, the king of the island, namely, Ovceyles [referring to the Isle of Man?]—bore four sons, namely Rhodri, Llywelyn, Owain Rufus, and Dafydd *Avenwen*. Dafydd, however, captured his brother Gruffudd on behalf of Llywelyn ab Iorwerth and imprisoned him for two years before the death of their father, first in his prison, afterwards in the king's prison in London. While Gruffudd was being held in the king's prison in London, their father Llywelyn died. Because of the death, his aforementioned son Dafydd, with his brother Gruffudd located in prison, acquired North Wales for himself by slaughter, and he made [people] do homage and take an oath of fealty to him, which thus he held by himself as king or prince of North Wales, and reigned for six years. In the meantime, Gruffudd died in the king's prison. With six years having elapsed, the same Dafydd, brother of Gruffudd, died, without naming an heir begotten legitimately of his body. He was succeeded into the kingdom or principality of Wales by Llywelyn, son of Gruffudd and Cenina. This Llywelyn led into marriage Eleanor, daughter of Simon de Montfort, earl of Leicester, from whom he bore an heir who did not live for long. Meanwhile, Owain Rufus died without children in the year of our Lord 1267, and Dafydd his brother was killed in the following year in Shropshire. And that Llywelyn, king or prince of Wales, was killed on the 3rd Ides of December [11 December] in the year of our Lord 1272, in the land of Buellt. And with his army, King Edward, son of King Henry, with his heir, obtained the principality of Wales.'

Appendix B

Pedigree of Gwladys Ddu

Chicago, University Library, MS 224, fols. 51^v–52^r

Incipit genealogia d*omi*ne Gwladuse filie *et* heredis Lewelini quondam principis Wallie uxoris nobilis uiri d*omi*ni Radulphi de Mortuo Mari d*omi*ni de Wyggemore.[1]

Gwladusa filia Lewelini principis Wallie, sercles[2] de Aberfraw Wallice Thalleythiawc, filii Ierwerth Drwyndwn, filii Yweyn Gwyned, filii Gruffyth, filii Kynan, filii Iago, filii Idwal, filii Meuryc, filii Idwal Voel, filii Anarawt, filii Rodri Mawr, filii Essillt, filie Kynan Dindaethwy, filii Rodry Maelwynawt, filii Idwal Iwrch, filii Cadwaladre Vendigait **ultimi regis Brittonu*m*,** filii Cadwallon, filii Cadvan, filii Iago, filii Bely, filii Run, filii Maelgwn Gwyned, filii Cadwallon Llawyr, filii Eynyon Yrth, filii Kunedda Weledic, filii Edern, filii Padarn Peisrud, filii Tegit, filii Iago, filii Kuneddawt, filii Kayn, filii Gwrgain, filii Doly, filii Gwrddoly, filii Dwyn, filii Gorddwyn, filii Anylwyd **ducis Cornubie patris Iugerne Wallice Eygyr matris Arthuri, qui Anylwyd fuit filius,** Anwerydde, filii Onwedde, filii Dwnger, filii Brychwayn, filii Ywayn, filii Avallath, filii

---

[1] In this text, rubrications are indicated in bold type. The incipit is in a single-column layout. The rest of the text is in triple-column layout. 'Here begins the genealogy of Lady Gwladys, daughter and heir of Llywelyn, formerly prince of Wales, wife of the nobleman Lord Ralph de Mortimer, lord of Wigmore.'

[2] Perhaps Anglo-Norman French *sercle* 'circle, ring, hoop, circlet, coronet'. *Anglo-Norman Dictionary*, s.v. *cercle* 2.1, *Online Edition*, http://www.anglo-norman.net/D/cercle, accessed 3 March 2022.

Affleth, filii Bely Mawre, filii Mynogan, filii Enayt, filii Kerwyt, filii Kryden, filii Dyfnach, filii Pryden, filii Aed Mawr, filii Antony, filii Seyrioel, filii Gwrrwst, filii Rywallon, filii Kvnedda, filii[3] Regaw, filia[4] Llyr, filii Bleydvt, filii Rvn, filii Leon **fundatoris Westcestrie**, filii Bruti Ysgwydhyr, filii Ewrawc **edificatoris Ebor*acum***, filii Mymbyr, filii Madoc, filii Locrini, filii Bruti *primi regis Britanie*, filii Syluii, filii Ascaniii,[5] filii Enee Ysgwytwyn, filii Enchiches, filii Capys, filii Assaraci, filii Troii, filii Heri[c]tonii, filii Mercurii, filii Dardani, filii Iouis, filii Saturni, filii Celii,[6] filii Creti, filii Ciprii, filii Settim, filii Iaun, filii Iapheth, filii Noe Hen, filii Lamech, filii Matussale, filii Ennok, filii Iareth, filii Malaleel, filii Kaynan, filii Enos, filii Seth, filii Ade **primi prothoplausti**.[7]

---

[3] This word is corrected by a later hand to 'filia'.

[4] A later hand replaces 'i' with 'a', correcting to 'filia'.

[5] There are one too many minims in this word; there should only be only two dotted 'i's.

[6] *MS* Relii.

[7] This marks the end of the genealogy; the following text continues to discuss her ancestry.

BIBLIOGRAPHY

The Abridged English Metrical Brut edited from London, British Library MS Royal 12 C. XII, ed. Una O'Farrell-Tate (Heidelberg, 2002).
The Acts of the Welsh Rulers, 1120–1283, ed. Huw Pryce (Cardiff, 2005).
Allan, Alison, 'Yorkist Propaganda: Pedigree, Prophecy and the "British History" in the Reign of Edward IV', in Charles Ross (ed.), *Patronage, Pedigree, and Power in Later Medieval England* (Gloucester and Totowa, NJ, 1979), 171–92.
Allen, Rosamund, '*The Awntyrs off Arthure*: Jests and Jousts', in Jennifer Fellows et al. (eds), *Romance Reading on the Book: Essays on Medieval Narrative Presented to Maldwyn Mills* (Cardiff, 1996), 129–42.
Anglo-Norman Dictionary, Online Edition, http://www.anglo-norman.net/, accessed 3 March 2022.
Anglo, Sydney, 'The *British History* in Early Tudor Propaganda: With an Appendix of Manuscript Pedigrees of the Kings of England, Henry VI to Henry VIII', *Bulletin of the John Rylands Library*, 44 (1961–2), 17–48.
Annales Cestrienses: Or, Chronicle of the Abbey of S. Werburg at Chester, ed. and trans. R. C. Christie (London, 1887).
Anzaldúa, Gloria, *Borderlands/La Frontera: The New Mestiza* (San Francisco, 1987).
Arner, Lynn, 'The Ends of Enchantment: Colonialism and Sir Gawain and the Green Knight', *Texas Studies in Literature and Language*, 48/2 (2006), 79–101.
Aronstein, Susan, 'Becoming Welsh: Counter-Colonialism and the Negotiation of Native Identity in *Peredur vab Efrawc*', *Exemplaria*, 17/1 (2005), 135–68.
Ashe, Laura, 'William Marshal, Lancelot, and Arthur: Chivalry and Kingship', *Anglo-Norman Studies*, 30 (2008), 19–40.
Aurell, Martin, *Le Chevalier lettré: Savoir et conduite de l'aristocratie aux XIIe et XIIIe siècles* (Paris, 2011).
The Awntyrs off Arthure at the Terne Wathelyn: An Edition Based on Bodleian Library MS. Douce 324, ed. Ralph Hanna (Manchester, 1974).
The Awntyrs off Arthure at the Terne Wathelyne: Modern Spelling Edition, ed. Helen Phillips (Lancaster, 1988).
Babcock, Robert S., 'Rhys ap Tewdwr, King of Deheubarth', *Anglo-Norman Studies*, 14 (1994), 21–36.
Barth, Fredrik (ed.), *Ethnic Groups and Boundaries: The Social Organization of Culture Difference* (Boston, 1969).

Bartlett, Robert, 'Gerald of Wales and the *History of Llanthony Priory*', in Georgia Henley and A. Joseph Mcmullen (eds), *Gerald of Wales: New Perspectives on a Medieval Writer and Critic* (Cardiff, 2018), 81–96.

Beal, Jane, *John Trevisa and the English Polychronicon*, Arizona Studies in the Middle Ages and Renaissance, 37 (Turnhout, 2013).

——, 'Mapping Identity in John Trevisa's English *Polychronicon*: Chester, Cornwall and the Translation of English National History', *Fourteenth Century England*, 3 (2004), 67–82.

Bellon-Méguelle, Hélène, 'Une œuvre protéiforme: Mises en prose et dérimage des *Grantz Geanz*', in Paola Cifarelli, Maria Colombo Timelli, Matteo Milani, and Anne Schoysman (eds), *Raconter en prose. xive-xvie siècle*, Encounters 279, Medieval Civilization, 21 (Paris, 2017), 355–66.

Benskin, Michael, Margaret Laing, Vasilis Karaiskos, and Keith Williamson (eds), *An Electronic Version of a Linguistic Atlas of Late Mediaeval English* (Edinburgh, 2013), http://www.lel.ed.ac.uk/ihd/elalme/elalme.html, accessed 5 December 2021.

Bezant, Jemma, 'The Medieval Grants to Strata Florida Abbey: Mapping the Agency of Lordship', in Janet Burton and Karen Stöber (eds), *Monastic Wales: New Approaches* (Cardiff, 2013), 73–88.

Bhabha, Homi, *The Location of Culture* (London and New York, 1994).

Birkholz, Daniel, 'Harley Lyrics and Hereford Clerics: The Implications of Mobility, c.1300–1351', *Studies in the Age of Chaucer*, 31 (2009), 175–230.

Blacker, Jean, 'Where Wace Feared to Tread: Latin Commentaries on Merlin's Prophecies in the Reign of Henry II', *Arthuriana*, 6/1 (1996), 36–52.

Blair, Claude, 'The Wooden Knight at Abergavenny', *Church Monuments: Journal of the Church Monuments Society*, 9 (1994), 33–52.

Brady, Lindy, 'The Fluidity of Borderlands', *Offa's Dyke Journal*, 4 (2022), 3–15.

——, *Multilingualism in Early Medieval Britain*, Cambridge Elements: Elements in England in the Early Medieval World (Cambridge, 2023).

——, *Writing the Welsh Borderlands in Anglo-Saxon England* (Manchester, 2017).

Breeze, Andrew, '"The Awntyrs off Arthure", Caerphilly, Oysterlow, and Wexford', *Arthuriana*, 9/4 (1999), 63–8.

Bridges, Venetia, *Medieval Narratives of Alexander the Great: Transnational Texts in England and France*, Studies in Medieval Romance, 20 (Cambridge, 2018).

Bruce, Mark P., and Katherine H. Terrell, 'Introduction: Writing Across the Borders', in Mark P. Bruce and Katherine H. Terrell (eds), *The Anglo-Scottish Border and the Shaping of Identity, 1300–1600* (New York, 2012), 1–14.

The Brut: Or, The Chronicles of England, ed. Friedrich W. D. Brie, 2 vols, Early English Text Society, os 131, 136 (London, 1906–8; repr. 1960).

Brut y Tywysogion, or, the Chronicle of the Princes: Peniarth MS 20 Version, ed. Thomas Jones (Cardiff, 1952).

Brut y Tywysogyon, or The Chronicle of the Princes, Red Book of Hergest Version, ed. and trans. Thomas Jones (Cardiff, 1955).

Brut y Tywysogion, Peniarth MS 20, ed. Thomas Jones (Cardiff, 1941).

Busby, Keith, 'Multilingualism, the Harley Scribe, and Johannes Jacobi', in Connolly and Radulescu (eds), *Insular Books*, 49–60.

Byrne, Aisling, and Victoria Flood (eds), *Crossing Borders in the Insular Middle Ages*, Texts and Cultures of Northern Europe, 30 (Turnhout, 2019).

Calendar of Patent Rolls, Henry III, volume 3. *1232–1247* (London, 1906).

Carley, James P., and Julia Crick, 'Constructing Albion's Past: An Annotated Edition of *De origine gigantum*', *Arthurian Literature*, 13 (1995), 41–114.

Carruthers, Mary, *The Book of Memory: A Study of Memory in Medieval Culture*, 2nd edn (Cambridge, 2008).

Cartae et Alia Munimenta quae ad Dominium de Glamorgan Pertinent, vol. iv. *1215–1689*, ed. G. T. Clark (Cardiff, 1893).

Cavell, Emma, 'Aristocratic Widows and the Medieval Welsh Frontier: The Shropshire Evidence', *TRHS* 17 (2007), 57–82.

——, 'Bohun, Margaret de [née Margaret of Gloucester] (c.1121–1196/7)', *ODNB*, https://doi.org/10.1093/ref:odnb/102428, accessed 2 February 2022.

——, '*Fouke le Fitz Waryn*: Literary Space for Real Women?' *Parergon*, 27/2 (2010), 89–109.

——, 'Intelligence and Intrigue in the March of Wales: Noblewomen and the Fall of Llywelyn ap Gruffudd, 1274–82', *Historical Research*, 88/239 (2015), 1–19.

Charles, B. G., 'An Early Charter of the Abbey of Cwmhir', *Transactions of the Radnorshire Society*, 40 (1970), 68–74.

Chism, Christine, *Alliterative Revivals* (Philadelphia, 2002).

Chronica Monasterii S. Albani. Thomæ Walsingham, quondam monachi S. Albani, Historia Anglicana, ed. Henry Thomas Riley, 2 vols (London, 1863–4).

The Chronicle of Adam Usk, 1377–1421, ed. and trans. Chris Given-Wilson (Oxford, 1997).

Clanchy, M. T., *From Memory to Written Record: England 1066–1307*, 2nd edn (Oxford, 1993).

Clarke, Catherine A. M. (ed.), *Mapping the Medieval City: Space, Place and Identity in Chester c.1200–1600* (Cardiff, 2011).

Cleaver, Laura, 'Past, Present and Future for Thirteenth-Century Wales: Two Diagrams in British Library, Cotton Roll XIV.12', *Electronic British Library Journal* (2013), 1–26.

Cohen, Jeffrey Jerome, 'Hybrids, Monsters, Borderlands: The Bodies of Gerald of Wales', in Jeffrey Jerome Cohen (ed.), *The Postcolonial Middle Ages* (New York, 2000), 85–104.

Colker, Marvin L., 'The "Margam Chronicle" in a Dublin Manuscript', *Haskins Society Journal*, 4 (1992), 123–48.

Connolly, Margaret, and Raluca Radulescu (eds), *Insular Books: Vernacular Manuscript Miscellanies in Late Medieval Britain*, Proceedings of the British Academy, 201 (Oxford, 2012).

Coote, Lesley A., *Prophecy and Public Affairs in Later Medieval England* (Woodbridge, 2000).

Courtney, Paul, 'The Norman Invasion of Gwent: A Reassessment', *JMH* 12/4 (1986), 297–313.

Crane, Susan, 'Anglo-Norman Romances of English Heroes: "Ancestral Romance"?' *Romance Philology*, 35/4 (1982), 601–8.

Crouch, David, 'Marshal, William [*called* the Marshal], fourth earl of Pembroke', *ODNB*, https://doi.org/10.1093/ref:odnb/18126, accessed 2 February 2022.

——, 'The Transformation of Medieval Gwent', in Ralph A. Griffiths, Tony Hopkins, and Ray Howell (eds), *The Gwent County History*, volume 2. *The Age of the Marcher Lords, c.1070–1536* (Cardiff, 2008), 1–45.

——, *William Marshal: Court, Career, and Chivalry in the Angevin Empire, 1147–1219* (London, 1990).

——, 'Writing a Biography in the Thirteenth Century: The Construction and Composition of the "History of William Marshal"', in David Bates, Julia Crick, and Sarah Hamilton (eds), *Writing Medieval Biography, 750–1250: Essays in Honour of Professor Frank Barlow* (Woodbridge, 2006), 221–35.

Crump, J. J., 'The Mortimer Family and the Making of the March', in Michael Prestwich, R. H. Britnell, and Robin Frame (eds), *Thirteenth Century England VI: Proceedings of the Durham Conference 1995* (Woodbridge, 1997), 117–26.

——, 'Mortimer, Roger de, lord of Wigmore', *ODNB*, https://doi.org/10.1093/ref:odnb/19352, accessed 29 December 2021.

Curtius, Ernst Robert, *European Literature and the Latin Middle Ages*, trans. Willard R. Trask, Bollingen Series, 36 (Princeton and Oxford, 1953; repr. 2013).

DafyddapGwilym.net, http://www.dafyddapgwilym.net/eng/3win.htm, accessed 18 March 2022.

Danbury, Elizabeth, 'The Intellectual Life of the Abbey of St Werburgh, Chester in the Middle Ages', in Alan T. Thacker (ed.), *Medieval Archaeology, Art and Architecture at Chester*, The British Archaeological Association Conference Transactions, 22 (Leeds, 2000), 107–20.

Davies, John Reuben, *The Book of Llandaf and the Norman Church in Wales*, Studies in Celtic History, 21 (Woodbridge, 2003).

——, 'The Saints of South Wales and the Welsh Church', in Alan Thacker and Richard Sharpe (eds), *Local Saints and Local Churches in the Early Medieval West* (Oxford, 2002), 361–95.

Davies, R. R., *The Age of Conquest: Wales, 1063–1415* (Oxford, 2000).

——, *Conquest, Coexistence and Change: Wales, 1063–1415* (Oxford, 2000).

——, *Domination and Conquest: The Experience of Ireland, Scotland, and Wales, 1100–1300* (Cambridge, 1990).

——, *The First English Empire: Power and Identities in the British Isles, 1093–1343* (Oxford, 2000).

——, 'Kings, Lords and Liberties in the March of Wales, 1066–1272', *TRHS* (Fifth Series), 29 (1979), 41–61.

——, 'The Law of the March', WHR, 5 (1970), 1–30.

——, *Lordship and Society in the March of Wales, 1282–1400* (Oxford, 1978).

——, 'Mortimer, Roger, fourth earl of March and sixth earl of Ulster', *ODNB*, https://doi.org/10.1093/ref:odnb/19356, accessed 29 December 2021.

Davies, R. R., *The Revolt of Owain Glyn Dŵr* (Oxford, 1995).

Davies, Wendy, 'Land and Power in Early Medieval Wales', *Past and Present*, 81 (1978), 3–23.

——, 'Property Rights and Property Claims in Welsh "Vitae" of the Eleventh Century', in Evelyne Patlagean and Pierre Riché (eds), *Hagiographie, cultures et sociétés Ive–VIIe siècles: Actes du colloque organisé à Nanterre et à Paris (2–5 mai 1979)* (Paris, 1981), 515–33.

Davies, Wendy, *Small Worlds: The Village Community in Early Medieval Brittany* (London, 1988).

Davies, Wendy, *Wales in the Early Middle Ages* (Leicester, 1982).

Dickinson, J. C., and P. T. Ricketts, 'The Anglo-Norman Chronicle of Wigmore Abbey', *Transactions of the Woolhope Naturalists' Field Club*, 39 (1967–9), 413–45.

Dolmans, Emily, 'Locating the Border: Britain and the Welsh Marches in *Fouke le Fitz Waryn*', *New Medieval Literatures*, 16 (2016), 109–34.

——, *Writing Regional Identities in Medieval England: From the Gesta Herwardi to Richard Coer de Lyon* (Cambridge, 2020).

Dryburgh, Paul, and Philip Hume (eds), *Mortimers of Wigmore 1066–1485: The Dynasty of Destiny* (Eardisley, 2023).

Dwyer, Richard A., 'Some Readers of John Trevisa', *Notes & Queries*, 212 (1967), 291–2.

Early Welsh Genealogical Tracts, ed. Peter C. Bartrum (Cardiff, 1966).

Early Welsh Saga Poetry: A Study and Edition of the Englynion, ed. and trans. Jenny Rowland (Cambridge, 1990).

Echard, Siân, 'Navigating Absence in the Digital Realm', in Benjamin Albritton, Georgia Henley, and Elaine Treharne (eds), *Medieval Manuscripts in the Digital Age* (London, 2020), 82–90.

Edwards, A. S. G., 'The Influence and Audience of the *Polychronicon*: Some Observations', *Proceedings of the Leeds Philosophical and Literary Society*, 17/6 (1980), 113–19.

Eley, Penny, 'The Myth of Trojan Descent and Perceptions of National Identity: The Case of *Eneas* and the *Roman de Troie*', *Nottingham Medieval Studies*, 35 (1991), 27–40.

Elliott, Ralph, 'The Materials of Culture: Landscape and Geography', in Derek Brewer and Jonathan Gibson (eds), *A Companion to the Gawain-Poet*, Arthurian Studies, 38 (Cambridge, 1997), 104–17.

An English Chronicle, 1377–1461: Edited from Aberystwyth, National Library of Wales MS 21068 and Oxford, Bodleian Library MS Lyell 34, ed. William Marx (Woodbridge, 2003).

Español, Alicia, Giuseppina Marsico, and Luca Tateo, 'Maintaining Borders: From Border Guards to Diplomats', *Human Affairs*, 28/4 (2018) 443–60.

Faletra, Michael A., 'Once and Future Britons: The Welsh in Lawman's *Brut*', *Medievalia et Humanistica*, 28 (2002), 1–23.

——, *Wales and the Medieval Colonial Imagination: The Matters of Britain in the Twelfth Century* (New York, 2014).

Faraday, Michael, *Ludlow, 1085–1660: A Social, Economic, and Political History* (Chichester, 1991).

Fein, Susanna, 'Compilation and Purpose in MS Harley 2253', in Scase (ed.), *Essays in Manuscript Geography*, 67–94.

——, 'Literary Scribes: The Harley Scribe and Robert Thornton as Case Studies', in Connolly and Radulescu (eds), *Insular Books*, 61–79.

Fein, Susanna (ed.), *Studies in the Harley Manuscript: The Scribes, Contents, and Social Contexts of British Library MS Harley 2253* (Kalamazoo, 2000).

Fisher, Matthew, 'Genealogy Rewritten: Inheriting the Legendary in Insular Historiography', in Radulescu and Kennedy (eds), *Broken Lines*, 123–42.

——, *Scribal Authorship and the Writing of History in Medieval England* (Columbus, 2012).

Flood, Victoria, 'Prophecy as History: A New Study of the Prophecies of Merlin Silvester', *Neophilologus*, 102/4 (2018), 543–59.

——, *Prophecy, Politics and Place in Medieval England: From Geoffrey of Monmouth to Thomas of Erceldoune* (Woodbridge, 2016).

Fouke Le Fitz Waryn, ed. E. J. Hathaway, P. T. Ricketts, C. A. Robson, and A. D. Wilshere, Anglo-Norman Texts Society, 26–28 (Oxford, 1975).

Fowler, David C., *John Trevisa* (Aldershot, 1993).

Fulton, Helen, 'Class and Nation: Defining the English in Late-Medieval Welsh Poetry', in Kennedy and Meecham-Jones (eds), *Authority and Subjugation*, 191–212.

——, 'The Geography of Welsh Literary Production in Late Medieval Glamorgan', *JMH* 41/3 (2015), 325–40.

——, 'Literary Networks and Patrons in Late Medieval Wales', in Helen Fulton and Geraint Evans (eds), *The Cambridge History of Welsh Literature* (Cambridge, 2019), 129–54.

——, 'Literature of the Welsh Gentry: Uses of the Vernacular in Medieval Wales', in Elizabeth Salter and Helen Wicker (eds), *Vernacularity in England and Wales, c.1300–1550*, Utrecht Studies in Medieval Literacy, 17 (Turnhout, 2011), 199–223.

——, 'Mapping the March: Medieval Wales and England, c.1282-1550: Mapping Literary Geography in a British Border Region', https://blog.mowlit.ac.uk/, accessed 29 December 2023.

——, 'The Outside Within: Medieval Chester and North Wales as a Social Space', in Clarke (ed.), *Mapping the Medieval City*, 149–68.

——, 'Owain Glyn Dŵr and the Uses of Prophecy', *SC* 39 (2005), 105–21.

——, 'The Red Book and the White: Gentry Libraries in Medieval Wales', in Byrne and Flood (eds), *Crossing Borders*, 23–46.

——, 'Tenth-Century Wales and *Armes Prydein*', *Transactions of the Honourable Society of Cymmrodorion*, 7 (2001), 5–18.

——, 'Translating Europe in Medieval Wales', in Aidan Conti, Orietta Da Rold, and Philip Shaw (eds), *Writing Europe, 500–1450: Texts and Contexts*, Essays and Studies, 68 (Cambridge, 2015), 159–74.

Geoffrey of Monmouth, *De gestis Britonum*, ed. Michael Reeve, trans. Neil Wright, *Geoffrey of Monmouth: The History of the Kings of Britain: An Edition and Translation of De Gestis Britonum (Historia regum Britanniae)* (Woodbridge, 2007).

Gerald of Wales, *Descriptio Kambriae*, ed. J. F. Dimock, *Giraldi Cambrensis Opera*, 6 (London, 1868).

Gerald of Wales, *Expugnatio Hibernica*, ed. and trans. A. B. Scott and F. X. Martin, *Expugnatio Hibernica: The Conquest of Ireland by Giraldus Cambrensis*, A New History of Ireland, Ancillary Publications, 3 (Dublin, 1978).

Gerald of Wales, *Itinerarium Kambriae*, ed. J. F. Dimock, *Giraldi Cambrensis Opera*, 6 (London, 1868).

Giffin, Mary E., 'Cadwalader, Arthur, and Brutus in the Wigmore Manuscript', *Speculum*, 16 (1941), 109–20.

——, 'The Wigmore Manuscript and the Mortimer Family' (unpublished Ph.D. dissertation, University of Chicago, 1939).

——, 'A Wigmore Manuscript at the University of Chicago', *NLWJ* 7/4 (1952), 316–25.

Gillingham, John, *The English in the Twelfth Century: Imperialism, National Identity, and Political Values* (Woodbridge, 2000).

——, 'War and Chivalry in the *History of William the Marshal*', *Thirteenth Century England*, 2 (1998), 1–13.

Given-Wilson, Chris, 'Chronicles of the Mortimer Family, c.1250–1450', in Richard Eales and Shaun Tyas (eds), *Family and Dynasty in Late Medieval England: Proceedings of the 1997 Harlaxton Symposium* (Donington, 2003), 67–86.

Goodman, Anthony, 'The Anglo-Scottish Marches in the Fifteenth-Century: A Frontier Society?' in Roger A. Mason (ed.), *Scotland and England: 1286–1815* (Edinburgh, 1987), 18–33.

Gough-Cooper, Henry W., 'Annales Cambriae: The B Text, from London, National Archives, MS E164/1, pp. 2–26', Welsh Chronicles Research Group, Bangor University, http://croniclau.bangor.ac.uk/editions.php.en, accessed 3 March 2022.

——, 'Annales Cambriae: The C Text, from London, British Library, Cotton MS Domitian A. i, ff. 138^r–155^r, with an Appended Concordance of Intercalated Notices', Welsh Chronicles Research Group, Bangor University, http://croniclau.bangor.ac.uk/editions.php.en, accessed 3 March 2022.

Gullick, Michael, 'Professional Scribes in Eleventh- and Twelfth-Century England', *English Manuscript Studies*, 7 (1998), 1–24.

GutorGlyn.net, Aberystwyth: Centre for Advanced Welsh and Celtic Studies, 2013, http://www.gutorglyn.net/gutorglyn/poem/?poem-selection=029&first-line=%23, accessed 18 March 2022.

Guy, Ben, 'The Changing Approaches of English Kings to Wales in the Tenth and Eleventh Centuries', *Offa's Dyke Journal*, 4 (2022), 86–106.

——, '*Epitome Historiae Britanniae*', Welsh Chronicles Research Group, Bangor University, http://croniclau.bangor.ac.uk/hist-britanniae.php.en, accessed 3 February 2022.

——, 'Historical Scholars and Dishonest Charlatans: Studying the Chronicles of Medieval Wales', in Guy et al. (eds), *Chronicles of Medieval Wales*, 69–106.

——, 'The Life of St Dyfrig and the Lost Charters of Moccas (Mochros), Herefordshire', *CMCS* 75 (2018), 1–37.

——, *Medieval Welsh Genealogy: An Introduction and Textual Study*, Studies in Celtic History, 42 (Woodbridge, 2020).

——, Georgia Henley, Nia Wyn Jones (published under Owain Wyn Jones), and Rebecca Thomas (eds), *The Chronicles of Medieval Wales and the March: New Contexts, Studies and Texts*, Medieval Texts and Cultures of Northern Europe, 31 (Turnhout, 2020).

——, Howard Williams, and Liam Delaney (eds), 'Borders in Early Medieval Britain', *Offa's Dyke Journal*, 4 (2022).

Gwaith Bleddyn Fardd a beirdd eraill ail hanner y drydedd ganrif ar ddeg, ed. Rhian M. Andrews and Catherine McKenna, Cyfres Beirdd y Tywysogion, 7 (Cardiff, 1996).

Gwaith Iolo Goch, ed. D. R. Johnston (Cardiff, 1988).

Gwaith Lewys Glyn Cothi, ed. Dafydd Johnston (Cardiff, 1995).

Gwaith Tudur Aled, ed. T. Gwynn Jones, 2 vols (Cardiff, 1926).

Hamilton, J. S., 'Bohun, Humphrey de, fourth earl of Hereford and ninth earl of Essex (*c*.1276–1322)', *ODNB*, https://doi.org/10.1093/ref:odnb/27777, accessed 22 October 2021.

Hanna, Ralph, '*The Awntyrs off Arthure*: An Interpretation', *Modern Language Quarterly*, 31 (1970), 275–97.

——, 'The Matter of Fulk: Romance and History in the Marches', *Journal of English and Germanic Philology*, 110/3 (2011), 337–58.

——, 'Sir Thomas Berkeley and his Patronage', *Speculum*, 64/4 (1989), 878–916.

Harbus, Antonina, 'Embodied Emotion, Conceptual Metaphor, and the Aesthetics of Reading Old English Poetry', in Michael Champion and Andrew Lynch (eds), *Understanding Emotions in Early Europe*, Early European Research, 8 (Turnhout, 2015), 127–49.

Haycock, Marged, 'Some Talk of Alexander and Some of Hercules', *CMCS* 13 (1987), 7–38.

Hays, Rhŷs W., *The History of the Abbey of Aberconway, 1186–1537* (Cardiff, 1963).

Helbert, Daniel, *Arthur between England and Wales: Arthurian Literature in the Anglo-Welsh Borderlands* (Liverpool, forthcoming).

Henley, Georgia, 'The "Cardiff Chronicle" in London, British Library, Royal MS 6 B. xi', in Guy et al. (eds), *Chronicles of Medieval Wales*, 231–87.

——, 'Chaucer's Vision of the British Past: Literary Inheritance and Historical Memory in Chaucer's *Canterbury Tales*', *Neophilologus*, 106 (2022), 331–47.

——, 'From "The Matter of Britain" to "The Matter of Rome": Latin Literary Culture and the Reception of Geoffrey of Monmouth in Wales', *Arthurian Literature*, 33 (2016), 1–28.

——, 'Networks of Chronicle Writing in Western Britain: The Case of Worcester and Wales', in Francesca Tinti and David Woodman (eds), *Constructing*

History through the Conquest: Worcester c.1050–c.1150 (Woodbridge, 2022), 227–70.

——, 'The Reception of Geoffrey of Monmouth as Political Influence', in Ben Guy and Patrick Wadden (eds), *Propaganda and Pseudo-History in the Medieval Celtic World: Interrogating a Paradigm* (forthcoming).

——, 'The Reception of Gerald of Wales in Welsh Historical Texts', in Sadie Jarrett, Katharine Olson, and Rebecca Thomas (eds), *Memory and Nation: Writing the History of Wales* (Cardiff, forthcoming).

——, 'Rhetoric, Translation and Historiography: The Literary Qualities of Brut y Tywysogyon', *Quaestio Insularis*, 13 (2012), 78–103.

——, 'Scribal Authority and Hagiographical Adaptation in London, British Library, Cotton Titus D. xxii', in Myriah Williams, Silva Nurmio, and Sarah Waidler (eds), *Medieval Wales and the Medieval World: Context and Approaches, Knowledge and Exchange* (Turnhout, forthcoming).

Heyman, Josiah McC., 'Culture Theory and the US–Mexico Border', in Thomas M. Wilson and Hastings Donnan (eds), *A Companion to Border Studies* (Chichester, 2012), 48–65.

Hill, Ordelle G., *Looking Westward: Poetry, Landscape, and Politics in Sir Gawain and the Green Knight* (Newark, 2009).

The History of Llanthony Priory, ed. and trans. Robert Bartlett (Oxford, 2022).

A History of Shropshire, Volume III, ed. G. C. Baugh, The Victoria History of the Counties of England (London and Oxford, 1979).

The History of William Marshal, ed. A. J. Holden, trans. S. Gregory, with notes by David Crouch, Anglo-Norman Text Society, Occasional Publications Series, 4, 3 vols (London, 2002–6).

Holden, Brock W., *Lords of the Central Marches: English Aristocracy and Frontier Society, 1087–1265* (Oxford, 2008).

——, 'The Making of the Middle March of Wales, 1066–1250', *WHR* 20/2 (2000), 207–26.

Hollister, C. Warren, 'Anglo-Norman Political Culture and the Twelfth-Century Renaissance', in C. Warren Hollister (ed.), *Anglo-Norman Political Culture and the Twelfth-Century Renaissance* (Woodbridge, 1997), 1–316.

Hume, Philip, 'The Arrival of the Normans 1066–1100 and Establishment of Early Marcher Lordships', in Hume (ed.), *Welsh Marcher Lordships*, 41–56.

——, 'The Lordships of Radnorshire and North Herefordshire', in Hume (ed.), *Welsh Marcher Lordships*, 129–88.

——, 'The Marcher Lordships and their Distinctive Features', in Hume (ed.), *Welsh Marcher Lordships*, 1–9, 13–17.

—— (ed.), *The Welsh Marcher Lordships*, i. *Central & North* (Eardisley, 2021).

Huws, Daniel, *Medieval Welsh Manuscripts* (Aberystwyth, 2000).

------, *A Repertory of Welsh Manuscripts and Scribes*, c.800–c.1800, 3 vols (Aberystwyth, 2022).

Ingham, Patricia Clare, *Sovereign Fantasies: Arthurian Romance and the Making of Britain* (Philadelphia, 2001).

The Inventory of Historic Battlefields in Wales (Aberystwyth, 2017), http://battlefields.rcahmw.gov.uk/, accessed 12 October 2022.

Iolo Goch: Poems, trans. Dafydd Johnston (Llandysul, 1993).

Jacobs, Nicolas, 'The Green Knight: An Unexplored Irish Parallel', *CMCS* 4 (1982), 1–4.

Jenkins, Manon Bonner, 'Aspects of the Welsh Prophetic Verse Tradition in the Middle Ages: Incorporating Textual Studies of Poetry from "Llyfr Coch Hergest" (Oxford, Jesus College, MS cxi) and "Y Cwta Cyfarwydd" (Aberystwyth, National Library of Wales, MS Peniarth 50)' (unpublished Ph.D. thesis, University of Cambridge, 1990).

Johnston, Dafydd, 'The Aftermath of 1282: Dafydd ap Gwilym and his Contemporaries', in Helen Fulton and Geraint Evans (eds), *The Cambridge History of Welsh Literature* (Cambridge, 2019), 112–28.

------, *Llên yr Uchelwyr: Hanes Beirniadol Llenyddiaeth Gymraeg, 1330–1525* (Cardiff, 2005).

Jones Nerys Ann, 'Canu Mawl Beirdd y Tywysogion i'r Arglwydd Rhys', in Pryce and Jones (eds), *Yr Arglwydd Rhys* (Cardiff, 1996), 129–44.

Jones, Aled Llion, *Mab Darogan: Prophecy, Lament, and Absent Heroes in Medieval Welsh Tradition* (Cardiff, 2013).

Jones, Thomas, '"Cronica de Wallia" and Other Documents from Exeter Cathedral Library MS 3514', *Bulletin of the Board of Celtic Studies*, 12 (1946), 27–44.

Jones, Timothy, 'Geoffrey of Monmouth, "Fouke le Fitz Waryn", and National Mythology', *Studies in Philology*, 91/3 (1994), 233–49.

Kaeuper, Richard W., 'William Marshal, Lancelot, and the Issue of Chivalric Identity', in Christopher Guyol (ed.), *Kings, Knights and Bankers: The Collected Articles of Richard W. Kaeuper* (Leiden, 2016), 221–42.

Karasawa, Kazutaka, 'John Trevisa's Middle English Translation of Ranulph Higden's *Polychronicon* Based on Senshu University Library, MS 1-A Diplomatic Edition', *Journal of the Faculty of Letters, Komazawa University*, 69 (2011), 23–59; 70 (2012), 1–85; 71 (2013), 21–101; 72 (2014), 1–97; 75 (2017), 29–89; 76 (2018), 29–90.

Keating, AnaLouise (ed.), *Entre Mundos/Among Worlds: New Perspectives on Gloria E. Anzaldúa* (New York, 2005).

Kennedy, E. D., and Raluca Radulescu, 'Genealogical Chronicles in English and Latin', Graeme Dunphy and Cristian Bratu (eds), *Brill Encyclopedia of the Medieval Chronicle* (Leiden, 2016), http://doi.org/10.1163/2213-2139_emc_SIM_01076, accessed 7 March 2022.

Kennedy, Ruth, and Simon Meecham-Jones (eds), *Authority and Subjugation in Writing of Medieval Wales* (New York, 2008).

Ker, Neil R., *Medieval Libraries of Great Britain: A List of Surviving Books*, 2nd edn (London, 1964).

King Horn: An Edition Based on Cambridge University Library MS Gg. 4.27, ed. Rosamund Allen, Garland Medieval Texts, 7 (New York, 1984).

King, Andy, 'Best of Enemies: Were the Fourteenth-Century Anglo-Scottish Marches a "Frontier Society"?', in Andy King and Michel Penman (eds), *England and Scotland in the Fourteenth Century: New Perspectives* (Woodbridge, 2007), 116–35.

Knight, Jeremy K., 'The Anglo-Norman Conquest of Gwent and Glamorgan', in N. J. G. Pounds (ed.), *The Cardiff Area: Proceedings of the 139th Summer Meeting of the Royal Archaeological Institute, 1993*, Supplement to the Archaeological Journal, 150 (London, 1993), 8–14.

Knight, Stephen, 'Resemblance and Menace: A Post-Colonial Reading of *Peredur*', in Sioned Davies and Peter Wynn Thomas (eds), *Canhwyll Marchogyon: Cyd-destunoli Peredur* (Cardiff, 2000), 128–47.

Konrad, Victor A., and Anne-Laure Amilhat Szary, *Border Culture: Theory, Imagination, Geopolitics* (Abingdon and New York, 2023).

Lamont, Margaret, 'Becoming English: Ronwenne's Wassail, Language, and National Identity in the Middle English Prose *Brut*', *Studies in Philology*, 107 (2010), 283–309.

Lampitt, Matthew Siôn, 'Networking the March: A History of Hereford and its Region from the Eleventh through Thirteenth Centuries', *Journal of the Mortimer History Society*, 1 (2017), 55–72.

——, 'Networking the March: The Literature of the Welsh Marches, c.1180–c.1410' (unpublished Ph.D. dissertation, King's College London, 2019).

Lapidge, Michael, 'The Welsh–Latin Poetry of Sulien's Family', *SC* 8 (1973), 68–106.

Lavezzo, Kathy, *Angels on the Edge of the World: Geography, Literature, and English Community, 1000–1534* (Ithaca, NY, 2006).

Layamon: Brut: Edited from British Museum Ms Cotton Caligula A. IX and British Museum Ms Cotton Otho C. XIII, ed. G. L. Brook and R. F. Leslie, 2 vols (London, 1963–78).

Laynesmith, J. L., 'Anne Mortimer's Legacy to the House of York', in Dryburgh and Hume (eds), *Mortimers of Wigmore*, 212–41.

Le Saux, Françoise, 'Laȝamon's Welsh Sources', *English Studies*, 67/5 (1986), 385–93.

Legge, M. Dominica, *Anglo-Norman Literature and its Background* (Oxford, 1963).

Lewis, C. P., 'The Shape of the Norman Principality of Gwynedd', in K. J. Stringer and A. Jotischky (eds), *The Normans and the 'Norman Edge': Peoples, Polities and Identities on the Frontiers of Medieval Europe* (London, 2019), 100–28.

Lewis, Ceri W., 'The Literary Tradition of Morgannwg down to the Middle of the Sixteenth Century', in Pugh (ed.), *Glamorgan County History*, iii.449–554.

Lieberman, Max, 'The English and the Welsh in *Fouke le Fitz Waryn*', *Thirteenth-Century England*, 12 (2009), 1–11.

——, *The March of Wales, 1067–1300: A Borderland of Medieval Britain* (Cardiff, 2008).

——, *The Medieval March of Wales: The Creation and Perception of a Frontier, 1066–1283*, Cambridge Studies in Medieval Life and Thought, 78 (Cambridge, 2010).

——, 'The Medieval "Marches" of Normandy and Wales', *EHR* 115/517 (2010), 1357–81.

The Life, Diary, and Correspondence of Sir William Dugdale, ed. William Hamper (London, 1827).

Lives of the Cambro-British Saints, ed. and trans. W. J. Rees (London, 1853).

Livingston, Michael, 'Owain Glyndŵr's Grand Design: "The Tripartite Indenture" and the Vision of a New Wales', *Proceedings of the Harvard Celtic Colloquium*, 33 (2013), 145–68.

Lloyd-Morgan, Ceridwen, 'Lancelot in Wales', in Karen Pratt (ed.), *Shifts and Transpositions in Medieval Narrative: A Festschrift for Dr Elspeth Kennedy* (Cambridge, 1994), 169–79.

——, 'Prophecy and Welsh Nationhood in the Fifteenth Century', *Transactions of the Honourable Society of Cymmrodorion* (1985), 9–26.

——, and Erich Poppe, 'The First Adaptations from French: History and Context of a Debate', in Ceridwen Lloyd-Morgan and Erich Poppe (eds), *Arthur in the Celtic Languages: The Arthurian Legend in Celtic Literatures and Languages*, Arthurian Literature in the Middle Ages, 9 (Cardiff, 2019), 110–16.

Lloyd, J. E., *A History of Wales from the Earliest Times to the Edwardian Conquest*, 2 vols, 2nd edn (London, 1912).

——, 'Rhys ap Tewdwr (d. 1093)', rev. David E. Thornton, *ODNB*, https://doi.org/10.1093/ref:odnb/23463, accessed 14 March 2022.

Luft, Diana, 'The NLW Peniarth 32 Latin Chronicle', *SC* 44 (2010), 47–70.

Lumbley, Coral, 'Geoffrey of Monmouth and Race', in Georgia Henley and Joshua Byron Smith (eds), *A Companion to Geoffrey of Monmouth*, Brill's Companions to European History, 22 (Leiden, 2020), 369–96.

McKenna, Catherine, 'Reading with Rhydderch: *Mabinogion* Texts in Manuscript Context', in Anders Ahlqvist and Pamela O'Neill (eds), *Language and Power in the Celtic World: Papers from the Seventh Australian Conference of Celtic Studies* (Sydney, 2011), 205–30.

McKisack, May, *The Fourteenth Century, 1307–1399* (Oxford, 1959).

McSparran, Frances, 'The Language of the English Poems', in Fein (ed.), *Studies in the Harley Manuscript*, 391–426.

Manion, Lee, 'Sovereign Recognition: Contesting Political Claims in the *Alliterative Morte Arthure* and *The Awntyrs off Arthur*', in Robert S. Sturges (ed.), *Law and Sovereignty in the Middle Ages and the Renaissance* (Turnhout, 2011), 69–91.

Mann, Kevin, 'The March of Wales: A Question of Terminology', *WHR* 18 (1996), 1–13.

Marchant, Alicia, 'Narratives of Death and Emotional Affect in Late Medieval Chronicles', *Parergon*, 31/2 (2015), 81–98.

Marx, William, 'Aberystwyth, National Library of Wales, MS 21608 and the Middle English Prose *Brut*', *Journal of the Early Book Society*, 1/1 (1997), 1–16.

Matheson, Lister M., *The Prose Brut: The Development of a Middle English Chronicle* (Tempe, 1998).

Matonis, A. T. E., 'An Investigation of Celtic Influences on MS Harley 2253', *Modern Philology*, 70/2 (1972), 91–108.

——, 'The Rhetorical Patterns in *Marwnad Llywelyn ap Gruffudd* by Gruffudd ab yr Ynad Coch', *Studia Celtica*, 14/1 (1979), 188–92.

Maund, K. L., 'Neufmarché, Bernard de (d. 1121×5?)', *ODNB*, https://doi.org/10.1093/ref:odnb/2236, accessed 2 February 2022.

A Mediaeval Prince: The Life of Gruffudd ap Cynan, ed. and trans. D. Simon Evans (Lampeter, 1990).

Meecham-Jones, Simon, 'Where Was Wales? The Erasure of Wales in Medieval English Culture', in Kennedy and Meecham-Jones (eds), *Authority and Subjugation*, 27–56.

Meisel, Janet, *Barons of the Welsh Frontier: The Corbut, Pantulf, and Fitz Warin Families, 1066–1272* (Lincoln, 1980).

Miller, Jennifer, 'Laȝamon's Welsh', in Rosamund Allen, Jane Roberts, and Carole Weinberg (eds), *Reading Laȝamon's Brut: Approaches and Explorations* (Amsterdam, 2013), 589–622.

Monasticon Anglicanum: Or, The history of the ancient abbies, monasteries, hospitals, cathedral and collegiate churches, with their dependencies, in England and Wales, ed. William Dugdale, 6 vols (London, 1718; repr. 1846).

Monroe, W. H., 'Thirteenth- and Early Fourteenth-Century Illustrated Genealogical Manuscripts in Roll and Codex: Peter of Poitiers' *Compendium, Universal Histories* and *Chronicles of the Kings of England*' (unpublished Ph.D. thesis, University of London, 1989).

Morgan-Guy, John, 'Arthur, Harri Tudor and the Iconography of Loyalty', in Steven Gunn and Linda Monckton (eds), *Arthur Tudor, Prince of Wales: Life, Death and Commemoration* (Woodbridge, 2009), 50–63.

Mortimer, Ian, 'The Chronology of the de Mortemer Family of Wigmore, c.1075–1185, and the Consolidation of a Marcher Lordship', *Historical Research*, 89/246 (2016), 613–35.

Naples, Nancy A., 'Borderland Studies and Border Theory: Linking Activism and Scholarship for Social Justice', *Sociology Compass*, 4/7 (2010), 505–18.

O'Donnell, Thomas, Jane Gilbert, and Brian Reilly, 'Introduction', in Thomas O'Donnell, Jane Gilbert, and Brian Reilly (eds), *Medieval French Interlocutions: Shifting Perspectives on a Language in Contact* (York, forthcoming).

The Oldest Anglo-Norman Prose Brut Chronicle, ed. and trans. Julia Marvin, Medieval Chronicles, 4 (Woodbridge, 2006).

O'Rourke, Jason, 'Imagining Book Production in Fourteenth-Century Herefordshire: The Scribe of British Library, MS Harley 2253 and his "Organizing Principles"', in Stephen Kelly and John J. Thompson (eds), *Imagining the Book*, Medieval Texts and Cultures of Northern Europe, 7 (Turnhout, 2005), 45–69.

'Original Documents: Edward I Parliaments, Roll 5', in *Parliament Rolls of Medieval England*, ed. and trans. Chris Given-Wilson et al. (Woodbridge, 2005), *British History Online*, http://www.british-history.ac.uk/no-series/parliament-rolls-medieval/roll-5, accessed 27 October 2022.

'Original Documents: Edward I Parliaments, Roll 11', in *Parliament Rolls of Medieval England*, ed. and trans. Chris Given-Wilson et al. (Woodbridge, 2005), *British History Online*, http://www.british-history.ac.uk/no-series/parliament-rolls-medieval/roll-11, accessed 27 October 2022.

Original Letters Illustrative of English History, ed. Henry Lewis, 4 vols (London, 1827).

Otter, Monika, *Inventiones: Fiction and Referentiality in Twelfth-Century English Historical Writing* (Chapel Hill, 1996).

Over, Kristen Lee, 'Transcultural Change: Romance to *Rhamant*', in Helen Fulton (ed.), *Medieval Celtic Literature and Society* (Dublin, 2005), 183–204.

Parkinson, B. J., 'The Life of Robert de Bethune by William de Wycombe: Translation with Introduction and Notes' (unpublished B.Litt. dissertation, University of Oxford, 1951).

Parry, Graham, 'Dugdale, Sir William (1605–1686)', *ODNB*, https://doi.org/10.1093/ref:odnb/8186, accessed 22 October 2021.

Parsons, David N., 'Pre-English River Names and British Survival in Shropshire', *Nomina*, 36 (2013), 107–23.

——, *Welsh and English in Medieval Oswestry: The Evidence of Place-Names* (Nottingham, 2023).

Patterson, Robert B., 'The Author of the "Margam Annals": Early Thirteenth-Century Margam Abbey's Compleat Scribe', *Anglo-Norman Studies*, 14 (1992), 197–210.

Pensom, Roger, 'Inside and Outside: Fact and Fiction in *Fouke le Fitz Waryn*', *Medium Ævum*, 63 (1994), 53–60.

Powicke, F. M., 'Notes on Hastings Manuscripts', *Huntington Library Quarterly*, 3 (1938), 247–76.

Price, Adrian, 'Welsh Bandits', in Helen Phillips (ed.), *Bandit Territories: British Outlaw Traditions* (Cardiff, 2008), 58–72.

Pryce, Huw, 'Y Canu Lladin', in Pryce and Jones (eds), *Yr Arglwydd Rhys*, 212–23.

——, and Nerys Ann Jones (eds), *Yr Arglwydd Rhys* (Cardiff, 1996).

Pugh, T. B. (ed.), *Glamorgan County History*, vol. iii. *The Middle Ages* (Cardiff, 1971).

——, 'The Marcher Lords of Glamorgan, 1317–1485', in Pugh (ed.), *Glamorgan County History*, iii.167–204.

Putter, Ad., and Judith Jefferson (eds), *Multilingualism in Medieval Britain (c.1066–1520): Sources and Analysis*, Medieval Texts and Cultures of Northern Europe, 15 (Turnhout, 2012).

Radulescu, Raluca L., and Edward Donald Kennedy (eds), *Broken Lines: Genealogical Literature in Medieval Britain and France*, Medieval Texts and Cultures of Northern Europe, 16 (Turnhout, 2008).

Ranulph Higden, *Polychronicon*, and John Trevisa, *Polychronicon*, ed. Churchill Babington and Joseph Rawson Lumby, *Polychronicon Ranulphi Higden monachi Cestrensis*, 9 vols (London, 1865–86).

Ray, Keith, 'The Organisation of the Mid–Late Anglo-Saxon Borderland with Wales', *Offa's Dyke Journal*, 4 (2022), 132–53.

Ray, Roger D., 'Medieval Historiography through the Twelfth Century: Problems and Progress of Research', *Viator*, 5 (1974), 33–60.

Registrum Epistolarum Fratris Johannis Peckham, Archiepiscopi Cantuariensis, ed. Charles Trice Martin, 3 vols (London, 1882–5; repr. 1965).

Revard, Carter, 'Scribe and Provenance', in Fein (ed.), *Studies in the Harley Manuscript*, 21–110.

Richards, Melville, 'The Population of the Welsh Border', *Transactions of the Honourable Society of Cymmrodorion* (1970), 77–100.

Richter, Michael, 'Giraldus Cambrensis and Llanthony Priory', *SC* 12–13 (1977–8), 118–32.

——, 'William ap Rhys, William de Braose and the Lordship of Gower, 1289 and 1307', *SC* 32 (1998), 189–209.

Roberts, Brynley F., 'Geoffrey of Monmouth and Welsh Historical Tradition', *Nottingham Medieval Studies*, 20 (1976), 29–40.

——, 'The Treatment of Personal Names in the Early Welsh Versions of *Historia regum Britanniae*', *Bulletin of the Board of Celtic Studies*, 25 (1973), 274–90.

Roberts, Sara Elin, 'The Law of the March', in Philip Hume (ed.), *The Welsh Marcher Lordships*, 9–13.

Rock, Catherine, 'Fouke le Fitz Waryn and King John: Rebellion and Reconciliation', in Alexander L. Kaufman (ed.), *British Outlaws of Literature and History: Essays on Medieval and Early Modern Figures from Robin Hood to Twm Shon Catty* (Jefferson, NC, 2011), 67–96.

Roger of Wendover, *Flores historiarum*, ed. Henry Richards Luard, *Flores Historiarum*, 3 vols (London, 1890).

Roger of Wendover's Flowers of History: Comprising the history of England from the descent of the Saxons to AD 1235, Formerly ascribed to Matthew Paris, trans. J. A. Giles, 2 vols (London, 1849).

The Romance of Fergus, ed. Wilson Frescoln (Philadelphia, 1983).

Rosenwein, Barbara H., *Generations of Feeling: A History of Emotions, 600–1700* (Cambridge, 2016).

Rotuli parliamentorum, ut et petitiones, et placita in parliament, ed. J. Strachey, 6 vols (London, 1767–77).

Rudd, Gillian, '"The Wilderness of Wirral" in *Sir Gawain and the Green Knight*', *Arthuriana*, 23/1 (2013), 52–65.

Russell, Paul, '"Go and Look in the Latin Books": Latin and the Vernacular in Medieval Wales', in Richard Ashdowne and Carolinne White (eds), *Latin in Medieval Britain*, Proceedings of the British Academy, 206 (Oxford, 2017), 213–46.

Rutherford, Jonathan, 'The Third Space: Interview with Homi Bhabha', in Rutherford, *Identity: Community, Culture, Difference* (London, 1990), 207–21.

Rutter, Russell, 'Printing, Prophecy, and the Foundation of the Tudor Dynasty: Caxton's *Morte Darthur* and Henry Tudor's Road to Bosworth', in E. L.

Risden, Karen Moranski, and Stephen Yardell (eds), *Prophet Margins: The Medieval Vatic Impulse and Social Stability* (New York, 2004), 123–47.

Scase, Wendy (ed.), *Essays in Manuscript Geography: Vernacular Manuscripts of the English West Midlands from the Conquest to the Sixteenth Century*, Medieval Texts and Cultures of Northern Europe, 10 (Turnhout, 2007).

Schiff, Randy P., 'Borderland Subversions: Anti-Imperial Energies in *The Awntyrs off Arthure* and *Golagros and Gawane*', *Speculum*, 84 (2009), 613–32.

Shenton, Caroline, 'Edward III and the Coup of 1330', in J. S. Bothwell (ed.), *The Age of Edward III* (York, 2001), 13–34.

Sims-Williams, Patrick, *The Book of Llandaf as a Historical Source*, Studies in Celtic History, 38 (Woodbridge, 2019).

——, 'The Welsh Versions of Geoffrey of Monmouth's "History of the Kings of Britain"', in Axel Harlos and Neele Harlos (eds), *Adapting Texts and Styles in a Celtic Context: Interdisciplinary Perspectives on Processes of Literary Transfer in the Middle Ages: Studies in Honour of Erich Poppe*, Studien und Texte zur Keltologie, 13 (Münster, 2016), 53–74.

Sir Gawain: Eleven Romances and Tales, ed. Thomas Hahn (Kalamazoo, 1995).

Sir Gawain and the Green Knight, trans. Simon Armitage (New York, 2007).

Slack, W. J., *The Lordship of Oswestry, 1393–1607* (Shrewsbury, 1951).

Smith, J. Beverley, 'Dafydd ap Llywelyn (*c*.1215–1246)', *ODNB*, https://doi.org/10.1093/ref:odnb/7323, accessed 2 February 2022.

——, 'The Kingdom of Morgannwg and the Norman Conquest of Glamorgan', in Pugh (ed.), *Glamorgan County History*, iii.1–43.

——, *Llywelyn ap Gruffudd: Prince of Wales* (Oxford, 1998).

——, 'The Middle March in the Thirteenth Century', *Bulletin of the Board of Celtic Studies*, 24 (1970–2), 77–93.

——, *Yr Ymwybod â Hanes yng Nghymru yn yr Oesoedd Canol: Darlith Agoriadol/The Sense of History in Medieval Wales: An Inaugural Lecture* (Aberystwyth, 1991).

——, and T. B. Pugh, 'The Lordship of Gower and Kilvey', in Pugh (ed.), *Glamorgan County History*, iii.205–84.

Smith, Joshua Byron, 'Benedict of Gloucester's *Vita Sancti Dubricii*: An Edition and Translation', *Arthurian Literature*, 29 (2012), 53–100.

——, 'Fouke le Fitz Waryn', in Jocelyn Wogan-Browne, Thelma Fenster, and Delbert W. Russell (eds), *Vernacular Literary Theory from the French of Medieval England: Texts and Translations, c.1120–c.1450* (Cambridge, 2016), 293–302.

——, 'Madog of Edeirnion's *Strenua cunctorum*: A Welsh–Latin Poem in Praise of Geoffrey of Monmouth', *North American Journal of Celtic Studies*, 6/1 (2022), 1–14.

——, '"Til þat he neȝed ful neghe into þe Norþe Walez": Gawain's Postcolonial Turn', *Chaucer Review*, 51/3 (2016), 295–309.

——, *Walter Map and the Matter of Britain* (Philadelphia, 2017).

Smith, Llinos Beverley, 'The Death of Llywelyn ap Gruffudd: The Narratives Reconsidered', *WHR* 11 (1982–3), 200–13.

——, 'Glyn Dŵr [Glyndŵr], Owain [Owain *ap* Gruffudd Fychan, Owain Glendower]', *ODNB*, https://doi.org/10.1093/ref:odnb/10816, accessed 4 May 2022.

——, 'Llywelyn ap Gruffudd and the Welsh Historical Consciousness', *WHR* 12/1 (1984), 1–28.

Spearing, A. C., '*The Awntyrs off Arthure*', in Bernard S. Levy and Paul E. Szarmach (eds), *The Alliterative Tradition in the Fourteenth Century* (Kent, OH, 1981), 183–200.

——, 'Central and Displaced Sovereignty in Three Medieval Poems', *Review of English Studies*, 33/131 (1982), 247–61.

Spence, John, 'Genealogies of Noble Families in Anglo-Norman', in Radulescu and Kennedy (eds), *Broken Lines*, 63–78.

——, *Reimagining History in Anglo-Norman Prose Chronicles* (Woodbridge and Rochester, 2013).

Steiner, Emily, 'Compendious Genres: Higden, Trevisa, and the Medieval Encyclopedia', *Exemplaria*, 27/1–2 (2015), 73–92.

——, 'Radical Historiography: Langland, Trevisa, and the *Polychronicon*', *Studies in the Age of Chaucer*, 27 (2005), 171–211.

Stephenson, David, *The Aberconwy Chronicle*, Kathleen Hughes Memorial Lectures on Mediaeval Welsh History, 2 (Cambridge, 2002).

——, '*Fouke le Fitz Waryn* and Llywelyn ap Gruffudd's Claim to Whittington', *Transactions of the Shropshire Historical and Archaeological Society*, 78 (2002), 26–31.

——, 'Llywelyn Fawr, the Mortimers, and Cwmhir Abbey: The Politics of Monastic Rebuilding', *Transactions of the Radnorshire Society*, 80 (2010), 29–41.

——, *Medieval Powys: Kingdom, Principality and Lordships, 1132–1293* (Woodbridge, 2016).

——, *Medieval Wales, c.1050–1332: Centuries of Ambiguity* (Cardiff, 2019).

——, *Patronage and Power in the Medieval Welsh March: One Family's Story* (Cardiff, 2021).

——, 'The Politics of Powys Wenwynwyn in the Thirteenth Century', *CMCS* 7 (1984), 39–61.

——, 'Welsh Lords in Shropshire: Gruffydd ap Iorwerth Goch and his Descendants in the Thirteenth Century', *Transactions of the Shropshire Archaeological Society*, 77 (2002), 32–7.

Stock, Markus (ed.), *Alexander the Great in the Middle Ages: Transcultural Perspectives* (Toronto, 2015).

A Summary Catalogue of Western Manuscripts in the Bodleian Library at Oxford, ed. Falconer Madan and H. H. E. Craster, vol. ii, part 2 (Oxford, 1937).

Suppe, Frederick, 'Interpreter Families and Anglo-Welsh Relations in the Shropshire–Powys Marches in the Twelfth Century', *Anglo-Norman Studies*, 30 (2008), 192–212.

——, *Military Institutions on the Welsh Marches: Shropshire, AD 1066–1300*, Studies in Celtic History, 14 (Woodbridge, 1994).

Tahkokallio, Jaakko, *The Anglo-Norman Historical Canon: Publishing and Manuscript Culture*, Cambridge Elements: Elements in Publishing and Book Culture, (Cambridge 2019).

Taylor, John, *English Historical Literature in the Fourteenth Century* (Oxford, 1987).

Thompson, John J., 'Mapping Points of West of West Midlands Manuscripts', in Wendy Scase (ed.), *Vernacular Manuscripts of the English West Midlands from the Conquest to the Sixteenth Century* (Turnhout, 2007), 113–28.

Thornton, David E., 'A Neglected Genealogy of Llywelyn ap Gruffudd', *CMCS* 23 (1992), 9–23.

Thornton, Tim, 'Wales in Late Medieval and Early Modern English Histories: Neglect, Rediscovery, and their Implications', *Historical Research*, 90/250 (2017), 663–858.

Tristram, Hildegard L. C., 'More Talk of Alexander', *Celtica*, 21 (1990), 658–63.

Turvey, Roger, *The Lord Rhys: Prince of Deheubarth* (Llandysul, 1997).

Turville-Petre, Thorlac, *England the Nation: Language, Literature, and National Identity, 1290–1340* (Oxford, 1996).

Two Medieval Outlaws: Eustace the Monk and Fouke Fitz Waryn, trans. Glyn S. Burgess (Cambridge, 1997).

Tyler, Elizabeth M. (ed.), *Conceptualizing Multilingualism in England, c.800–c.1250*, Studies in the Early Middle Ages, 27 (Turnhout, 2011).

Tyson, Diana B., 'The Adam and Eve Roll: Corpus Christi College Cambridge MS 98', *Scriptorium*, 52/2 (1998), 301–16.

——, 'A Medieval Genealogy of the Lords of Brecknock', *Nottingham Medieval Studies*, 48 (2004), 1–14.

Vila, Pablo, 'The Limits of American Border Theory', in Pablo Vila (ed.), *Ethnography at the Border* (Minneapolis, 2003), 306–41.

Vincent, Nicholas, 'Cantilupe, Sir George de (1251–1273)', *ODNB*, https://doi.org/10.1093/ref:odnb/4566, accessed 2 February 2022.

Vita Griffini Filii Conani: The Medieval Latin Life of Gruffudd ap Cynan, ed. and trans. Paul Russell (Cardiff, 2005).

'Vita Sancti Dubricii (Liber Landavensis / Vespasian A. xiv)', ed. and trans. Ben Guy, *Seintiau: The Cult of Saints in Wales* (Aberystwyth, 2019), https://saint2.llgc.org.uk/texts/prose/VDub_LL-V/edited-text.eng.html, accessed 4 May 2022.

Waldron, Ronald, *John Trevisa's Translation of the Polychronicon of Ranulph Higden, Book VI: An Edition Based on British Library MS Cotton Tiberius D. VII*, Middle English Texts, 35 (Heidelberg, 2004).

——, 'The Manuscripts of Trevisa's Translation of the *Polychronicon*: Towards a New Edition', *Modern Language Quarterly*, 51/3 (1990), 281–317.

——, 'Trevisa's "Celtic Complex" Revisited', *Notes & Queries*, 36/3 (1989), 303–7.

——, 'Trevisa's Translation of Higden's *Polychronicon*, Book I, Chapter 38, *De Wallia*: An Edition', in Kennedy and Meecham-Jones (eds), *Authority and Subjugation*, 99–135.

Warren, Michelle R., *History on the Edge: Excalibur and the Borders of Britain, 1100–1300* (Minneapolis, 2000).

——, 'Making Contact: Postcolonial Perspectives through Geoffrey of Monmouth's "Historia regum Britannie"', *Arthuriana*, 8/4 (1998), 115–34.

Watson, Fiona, 'Hastings, John, first Lord Hastings (1262–1313)', *ODNB*, https://doi.org/10.1093/ref:odnb/12578, accessed 2 February 2022.

Waugh, Scott L., 'Bohun, Humphrey de, third earl of Hereford and eighth earl of Essex (c.1249–1298)', *ODNB*, https://doi.org/10.1093/ref:odnb/2776, accessed 22 October 2021.

Wiggins, Alison, 'Middle English Romance and the West Midlands', in Scase (ed.), *Essays in Manuscript Geography*, 239–56.

Williams, Alison, 'Stories within Stories: Writing History in *Fouke le Fitz Waryn*', *Medium Ævum*, 81/1 (2012), 70–87.

Williams, David H., *The Welsh Cistercians* (Leominster, 2001).

Williams, Glanmor, 'The Church in Glamorgan from the Fourteenth Century to the Reformation', in Pugh (ed.), *Glamorgan County History*, iii.135–66.

Williams, Gruffydd Aled, 'The Bardic Road to Bosworth: A Welsh View of Henry Tudor', *Transactions of the Honourable Society of Cymmrodorion* (1986), 7–31.

——, 'Welsh Raiding in the Twelfth-Century Shropshire/Cheshire March: The Case of Owain Cyfeiliog', *SC* 40 (2006), 89–115.

Wilshere, A. D., 'The Anglo-Norman Bible Stories in MS Harley 2253', *Forum for Modern Language Studies*, 24 (1988), 78–89.

Wogan-Browne, Jocelyn (ed.), *Language and Culture in Medieval Britain: The French of England c.1100–c.1500* (York, 2009).

The Works of the Gawain Poet: Sir Gawain and the Green Knight, Pearl, Cleanness, Patience, ed. Ad Putter and Myra Stokes (London, 2014).

Zeiser, Sarah, 'Latinity, Manuscripts, and the Rhetoric of Conquest in Late-Eleventh-Century Wales' (unpublished Ph.D. dissertation, Harvard University, 2012).

GENERAL INDEX

Aberconwy Abbey, 70, 73, 170
Abergavenny
   lords of, 119, 136–7, 143
   lordship of, 3 n.9, 118 n.4, 122, 139, 143
   priory, 139 n.55
Aberystwyth castle, 49
Achilles, 200, 211, 214 n.51
Acts of Union, 17
Ada of Huntingdon, 136, 144, 145
Adam, 88, 93, 97, 100, 251
Aedd Mawr (Antonius), 98, 243, 251
Aelmayl, king, 245
Aeneas *see* Eneas Ysgwydwyn
Afallach, 98, 243, 250, 251
Afan, 46
affect/affective experience, 195–8, 200–1, 206–7, 220–2, 224–5, 227
Africa, 45
Ajax, 199–200, 211, 214 n.51
Albanactus, 1, 85, 93, 94 n.51, 204
Alberbury Priory, 156
Albion, 51, 166, *see also* giants
Alexander the Great, 45 n.29, 183, 192 n.121, 203–4, 207–8, 222
Alice de Lusignan, 147, 149
Allesley, 137
alliterative romance, 157, 185
Amlawdd, duke of Cornwall, 98, 113 n.100, 250
Amweryd, 98, 243, 250
Amys and Amylion, 163
Anarawd ab Idwal Foel, 98, 112 n.96
Anarawd ap Rhodri Mawr, 98, 110, 247, 250
Anchises, 98, 99 n.69, 251
Anglesey, 16, 49, 2177, 237–8, 248
Anglo-Norman
   ancestry, 4, 8, 11–13, 19–22, 47, 61, 73, 79, 81, 161, 184, 229, 230–1

   genealogies, 119 n.6, 119 n.7, 134
   identity terms, 13, 18
   kings, 67, 86
   language *see* French, language
   monasteries, 15
   see also Brut, Anglo-Norman Prose; Norman; Normandy
Yr Anghrist a Dydd y Farn, 37
Anglo-Saxon Chronicle, 196 n.2
Annales Cambriae, 112, 114, 196 n.2, *see also Cronica de Wallia*
Annals of Chester, 170 n.56, 223
Annals of the Four Masters, 196 n.2
Annals of Tigernach, 196 n.2
Annals of Ulster, 196 n.2
Annals of Waverley, 67
Annals of Worcester, 67
Anne, daughter of Richard of York, 101
Aoife, daughter of Diarmait Mac Murchada, 178, *see also* Clare, Richard (Strongbow)
Arabic, 163
Archenfield, 3 n.9, 36 n.7, 49, *see also* Ergyng
Armes Prydein Vawr, 224 n.77
Arthen, 112 n.98, 246
Arthur, king
   in *The Awntyrs off Arthure at the Terne Wathelyn*, 186–93
   in *De gestis Britonum*, 56
   in *Epitome historiae Britanniae*, 43–4, 45 n.29, 69
   in *Fouke le Fitz Waryn*, romance of, 167–8
   in *History of William Marshal*, 183–4
   in lament for Rhys ap Gruffudd, 203–4
   in Ludlow Annal, 67, 73
   in Middle English Prose *Brut*, 73
   Mortimer interest in, 95, 115, 250

in *Sir Gawain and the Green Knight*, 233–8
  Tudor use of, 115
  in Welsh poetry, 104 n.85
Arthurian literature, 6, 32, 73, 153–4, 182–93, 227, 232–40, *see also* romance, genre
Arviragus ap Maelgwn Gwynedd, 91, 244
Ascanius, 98, 251
Asia, 45
Assaracus, 98, 251
Athelston, 159
Augustine of Canterbury, saint, 67
Augustine of Hippo, saint, 207
Augustinian order, 59 n.67, 60, 78, 212
Aurelius Ambrosius, 42
Avalon, 43, 67
The Awntyrs off Arthure at the Terne Wathelyn, 32, 154, 185–93

Bala, 174
Balliol
  Eustace, 146
  Hugh, 148
barbarity, 190, 212–13, 220, 240, *see also* civility
Barbary, 156
Bath, 98, 216
Batman, Stephen, 213
Battle Abbey, 131
Battle of Bosworth, 115
Battle of Bryn Glas, 49
Battle of Lewes, 157 n.13
Battle of Mynydd Carn, 15
Beatrice de Clermont, 148
Beauchamp, family, 215 n.53
  Isabel, 146
Bede, 67, 218–19
Bedford, 95
Beli ap Rhun [Hir], 98, 109, 247, 250
Beli Mawr, 98, 243, 251
Benedictine order, 15, 40 n.10, 48 n.39, 208, 212

Bernard de Neufmarché, 14–15, 122, 124, 128, 130–1
Bertha, daughter of Miles fitz Walter, 127–8, 131 n.36, 139–40, *see also* Braose, William II; Miles fitz Walter
Bertilak, 240
Bevis of Hampton, 159
Bible, 63, 88, 90, 200, 227
  history, 37, 44, 45 n.29, 50, 69
  see also Adam; Eve
Bigot
  Hugh, 147
  Roger, 147
Bishop's Castle, 3 n.9
Black Death, 44
Blaenau Morgannwg, 46
Blaenllyfni, 3 n.9, 140–1
Blanche Launde, 162, 164 n.37, 166–8, *see also* Whittington (*Blancheville*)
Bleddudd (Bladud), 98, 106–8, 113 n.100, 242, 246, 251
Bleddyn, king, 246
Boethius, 199
Bohun, family, 17, 120, 122, 126–30, 143
  Eleanor (d. 1314), 128, 130
  Frank, 150
  Gilbert, 128
  Humphrey II (d. 1164/5), 127–8, 131 n.36, 140
  Humphrey V (d. 1265), 122, 122 n.14, 128–30, 138, 146, 150
  Humphrey VI (c.1249–98), 128–30, 150, 169
  Humphrey VII (c.1276–1322), 137, 150
  Humphrey VIII (1309–61), 233
  John, 150
  John II, 150
  Maud, 128, 130
  see also Braose, Eleanor; Margaret, daughter of Miles fitz Walter
Boniface VIII, pope, 186
Book of Llandaf *see* Index of Manuscripts, Aberystwyth, National Library of Wales, 17110E (Book of Llandaf)

border, 4–29, 60–1, 160, 195, 209, 212, 239–40
  culture, 5–7, 13, 19–23, 30, 32, 34–6, 76, 114, 119–20, 152–5, 170–1, 184, 186–94, 209–10, 229–40
  theory, 19–22
  zone, 3 n.9, 5–6, 8, 10–11, 14 n.38, 26, 31, 46, 188 n.109
  see also March of Wales; marches, Anglo-Scottish
borderland, 3–34, 46, 75–6, 80–1, 114, 119, 154, 161, 185–8, 191, 193–4, 198, 209–10, 212, 221, 227–30, 236–40
  definition of, 3 n.9, 10–13, 19–26
  see also March of Wales; marches, Anglo-Scottish
Bowus, king, 244
Bran, king, 165
Braose, family, 15, 67, 69, 78 n.8, 122, 127, 130, 136–43, 160, 169
  Alice, 146
  Eleanor, 122, 122 n.14, 128–30, 138, 146, 150
  Eve, 128–9, 138, 143, 146, 150
  Giles, 122, 127–8, 141–2
  Isabel, daughter of Reginald, 146
  Isabel, daughter of William V, 122, 128–9, 138, 146
  Joan, 146
  Margery, 146
  Maud (d. 1300/1), daughter of William V, 78 n.8, 128–9, 138, 146, 150
  Maud de Saint Valéry, wife of William III, 127–8
  Reginald, 78, 87, 122, 127–8, 136, 139, 141–2, 144, 146
  William II, 127–8, 131 n.36, 140, 140 n.58
  William III (d. 1211), 127–8, 141–2
  William IV (d. 1210), 127–8
  William V (d. 1230), 127–9, 136, 138–9, 143, 146, 150
  William VI, 27–8
  see also Bertha, daughter of Miles fitz Walter; Marshal, Eve
Brecon, 3 n.9, 14–15, 17, 31, 47, 118 n.4, 119–22, 127–31, 134–5, 139–44, 169, 201 n.19, 230, 246
  see also Brycheiniog; *Genealogy of the Lords of Brecknock*
Breton
  cartularies, 112 n.97
  people, 4, 11
  see also Brittany
Brewer
  Griselle, 144, 146
  William, 136, 144, 146
  William II, 146
Bristol, 60
Britain, 1–5, 10, 14 n.38, 18, 21 n.65, 29–30, 32, 36, 41–3, 45, 51, 53, 56–7, 67, 77, 80, 88, 91, 93–4, 99, 101–2, 104–5, 108, 114, 117, 119, 160–2, 164, 166, 168–9, 185, 192, 194, 202, 208, 215–16, 220, 228, 231–6, 239, 241
  division into three parts, 1–2, 81 n.18, 93–4
  legendary history of, 1–3, 5, 10, 29–30, 35–6, 41–3, 45, 51, 53, 56, 59, 67, 69, 73–7, 81 n.18, 88, 93–4, 99, 101–2, 108–11, 114, 160–2, 164–9, 192–4, 202, 215–16, 220, 232–6, 239
  literary history of, 9–10
  peoples of, 9, 18, 91, 96, 114, 231
  political landscape of, 3–4, 9, 29, 32, 241
  Roman, 14 n.38
  unification of, 29, 94, 104–5, 184, 232
  see also Brutus; Geoffrey of Monmouth
British-Welsh history, 3–5, 8, 29–36, 50, 58–60, 64, 66, 73–4, 76, 91, 102–5, 116, 228–32, 241
Britons, 36, 42–3, 45, 51, 53, 64, 67, 91, 104, 165–7, 209, 215–16, 220, 224 n.78, 232–3, 235–6, 246 n.14, *see also* Brutus; Geoffrey of Monmouth
Brittany, 156, 189, 191
  dukes of, 112 n.97
  see also Breton
Bromfield and Yale, 3 n.9, 16–17
Bro Morgannwg, 46

GENERAL INDEX | 277

Bronllys castle, 126, 134
Brut
  Anglo-Norman Prose, 42 n.19, 75, 79–80, 101–2
  Latin Prose, 77, 79–80, 85, 91, 164, 182–3
  Middle English Prose, 42 n.19, 43 n.20, 43 n.24, 59, 73, 79–85, 87 n.36, 99 n.70, 104, 114, 223, 232, 235
    Arthur in, 73
    Herefordshire in, 80–5, 114
    Mortimers in, 81–3
    as product of March of Wales, 80–1
Brut y Brenhinedd, 50, 75, 106–7
Brut y Tywysogion, 24, 181 n.89, 196 n.2, 202–6
Brutus, 1, 64, 81, 93–4, 98, 182, 204, 215
  in *Epitome historiae Britanniae*, 36, 41–2, 51, 58, 69
  in *Fouke le Fitz Waryn*, romance of, 156, 162–4, 166, 166 n.47
  in genealogies and lists, 85–6, 90, 91, 94, 106–8, 202, 242, 251
  in *Sir Gawain and the Green Knight*, 233–5, 237
Brutus Darianlas/Ysgwydhir, 98, 106–7, 242, 251
Brycheiniog, 14, 120, 122, 124, 126, 246, *see also* Brecon
Brychwain, 98, 113 n.99, 243, 250
Bryceath, king, 244
Buellt, 92–3, 249
Builth, 3 n.9
Burgh
  John, 149
  Maud, 149

Cadell ap Rhodri Mawr, 110, 112 n.98, 247
Cadfan ab Iago, 98, 109, 247, 250
Cadfan, king, 245
Cadog, saint, life of, 37
Cadwaladr Fendigaid (Kadwaladrus), 41, 43, 54, 67, 86, 98, 109, 245, 247, 250
Cadwallon ap Cadfan, 98, 109, 247, 250
Cadwallon Lawhir, 98, 244, 250

Cadwallon, king, 245
Caerleon, 3 n.9, 56, 179 n.80, 181–2
Caernarfon, 16
  castle, 49, 226
Caernarfonshire, 16, 233
Caerphilly castle, 191
Caesar, Julius, 204, 215
Cainan, 98, 251
Cain ap Gwrgain, 98, 244, 250
Camber, 1–2, 81 n.18, 91, 93–4, 203–4, 242
Cambria, 2, 44, 81 n.18, 91, 93, *see also* Wales
Camden, William, 214
Camelot, 238
Cantilupe
  George, 138, 143, 150
  Joanna, 138–9, 143–4, 150
  Millicent, 138–9, 143, 150
  William, 128–9, 138, 143, 146, 150
Cantref Bychan, 3 n.9, 16
Cantref Selyf, 26
Canu Urien, 206–7
Capys, 98, 251
Caradog, 109, 112 n.98, 246, 247
Cardiff
  castle, 49
  chronicle, 68
  priory, 40 n.10, 48 n.39
  town, 40 n.10, 45, 48 n.39, 67
Careticus see Kareticus
Carlisle, 186, 187 n.104
Carmarthen, 16, 179, 217
Carmarthenshire, 27–8, 198
Catercus, king, 245
Catrin, daughter of Owain Glyndŵr, 79 n.11, *see also* Mortimer, Edmund IV (1376–1408/9)
Caus, 3 n.9, 61, 64
Caxton, William, 213
Ceaulinus, king, 216
Cecil, William, 213
Cedewain, 3 n.9, 16
Celius, 98, 251
Cemais, 3 n.9, 138, 144 n.65

Ceredigion, 14, 16, 27 n.91, 47 n.36, 48 n.37, 49, 58, 70, 118 n.4, 179 n.80, 199, 246
Ceri, 3 n.9, 16
Cerwyd ap Crydon, 98, 243, 251
Cetim, 251
chancery, 25, 28
chanson de geste, 159
Charlemagne, 45 n.29, 159
Charles VI, king of France, 49
Chaucer, Geoffrey, 75, 213, 235 n.5
  Canterbury Tales, 63, 63 n.86
Chaworth
  Eve, 146
  Maud, 146
  Patrick (d. 1258), 146
  Patrick II, 146
  Payn, 146
  Payn II, 146
Chenclern, king, 245
Chepstow (Striguil), 3 n.9, 118 n.4, 179
Cheshire, 3 n.9, 212–13, 233, 235, 238–40
Chester
  city, 195, 208–12, 226, 239, 251
  earldom of, 14
  see also Annals of Chester; Higden, Ranulph, *Polychronicon*
Chirk, 3 n.9, 16
chivalry, 95, 175, 178, 182, 188, 190–3, 214 n.51
Chrétien de Troyes
  Cligés, 192 n.121
  Perceval, 190
Christ, 40 n.13, 41, 67, 133–4, 207
Christianity, 42, 50–1, 53, 67, 166, 186, 197, 216, 238
chronicle, 5, 8, 32, 59 n.66, 75, 77, 103, 108, 112, 114, 117, 131, 136, 159, 171, 193, 195–8, 200, 220–3, 227, 228–9, see also *Annales Cambriae*; *Brut y Brenhinedd*; *Brut y Tywysogion*; *Brut*; *Epitome historiae Britanniae*; Higden, Ranulph, *Polychronicon*; Usk, Adam, chronicle of

Chronicle of John of Worcester, 178 n.74, 202 n.19
Cibwr, 47
Cilgerran, 3 n.9, 143, 179 n.80
Ciprius, 98, 251
Cirencester, 43
Cistercian order, 70, 78, 99, 212
civility, 13, 190, 217–18, 227, 238, 240, see also barbarity
Clare, family, 16, 44 n.27, 46, 67, 69, 136
  Bogo, 149
  Eleanor, 149
  Elizabeth, 149
  Gilbert (c.1180–1230), 149
  Gilbert II (1243–95), 130, 149
  Gilbert III (1291–1314), 149
  Gilbert IV (d. 1308), 149
  Isabel (1171×6–1220), daughter of Strongbow, 144, 178–80
  Isabel (1240–c.1271), daughter of Richard, 149
  Isabel (1263–1338), daughter of Gilbert, 149
  Isabel de Montferrat (1240–c.1271), 149
  Joan, 149
  Margaret (1249–1312), 149
  Margaret (1291/2?–1342), 149
  Margaret, daughter of Thomas, 149
  Maud, 149
  Richard (1222–62), 149
  Richard (d. 1318), 149
  Richard (Strongbow), 178
  Rose, 149
  Thomas, 149
Clarice d'Auberville, 156, 158
classical era, 36, 45 n.29, 198–200, 212, 214, 222, 225, see also Rome; Romans; Troy; Trojans
Clifford, 3 n.9, 26
Clun, 3 n.9, 61, 64
code-switching, 22, 38, 155, 206, see also multilingualism
Coety, 47
colonization, 7–8, 11–12, 14–15, 18, 21–2, 30 n.97, 33–5, 115, 151–4, 177, 184–5,

195–8, 208–10, 212–16, 220, 222, 226–7, 230, 232, 238
  in *The Awntyrs off Arthure at the Terne Wathelyn*, 185, 190–3
  colonial aristocracy, 3, 214–15
  colonial subject, 8, 11–12, 190–1
  of Glamorgan, 33–6, 45–51
  in Trevisa, 214–18, 226
  see also conquest; postcolonial studies/theory; Wales, colonization of
Comyn
  Joanne, 148
  John, 148
  William, 148
conquest, 2–3, 5, 10, 15, 21–2, 29–30, 33–5, 144, 220
  in *The Awntyrs off Arthure at the Terne Wathelyn*, 185–193
  of Britain, 166–7, 202, 215
  as historiographical theme, 2–3, 33, 54–5, 58, 104–5, 212–13, 215, 220, 229
  of Wales *see* Wales, conquest of
  see also Norman conquest
conversion, 42, 51, 67, 126, 216 n.58
Conwy castle, 49
Corbet, family, 15, 61
Corfe castle, 127
Corineus, 162, 164–6, 166 n.47
Cornish
  language, 214 n.49
  people, 91
Cornwall, 85, 162, 164, 214, 214 n.49
Cotton, Robert, 68
Coventry, 137, 139 n.55
Cranlon, king, 244
Cretus, 98, 251
Croes Neide, 44
Cronica de Wallia, 198–201, 205–6, 210–11, 214 n.51
cross-cultural contact, 7–8, 213–14, *see also* March of Wales, cultural contact in
Crydon ap Dyfnarch, 98, 243, 251

Cumbria, 186
Cunedda (Cunedagius), 98, 243, 251
Cunedda Wledig, 98, 113 n.100, 244, 250
Custennin, king, 245
Cwmhir Abbey, 78
Cwmwd Deuddwr, 3 n.9
Y Cwtta Cyfarwydd see Index of Manuscripts, Aberystwyth, National Library of Wales, Peniarth 50 (*Y Cwyta Cyfarwydd*)
Cyfoesi Myrddin, poem, 54
Cymaron, 78
Cynan Dindaethwy, 98, 109, 247, 250
Cynan ab Iago, 98, 111, 247, 250
Cynan ab Idwal Foel, 112 n.96
cywyddwyr, 55

Dafydd ap Gruffudd, 44, 44 n.27, 223, 248–9
Dafydd ap Gwilym, 175
Dafydd ap Llywelyn, 92, 128–9, 131, 138, 146, 248–9
Danes, 104, 215
Dardanus, 98, 104 n.85, 251
David, bible, 45 n.29
David fitz Gerald, bishop of St Davids, 126, 134
David I, king of Scots, 145
David, saint
  birth of, 67
  Welsh life of, 37
  see also St Davids
David of Scotland, earl of Huntingdon, 144–5
David Winchcombe, abbot of Aberconwy, 36 n.5, 70
Dee, river, 209
De gestis Britonum see Geoffrey of Monmouth, *De gestis Britonum*
De origine gigantum, 164
De primo et statu Landauensis ęcclesię, 43 n.21, 57, *see also* Index of Manuscripts, Aberystwyth, National Library of Wales, 17110E (Book of Llandaf)

Deheubarth, 14, 44, 91, 112 n.97, n.98, 179 n.80, 198, 208, 217
Denbigh, 3 n.9, 16
Denbighshire, 87 n.36, 165 n.41, 223
Des grantz geanz, 80, 164
Despenser, family, 17, 33, 46, 67, 215
  Hugh the Younger, 149, 159
devil, 165-7
digna memoria, 197
Dinas Brân, 165 n.41
Dinorben, 175
disinheritance/dispossession, 44 n.27, 50-1, 53
  in *The Awntyrs off Arthure at the Terne Wathelyn*, 185-90, 192-3
  in *Fouke le Fitz Waryn*, romance of, 153, 156, 166, 168, 171-4
  in *Genealogy of the Lords of Brecknock*, 125, 134
  in *History of William Marshal*, 185
  see also inheritance
Diwanus, 42, 67
Doli, 98, 244, 250
Domesday Book, 24, 24 n.76, 60
dragons, 42 n.19, 95-6, 103, 115, 156, *see also* prophecy
Dru, lord of Ballon, 136
Dugdale, William, 134 n.46, 135-7, 143
Dwfn, 98, 243, 250
Dwnger (Dubun), 98, 243, 250
Dyfed, 14
Dyffryn Clwyd, 3 n.9, 16
Dyfnarch ap Prydain, 98, 243, 251
Dyfrig, saint, 36 n.7, 40 n.11, 43, 45, 56-8
  first life by Lifris of Llancarfan, 36, 40, 43, 56-8
  second life by Benedict of Gloucester, 58 n.63

Ebostol y Sul, 37
Ebraucus *see* Efrog (Ebraucus)
Edern ap Padarn Peisrudd, 98, 244, 250
Edward I, king, 1-2, 15-16, 23 n.72, 27, 44, 52, 68-9, 92-4, 163, 186-92, 197, 222, 226, 248-9, *see also* Wales, conquest of
Edward II, king, 17, 61, 79, *see also Vita Edwardi Secundi*
Edward III, king, 79, 86, 94, 100-2, 238
Edward IV, king, 4, 77, 99-103, 104 n.85, 105, 115, 241
Edward the Confessor, 101
Efrog (Ebraucus), 98, 106, 242, 251
Eigr (Igerna), 250
Einion ab Owain, 111, 112 n.98, 247
Einion, king, 245
Einion Yrth, 98, 244, 250
Eldoc, king, 245
Eleanor, daughter of King John, 147, *see also* Marshal, William II (c.1190-1231)
elegy, 32, 55, 84 n.24, 151, 195-214, 218-22, 227, *see also* Rhys ap Gruffudd, lord
Eleutherius, pope, 42
Elfael, 3 n.9
Elgar, saint, 57
Elissed, 111
Emlyn, 3 n.9
Enaid ap Cerwyd, 98, 243, 251
Eneas Ysgwydwyn (Aeneas), 98, 98 n.67, 202, 234, 251
England, 1, 18, 22, 25, 31, 61, 64, 67, 73, 75, 87, 93-4, 99, 102, 104, 127, 141-2, 159-60, 164, 179, 185, 188, 191, 195-8, 213-14, 222, 232, 235, 241
  border with Wales, 10-12, 230, 233
  in Geoffrey of Monmouth, 1-2, 81 n.18, 93, 204, 237
  in Higden, 209, 212-13, 216-17
  relations with March of Wales, 3-4, 4 n.9, 10-17, 21-2, 25-6, 28-9, 61, 75-9, 86 n.31, 87, 93-4, 160, 196, 209, 241
  relations with Wales, 1-3, 4 n.9, 5-13, 21-2, 28-9, 32, 160, 195-8, 204, 218, 241
  and *Sir Gawain and the Green Knight*, 235, 237, 238-9

in Trevisa, 216–17 *see also* Crown; Mortimers, and England
English
  culture, 11, 17–18, 29, 34, 154–5, 210, 212–13, 216–18, 222, 226–7
  exceptionalism, 213, 216
  governance, 16–17, 25–8, 61, 116, 151–2, 186–7, 191–2, 217, 226, 238
  history and historical narrative, 2–3, 5, 67, 68 n.94, 91, 162, 208–9, 213–18, 220–4, 227
  identity, 15 n.43, 17–18, 21–2, 73, 76–7, 81, 81 n.16, n.17, 104, 154–5, 187, 192, 216–18, 218 n.63, 230–2, 235, 239–40
  interest in Wales, 1–3, 10, 31–2, 64–74, 99–105, 152, 195–8, 208–27, 238–40
  language, Middle, 24–5
    Cheshire dialect, 240 n.17
    Herefordshire dialect, 80, 233
    literature, 6–7, 9–10, 12–13, 32, 43, 43 n.20, 62–4, 73, 75, 80–3, 84, 104, 114, 154, 157–9, 163, 185–92, 213–18, 223, 226, 232–40
    northern dialect, 185
    Shropshire dialect, 63
    West Midlands dialect, 13, 62, 232–40
    see also The Awntyrs off Arthure at the Terne Wathelyn; *Brut*, Middle English Prose; England; English; *Sir Gawain and the Green Knight*; Trevisa, John
  language, Old, 11
  literary history, 5–7, 9–10, 12–13, 32, 75, 228
  people, 3 n.9, 5, 11–12, 17–19, 21–2, 46–7, 60–1, 69, 73, 80–1, 81 n.18, 94, 104, 161, 167, 184, 195, 204, 209–10, 210 n.37, 217, 220, 222–7, 229–31, 239–40
  royalty, 4, 25–6, 67, 85, 93–4, 101–5, 115–16, 139, 161, 183–4, 186–7, 191–3, 229, 232, *see also* Crown
Enoch, 98, 251

Enos, 98, 99 n.69, 251
epitaph, 118, 151, 195–6, 204–6, 222–7
Epitome historiae Britanniae, 31, 33–73, 160, 208
Ergyng, 14 n.38, 36 n.7, *see also* Archenfield
Erichthonius, 98, 99 n.69, 251
Erispoe (Horispois), 112 n.97, 245
Ernalt de Lyls, 157
Essyllt ferch Cynan Dindaethwy, 98, 110, 113 n.99, 247, 250
Euryalus, 199–200, 210, 214 n.51
Eve, bible, 101
Ewenny, 48 n.39
Ewyas Lacy, 3 n.9, 27 n.91, 118 n.4
Exeter College, Oxford, 214 n.49

Faganus, 42, 67
Ferrers
  Agatha, 150
  Agnes, 150
  Eleanor, 150
  Isabel, 150
  Joan, 150
  John, 150
  John II, 150
  Maud, 150
  Sibyl, 150
  Sibyl II, 150
  William, 150
Fford Gam Elen, 174
First Barons' War, 181
Fitz Alan, family, 15, 61
Flemings, 4, 19, 21, 91, 218 n.63
Flint, 3 n.9
Flintshire, 16
Flood, Noah's, 44
Forest of Dean, 126–7, 140, 179
Fortuna, 199
Fouke fitz Waryn, literary character, 154–8, 160, 162, 166–77, 185 n.97, 189, 193
  daughter Eve, 169–70
  in Welsh literature (*Ffwg*), 157, 175–6
  see also Warin de Metz

Fouke I fitz Warin (d. 1171), 158
  wife Eva, 158
Fouke II fitz Warin (d. 1197), 158, *see also* Hawise de Dinan
Fouke III fitz Warin (d.1258), 153–8
  wife Matilda, 158
  see also Clarice D'Auberville
Fouke IV fitz Warin (d. 1264), 157 n.13, 158
  wife Constance, 158
Fouke le Fitz Waryn, romance of, 32, 62, 64, 152–7, 181–3, 185 n.97, 192–3, 237, 240
Fouke V fitz Warin, 157 n.13, 158
France, 49, 97, 99, 154, 177, 179, 181, 184, 193 n.125, 234
French
  identity, 21, 96, 102, 104, 114
  language, 8–9, 11, 15 n.43, 24, 75, 80–1, 119–21, 124, 130 n.31, 134–5, 153 n.1, 250 n.2
  literature, 8–9, 47 n.36, 62–4, 75–6, 80, 82 n.20, 85–6, 101–2, 119–36, 142–3, 153–4, 232
  people, 21, 96–7, 102, 104
  see also Anglo-Norman; *Fouke le Fitz Waryn*, romance of
  frontier, 11–13, *see also* border; borderlands
Fundationis eiusdem Historia, 86 n.32
Fundationis et Fundatorum Historia, 82 n.20, 83, 84 n.24, 86, 201 n.14

gaainable tere, 166, 213 n.46
Galaes, daughter of Ebraucus, 242
Galeron of Galloway, 186–93
Galloway, 185 n.97, 186–8, 188 n.109
Gamelyn, 159
Gawain, 186–91, 193 n.124, 233–40, *see also Sir Gawain and the Green Knight*
Geffrei Gaimar, *Estoire des Engleis*, 80
genealogy, 5, 9, 15, 116, 159–60
  of Edward IV, 4, 99–105, 115, 241
  marcher, 4, 8, 17, 31, 116–52, 169–70, 228–9

  Mortimer, 73–8, 85–115, 159–60, 236, 241, 242–9
  Welsh, 35, 39, 73, 75–8, 85, 87–99, 104–14, 116, 170 n.56, 202, 228–9, 235, 241–9
Genealogical Chronicle of the Kings of England, 103–4
Genealogy of earls of Hereford, 119–20, 135–50, 159, 169–70
Genealogy of the Lords of Brecknock, 120–35, 139–44, 147, 150–2, 170
Geneddog, 98, 244, 250
Geneville, family, 60, 64, 67, Joan, 62, 79 n.9
Geoffrey of Monmouth
  De gestis Britonum, 9, 42 n.15, n.16, 43 n.20, n.24, 56 n.57, 57 n.59, 58 n.63, 75, 106–7, 16–7, 183 n.93, 202, 204
  afterlives of, 1–4, 31–45, 48–59, 67–116, 153–4, 161–8, 181, 184, 202, 204, 215–16, 228–36, 241–3, 247, 250–1
  division of Britain in, 1–2, 81 n.18, 93–4, 204, 237
  Llywelyn ap Gruffudd and John Peckham's use of, 1–2
  marcher interest in, 3–4, 29–45, 48–60, 67–99, 104–15, 153–4, 161–8, 184, 215–16, 228–43, 247, 250–1
  Owain Glyndŵr's use of, 54 n.52
  reception in Wales, *see* Welsh, historical narrative
  title of work, 1 n.2
  Prophetiae Merlini, 29, 42 n.19, 51, 66, 68 n.94, 103, 162, 163, 165–8
  see also Arthur; Britain; *Brut y Brenhinedd*; *Brut*, Anglo-Norman Prose; *Brut*, Latin Prose; *Brut*, Middle English Prose; Brutus; *Epitome historiae Britanniae*; Higden, Ranulph, *Polychronicon*; Merlin; prophecy; Trevisa, John; Vortigern

geography, 80, 177, 204, 221, 227, 241
  of March of Wales, 4, 10–13, 16–21,
    23–6, 36, 119, 152, 160, 209–10,
    212–13, 232
  in *Sir Gawain and the Green
    Knight*, 233, 238–40
  of Wales, 95 n.52, 134
  of world, 41, 44–5
Gerald of Wales, 8, 120, 198
  Descriptio Kambriae, 44 n.25, 92 n.43,
    174, 209 n.35, 217
  Expugnatio Hibernica, 30 n.96, 231
  History of Llanthony Priory, 121, 131–5
  Itinerarium Kambriae, 124–7, 130 n.31,
    134, 139, 209 n.35
  and marchers, 13, 24–5, 30 n.96, 231
  reception in Higden, 209 n.35
Germanus of Auxerre, 42, 56–7, 57 n.59
giants, 42, 51, 156, 162, 164–6, 215, 238, 240,
    242, 242, *see also* Goemagog
Glamorgan, 3 n.9, 33–6, 44 n.27, 46–8, 59,
    61, 68, 113–14, 118 n.4
  in *The Awntyrs off Arthure at the Terne
    Wathelyn*, 191
  and *Epitome historiae Britanniae*, 33–7,
    40, 41, 45–8, 59–60, 68–9, 73
  and Owain Glyndŵr, 48 n.39
Glasbury, 3 n.9, 26
Gloucester, 68, 126, 178 n.74, 179, 216, 233
  earldom of, 31, 119, 130, 215
Gloucestershire, 35, 70, 120–1, 132–3,
    214–15
Glover, Robert, 135
Glynrhondda, 47
Godfrey of Bouillon, 45 n.29
Goemagog, 162, 164–5, *see also* giants
Golagros and Gawain, 193 n.126
Gordenon, king, 245
Gormundus, 43, 216
Gortegu, king, 245
Gotland, 156
Gower, 3 n.9, 27 n.91, 47, 49, 68, 112 n.98,
    179
  and Hopcyn ap Tomas, 47 n.36, 48 n.37
  and William VI de Braose, 27–8, 175

Grey, Roger, 138, 144 n.65, 148
Grosmont, 27 n.91
Gruffudd ab yr Ynad Coch, 206, 225
Gruffudd ap Cynan, 78, 81, 91 n.42, 98,
    105, 105 n.89, 106, 111, 112 n.96, 247,
    250, *see also Historia Gruffud vab
    Kenan*, *Vita Griffini Filii Conani*
Gruffudd ap Llywelyn (d. 1064), 125, 125
    n.18
Gruffudd ap Llywelyn ab Iorwerth, 92,
    248–9
Gruffudd ap Rhys, 200 n.13, 246
Gruffudd Fychan, 16
Gruffudd, king, 246
Grwst (Gurgustius), 98, 106, 243, 251
Guehic, king, 245
Guethfynauc, king, 245, 246
Guinevere, 186
Guto'r Glyn, 99 n.72, 175, 175 n.69
Guy of Warwick, 159
Gwehelyth Morgannwg, 40, 40 n.11, 42
    n.18, 43 n.22
Gwent, 36 n.7, 44 n.27, 177, 181 n.85
Gwenwynwyn ab Owain Cyfeiliog, 154,
    157, 173–5, 193
Gwerthrynion, 3 n.9, 78
Gwladys Ddu, 78, 78 n.8, 80, 87, 88 n.38
  in Mortimer genealogy, 78, 87–8,
    102–13, 169, 241, 248–51
  in praise poetry, 104 n.85
  in York and Tudor genealogy, 101–4
Gwrddoli, 98, 243, 250
Gwrddwfn, 98, 243, 250
Gwrgain, 98, 244, 250
Gwynedd, 15, 44, 70, 78, 87, 92, 96, 104
    n.85, 112 n.98, 113, 113 n.99, 156, 174,
    209, 217, 223
  conquest of, 16–17, 52, 92–4, 97, 222, *see
    also* Wales, conquest of
  genealogies, 88, 97, 102, 105, 108–13
  people of, 96 n.57
  see also Llywelyn ap Gruffudd;
    Llywelyn ab Iorwerth; Wales,
    North
Gwynllŵg, 3 n.9, 47

284 | GENERAL INDEX

Gwynllyw, saint, 37
Gwythaul, king, 245

Hailes Abbey, 35, 36 n.5, 70–3
   chronicle of, 35–6, 70–3
Harlech castle, 49
Harley lyrics, 7, 62–3
Harley scribe, 61–4, 153–5, 158–9, 163, 168 n.52, 232
Harrowing of Hell, 62
Hastings, family, 136–9, 143–4
   Elizabeth, 138, 144 n.65, 148
   Henry (d. 1250), 145
   Henry II (d. 1269), 138–9, 143–4, 147, 150
   Henry III, a cleric, 138, 144 n.65, 148
   Joan, 138, 144 n.65, 148
   John I (1262–1313), 136–9, 139 n.55, 143–4, 148, 150
   John II (1287–1325), 136–9, 139 n.55, 144, 148, 150
   John III (1372–89), 83 n.22
   Margaret, 138, 144 n.65, 148
   Theophilus, 137 n.54
   William, 136, 138, 144 n.65, 148
Hautdesert, 237–9
Havelok the Dane, 159
Haverford, 3 n.9, 179
Hawarden, 3 n.9
Hawise de Dinan, 158
Hawise de Londres, 146
Hay, 3 n.9
Hector, 45 n.29, 84 n.24, 199–201, 201 n.14, 210–11, 214 n.51
Helen of Sparta, 224
Hengist, 42, 67, 91
Henry I, king, 125
Henry II, king, 78, 127, 140, 172, 179, 198
Henry III, king, 26, 87 n.37, 93, 147, 163, 219, 249
Henry IV, king, 49, 86
Henry V, king, 49
Henry VI, king, 101–3
Henry VII, king, 4, 77, 105, 115, 241
Henry, earl of Lancaster, 146

Henry, earl of Northumberland, 145
Henry de Ferlington, 146
Henry, Young King, 182–4
heraldry, 86, 115
Herbert, family, 22
   Richard, 104 n.85
   William, 95 n.54, 104 n.85
Herbert fitz Herbert, 127–8, 131 n.36, 140, *see also* Peter fitz Herbert
Hercules, 199–200, 210–11, 222
Hereford
   diocese, 58, 121, 127–8, 132, 135
   earldom, 14, 31, 119–20, 131 n.36
   earls of, 119–21, 126, 133, 135–43
   town, 60, 63
   see also Genealogy of the Earls of Hereford
Herefordshire, 3 n.9, 24, 26 n.88, 27 n.91, 36 n.7, 68, 78–82, 153, 233
   Middle English Prose *Brut* in, 80–2, 82 n.20, 85, 114
hero/heroism, 96 n.56, 192–3, 197–204, 209, 212, 214, 221–2, 227
Higden, Ranulph, *Polychronicon*, 201 n.19, 208–27
Historia Gruffud vab Kenan, 88 n.39, 91 n.42, 105 n.89, 106–14, 243 n.8, *see also* Gruffudd ap Cynan, *Vita Griffini Filii Conani*
Historia regum Britanniae see Geoffrey of Monmouth, *De gestis Britonum*
History of Llanthony Priory see Gerald of Wales
History of William Marshal, 24, 32, 154, 177–85, 190, 192–3, *see also* Marshal, William I (*c*.1146–1219)
Holyhead, 238
Hopcyn ap Tomas, 47 n.36, n.37, 54 n.52
Hopedale, 3 n.9, 16
Horsa, 68, 90
Hundred Years' War, 139
Huntington, 3 n.9
hybridity, 5–6, 8, 10, 12, 19, 21–2, 76–7, 184, 231
Hywel ap Cadell, 112 n.98

Hywel ap Hywel, 110, 112 n.98, 247
Hywel Dda, 112 n.98
Hywel, king, 245

Iago ab Idwal Foel, 98, 110, 112 n.96, 247, 250
Iago ap Beli, 98, 112 n.98, 109, 247, 250
Iago ap Geneddog, 98, 244, 250
Iago, king, 246
identity, 3, 6, 12–13, 17–24, 47–8, 50, 70, 104, 160–1, 170 n.57, 172–3, 231, *see also* Anglo-Norman, identity; English, identity; French, identity; marcher, identity; Welsh, identity
Idwal Foel, 98, 110, 112 n.96, 247, 250
Idwal Fychan ab Idwal Foel, 98, 112 n.96, 250
Idwal Iwrch, 98, 112 n.96, 247, 250
Idwal, king, 245, 246
Ieuaf ab Idwal Foel, 110, 112 n.96, 247
Ifor Hael, 47 n.36, 175 n.69
Inglewood Forest, 186
inheritance, 30, 32, 55, 117–18, 122, 127, 129–31, 139–40, 143–4, 186, 189, 192–3, 228, 234
  British, 2, 10, 35, 81–2, 93, 97, 99, 102, 104, 115, 231–2, 235 n.5, 236
  in *Fouke le Fitz Waryn*, romance of, 156, 161, 169, 171–2, 175–8, 180, 184, 193, 230–1 *see also* disinheritance/dispossession
insular world, 7–8, 162, 185, 196
Iolo Goch, 34, 55, 95–7, 99, 175
Iorwerth Drwyndwn, 98, 111, 248, 250
Ireland, 25, 60–1, 67, 78–9, 82–4, 86 n.31, 87, 156, 177, 179–80, 184, 188–92, 196 n.2, *see also* Leinster, Ulster
Irish, people, 4, 19, 21, 82–4, 96–7
Isabel of Huntingdon, 145
Isabella of France, queen of England, 68, 79–80
Iscennen, 3 n.9, 16

Japheth, 98, 99 n.69, 251
Jared, 98, 99 n.69, 251

Javan, 98, 251
Jean d'Avesnes, 148
Joan, daughter of Edward I, 149
Joan, daughter of King John, 78, 87, 92, 129, 149, 156 n.6, 169–70, 248–9, *see also* Llywelyn ab Iorwerth
Joan, daughter of Warin de Munchensy, 148
John ap Hywel, abbot of Llantarnam, 58
John of Earley, 177–8
John, king, 27, 87 n.37, 94, 141–2, 181, 193
  in *Fouke le Fitz Waryn*, romance of, 156, 167–8, 170–5, 179 n.79, n.80
  in *Genealogy of the Lords of Brecknock*, 127
  see also Joan, daughter of King John
John of Scotland, earl of Huntingdon, 145
Joshua, 45 n.29
Juliana de Leybourne, 138, 140, 144 n.65, 148
Juliana, daughter of Maurice fitz Maurice, 149, *see also* Clare, Thomas
Julius Caesar, 45 n.29, 204, 215
Jupiter, 85, 98, 251
justice/injustice, 27, 51, 133, 166–8, 185–8, 192–4

Kareticus, 43, 216
Katherine, saint, Welsh life of, 37
Kei, Sir, 183
Kellistown, 83
Kells, 83
Kenfig, 47
Kenilworth, 95
Kidwelly, 3 n.9, 27 n.91
King Horn, 62
Kynacus, king, 246
Kyng Alisaunder, 63 n.86
Kynwynus, king, 246
Lacy, family, 15, 60, 76, 69, 102, 130, 136
  Henry, 138
  Hugh, 121
  John, 147
  Maud, 149

Lamech, 98, 251
Langland, William *see Piers Plowman*
Langobard, 234
Latin, language, 8–11, 24, 25, 25 n.81, 62, 64, 75–7, 80–6, 91, 103, 105 n.89, 106–7, 119, 121, 130–1, 134–6, 139, 141–3, 153 n.1, 158, 163–4, 196–7, 212, 213–14, 214 n.51, 222–7, 232, 235, 239
   in Wales, 24 n.78, 37–8, 40, 50, 54, 57 n.61, 106–7, 112, 198–201, 204–7, 225
   see also Brut, Latin Prose; classical era; Higden, Ranulph, *Polychronicon*; leonine hexameter
Laugharne, 3 n.9
law, 4, 11–13, 18, 25–9, 33, 46 n.32, 54, 61, 69–70, 206 n.28, 223–4, 226, 229, 240, *see also* marcher, liberties; outlaw; Welsh, law
Laȝamon, *Brut*, 7, 43 n.20, n.24, 75
Lebor Gabála Érenn, 196 n.2
Leicester, 98, 249 n.19
Leinster, 179–80
Leir, *see* Llŷr (Leir)
Leland, John, 157
leonine hexameter, 202
Les Quatre Fils Aymoun, 159
Lewys Glyn Cothi, 103–4
Lionel, duke of Clarence, 79, 100–1
Llanbadarn Fawr, 202, 206 n.28
Llanblethian, 47
Llandaf, 33–4, 26, 29, 42–8, 56–9, 64, 68–9
Llangollen, 165 n.41
Llanstephan, 3 n.9
Llantarnam, 41, 58
Llanthony, general, 31, 119–20, 131–5, 144
   Prima, 121, 132–3
   Secunda, 120–2, 130–3, 135
   see also Gerald of Wales, *History of Llanthony Priory*
Llawhaden, 3 n.9
Lleon (Leil), 98, 99 n.69, 107, 113 n.100, 242, 251
Llŷr (Leir), 98, 107, 243, 251

Llywarch ap Brân, 248–9
Llywelyn ab Iorwerth, 84 n.25, 86–7, 87 n.37, 91 n.42, 92, 98, 101–2, 106–11, 112 n.96, n.98, 113, 127, 129, 134, 139, 156, 156 n.6, 157, 179 n.80, 219, 248–50
   in *Fouke le Fitz Waryn*, romance of, 156, 160, 169–75
   and Gwladys Ddu, 78, 87–9, 91–4, 169
   in *History of William Marshal*, 181–2
Llywelyn ap Gruffudd, 16, 70, 91–2, 111, 130, 157, 195–6
   death of, 2, 36, 44, 52–3, 69, 92–3, 97, 208
   epitaphs and laments for, 206, 222–7
   genealogies of, 88 n.39, 91–5, 108–13, 248–9
   letter to John Peckham, 1–2
Llywelyn Bren, 44, 44 n.27, 69
Llywelyn, king, 246
Locrinus, 12, 81 n.18, 93–4, 98, 101, 203–4, 237, 251
Loegria, 81 n.18, 93, 237
London, 13, 42, 49, 60, 136, 248–9
Louis VIII, king of France, 181, 192
loyalty, 48 n.39, 70, 82, 178, 181
Lucius legend, 42, 67
Lucy, daughter of Miles fitz Walter, 122, 127–8, 131 n.36, 139–40, *see also* Herbert fitz Herbert; Miles fitz Walter; Peter fitz Herbert
Ludlow
   castle, 62, 79 n.9, 102
   priory, 60
   town, 34–5, 59–70, 73, 113, 155, 157, 159
Ludlow Annal, 59–61, 64–70, 74
Lupus of Troyes, 42, 56–7, 57 n.59
Lydgate, John, 75, 213

mab darogan, 51, 96
Mabinogion, 232, 241
Maccabeus, 45 n.29
Machynlleth, 49
Madog (Maddan), 98, 106, 242, 251
Madog ab Idnerth, 78

Madog ap Llywelyn, 226
Madog ap Maredudd, 44 n.25
Madog Fychan, 47 n.36
Madog of Edeirnion, 223 n.74
Maelgwn Gwynedd, 78, 88, 91, 92 n.43, 98, 109, 112 n.97, 244, 247, 250
Maelienydd, 3 n.9, 49, 78, 95 n.52
Maelor Saesneg, 3 n.9, 16
Magna Carta, 25 n.83
Mahalalel, 98, 251
Mahel (Mael), son of Bernard de Neufmarché, 125, 128, 134
Malcolm IV, king of Scots (1141–65), 145
Malcolm, a king of Scotland, 85
Malgo, king, 245
manuscript
  of *The Awntyrs off Arthure at the Terne Wathelyn*, 185
  containing Mortimer genealogy, 76, 85–91, 97, 99, 101, 115, 242–51
  containing Welsh literature, 47 n.37, 52, 202, 206 n.28, 223 n.74
  containing Welsh prophecy, 54
  of *De gestis Britonum*, 1 n.2
  by Dugdale, William, 135–9, 141, 143–4
  of *Epitome historiae Britanniae*, 37–41, 44–5, 45 n.28, 46, 56 n.57, 57 n.61, 58–60, 59 n.66, n.67, 64–6, 69
  of *Genealogical Chronicle of the Kings of England*, 103
  of *Genealogy of the Lords of Brecknock*, 121, 122 n.16, 123–4, 129–32, 132 n.40, 133–5
  by Harley scribe, 61–3, 155, 157–9, 162–3
  of Higden's *Polychronicon*, 213–14, 221 n.68
  of *History of William Marshal*, 178
  of Middle English Prose *Brut*, 80 n.15, 81–2, 87 n.36, 223 n.74
  production, 116–20, 134–5, 147, 150–2, *see also* chancery
  of romance of *Fouke le fitz Waryn*, 155, 157–9, 162–3, 168, 168 n.52
  from Shropshire, 63–4, 233
  of Trevisa's *Polychronicon*, 214

  see also Index of Manuscripts
March, earls of, 34, 61, 73, 76, 78–9, 79 n.9, 80, 82–4, 86–7, 100–2, 104, *see also* Mortimer
March of Wales
  boundaries, 3 n.9, 10–13, 16–17, 25, 160, 209–10, 238–40
  cultural contact in, 4–7, 9–13, 15, 33–6, 35 n.4, 46–8, 60, 88–115, 157–8, 195–8, 208–29, 232, 241
  definition of, 3–4, 3 n.9, 10–17, 20–9
  history, 10–17, 77–9
  identity *see* marcher, identity
  law *see* marcher, liberties
  lordships *see* marcher, lordships
  multilingualism in, 4, 6–7, 6 n.12, 9–10, 18, 20–1, 31, 33–4, 47–8, 62–4, 80–1, 84–5, 153 n.1, 157–9, 163, 230–2, 239
  as peripheral or central, 4, 12–13, 21 n.65, 63, 160, 232
  relationship with Wales and Welsh, 2–5, 10–23, 29–36, 44 n.27, 59–61, 68–115, 126, 156 n.6, 160–1, 170–84, 193, 195–8, 208–32, 239–41
  ruling families of *see* marcher, lords
  scholarship about, 5–8
  society *see* marcher, society and culture
  women in, 29, 118–19, 118 n.5, 143, 154, 161, 168–70
  see also border; borderlands; frontier; third category/space
marcher
  identity, 17–23, 29–30, 30 n.96, 31–5, 60, 75–6, 84–5, 97, 114–19, 152–5, 160–1, 175–7, 193–4, 228–32
  interest in dual ancestry, 5, 10, 13, 76–7, 81 n.18, 104–5
  interest in and use of British and Welsh history, 3–5, 9, 15, 29–32, 35–119, 154, 161–8, 176–7, 195–8, 208–32, 235–41, *see also* March of Wales, relationship with Wales and the Welsh
  intermarriage with Welsh, 4, 13, 79

marcher (*Continued*)
  liberties, 3 n.9, 11, 23 n.72, 25–9, 61, 173, 175–6, 184, 230
  literature, 4–7, 8 n.22, 9–10, 31–2, 80–1, 116–17, 159–61, 184–5, 232, *see also Brut*, Middle English Prose; *Epitome historiae Britanniae*; *Fouke le Fitz Waryn*, romance of; Geoffrey of Monmouth, *De gestis Britonum*; *Genealogy of the Lords of Brecknock*; *History of William Marshal*; *Sir Gawain and the Green Knight*
    definition of, 29–30
    key themes, 29–30, 32, 73–4, 116, 118–19, 151–4, 161–2, 168–72, 178, 180–1, 184–5, 228–9, 233–41
    transmission *see* March of Wales, cultural contact in
  lords, 2–5, 8 n.22, 13, 15 n.43, 15–17, 25–9, 48, 61, 64, 67, 73, 76–105, 117–19, 121–2, 125–31, 136–44, 146–61, 166–84, 193, 228–30, *see also* Bohun; Braose; Brecon; Clare; Fouke fitz Waryn; Hereford, earls of; Lacy; Marshal; Mortimer
    affiliation with Welsh princes, 170–7
    and Gerald of Wales, 13, 24–5, 30 n.96, 231
    as patrons of churches *see* patronage, of churches
    as patrons of literature *see* patronage, of texts
    role in conquest of Wales, 8 n.22, 13, 16–17, 23 n.72, 118–19, 178–9, 181–4, 208
  lordships, 3 n.9, 14–17, 25–9, 33–4, 46–8, 47 n.37, 61, 68–70, 95 n.52, 118 n.4, 119, 122–31, 137–44, 161, 169, 178–9, 191, 228–32
  society and culture, 3–5, 10–13, 15–23, 25–30, 34–6, 35 n.4, 46–8, 61, 77, 80–1, 85, 104–5, 114–15, 118–19, 144, 151–5, 160, 171, 184, 192, 212–13, 229–32, 238–40

  see also border; borderlands; frontier; genealogy, marcher; third category/space
marches, Anglo-Scottish, 25 n.81, 32, 154, 185, 185 n.96, n.97, 186–7, 189–90
Maredudd ap Bleddyn, 167
Maredudd ap Rhys, 200 n.13
Maredudd, king, 245–6
Margadud, king, 245
Margam, 47, 47 n.37, 48 n.39, 68, 68 n.92
Margaret, daughter of David, earl of Huntingdon, 145
Margaret, daughter of Miles fitz Walter, 122 n.14, 127–8, 131 n.36, 139–40, *see also* Bohun, Humphrey II (d. 1164/5); Miles fitz Walter
Margaret, saint, Welsh life of, 37, 84
Marjorie, sister of the king of Scots, 147, *see also* Marshal, Gilbert
Marshal, family, 16, 79 n.8, 102, 136, 139
  Anselm, 147
  Eve, 128–9, 138, 146, 150
  Gilbert, 147
  Isabel, 149
  Joan, 148
  Maud, 147
  Richard, 129, 147, 219
  Sibyl, 150
  Walter, 147
  William I (*c*.1146–1219), 24, 32, 129 n.28, 136, 144, 147–50, 154, 177–84, 192–3, 193 n.125, 230
  William II (*c*.1190–1231), 147, 177, 180
  see also History of William Marshal; Isabel (1171×6–1220), daughter of Strongbow; John of Earley
Martin
  Edmund, 138, 144 n.65, 148
  Eleanor, 138, 144 n.65
  William, 138, 144 n.65, 148
Mary, Virgin, 163, 165
Matilda, empress, 132
Matusalem, 98, 251
Maud de Burgh, 149

Maud, daughter of David, earl of
    Huntingdon, 145
Maud de Saint Valéry *see* Braose, Maud de
    Saint Valéry
Maurice fitz Gerald, 148
Maximus, 216
medical diagrams and notes, 162–3
Meirionnydd, 16
Meisgyn, 47
Membyr (Mempricius), 98, 106, 242, 244,
    251
memory, 29, 195, 197
   family, 31, 118–20, 135, 144–52
   historical, 3, 214, 218, 222, 227
Mercia, 11, 14
Mercurius, 98, 251
Merfyn Frych, 110, 112 n.97, 113 n.99, 247
Merionethshire *see* Meirionnydd
Merlin, 42–3, 51–3, 55, 58, 68–9, 73, 156,
    162–3, 165–8, 176, 182–3, *see also*
    Cyfoesi Myrddin; Geoffrey of
    Monmouth, *Prophetiae Merlini*;
    prophecy
Mersey, river, 209
mestiza consciousness, 20
Methodius, 162 n.34
Meurig ab Idwal Foel, 98, 108, 110, 112, 112
    n.96, 247, 250
Meurig ap Tewdrig, king of Morgannwg, 42, 56–7, 57
    n.59
Miles fitz Walter, 121–2, 125–33, 136,
    139–40
Mirk's Festial, 63 n.86
Moch Daw Byd, poem, 54
Mohun
   John, son of John, 150
   John, son of Reginald, 146, 150
   Reginald, 146, 150
   William, 150
Mold, 3 n.9
monasteries, 58–9, 67, 69, 75, 78, 135–6,
    200, 221–2, 227
   libraries, 9, 174, 219

   patronage, 31, 117–20, 130–3, 135, 147,
      150–2
   role in literary contact, 9–10, 15, 31, 114,
      117–18, 212, 227
   see also Augustinian order; Benedictine
      order; chronicle; Cistercian order
Monmouth, 3 n.9
Monmouthshire, 11, 40, 58–9, 121, 179
Montfort
   Eleanor, 92, 248–9
   Simon, 248–9
Montgomery, 3 n.9
Mordred, 43, 67, 187
Morgan ap Hywel, 179 n.80, 181–2, 189,
    192–3
Morgan ap Maredudd, 44, 44 n.27
Morgannwg, 42, 46 n.32, 56–7, *see also*
    Glamorgan
Moris (Meurig), son of Roger de
    Powys, 156, 172, *see also* Fouke le
    fitz Waryn, romance of
Mortimer, family, 15, 17, 22, 34, 41, 59–61,
    64, 76–81, 114–15, 152, 160, 184
   Anne, 100, 101
   in chronicle of Adam Usk, 97–9, 102
   claim to throne, 31, 73, 76–9, 82–7,
      93–5, 99, 102, 116, 169, 230, 241
   Edmund I (d. 1304), 52 n.46, 69, 80, 93
      n.46, 98, 150
   Edmund II (d. 1331), 80, 98
   Edmund III, 3rd earl of March
      (1352–81), 79–80, 97–8, 100–1
   Edmund IV (1376–1408/9), 49, 79 n.11
   Edmund V, 5th earl of March
      (1391–1425), 80, 83, 100
   and England, 31, 73–4, 78–9, 82–3, 85
      n.31, 87, 94, 99, 102
   Hugh I (d. 1185), 78, 80
   Hugh II (d. 1227), 78
   interest in British history, 75–7, 79–81,
      84–99, 104–5, 114, 230, 236
   interest in Welsh ancestry, 31, 34, 76–7,
      85–192, 104–15, 169
   in Ludlow Annal, 64, 67–9
   in Middle English Prose *Brut*, 79–84

Mortimer, family (*Continued*)
  Ralph I (fl. c.1080–after 1115), 77, 80
  Ralph II (d. 1246), 78, 78 n.8, 80, 87–8, 92, 102–3, 241, 248–50
  rise to prominence, 77–9
  Roger I (fl. 1054–c.1080), 80
  Roger II (d. 1214), 77–8, 80
  Roger III (1231–82), 52, 80, 95, 128–9, 138, 146, 150
  Roger IV, 1st earl of March (1287–1330), 60, 62, 68, 79–80, 79 n.9, 82 n.20, 98, 150
  Roger V (1328–60), 80, 98
  Roger VI, 4th earl of March (1374–98), 31, 34, 73, 76–87, 93–102, 169, 201 n.14, 236, 241
  Welsh poetry about, 22, 34, 95–7, 99 n.72, 103
  and York genealogies, 99–104, 115
  see also Fundationis et Fundatorum Historia; Maelienydd; genealogy, Mortimer; Gwladys Ddu; Ludlow; Wigmore
Morwynus (Morpidus), king, 242
Morwynus ap Rhodri Mawr, 110, 112 n.98, 247
Morwyth, king, 245
Mouhaut, John de, 138, 150
multilingualism, *see* March of Wales, multilingualism in
Munchensy
  Joan, 148
  Warin, 148
Mynogan (Manogan), 98, 243, 251

Narberth, 3 n.9
Neath, 47, 47 n.37, 48 n.39, 68
Nest, wife of Bernard de Neufmarché, 125, 128, 134
Nestor, 199–200, 210–11, 214 n.51
Netherwent, 181 n.85
network, transmission, 10, 35, 63, 73, 116–17, 212, 227, 241
New Abbey, 156
New Troy, 42, *see also* London

Newcastle, 47
Noah, 45, 98, 251
Nomenoe (Numeneus) (Welsh King List), 112 n.97, 245
Norman
  conquest, 14–15, 18, 166, 184, 215
  people, 11, 13–15, 19, 21–2, 47, 73, 79, 91, 99 n.71, 104, 114, 126, 151, 161, 166–7, 175–6, 184, 215
  see also Anglo-Norman; Bernard de Neufmarché
Normandy, 25, 101
North Wales *see* Gwynedd; Wales, North
Norway, 156
Norwich, priory, 218–19, 227

Of Arthour and of Merlin, 63 n.86
Offa's Dyke, 14 n.38
Old Testament Stories, 63
Onwed, 98, 243, 250
Orosius, 67
Oswestry, 3 n.9, 22, 61, 64, 69–70, 118 n.4, 170, 176
Otherworld, 239
outlaw, 55, 155–6, 159, 161, 171, 238
Owain ab Afallach, 98, 243, 250
Owain ap Gruffudd, 111
Owain Glyndŵr, 79 n.11, 197
  in poetry, 54, 54 n.52
  rebellion of, 33, 35–6, 40, 40 n.10, 48 n.39, 48 n.39, 49, 58, 215, 221
  Tripartite Indenture, 49, 54 n.52
Owain Gwynedd, 54 n.52, 98, 111, 112 n.98, 247–8, 250
Owain, king, 245
Owain Lawgoch, 54 n.52
Owain Rufus ap Gruffudd, 248–9
Owain Tudur, 105, 115, *see also* Henry VII, king; Tudor, Jasper
Oysterlow castle, 191

Padarn Peisrudd, 98, 244, 250
Padarn, saint, 206 n.28

panegyric/praise, 34–5, 55, 83–4, 95–7, 104 n.85, 175–6, 175 n.69, 198–201, 204, 206, 224
Paris, city, 127
Paris, prince of Troy, 2, 199–201, 210–11, 214 n.51, 224
Pascuethen (Pasceuth), 112 n.97, 245
Patrick, saint, 67
patronage
　of churches, 15, 31, 70, 76, 116–22, 129–35, 144–52, 199
　of texts, 4–5, 29, 33, 47 n.36, 54 n.52, 62, 97, 113, 116–17, 119–20, 134–5, 137, 144–7, 169, 180, 214–15, 241
Payn Peverel, 165–7, 169
peace, 43, 51, 127, 172, 180–2, 190, 192
Pebidiog, 3 n.9
Peckham, John, archbishop of Canterbury, 1–2, 224 n.78, 226
Pelagian heresy, 42, 56, 57 n.59, 216
Pembroke, 3 n.9
　castle, 219
　earls of, 83 n.22, 139, 143–4, 154, 177, 179, *see also* Marshal
Pembrokeshire, 24, 115
Percy
　Agnes, 146
　Alice, 146
　Anastasia, 146
　Henry 'Hotspur', 49
　Joan, 146
　[William], 146
Peredur vab Efrawc, 190–1
Peter fitz Herbert, 122, 127–8, 140–2, *see also* Herbert fitz Herbert
Philippa of 79–80, 100–1, *see also* Lionel, duke of Clarence; Mortimer, Edmund III, 3rd earl of March (1352–81)
Picts, 215
Piers Gaveston, 149
Piers Plowman, 63 n.86, 232–3, 240–1, 241 n.19
piety, 118, 121, 131, 133–4, 149, 186, 224
plague, 17, 44

Poitevin conflict, 219
postcolonial studies/theory, 8
Powys, 16, 44, 126, 156, 167, 173–5, 212, 217
Prick of Conscience, 63 n.86
print, early English, 213–14, 227
propaganda, 103–4, 115
prophecy
　genre, 2–3, 5, 29, 33, 35, 43, 51, 53–6, 68, 76, 95–7, 115, 161–3, 166–7, 229, 241
　Prophecies of Merlin, general, 42–3, 42 n.19, 48, 51, 53–5, 58, 68, 156, 162–3, 165–8, 176–7, 183
　Prophecy of Merlin Silvester, 48, 68
　Prophetiae Merlini by Geoffrey of Monmouth *see* Geoffrey of Monmouth, *Prophetiae Merlini*
　see also Armes Prydein Vawr; *mab darogan*; Merlin; Owain Glyndŵr; Welsh, prophecy
Prydain, 98, 113 n.99, 243, 251
purgatory, 186

Quincy
　Margaret, 147
　Roger, 150

Radnor, 3 n.9, 122
Ralph de Harangaud, 146
Ralph fitz Ralph, 146
Red Book of Hergest *see* Index of Manuscripts, Oxford, Jesus College, 111 (Red Book of Hergest)
Regau, 98, 107, 243, 251
Reginald fitz Piers, 146
Register and Chronicle of the Abbey of Aberconwy, 35–6, 70–3
Rhiwallon (Riuallo), 98, 106, 243, 246, 251
Rhodri ab Idwal Foel, 110, 247
Rhodri ap Gruffudd, 248–9
Rhodri Mawr, 36, 44, 44 n.25, 53, 70, 78, 88, 92 n.43, 98, 112 n.97, n.98, 202, 243 n.8, 247, 250
Rhodri Molwynog, 98, 109, 245, 247, 250
Rhos, 175

Rhuddlan, 1, 172
  Statute of, 28 n.95
Rhun [Hir], 91–2, 98, 109, 244, 247, 250
Rhun Baladr Bras (Rud Hudibras), 98, 107, 113 n.100, 243, 251
Rhun, king, 245
Rhydderch ab Ieuan Llwyd, 47 n.36
Rhydderch, king, 246
Rhygyfarch ap Sulien, 224 n.77
Rhys ap Gruffudd, lord, 44, 86, 91–2, 112 n.97, 246, 248–9
  elegies for, 84 n.24, 195–6, 198–208, 210–14, 214 n.51, 218–22, 225–7
Rhys ap Maredudd, 69
Rhys ap Tewdwr, 14, 122, 201 n.19
Rhys Gryg, 112 n.97
Rhys, king, 246
Rich, Edmund, archbishop of Canterbury, 163
Richard I, king, 127, 179
Richard II, king, 76, 82–3, 86, 87 n.36
Richard III, king, 100, 105, 115
Richard of Conisburgh, 100–1
Richard Neville, earl of Warwick, 46
Richard of York, 100–1
Robert of Bethune, bishop of Hereford, 121, 132, 133 n.43
Roger, earl of Hereford, 126, 128, 133
Robert fitz Hamon, 15, 33
Roger fitz John de Grey, 148
Robert fitz Sampson, 156
Roger Montgomery, 61
Roger de Powys, 156
Roger of Wendover, *Flores historiarum*, 218–20, 227
Roman de Fergus, 185 n.97
romance, genre, 3, 5, 47 n.36, 62–4, 75, 153–4, 227, 232–40, *see also* The Awntyrs off Arthure at the Terne Wathelyn; Fouke le fitz Waryn, romance of; History of William Marshal; King Horn; Sir Gawain and the Green Knight
Romans, 104, 215
Rome, 50, 67, 187–8, 234

Romulus, 234
Roteland, Hue de, 160 n.25
Round Table, 95, 186–7, 189–90, 235, *see also* Arthur
Rudaucus, king, 242
Ruthin, 46 n.32, 47, 49, 54 n.52, 87 n.36
  lords of, 138, 144 n.65

Salisbury, Robert, 176 n.69
Salomon, duke of Brittany, 112 n.97, 245
Sampson, 199–200, 210–11, 214 n.51
Saracens, 67
Saturnus, 98, 251
Saxons, 42–3, 51, 67, 85, 104, 112 n.98, 162, 202, 215–17, 220
scientific verses, 162
Scotland, 1, 1 n.3, 25, 68, 85, 87, 93–4, 144, 156, 185–6, 188, 194, 204
  borderlands of *see* marches, Anglo-Scottish
Scots
  language, 193 n.126
  people, 145, 147, 215, *see also* Albanactus
scribe, 35, 38, 45 n.28, 58, 68 n.93, 70, 76, 85, 113–14, 117, 129, 168, 219, 246 n.13, *see also* Harley scribe; manuscript; network
Seege or Batayle of Troye, 63 n.86, 233
Seisyll ap Cynan, 109, 112 n.98, 247
Seisyll, Seyrioel (Sisillius), 91, 98, 107, 243, 251
Senena, wife of Gruffudd ap Llywelyn, 248–9
Senghenydd, 46, 46 n.32, 47
Seth, 98, 251
The Seven Joys of Our Lady, 63 n.86
Severn river, 60, 156, 214, 216
Shire-Fee, 47
Short English Metrical Chronicle, 62, 162–3, 168
Shrewsbury
  earldom, 14
  town, 49, 60, 174, 217
Shropshire, 3 n.9, 12, 16, 24, 31, 33–5, 49, 59–70, 77, 79, 153, 160–2, 164 n.37,

169–70, 173, 175–6, 184, 233, 249, *see also* Ludlow
Sibyl, daughter of Bernard de Neufmarché, 125–6, 128, 131, *see also* Miles fitz Walter
Simon Bozoun, prior of Norwich, 218 n.64, 219, *see also* Norwich, priory
Sir Gawain and the Green Knight, 7, 232–40
Sir Orfeo, 239
Snowdonia, 1
Solomon, bible, 199–200, 210–11, 214 n.51
Spain, 99, 156
Spaniards, 104
St Augustine's Canterbury, 221
St Clears, 3 n.9
St Davids, 58, 126, 202
St Enoder, Cornwall, 214
Stanzaic Life of Christ, 63 n.86
Stater, king, 245
Stephen, king, 132
Strata Florida Abbey, 58, 68, 70, 198–9, 202
succession, 29–30, 32, 116, 119, 147–54, 161, 184, 196, 228
    of Brecon, 120, 122, 127, 131, 143–52
    of Deheubarth, 112 n.97, 244–6
    dispute, 87, 102, 112, 122, 129, 135, 143–4, 168–70
    in *Fouke le Fitz Waryn*, romance of, 161, 168–70
    of Gwynedd, 92, 112–13, 247–9
    in *History of William Marshal*, 178–80
    of kingdom of Britain, 64, 69, 73–4, 90
    see also Mortimer, claim to throne; women, and inheritance
Sylvius, 98, 251
Syre Gawene and the Carle of Carelyle, 233

Talgarth, 141
Talyfan, 47
Tangwystl, 248–9
Tarn Wadling, 186
Tegid ab Iago, 98, 244, 250
Teigengl, 16

Teilo, saint, 43, 56 n.57
    life of, 56–7
third category/space, 11–13, 19–21, 34, 115, 154–5, 231, *see also* borderlands; March of Wales; marcher
Thomas Holland, earl of Kent, 87
Thomas of Lancaster, 163
Thomas, Lord Berkeley, 214–16, 221
Tintern, 48 n.39
Tiptoft, Robert, 146
Tiriarll, 47, 47 n.36
Trahaearn, king, 246
transmission of texts, 5–10, 15, 29, 31, 34–6, 59–60, 63–4, 73–4, 77–8, 105–17, 194–8, 208, 212, 218–19, 227–9, 232, 241, *see also* marcher families, role in textual transmission
Treaty of Aberconwy, 28 n.95
Treaty of Montgomery, 157
Trevisa, John, 209 n.36, 213–18, 222–3, 226–7
Trojans, 2, 5, 164, 200, 201–2, 227
    Welsh descent from, 2, 5, 45, 50, 53, 88, 90, 93, 98–9, 99 n.71, 101, 201–2, 204, 215, 223–4, 226, 235 n.5
    see also Ascanius; Brutus; Eneas Ysgwydwyn; Hector; Paris; Sylvius
Tros, 98, 99 n.69, 251
Troy, 50–1, 67, 88 n.39, 99, 164, 202, 215, 233–4
Tudur Aled, 175, 176 n.69
Tudur Fychan, 55
Tudor, Henry *see* Henry VII, king
Tudor, Jasper, 46
Tydeus, 199–200, 210–11, 214 n.51

uchelwyr, 30 n.97, 31, 33–4, 35 n.4, 36, 47, 53, 55, 176
Ulster, 191
    earldom of, 79, 82–3
    see also Annals of Ulster; Ireland
Ulysses, 199–200, 210–11, 214 n.51
Urien of Rheged, 207–8
Usk, Adam, 97–9, 102
Usk, lordship, 3 n.9, 118 n.4

Usk, Thomas, 213
Uther Pendragon, 42

Vale of Ewyas, 132, 134
Valence
    Agnes, 148
    Aymer, 148
    Isabel, 138, 143–4, 148, 150
    Joan, 148
    John, 148
    William (d. 1296), 139, 143, 148
    William II (d. 1282), 148
Valle Crucis Abbey, 212
Vaughan, Robert, 37 n.9
Verdun family, 60, 64
vernacular language, 3, 7, 9–10, 24, 47–8, 47 n.36, 75, 81, 134, 153, 158, 183, 202, 206, 213, 225–6, 239, *see also* English, language, Middle; French; Scots, language; Welsh, language, Middle
Vesci
    Agnes, 150
    William, 150
Virgil, *Aeneid*, 199 n.11
Vita Edwardi Secundi, 53–4
Vita Griffini Filii Conani, 105–11, 113, 243 n.8, *see also* Gruffudd ap Cynan; *Historia Gruffud vab Kenan*
Vortigern, 42, 51, 53

Wace, *Brut*, 42 n.19, 75, 80, 183 n.93
Wake
    Baldwin, 146
    Baldwin II, 146
    Hugh, 146
    John, 146
    Thomas, 146
Waldef, 159
Wales, 86 n.31, 87, 105–6, 121 n.11, 141, 153–4, 189–90, 192 n.121, 206–7, 219–20
    in *The Awntyrs off Arthure at the Terne Wathelyn*, 188–92

bilingual manuscripts from, 37, 206, 206 n.28
colonization of, 8 n.22, 14–17, 16 n.46, 22–3, 33, 43–51, 77–9, 115, 151–4, 177, 179, 182, 184, 195–8, 207–10, 212–18, 220–2, 227, 230, 232, 238
conquest of, 1–3, 5, 8 n.22, 14–17, 16 n.46, 18, 22–3, 23 n.72, 27, 28 n.95, 30 n.97, 32–4, 35 n.4, 36, 44, 52–5, 69, 91–4, 104, 126, 151, 161, 197, 201 n.19, 207–8, 215–16, 220, 222, 226–7, *see also* Edward I; Llywelyn ap Gruffudd
conquest territories of, 10, 26–30, 46, 116, 147, 151–2, 170, 215, 232
division of, 44, 44 n.25, 91, 92 n.43, 104, 217, 244, 244 n.12
in elegy, 119–207, 214 n.51
in Geoffrey of Monmouth, 43–4, 64, 81 n.18, 91, 93, 167, 232
in Higden's *Polychronicon*, 201 n.19, 208–14, 221–5
independent, 1–2, 13–15, 36, 44, 46 n.32, 173, 175, 220, 221, *see also* Owain Glyndŵr
in Ludlow Annal, 68–9
North, 1, 14–17, 44, 48–9, 60, 70, 86, 88, 90–1, 93, 97–8, 105, 114, 209, 222, 226, 237, 238–40, 244, 244 n.12, 246–9, 249 n.19, *see also* Gwynedd
principality of, 1, 16, 44, 52, 92–3, 222, 248–9, 249 n.19
relationship with England, 2–17, 29, 60–1, 69, 115, 195–8, 207–8, 214–22, 241
relationship with March of Wales *see* March of Wales, relationship with Wales and the Welsh
in romance of *Fouke le Fitz Waryn*, 153–5, 160–77
saints of *see* Cadog, saint; David, saint; Dyfrig, saint; Elgar, saint; Gwynllyw, saint; Padarn, saint; Teilo, saint

South, 13–14, 16, 31, 33, 36, 36 n.7, 49, 56–8, 59 n.66, 69, 73, 86, 90–2, 97, 112 n.97, 120, 130, 167, 170, 191, 197–8, 207–8, 215, 232, 238, 244–6, 244 n.12, 246 n.14, 248–9, 249 n.19, *see also* Deheubarth
  in Trevisa's *Polychronicon*, 214–18, 221–2, 226–7
  see also Britain; Britons; Camber; Deheubarth; Gwynedd; Powys; Welsh, language, Middle
Walgayenus/Walganus, king, 109, 245, 247
Walter de Clifford, 26–7
Walter Constable, 133–4
Walter of Pederton, 27
war, 5, 26, 84, 132, 165–6, 172, 174–5, 178–9, 181, 187–9, 192–3, 199–200, 207, 210–11, 215, 220, 226, *see also* First Barons' War; Hundred Years' War; Owain Glyndŵr; Wars of the Roses
Warenne
  John, 147
  William, 147
Warin de Metz, 158, *see also* Fouke fitz Waryn
Warin family *see* Fouke fitz Waryn
Wars of the Roses, 17, 33, 99, 115, 139, 228, 241, *see also* York, house of
Warwick family *see* Richard Neville, earl of Warwick
Warwickshire, 135–7, 215 n.53
Waterford, 191
Welsh King List, 77, 85–7, 90–2, 94–5, 105–15, 242–9
Welsh Marches *see* March of Wales
Welsh
  absence in Middle English literature, 7, 10, 12–13
  culture and customs, 4, 12–13, 30, 30 n.97, 34, 95, 154, 161, 171, 174 n.66, 177, 184, 193, 217–18, 228–31

  external perceptions of barbarity, 212–13, 217–18, 220, 226–7
  genealogy *see* genealogy, Welsh
  gentry *see* uchelwyr
  historical narrative, 1–5, 3 n.8, 8, 15, 29, 30 n.97, 31–61, 64, 70, 73–5, 91, 104, 108, 117, 177, 201–2, 214, 220, 228–9, 232, 241, *see also* Annales Cambriae; Brut y Brenhinedd; Brut y Tywysogion; Epitome Historiae Britanniae; Geoffrey of Monmouth
  themes of, 5, 50–3, 59, 73, 126–7
  identity, 18, 21 n.68, 30 n.97, 31, 50, 53, 105, 114–15, 167, 171, 174–5, 177, 184, 193, 231
  kingdoms, 4, 14–15, 14 n.38, 30 n.97, 33, 36 n.7, 44, 53, 78, 91, 94, 96, 113, 119–20, 192 n.121, 198, 231
  language, Middle, 24, 32 n.98, 37–9, 47 n.37, 50, 54–5, 58–9, 75, 84–5, 96–7, 105 n.89, 106–7, 153 n.1, 157, 175–6, 181 n.85, 190, 196 n.2, 201 n.19, 205–7, 225, 232, *see also* Yr Anghrist a Dydd y Farn; Armes Prydein Vawr; Brut y Brenhinedd; Brut y Tywysogion; Canu Urien; Latin; Mabinogion; Peredur vab Efrawc
  law, 4, 13, 18, 28, 33, 46 n.32, 206 n.28
  literature, 7, 9–10, 13, 18, 32 n.98, 33, 47, 47 n.36, n.37, 55, 64, 177, 232, 240–1, *see also* Armes Prydein Vawr; Brut y Brenhinedd; Canu Urien; Mabinogion; panegyric/praise; Peredur vab Efrawc
  nobility *see* uchelwyr
  people, 2–4, 7–8, 11–13, 17–18, 29–30, 33–5, 44, 46 n.30, 46–55, 60–1, 64, 69–70, 80–1, 90–7, 104–5, 121, 126, 132, 134, 183–4, 197–8, 202, 210, 212–18, 220, 223–4, 226–31, 236
  poetic conventions, 200 n.14, 201–2, 206–7

Welsh (*Continued*)
  poetry, 47 n.36, 54–5, 95–7, 99 n.72, 104 n.85, 175–6, 198, 200 n.14, 201–2, 203–8, 206 n.28, 223 n.74, 224 n.77, 225, *see also cywyddwyr*; Dafydd ap Gwilym; Guto'r Glyn; Gruffudd ab yr Ynad Coch; Iolo Goch; Lewys Glyn Cothi; Tudur Aled
  princes, 11 n.24, 25, 30 n.97, 30–2, 64, 88, 91–4, 101, 105, 116, 151, 154, 161, 170 n.57, 171–8, 179 n.80, 181–2, 193–229, 235, *see also* Dafydd ap Gruffudd; Dafydd ap Llywelyn; Gruffudd ap Cynan; Gwenwynwyn ab Owain Cyfeiliog; Llywelyn ap Gruffudd; Llywelyn ab Iorwerth; Madog ap Maredudd; Morgan ap Hywel; Rhodri Mawr; Rhys ap Gruffudd, lord; Rhys Gryg; Rhys ap Maredudd
  prophecy, 2–3, 33, 35, 42–3, 48, 51, 53–6, 58, 68, 103, *see also Armes Prydein Vawr*; *Cyfoesi Myrddin*; Geoffrey of Monmouth, *Prophetiae Merlini*; *mab darogan*; Merlin; prophecy
Welshpool, 49
Welshry, 141–2
West Midlands, 10, 13, 63, 232–3, 235, *see also* English, language, Middle, West Midlands dialect
Westminster Abbey, 44 n.26, 82
Wexford, 191
Whitchurch, 170
Whitland Abbey, 198
Whittington (*Blancheville*), 156–7, 165 n.41, 166, 168–9, 175, *see also* Blanche Launde
Wigmore, 3 n.9, 17, 60, 95, 248–50
  abbey, 60, 76–8, 83–5, 88, 95, 114–15, 241
  genealogies, 85–115, 241
  Register, 136

  see also Fundationis et Fundatorum Historia; Mortimer
William the Conqueror, 14, 77, 165–7
William Constable, 126, 128, 134
William, founder of Llanthony Prima, 121, 134
William de la Frette, 146
  daughter Gundred, 146
William de Huntingfield, 138, 144 n.65, 148
William, king of Scots, 145
William of Malmesbury, 42 n.16
William of Palerne, 233
William Rufus, king, 67
William of Wycombe, prior of Llanthony Secunda, 121, 121 n.11, 132 n.40, 133, 133 n.43
Winchcombe, 70
Windsor castle, 127
Wirral, 237–40
women, 132, 170, 179–80
  and inheritance, 29, 118, 143, 154, 161, 168–70, 228
  in March of Wales, 29, 118 n.5, 161, 179–80
Worcester, town, 60, *see also* Annals of Worcester; Chronicle of John of Worcester
Worcestershire, 77
Wyclif, John, 213
Wynkyn de Worde, 213

Yaul, king, 245
Ynys Enlli (Bardsey Island), 43, 57
Ynysforgan, 48 n.37
York
  city of, 98, 251
  house of, 99–104, 115, 228, 241
Yorkshire, 63
Ystlwyf, 3 n.9, 191 n.120
Ystrad Tywi, 14, 49

Zouche
  Eudo, 134, 138, 143 n.63, 150
  William, 150

INDEX OF MANUSCRIPTS

Aberystwyth, National Library of Wales, 3036B (Mostyn 117), 88 n.39, 108 n.95, 109–11, 113 n.99

Aberystwyth, National Library of Wales, 17110E (Book of Llandaf), 40, 42 n.16, 43 n.21, 56–8, 206 n.28

Aberystwyth, National Library of Wales, 21608D, 87 n.36, 223 n.74

Aberystwyth, National Library of Wales, Peniarth 4 and 5 (White Book of Rhydderch), 47 n.37

Aberystwyth, National Library of Wales, Peniarth 20, 202, 202 n.22, 212

Aberystwyth, National Library of Wales, Peniarth 32 (*Y Llyfr Teg*), 37 n.8, 40, 40 n.13, 41, 56 n.58, 58

Aberystwyth, National Library of Wales, Peniarth 50 (*Y Cwyta Cyfarwydd*), 54

Aberystwyth, National Library of Wales, Peniarth 383, 37 n.9

Cambridge, Corpus Christi College, 98, 101–2

Cambridge, Corpus Christi College, 199, 206 n.28

Cambridge, Corpus Christi College, 264, 218–19, 219 n.65

Cambridge, Corpus Christi College, 281, 223 n.74

Cambridge, University Library, Kk.1.12, 80 n.15, 82, 82 n.19

Chicago, University Library, 224, 76, 85–95, 97, 101–15, 201 n.14, 242–51

Dublin, Trinity College, 212, 241 n.19

Exeter, Cathedral Library, 3514, 88 n.39, 108 n.95, 109–11, 113 n.99

Lincoln, Lincoln Cathedral, 91, 187

London, British Library, Add. 10104, 97

London, British Library, Add. 18268A, 102–3

London, British Library, Add. 34779, 63 n.86

London, British Library, Add. 38666, 63 n.86

London, British Library, Cotton Julius D. x, 121, 122–4, 130–1, 134–5

London, British Library, Cotton Nero A. iv, 40 n.13, 41, 59, 64–6, 69

London, British Library, Cotton Roll XIV 12, 130–1, 144

London, British Library, Cotton Titus D. xxii, 37–9, 40 n.13, 40–1, 45, 45 n.28, 46, 46 n.30, 56 n.57, 57 n.61, 58, 59 n.66

London, British Library, Cotton Vespasian E. vii, 103

London, British Library, Egerton 1076, 103

London, British Library, Harley 273, 62, 159

London, British Library, Harley 1240, 136 n.50

London, British Library, Harley 2010, 63 n.86

London, British Library, Harley 2253, 62–3, 159

London, British Library, Harley 3725, 70–2

London, British Library, Royal 12 C. xii, 62–3, 155, 158–9, 162–3

London, British Library, Royal 14 C. xiii, 219

London, Lambeth Palace Library, 527, 68 n.93

London, Lincoln's Inn, Hale 150, 63 n.86

INDEX OF MANUSCRIPTS

Manchester, John Rylands Library, 90, 63 n.86

New York, Pierpont Morgan Library, M.888, 178

Oxford, Bodleian Library, Bodley 840, 80 n.15
Oxford, Bodleian Library, Dugdale 18, 135–9, 141, 143–4
Oxford, Bodleian Library, Rawlinson B. 171, 80 n.15
Oxford, Bodleian Library, Rawlinson B. 173, 80 n.15, 82 n.19
Oxford, Bodleian Library, Rawlinson Poet. 139, 63 n.86
Oxford, Bodleian Library, Rawlinson Poet. 141, 63 n.86
Oxford, Jesus College, 20, 113–14
Oxford, Jesus College, 111 (Red Book of Hergest), 48 n.37, 54, 113
Oxford, Trinity College, 16A, 63 n.86

Philadelphia, Free Library, Lewis E 201, 103

Southwell, Southwell Minster Library, VII, 63 n.86